Arguments for a New Left

I am the clerk, the technician, the mechanic, the driver.
They said, Do this, do that, don't look left or right,
don't read the text. Don't look at the whole machine. You
are only responsible for this one bolt. For this one rubber-stamp.
This is your only concern. Don't bother with what is above you.
Don't try to think for us. Go on, drive. Keep going. On, on.
So they thought, the big ones, the smart ones, the futurologists.
There is nothing to fear. Not to worry. Everything's ticking just fine.
Our little clerk is a diligent worker. He's a simple mechanic.
He's a little man.
Little men's ears don't hear, their eyes don't see.
We have heads, they don't.
Answer them, said he to himself, said the little man,
the man with a head of his own. Who is in charge? Who knows
where this train is going?
Where is their head? I too have a head.
Why do I see the whole engine.
Why do I see the precipice –
is there a driver on this train?
The clerk driver technician mechanic looked up.
He stepped back and saw – what a monster.
Can't believe it. Rubbed his eyes and – yes,
it's there all right. I'm all right. I do see
the monster. I'm part of the system.
I signed this form. Only now I am reading the rest of it.
This bolt is part of a bomb. This bolt is me. How
did I fail to see, and how do the others go on
fitting bolts. Who else knows?
Who has seen? Who has heard? – The emperor really is naked.
I see him. Why me. It's not for me. It's too big.
Rise and cry out. Rise and tell the people. You can.
I, the bolt, the technician, mechanic? – Yes, you.
You are the secret agent of the people. You are the eyes of the nation.

From *I Am Your Spy*, by Mordechai Vanunu, who worked as a technician in the Israeli underground atomic weapons plant in the Negev desert. He is serving an 18-year sentence in solitary confinement for making public his knowledge of Israel's secret nuclear weapons programme.

Arguments for a New Left

Answering the Free-Market Right

Hilary Wainwright

BLACKWELL
Oxford UK & Cambridge USA

First published 1994

Blackwell Publishers
108 Cowley Road
Oxford OX4 1JF
UK

238 Main Street
Cambridge, Massachusetts 02142
USA

British Library Cataloguing in Publication Data

A CIP catalogue record for this book is available from the British Library.

Library of Congress Cataloging-in-Publication Data

Wainwright, Hilary.
 Arguments for a new left: answering the free-market right / Hilary Wainwright.
  p. cm.
 Originally published: 1993.
 Includes bibliographical references and index.
 ISBN 0-631-19189-5 (alk. paper). – ISBN 0-631-19191-7 (pbk.: alk. paper)
 1. Social movements – Europe. 2. New left – Europe. 3. Europe – Politics and government – 1945– 4. Knowledge, Sociology of.
 I. Title.
 HN377.W35 1994
 303.48'4'094 – dc20   93-1481
                                                                                  CIP

Typeset in 11 on 12½ pt Garamond by Best-set Typesetter Ltd., Hong Kong
Printed in Great Britain by Hartnolls Ltd.

This book is printed on acid-free paper

In memory of Anne and Bob Warin, imagining the discussions – and arguments – we would have had.

CONTENTS

PREFACE

It was discussions with Mísa, Petr and other young organizers of the civic movements of Hungary and the former Czechoslovakia that spurred me get to grips with the resurrection of the free-market right. Their attraction to neo-liberalism pinned me to the tables of Manchester's John Rylands Library to read the works of Frederick Hayek. I felt I had to return to the foundation of free-market ideology to comprehend how its appeal in Central and Eastern Europe could be answered.

Like many who would identify themselves as part of a broadly defined new left in the West, my socialism was shaped by protesting at the Soviet invasion of Czechoslovakia as much as by marching to stop the American bombing of Vietnam. In July 1968, as the Moscow gerontocracy were preparing their ultimate sanction against popular revolt, I went to Sofia as a political hybrid of Young Liberal and revolutionary student, to attend the Soviet dominated 'World Festival of Youth'. The festival slogan was 'Mir, Drooszba and Solidarnos' (Peace, Friendship and Solidarity). The festival organizers got a rather different breed of Western youth than they had bargained for. The West German, Italian and British delegations were packed with '68ers' who saw the festival as an opportunity to fraternize behind enemy lines. Fraternization was difficult. Everyone was housed in blocks of flats, remote from each other, and anti-social in their architecture. The Czech delegation was held in effect in solitary confinement. Every attempt at protest, every debate or hint of democracy was suffocated by busloads of what we called 'spontaneous Bulgarian workers', shouting repeatedly and in unison, 'Mir, Drooszba and Solidarnos'.

After this experience, the political logic that produced the Soviet invasion became awesomely clear. For us it was the opposite of socialism. We identified with the students trying to stop the tanks, and the workers occupying their factories. We extended our list of those resisting the power elites of the world: 'Ho, ho, ho Chi Minh, London, Paris and Berlin', and now Prague.

I realize now that I also assumed that although these imagined friends had been defeated in their struggle for a democratic socialism, they would, in parallel with us, continue their thinking about a real socialism, a socialism based on the popular democracy that pushed itself above the soil during the Prague Spring; and that this process would be joined by a younger generation. Few of us made the effort, however, to make contact or keep in touch.[1] Their civil rights were one of our causes. A small minority did maintain contact but for most of us it was a matter of an imagined common bond.

My first encounters, 20 years later, with the post 1968 generation of opposition activists shattered such an unconscious presumption.[2] Mísa Neubauerova, a twenty-four-year-old secretary and translator for the Helsinki Citizens' Assembly, the Prague based forum for East–West co-operation between democratic social movements, explained what 1968 meant to her. She was one year old when Soviet tanks drove relentlessly down the streets of her city. But spring 1968 has been with her ever since: '68 lived with my family all my life'. Her father, an engineering worker, thought then that 'the Communist Party was really going to change'. For the first time in his life he thought seriously of joining it. But after the Prague Winter (in August) 'he grew old very quickly; he felt betrayed'. Mísa recalled that 'He withdrew from politics and made our garden beautiful'. He also learnt English and listened incessantly to the Voice of America and Radio Free Europe. Through these channels Mísa and her father came to associate liberty with Mrs Thatcher and Ronald Reagan. The names of Edward Thompson or Petra Kelly, for instance, meant nothing.

These experiences shaped Mísa's understanding of the word 'socialism' and words associated with it. 'It is a really awful word,' she said with feeling. 'For ordinary people, it has been destroyed completely.' I asked her what she felt about the socialism of the Western socialists with whom she worked in the Citizens' Assembly: 'I understand that you mean something very different from our experience – I wouldn't talk to you if you didn't. And I agree with the content of some of what you say. But the word acts as an interruption in our conversation.' What of the 'content' that she felt she could share? 'I believe in self-government. I am against arrogance and the remoteness both of multinational companies and the state. For this reason I like the idea of civic movements. They mean having the ability to participate, to influence social and political decisions. I'm not happy following the free market. But I don't see the alternative.' Mísa put the challenge to the Western new left in an unusually sympathetic way. She has worked with many of its activists in Prague and (briefly) in London; she now works for a Czech public relations company whose customers include some of the investment trusts leading the process of privatization.

I could not dismiss the free-market sentiments of people like Mísa as those of dyed-in-the-wool reactionaries, defending a vested interest in an unrestrained market. Neither could I sweep aside these dissonant moments in the conversation and concentrate on areas of agreement: any practical thinking on shared concerns unavoidably comes back to principles of economic and political organization. Nor could I walk away and limit my political collaboration only to those – very few – with explicitly democratic socialist views similar to my own.

Many of these young democrats, with their neo-liberal leanings, are among those principled oppositionists in Central and Eastern Europe who resisted authoritarian rule in its socialist guise and who are now regrouping to face up to authoritarian politicians rallying popular support in the name of nation or race. There is an urgent need for pan-European action to resist the forces of ethnic hatred being mobilized across the continent. This will involve the broadest possible base of co-operation between the Western left and democratic, internationalist citizens in the East. Already vital international networks of co-operation are growing. But they are precarious; their inner strength is important. A source of this is an ability to work practically together and at the same time argue over the consequences of our different histories.

Before 1989 the independent peace movement in the West and a part of the opposition movement in the East, through extensive dialogue in difficult circumstances, managed to overcome a profound wariness of each other.[3] They established at least a common language, if not an entirely shared perspective. This intellectual effort made the movements on both sides of the crumbling Wall considerably stronger. Now the circumstances for debate and dialogue are physically much easier. After 40 years, however, of cultural isolation and repression, other difficulties are coming to the fore: of political language, lack of common reference points, clashing priorities and diverging concerns. The least one can do is enter into the frames of debate of potential allies in the East, but not deferentially: arguing the integrity of one's own ideas, even if they have not been forged in such adversity.

The intention of this book is to begin to answer Mísa. There are many like her who are not yet involved with movements in the West and who, alongside a shared belief in internationalism and democratic civic movements, espouse

free-market ideas, and with greater commitment than Mísa. So the political
stimulus to the arguments of this book came from discussions in the course of
working with activists in Eastern Europe. The process of working to answer
the challenge from the East has led, however, to explorations of both a wider
relevance to politics after 1989 and to specific implications for responding to
the influence of free-market ideas in Britain and the US.

With regard to the first, my mental debates with Hayek provided tools
with which to begin to reground and re-establish the idea of 'the social' and
'the public' as distinct from, but in a critical relationship to, an accountable
state. Hayek's appeal to many of the Easterners with whom I talked lies in his
challenge to the social engineering state, and its presumption that it is able
to know and meet the needs of the people. My main challenge to Hayek is to
his theory of knowledge: not to his recognition of the importance of practical,
uncodifed knowledge that cannot by its nature be centralized, but to the idea
that this experience-based knowledge is necessarily exclusively individual in
character and cannot provide a basis for collective action.

My alternative view of knowledge is inspired by the assertion in the
practice of the recent democratic movements in the West of the social features
of practical, experience-based forms of knowledge, in combination with
knowledge of a theoretical kind. Many of the lasting organizations originating from these radical movements illustrate how, contrary to Hayek, this
practical knowledge is of a sharable, 'socializable' character; a knowledge
which provides a basis for challenging existing state institutions as the expert
diviners of social need, while insisting on the responsibility of government to
provide public resources in response to those needs.

The important point is then how these public resources are managed, how
far a democratic state is based on the direct participation of those who *can*
identify and satisfy such needs and be publically accountable for doing so.
Indeed the extent to which political institutions are constructed to make
possible popular participation in their administration should be one criterion
by which their democracy should be judged.

Democratic social movements, including parts of the trade union movement and the kind of radical 'voluntary sector' which these movements have
stimulated, could be central to such a perspective. Movements themselves do
not provide ready-made models of new institutions, but many of their principles of organization indicate ways of achieving a popular participation and
pooling of practical and theoretical knowledge that no conventional public or
party institution could conceive of. My argument grounds a 'bottom up'
approach to social transformation in a recognition that the knowledge shared
at the base of society is essential to a socially effective and just society.

Moreover, such knowledge can only be fully utilized if those at the base are involved in economic and social decisions. I have therefore emphasized the importance of democratic citizens' and workers' movements, not simply as a subordinate fourth estate or a way of keeping politicians on their toes, but as the basis of a new mentality of government.

The potential significance of this emerging mentality and the conventional political assumption that it challenges is illustrated in the aptly headlined 'Western blundering in the Balkans'.[4] A full explanation of Western failures in this first East European test of the vaunted 'new world order' would require many levels of analysis. The underlying problem (not something for which one can 'blame' Western governments, which would be like asking the cart-horse to become nimble) is that Western dealings in the Balkans were always with other politicians, state to state. Negotiators have talked only to war mongers, never to the victims of war and those among the victims organizing for peace and human rights. The strategic thought of these mediators treated states and societies as homogeneous, like single-coloured blobs on the board game of Risk. Internal differentiation and the emergence of popular opposition to opportunist, xenophobic politicians does not seem to have figured in their thinking. Western diplomacy has seen power relations exclusively in terms of power as military power; it has been uncomprehending of the possibility of building up the power of those who are challenging the legitimacy of force.

From the beginning such people existed in large numbers: the anti-war movement in Belgrade, with its permanent Anti-War Centre, and the Civil Resistance Movement formed during the first actions of the war, brought over 50,000 Serbians on to the streets against the war. A petition collected 70,000 signatures. In Serbia, Croatia and Bosnia Herzegovina, a brave and effective alternative press has been struggling to keep the voice of these and peace groups throughout the Balkans heard over the gunfire.

In 1991 Serbian peace and opposition groups, with the help of the Helsinki Citizens' Assembly, planned a joint conference which they invited EC mediators to attend as observers. Their hope was to enable the EC mediators to understand enough about what was going on inside the country to avoid victimizing a whole people. 'We wanted to show that there were forces in Serbia who could be a counterforce to Milosevic and we wanted to discuss how they might have given this opposition some support,' said Sonja Licht, one of the organizers and co-chair of the Helsinki Citizens' Assembly. At first the EC Presidency did not even reply. Eventually, after public criticism for this, they wrote refusing to attend on the grounds that the EC could not get involved with the affairs of another country.

In fact every move that EC Ministers have made over the Balkans has involved them in the internal affairs of these societies. The problem was that it has been an involvement informed by far too little inside knowledge and without any self-awareness of Western ignorance. Leading EC and US mediators flew weekly to Belgrade, but they never called in on the Centre for Action Against War, or the offices of the opposition magazine *Vreme*.

In 1992 peace groups from all the Balkan republics sent a delegation to see David Owen, present proposals coming from a conference of 175 Balkan municipalities, and follow up a campaign for safe havens in which 250,000 people from across Europe sent him postcards urging this initiative. Owen's response reveals with especial clarity the mentality that dominates conventional politics. He said: 'If you want to lobby me it would be more effective to do it through friends or through important people whom I can't ignore, like politicians.'[5]

The left has not been free of this all-knowing arrogance. One of the themes of this book is a retrieval of those ideas and practices of the new left which were critical of the social-engineering presumptions of both vanguard party and social democratic state. I say 'retrieval' because, in Britain at least, much of the nature of this libertarian critique has long been hijacked by the free-market right and flown in entirely different direction.

By the late seventies the idea of 'the state', or even the government, as instruments of social improvement was losing credibility under pressure from several directions. On the one hand, there were economic pressures, such as the erosion of national powers of macroeconomic management by the internationalization of major economic decisions. There were cultural and political challenges, such as the insistent pressure from excluded social groups demanding the rights whose claims to universality had given the liberal state its moral high ground. And there was the growth of alternative regional and international identities, weakening the national cultural unity that underpins the strength of existing state institutions. On the other hand, there were failures specific to actually existing socialism, East and West, both of which had held out the action of the state as the measure by which socialism should be judged. It was the suppression of individual and collective rights and the economic stagnation of the Soviet bloc which did most to undermine socialism as a programme of change led by the state. But in the West, unhappy day-to-day dealings with the welfare state, and experience of government interventions that repeatedly failed either to stimulate prosperity or to achieve social or ecological objectives, meant that a continuum could be credibly conjured up of failed social engineering, from the command economy to the National Enterprise Board.

The new conservative right, feeling cheated by Edward Heath's retreat from Selsdon Man in the early 1970s, had made a determined return
to their think-tanks to refuel their ideological onslaught on the corporatist institutions of the post-war settlement. As the 1974–9 Labour Governments stumbled on the economic potholes caused by the oil crisis and the
collapse of the boom, Thatcher and her team were ready with an intellectual framework that could articulate and capture the growing disaffection with government. A confident reassertion of free-market nostrums
blamed socialism and the Labour Party for failings in the post-war welfare
state and economic management. Labour was lumbered as the party of the
discredited state.

Throughout the 1970s there was much critical thinking among the new
left that emerged after 1968 (influenced by earlier generations[6]) about the
inadequacy of existing state institutions for meeting people's needs. But this
did not permeate the Labour establishment. As a result, and without any
springs of intellectual creativity of their own, the only terms on which Labour
leaders could distance themselves from the failings of state socialism were
those set by the new right. Labour manifestos and policy statements became
increasingly unconvincing admixtures of traditional defence of the most
popular parts of the welfare state with an acceptance of private market criteria
for efficiency and success.

The squeezing out of any left alternative to the failures of government was
intensified by the tendency of the Left of the Labour Party to react defensively
to the Labour leadership's adoption of market-oriented priorities. The Left's
instinctive stance was simply to stand firm in its traditional policies. There
were exceptions, including Tony Benn with his work in the 1970s on industrial democracy and his persistent stand for a republican constitution, and
Ken Livingstone with his opening up of London's County Hall. But as the
Labour leadership became more and more fixated with demonstrating its
respectability, such creative politicians, trapped in the polarizing logic of
inner party conflict, found it difficult to keep open this third space.

The result is that there are few effective voices in British politics advocating an alternative framework to that of a private market. There is no confident
assertion of the priority of social considerations; nor is there public debate
about the variety of democratic public institutions, state and non-state, by
which these priorities could be achieved.

The problem became clear to me after listening to a plummy-voiced
student called Georgina talk on Channel Four's *Comment* about how people 'no
longer felt the state was theirs'. She went on to argue that 'instead of
encouraging them to turn to the private sector we must encourage greater

scope for participation in the public sector'. The words, the sentiments too, sounded strangely familiar. They were the phrases of the radical left in the late 1960s and throughout the 1970s. Yet here they were coming out of the mouth of a Conservative student in her bluest best, defending the government's proposals to bring market mechanisms – student loans, for instance – into the education system. This episode has been repeated many times in all the announcements that the Conservative government is bringing 'choice' (to those who can afford it) into the public sector. It reminded me of how easily, in the absence of a genuinely pluralistic political culture (after all, the British Labour Party, an increasingly centralised political party, has a monopoly over the left's political representation in England at any rate), the experiments towards a participative, anti-paternalist view of socialism of fifteen, ten, even five years ago, have been forgotten. After the abolition of the Greater London Council, they had all but disappeared from public political debate. 'This is the new, modern socialism,' remarked Norman Tebbit, perceptively, of the Livingstone GLC, 'and we must kill it'. And they almost did.

One problem for this new left that has made it easier to be wiped from memory is that its attempts to create a variety of forms of democratic or co-operative management of public resources in housing, health, education and local government, and its initiatives in the trade unions, by way of co-operatives or in a variety of campaigns to illustrate alternatives to production for profit, have been very localized and particular. Principles can be drawn from these experiences and generalized but, except all too briefly at the GLC, there has not been the impetus of a national political presence to test and develop ideas for a wider public. Thatcherism was able sucessfully to appropriate the libertarianism of 1968, extracting its entrepreneurial spirit from its values of social solidarity.

It is necessary, therefore, to retrieve some of the fundamental innovations of the new left in the context of answering the same ideas associated with the revival of the right in Britain. I hope that this retrieval will help the left to regain its confidence. It will not give people a programme in their pocket or a slogan to wake up to every morning. But it might provide some tools for rethinking the agencies and institutions by which socialist values can be pursued, effectively and with integrity; tools which already have had some limited, unselfconscious testing in practice.

My intentions then in this book are political; my means of fulfilling these intentions aim to be scholarly, in the sense of involving a constant effort to be true, while knowing that I can only ever approximate to the truth. I began to test ideas from the practice of the new left in the West against certain themes of the neo-liberal right, unsure quite how the argument would end. This book, therefore, is really a way of thinking aloud. I hope its ommissions and contentious assertions will stimulate others to do the same.

Acknowledgements

In an effort to make this book manageable for writer and reader alike, I have pursued only one of the many tracks of argument needed to cover the ground that I have staked out above. I explain this argument, concerning the politics of knowledge, in the next part of the book. This track I have merely mapped, its detail remains to be analysed. Even so, this book seems to have been a mighty effort in which many friends and colleagues have been incredibly helpful and patient. Most patient and helpful have been Huw Beynon, Peter Halfpenny and the Sociology Department at Manchester University where I went for a year, as a Senior Simon Fellow, to write this book and where, apart from a few sojourns in the United States and on the continent, I remained like a legalized squatter for over three years. This book has benefitted enormously from a variety of overlapping critical intellectual and political communities which a cosmopolitan, regional capital like Manchester is able to host. I want to thank everyone associated with the International Centre for Labour Studies, based in the Faculty of Social Sciences, especially Huw Beynon, Diane Elson, David Howell, Paul Keleman, Jamie Peck and Linda Shaw for many useful discussions. I am also grateful to other members of the University for their friendship and comments on work in progress, especially Brian Doherty, Norman Geras, Daryl Glazier, Simon Miller, David Morgan, Sue Scott, Teodor Sharion, Rachel Thomson, Mike Waller, Elena Liven, Pat Devine and Ursula Vogel. I am grateful to Helen Brown, Secretary of the Sociology Department, other secretaries in the Department and Peter Blore of the Computer Training Workshop for all my use of their facilities and for being so friendly in the process. I also want to thank Di Parkin, Su Maddock, Annandi Ramamurthy, Tariq Mahommed Ali and Neil Swannick for their constant arguments, criticisms and support and for helping to make my years in Manchester so enjoyable that I decided to stay.

Three other institutions and groups of people have provided support, hospitality and a fertile intellectual environment as I was working on this book. For three months in 1991 I was a Visiting Scholar at the Center for Social Theory and Comparative History at the University of California, Los Angeles. I am grateful to Bob Brenner, the Center's director, Tom Mertes, the Center's erudite and courteous administrator, Carolyn Eickner, Perry Anderson, Carole and Roy Pateman, Ellen Dubois, Ruth Milkman, Mike

Davis and everyone in my graduate class, for their discussions and hospitality. And Philip Monihan for being such a stimulating assistant. The Transnational Institute supported me financially and encouraged me at an early stage of my work, especially on new left and green parties in Western Europe. They also helped at a later stage with a seminar of social movement activists from East and West, rather hopefully entitled 'New Forms of Democracy in Europe' – it was conceived in December 1989. Kate Thompson helped to compile the Directory of international new left networks which is included at the back of this book. I want especially to thank John Cavanagh, Diane De Veigh, Richard Healey, Joel Rocamero, Cora and Peter Weiss and Laurian Zwart for their support and help, and the TNI/Institute for Policy Studies 'family' more generally for the international debating chamber that they have created.

As I was finishing this book, I benefitted from a period with the Haven Centre at the University of Wisconsin, Madison. I would like to thank Allan Hunter, Laura McAnnaney, Linda Gordon, Harry Brighouse, Vincent Tucker, Boas Dos Santos, Andy Levine and Erik Olin Wright for their hospitality and discussion.

As the book developed my involvement on the continent moved East, especially through the work of the Helsinki Citizens' Assembly, which will itself figure in the following chapters, as will several of its creators and shapers. I must thank especially Mary Kaldor for persuading me to become involved in this East–West civic network. Her work and example has been a vital influence in the writing of this book. Through her, I met many others – Judit Kiss, Hannah Klemescova, Istvan Rev, Sonja Licht, Jan Kavan, Radha Kumar, Tadeusz Kowalik – without whose inspiration and challenge to my Western parochialism this book would have been impossible.

Finally I want to thank the numerous friends in addition to those mentioned above, who were willing to receive delivery of a telephone-directory-size manuscript and wade through unpruned ramblings, if only to force me to use 'spell check' more regularly. Michael Barratt Brown, Neil Belton and Julian Gowan provided very helpful criticisms at an early stage. Michael Safier and Richard Kuper, friends and comrades from the Socialist Society, provided patient, helpful responses to several drafts. Zdeněk Kavan and Laslo Andor provided detailed comments on a later draft. Anthony Arblaster, Irene Bruegel, Cynthia Cockburn, Martin Baldwin Edwards, Nick Clegg, Peter Gowan, Joost Lagendijk, John Lambert, Colin Lindsay, Stephen Marks, Frieder Otto Wolf, William Outhwaite, Andy Roberts, John Palmer, Steven Quilley and Kate Soper all gave me helpful comments at some or several stages of the drafting process. Anything useful about the book owes a lot to them. I also want to thank Anne MacDermid for her shrewd advice, and Denise Searle for making me edit myself.

Throughout the research for this book there have been many people who not only agreed to be interviewed for hours, but also provided me with a place to stay. They are acknowledged for their information and ideas in the stories and arguments to follow, but I also want to thank them all for their personal kindness.

Sheila Rowbotham, through numerous extravagant phone calls that neither of us could really afford, has been a constant reminder and source of confidence in the existence of a new left. Robin Blackburn and Andrew Gamble encouraged me in my reading of Hayek. Regular discussions with Robin Murray, Mike Rustin, Maureen MacIntosh, Vella Pillay, Doreen Massey, John and Joan Bohanna, Anthony Barnett, Jean McCrindle, Marion Kosack, Ralph Miliband, Lynne Segal, Dave Cook and Richard Wainwright helped me to locate my arguments in wider debates. Simon Prosser has been a wonderfully supportive editor, and Cameron Laux an extraordinarily discerning and patient copy-editor. Emma Gotch has been a skilled and patient production controller, and Sally Pearson and Kate Howard have approached the marketing and publicity for this book with incredible energy. I am very grateful to all for their help. My thanks, above all, must go to Roy Bhaskar, with whom I intend to write a book on the politics of critical realism that will, among other things, develop the arguments in chapter 4. For the present, I am grateful for his constant willingness to discuss and read this book at every twist and turn. But only I can take responsibility for what is to follow.

Finally, an apology to all at *Socialist/Red Pepper*, Frontline Books, Charter 88, the Socialist Society and Socialist Movement, and many dear friends and relations for being about as constant as the Scarlet Pimpernel.

Hilary Wainwright
Manchester
May 1993

Notes

1   Those who did keep in touch included a small network of Trotskyists of various kinds, including those who from the late 1970s produced *Labour Focus on Eastern Europe*; and peace and human rights groups, many of whom helped to create the European Campaign for Nuclear Disarmament (END) in the early 1980s.

2 There was a minority who did follow the path I had imagined. See the interview with Petr Uhl, the Czech opposition socialist jailed for his dissent, in *New Left Review*, 179.

3 Christopher Hitchens provides a vivid illustration of these difficulties in describing the arrest and detention in Prague in 1988 of all those attending a meeting of human rights activists from the East and disarmament movements from the West: 'Cretinismo Eroico', in *For the Sake of Argument* (London, 1993).

4 Article by Tony Barber, *Independent on Sunday*, 30 May 1993.

5 Report available from the Helsinki Citizens' Assembly, 7 Panska Street, Prague.

6 See Robin Archer et al., *Out of Apathy: Voices from the New Left* (London, 1990) for a fascinating discussion of the development of the new left from 1956 onwards.

THE ARGUMENTS: A NEW LEFT
AND THE DEMOCRATIZATION
OF KNOWLEDGE

Read about the transformations of Eastern Europe and you find yourself reading about a process in which the East aspires to join the West. The West itself appears to be unaffected by the changes; self-satisfaction is its official emotion, now giving way to a certain anxiety lest the post-revolutionary tumult in the East disturb the precariously prosperous Western peace.

The stimulus of unpredicted change has worked slowly in the West, sometimes imperceptibly. Certainly the consequences for left-wing thinking and practice are not immediately obvious. Many Western socialists felt at first that their own political beliefs would not be disturbed – might even be confirmed – by the turbulent events in the central and eastern parts of the continent. They had long believed that the regimes in these lands had little or nothing in common with socialism; that bureaucratic party elites had twisted the name and history of socialism to suit their own ends. These Western new leftists, socialists of an eco-, feminist, libertarian or Trotskyist variety, believed that they had experienced in their own movements and in the hidden histories of marginalized traditions, entirely different democratic arrangements through which people could gain control over the fruits of their labour.

Certainly this had been my response. In the autumn of 1989, I was beginning to write what I imagined would be a book exploring whether the Western new left, as it developed from its extra-parliamentary base to some engagement with the state (for example, leading a municipal authority like the Greater London Council, or creating a new party like the German Greens), had created new democratic forms. From an armchair in the television room of a university hall of residence, I applauded the demonstrators on the streets of Leipzig, Prague and finally Bucharest. From my reading of the writings of Eastern oppositionists in the years leading up to the breaching of the Berlin Wall, it seemed that a significant number of them had arrived by very different routes and often with a distinct and fresh use of language at concepts very similar to those of the movements that challenged the Cold War from the Western side of the Wall.

Most notable in this respect were the writings of those, like Vaclav Havel and Jaroslav Sabota of Charter 77, and George Konrad of the Hungarian opposition, who not merely savaged and satirized the regimes of the Soviet bloc but questioned the very basis of bloc politics itself.[1] Independent peace movements encroaching on the military blocs from both sides defined their mutual goal as inseparable from democracy and human rights. This definition of peace exposed the emptiness of Soviet 'peace' rhetoric. It also involved an understanding of democracy as something more powerful than the parliamentary institutions that co-existed with the Western arsenals of the Cold War. A further sense of familiarity came from the stress in the writing of some Eastern oppositionists on public activity autonomous from the state. This echoed the insistence of left-wing movements in the West, the women's liberation movement, black organizations and the radical shop stewards' movement, for instance, on autonomy from state and corporate management alike. Moreover, Vaclav Havel's idea of 'living the truth' seemed to express the political importance of the aspiration to personal integrity, one of the thoughts behind the Western feminist slogan: 'the personal is political'.

My book, I presumed, could end with a chapter of dialogue with Eastern oppositionists, with the latter commenting on the relevance of new democratic forms in the West.[2] Their perceptions would, again I presumed, tend to confirm rather than challenge the ideas of the libertarian new left in the West.

First encounters with students who had worked at the Civic Forum office during the November demonstrations in Prague made me think again. I recount these and other encounters of a similar kind in chapter 1 of this book. Here were organizers of a civic movement who had mobilized on the streets and in the factories and believed passionately in the continued importance of democratic 'civic initiatives', expressing a deeply held belief in the philosophy of the free market. It was not that they were drawn to particular pragmatic economic prescriptions. It was the moral and philosophical notions of neo-liberalism, above all its challenge to the all-knowing state and party, which attracted them.

There are many kinds of born-again free-marketeers in Eastern Europe. Much of the *nomenklatura* have simply exchanged ideological masters in order to remain in post or to exploit new openings. This is certaintly the reality behind the pervasiveness of the language of the free market in the East: a new yes-man's code replacing the similarly misleading Soviet rhetoric of 'peace, friendship and solidarity'. But it does not explain the lasting legacy amongst previously oppositional young people, with no posts to hold on to and a wary attitude to power, of reading of Hayek in samizdat and listening to speeches of Mrs Thatcher and Ronald Reagan on Radio Free Europe and Voice of America.

This espousal of free-market ideas is, it is true, unstable. The devastating social consequences of most of the Western, especially US, policies justified with these ideas has stimulated scepticism and debate alongside unrest. But in the present political circumstances of Central and Eastern Europe there is little public scope for such debate. Moreover, there is no inexorable logic driving what public debate there is towards egalitarian and democratic values. That would be to assume that it was just a matter of people seeing through the well-financed Cold War propaganda of the West and recognizing the undesirability and unfeasibilty of a political economy built on these values. The political cultural problem has roots deeper than propaganda. On the surface, there is the problem of words: most of the words with which Western leftists describe their alternatives, 'socialist', 'collective', 'publically supported', even 'co-operative' and 'social', are anathema to many in the East who nevertheless share principles with these Western leftists. Behind this is the poverty of concepts: in the absence of any pluralism of thought and speech, these words have no meaning, and contain no concept, other than that evoked by the hated realities of the previous regime. For most people, especially younger people, there are no conceptual alternatives other than the simple opposite of what went before. This poverty is the outcome not only of lack of debate and the suppression of free expression, but also distortions of national and international history and restrictions on travel and communications. Few people, again especially young people, have had any experience of such alternatives.[3]

The egalitarian and democratic left does have alternatives. As far as I can tell, however, they have yet to be theorized in a form that can directly counter the contemporary appeal of the free-market right. The last sustained responses to Hayek's neo-liberalism, by Barbara Wootton and, more indirectly, Anthony Crosland in the late 1940s and mid-1950s, do not adequately serve this purpose.[4] Wootton, particularly, makes the case for state planning in a mixed economy, showing how, with a parliamentary democracy and a private

sector, Hayek's fears that all state intervention in the market entails a tendency towards totalitarianism are groundless. But they both in their different
ways require us to place undue faith in the benevolent expertise and good
judgement of people like themselves.

In chapter 2 I reflect on Hayek's ability to bounce back, especially in the
East but also parts of the West. The search for an explanation to this required
me to return to the intellectual debates of liberals and socialists in the
Privatseminars of Vienna in the 1920s and 1930s in which Hayek first developed his arguments against socialism – which he understood in terms of state
intervention in the market. Hayek's resilience, I argue, lies in his theory of
knowledge: in his challenge to the presumption that all relevant social and
economic knowledge can in principle be centralized. In his view, this assumption lay behind all forms of 'socialist' state engineering. His argument rested
on demonstrating the distinctive importance of everyday practical knowledge: knowledge, in his words, 'of time and circumstance'. Also central to his
argument was the proposition that this knowledge is uniquely individual in
character.

Reading Hayek's early work on the economic uses of knowledge produced
an eerie sense of recognition. Here was this arch-right-winger, guru of
General Pinochet's Chile and spiritual tutor to Margaret Thatcher, writing
about knowledge in ways which I had come across already amongst radical
shop stewards, in the consciousness-raising groups of the early women's
liberation movement and amongst critical socialist philosophers. Here was
this right-wing philosopher giving credence to tacit skills and capacities,
ignored by conventional economists, 'those things we know but cannot tell';
or pointing to the importance of the 'body of very important but unorganized
knowledge which cannot possibly be called scientific in the sense of knowledge of general rules: knowledge of particular time and circumstance.'[5]

Hayek built his challenge to the social-engineering presumption that a
benevolent state could know the interests and needs of the people, from his
understanding that economic knowledge did not only consist of scientific
laws – understood by Hayek as generalizing from statistical regularities. He
recognized that a very significant quantity of economic knowledge was by its
very nature ephemeral, practical and often tacit. Such knowledge, argued
Hayek, unlike scientific knowledge, could not even in principle be centralized, but it was nevertheless no less valid and vital as a result. From this
understanding of the limits on scientific, public human knowledge he draws
the conclusion that individuals can never know the social consequences of
their action. According to Hayek, individuals enter the world socially blindfold. If they attempt, individually or collectively, to engineer the social

consequences of their action, they infringe the liberty of others. The only alternative to what is in his view an unavoidably dictatorial order of the economy from above, is the spontaneous co-ordination of producers and consumers brought about through the price mechanism of the unregulated market.

Chapter 2 of this book explores the logic of this argument and the way that it is echoed in many of the political agendas influential now in Central and Eastern Europe. I go on to show that Hayek's theory of knowledge and the ultimate grounds for his justification of the free market are flawed by a dogmatically individualist interpretation of the limits of human knowledge, a denial of knowledge as a social product (albeit an imperfect product). The linchpin of Hayek's argument is a denial that an individual can know or participate in knowledge about anything 'beyond his own small circle'. It is this denial that links his recognition of the limits on human knowledge to his conclusions that the outcome of human activity is haphazard, and that what social order exists – notably the private market – is the product of an evolutionary process with which there should be no interference. He consequently prescribes a strong state to protect the private market from the pressures of particularistic social interests (trade unions for example) and short-term electoral pressures.

This view of the individualistic character of human knowledge is a state of affairs which rings true for those in Eastern Europe who had been forced into a life of private exile. But it is a view of knowledge which leads Hayek, despite his libertarian starting point, to favour order – and ultimately a strong state to protect that order – over human creativity. This logic is apparent in the behaviour of Hayek's followers in the economic ministries of Central and Eastern Europe.[6]

Theories of knowledge might seem extremely abstract in the face of war in the Balkans, growing unemployment and widening economic divisions across the continent, and the rise of racism East and West. Reading Hayek, however, made me conscious of a dimension of the left movements in which I had been active – most especially the student movement of 1968, the women's movements and the radical shop stewards' movement – to whose importance I had not previously been sufficiently alert. It should, I will argue, contribute to new foundations for the left. In circumstances where professional politicians across the political spectrum failed, this dimension entrenches the importance of democratic civic organizations, in workplace, community and international affairs, as means through which practical knowledge is socialized, theoretical understanding is scrutinized and partially knowing, collective agents of change are forged.

In practice these Western movements were rebelling against the all-knowing authorities of the state and the corporation and holding out, in their ways of organizing and thinking, the value of socializing everyday understanding and combining and testing its insights with those of theoretical knowledge. The student movement and the movement against the war in Vietnam, for instance, challenged the confidence of Western (and Eastern) elites – military, industrial and political – that scientific knowledge could show the way forward, not only for physics, but also for society.

The notion of science influential in shaping state action in its very different forms, East and West, was based on the model of the natural sciences which aspired to formulate general laws describing regular conjunctions of events or phenomena. This provided the premisses from which science, social as well as natural, was thought to be able to make certain predictions and gain ever more perfect knowledge as discovery of generalizations progressed. Historically, in the Enlightenment of the eighteenth century, this positivistic model had a progressive impact, undermining the influence of religious faith and superstition as a basis for medical, physical and social action. However, it had come to underpin an unduly optimistic faith in scientific production, manipulation and control, and in the capacity of science to move forward, morally, socially and intellectually.[7] When applied to the study and reform of society, it presumed that general (in positivist terms, 'scientific') laws were the only valid form of knowledge. This in turn seemed to point to an engineering model for processes of social reform.

The problem with social engineering, whether by mechanics who heed the constraints of formal democracy, or by those of a more bullying character, is not that it aims at conscious social change. Rather, it presumes that the most effective operators of social change, whether a social democratic state or a Leninist party, are acting on society from the outside – just as on a positivistic model the social scientist analyses from outside, without any self-consciousness of the social relations and processes connecting them and the subject of their study. To varying degrees, society was understood as the material, the raw steel. The state, in the hands of social reformers, or the new state operated by the revolutionary party, were the engineers working the political machinery to transform the material. They were guided by what they presumed to be a scientific understanding of the material, based on past observance of the recurring patterns of its behaviour under certain circumstances.

The student and workers movements of the late 1960s, and even more so in consequent movements – most notably the women's, green and peace movements – implicitly challenged this methodology from several angles.

They questioned the inevitably progressive character of science and its application. Also, in their practice and to some extent in their theory, they both valued practical/tacit knowledge and demonstrated the social character of all forms of knowledge, everyday and theoretical. Their rejection of the superior position of scientific laws has some similarities to Hayek's iconoclasm: 'Today,' wrote Hayek in the 1940s, 'it is almost heresy to suggest that scientific knowledge is not the sum of all knowledge.'[8] Yet Hayek concluded from his analysis of the practical and tacit character of knowledge that it was necessarily and uniquely individual. The activities of new movements, by contrast, illustrate the scope for consciously sharing and socially building upon practical knowledge as a means of bringing about social change without presuming to be all-knowing. Of course, in the course of struggling to democratize and share knowledge, there has sometimes been an idealization of practical, everyday knowledge. But many of the lasting initiatives of recent left-wing movements have also pioneered new ways of combining theoretical and practical knowledge, which take account of the distinct and essential importance of each for a more adequate understanding of how to achieve social changes.

I argue that these movements were and are more or less practising a new understanding of knowledge. It is not always coherent; though feminist writers in particular have formulated coherent counter-interpretations of science.[9] There are certain themes in the practice of all the recent radical movements, including those parts of the workers' movement influenced by the radicalization of politics from the late 1960s, that I believe are politically important to investi-gate, or retrieve. The new understanding of science which their practice in-dicates views experience and theory, feeling and intellect in a relationship of mutuality; and that mutuality occurs as a process rather than a fixed moment of verification or falsification. Experience, rather than simply yielding facts which confirm or falsify general laws, provides clues to underlying structures and relationships which are not observable other than through the particular phenomena or events that they produce. The precise character of such structures can only be understood by paying attention to the details of experience of the events and phenomena that they generate, its variations as well its recurrences. Moreover, feelings can be signs of an inadequacy in an influential interpretation of experience; to be fruitful, however, there needs to be a context in which this doubt leads to the assessment of other theoretical interpretations and if necessary the forging of new analytic tools. The socializing of knowledge is in many ways about sharing these different sources of knowledge and stimuli to further inquiry, to explain a social problem and identify the resources for change.

In chapter 3 I show how in much (not all) of their practice, these movements spurned the seductive goal of gaining power either within or over all-knowing authorities. I go on to show how they turned to ways by which they themselves could become more knowing – the consciousness-raising groups of the women's movement, for example, and a vast variety of grassroots forms of information exchange – thereby stimulating new forms of power necessary to achieve purposeful social change. This assumes a view of knowledge as a social product, distributed, valued and appropriated in ways that are potentially transformable; and in turn implies that the possibilities of radical and democratic social change depend to a considerable extent on democratizing and socializing the organization of knowledge. This applies to its distribution and character in both the state and private sector and in the labour movement and the left itself.

What are the logical steps that lead to this politics of knowledge? I argue them like this. The people who inherit and daily maintain, or passively reproduce, social institutions also inherit and reproduce social cultures. These cultures in turn include presuppositions about the character of knowledge and how it is best organized. Generally such presuppositions are not publicly discussed or consciously espoused. Debates about the organization of knowledge, let alone the philosophy of knowledge, are not normally the stuff of politics. When movements emerge, however, expressing a counter-culture which people have produced in the course of trying to transform the institutions surrounding them, the old presuppositions are laid bare. Just so with the assumptions concerning the character of knowledge underpinning the economic and political institutions of the Cold War. The culture of these institutions was permeated by a highly positivistic understanding of knowledge as exclusively based on generalizations from the regularities of social variables or the codification of repeated observable behaviour.

This view of knowledge has long been the subject of philosophical questioning. But in the stasis of the Cold War, political and social change lagged far behind philosophical change. It is not surprising then that when the pressures of social change burst into the streets, notably from 1968 onwards, competing theories of knowledge – the critical theory of Marcuse and Habermas, the relativism and 'post-modernism' of Foucault and Derrida, and more recently the critical realism of Bhaskar and others – should become unusually central to the left's public political debate.

This is as it should be. As established institutions are toppled and their cultural foundations found to be rotten, the instigators of change will be more effective if they consciously consider what new foundations they should prepare, rather than try to build on the rubble from the past. In chapter 4 therefore I also discuss possible theoretical tools that might be used to develop the approach to knowledge implicit in much of the practice of recent movements on the left.

In the course of reading – from this practical, political point of view – a selection of texts from the main aspirants to the role of intellectual champion, avuncular critic or, in the case of critical realism, underlabourer for the radical movements, I sometimes felt that in certain respects they were driving in a similar direction. Critical theory, critical realism and post-modernism are all with varying degrees of success challenging the legacy of positivistic views of science, knowledge and culture. But they each have developed out of engagements with different aspects of positivism in distinct political and cultural circumstances. Critical theory draws attention to the culture of positivism as it has pervaded economic, political and educational institutions. Consequently, it has tended to mix substantive social and cultural theories with reflections within the philosophy of knowledge. Critical realism, by contrast, has emerged out of an engagement with positivist philosophy of science and is consequently explicitly methodological (or using a more technical term, 'metatheoretical') in its purpose. Post-modernism has come from a diversity of engagements: most influential have been the break with modernist art and architecture and debates within cultural theory.

In considering how far these theories enable us to understand the character of recent movements' attempts to bring about social change, I have found the insights of critical theory and critical realism most fruitful. The impetus of post-modernism to deconstruct the language of the Enlightenment and challenge the tendency of humanist concepts – 'the human race', 'the people', 'human rights' – and to glide over different identities, is an impetus shared by social movements; so also is its scepticism towards notions of scientific and rational progress. At times, however, post-modernists' concern to demonstrate the active role of language and ideology in the creation of material cultural influences has led them to deny the very possibility of objectivity. This in turn erodes the idea of truth even as a standard to which we might aspire and denies the possibility of argument and agreement about what is to be done. Yet some kind of objective reality, posited without any presumption that language or the present state of our knowledge can ever directly reflect it in the way that positivism imagined, is a necessary condition for any collective effort to resist the injustices and oppressions in which post-modernists have shown language and culture to be actively complicit.

Critical realism (explicitly) and critical theory (arguably implicitly) base themselves on a realist ontology without assuming that language is a mere expression of that reality. They enable us both to understand cultural changes (in theories of knowledge, for instance) and to arrive at an approximation to the truth about their consequences for other spheres of society (institutions of political and economic power, for instance). Their critical approach demands that truth must always be open to revision as a result of experiment, but allows that in the meantime truth provides a basis for action, including collective action, to transform institutions.

Not surprisingly, then, this investigation into the forms of rationality presumed by those who now exercise power and the alternatives held out by those determined to counter this power has radical implications for the character of democratic government. The idea of knowledge as practical as well as theoretical, and of the human capacity to know as socially variable and actively transformable, leads to strategies for transformation that no longer envisage the state as an external engineer but as the potential source of a democratic and egalitarian framework and provider of public support and protection for a variety of forms of popular self-government. In terms of traditional debates about democracy, such an approach would imply a combination of participative and representative forms. A vital criteria concerning both the level at which power should lie and the appropriate forms of democracy through which it should be exercised would be the level and the form in which the knowledge of those affected by such power can be fully utilized.

Chapters 5, 6 and 7 illustrate what can be gleaned from the practice of the women's movement, radical parts of the trade union movement and parties emerging from, or influenced by, the green movement and the new left more generally. Experiences described in these chapters show possibilities for the democratic management of public provision, co-ordination and regulation of the economy and organization of political parties of the left.

Firstly, the recognition of the importance of diverse sources of knowledge and of their socially determined character implies that any notion of democracy based exclusively on formal democratic procedures (the election of representatives and public voting on competing programmes and opinions) is far too narrow an understanding of democracy. If democracy is to take account of the tacit, practical character of knowledge then democratic organization must also include the processes – formal as well as informal – by which decisions are implemented and the day-to-day management of a service, company or party takes place. The 'democracy of doing' must complement the democracy of deciding. In chapter 5, I explore possible mechanisms for this dimension of participatory democracy and the conditions necessary for their success, through discussion of the problems facing a group of feminists running a womens' adult education college in Sweden. This is a detailed case study which has wider implications for the self-management of the work and community institutions of everyday life.

Secondly, moving from the participatory processes of workplace self-management to the problems of economic co-ordination: a recognition of the practical and ephemeral character of much economic knowledge contradicts the desirability of a single, integrated decision-making process, either for the economy as a whole or for a sector of it. On the other hand, an understanding of the possibilities of the social and transformable character of economic knowledge and its organization undermines the neo-liberal case for the unregulated market and opens up the possibility of forms of economic co-ordination and regulation based on sharing knowledge amongst those at the base of the economy. This would involve forms of co-operation between elected political authorities at different levels (continental, national, regional or local) and associations of citizens as workers, consumers, users of services, inhabitants of a physical environment as well as a social community.

In chapter 6, I investigate examples of the democratic networks and public but non-state forms of economic organization which a variety of 'economic activists' have created, often in the course of what were initially defensive struggles where conventional forms of regulation failed or did not exist. The dynamic of these organizations – international workplace trade union networks; international campaigns of homeworkers; projects inspired by radical technologists; campaigns and organizations which attempt to change the character of trade; initiatives attempting to mobilize the pressure of consumers – is not so much to replace the state or the market. The thrust of their work is towards a democratization of the state that involves direct expression of the expertise of grassroots organizations representing those whose needs the left-wing party in government is aiming to meet. On the other hand, much of their activity implies a socializing of the market so that the antagonistic nature of private competition is overcome and the market is one source amongst several of the information needed for enterprises and government to take appropriate decisions.

The vision of a democratic society and economy as involving different forms of democracy, state and non-state, at distinct levels has radical implications for political agency. These I explore in chapter 7, which traces how the need to achieve an open sharing of knowledge was an important impetus among feminists, green, peace movement, lesbian and gay and trade union activists to create non-party, 'horizontal' forms of organizing for common goals across institutions, localities and nations ('networks' has become the common description, though this is now the fashionable word for any informal way of organizing).

The history of left movements over the last twenty years indicates that they have been at their most effective when they have consciously organized on the basis of these horizontal networks – not denying the need, frequently, for a practical hierarchy in the execution of any particular operation. In order to have a lasting political impact, however, such networks need infrastructures and people who will take responsibility for maintaining the infrastructure: the means by which networks communicate, interconnect, articulate, extend themselves. Often such work is neglected, with the consequence that networks have frequently to be recreated, with much wastage of scarce energy and loss of historical memory. Moreover, the network-based movements have found they need political representation to follow through the changes and demands for change that they have made outside the political system.

But they have not sought to meet this need for a permanent public voice in the conventional manner, by turning themselves into pressure groups and lobbies on an established party of the left. They have experimented with forms of representation by which organizations through which people are taking extra-parliamentary action through a party that shares their objectives, can have a direct presence within the political system. In most West European countries, such extra-parliamentary organizations have found that they need political support and political platforms of a kind that traditional social democratic and Communists parties cannot reliably give. Partly in response to this need, there are signs of new kinds of parties haltingly emerging (sometimes out of old established parties) which do not assume a monopoly or even necessarily a leadership of the process of change from the left. Such parties – the greens in Germany, the Socialist People's Party in Denmark, the United Left in Spain for instance – have a different character from their electoral competitors in that they are concerned neither to represent purely the individual voter nor a corporate interest group, but rather to provide a platform for ideas and projects of social change whose most dynamic activity is outside of the political structures. As yet these parties do not represent a coherent, stable political paradigm, but they have pioneered innovative forms of representation that have shaken the political systems in which they warily participate.

My choice of illustrations for the arguments linking democracy and knowledge is, perhaps inevitably, a somewhat personal one, based both on my own direct involvement and on examples which seemed both to test and elaborate the importance for genuine democracy of the organization of social and economic knowledge.

This raises the issue of the methodology and style of this book. I should assure the reader that the book does not claim to describe some 'general view' of recent movements of the left. It is not written therefore as if it were the summary of a comprehensive survey of the West European social movement left. Rather, I attempt to put forward several hypotheses stimulated by the combination of my own experience of social movement politics (mainly in the West), an appreciation and critique of Hayek's theory of knowledge and my reading of anti-positivistic philosophies of science.

The hypotheses are, in summary, that social movement activists, in much of their more innovative practice, have pioneered an approach to knowledge which, like Hayek, appreciates its practical and tacit aspects but, unlike Hayek, treats these and its theoretical aspects as social products. The democratization of knowledge runs through their methods. This underpins a belief that genuine democracy involves popular power in the running of society, which in turn is only realistic if economic life is egalitarian and co-operative. This represents an alternative challenge to the all-knowing state to that posed by the neo-liberal right: a challenge that, in contrast to the right, retains the genuine possibility and legitimacy of conscious, partially knowing efforts to transform society. Thus in their practice, if not their theory, they provide the basis of an answer to the appeal of the free-market to Eastern democrats.

Given the origin and character of these arguments, the style of the book varies. The challenge to the Western left is presented in an anecdotal form, from my own experience. The exploration of the appeal of neo-liberalism in the East takes the form of an investigation and critique of Hayek which is inevitably a work of theory. The initial overview of the approach to knowledge implicit in the left social movements that first emerged in 1968 is analytic and includes several examples. The assessment of the competing approaches to knowledge influencing or influenced by the social movements is primarily a piece of theoretical exegesis. The subsequent chapters consist of description and analysis of the examples that test or elaborate my hypotheses. Prepare, then, for a bumpy ride.

How do the hypotheses that run through the different parts of the book contribute to a new foundation for the left in post-Cold War Europe?

First, I should explain my focus on Europe, beyond pragmatic considerations of personal resources and location. Europe was the continent in which capitalist economies first matured; and in reaction to the hardships that this predatory economic dynamic, it was also the continent in which working people and intellectuals generated some of the earliest recorded 'socialist' ideas and organizations. Europeans have been the first to experience governments that ruled in the name of socialism, including the government of the USSR.

There is no doubt that the wealth of Europe, especially North-western Europe, which has underpinned the bargaining power of working-class movements, depended on the exploitation of the natural and human resources of the rest of the world. Moreover, the cultures of Europe, including the cultures of the left, drew from the suppressed civilizations of Asia, Africa and the Americas.

Debates about the future of the left are increasingly international, partly because they are stimulated by the rapid globalization of economic relations. But the experiences of resistance and alternatives are shaped by continental histories and the national and regional variations that these contain. Thus my focus on the left in Europe does not necessarily restrict the wider relevance of my arguments, nor do I deny that my thesis would have been greatly enriched or altered by drawing on recent experiences of the left in Latin America, India or South Africa. My historically and geographically specific focus of course also means that the developments discussed in this book are not the only alternatives to liberal capitalism. On the one hand, distinct models of socialism are being fashioned through trial and error in a minority of countries in Latin America, Asia and Africa. On the other hand, a form of capitalist development led by strong authoritarian states proved in its own terms to be highly successful in Japan and is now being adapted in more extreme forms and apparently with equal success in Taiwan, South Korea, and other newly industrializing countries.

At the same time as the positivistic understandings of knowledge and the social-engineering conception of the state and its relation to society have been under challenge from the libertarian left and the neo-liberal right in Europe, nation states themselves in Western Europe have been under attack. Some of the powers of these nation states, as with others across the world, have been undermined from 'above', that is, from international economic organizations. West European nation states have been under attack also from below, from people in workplaces and communities frustrated by the impotence of national parliaments to respond to their needs, and from people recognizing the international nature of the main threats to human life and dignity. This book is predominantly about the challenge from below, a challenge to the methods as well as the spatial limits of contemporary national governments.

The networks of this new left aspire to be international: after all, they have developed out of efforts to track down and understand the new powers of multinationals and inter-governmental institutions, and to share common experiences of struggle and organization for which there are no national models. In chapter 8 I assess the importance of these movements as actors in contemporary European politics by examining what role they had in ending the Cold War. My conclusion is that they are actors whose sources of power, deriving in part from the networks and resources created by radical movements of the previous ten years, took established actors on both sides of the iron curtain by surprise. I present the evidence for concluding that the peace movements of the early eighties were, across Europe, a real material force in creating a political climate (against the pressures from the Pentagon and NATO) favourable to Gorbachev's dramatic moves towards disarmament, thereby easing the way for Perestroika and what turned out to be the end of the polarization of Europe. The one-sided way in which the Cold War ended, however, was not wholly as the majority of peace activists wanted.

The sources of power that the movements could draw on in the early 1980s can only under special circumstances be mobilized. Frequently this new left politics is marginal and sometimes self-marginalizing. The absence of a democratic pan-European political framework contributes to their invisibility. The distinctively European or at least transnational campaigns and initiatives of, for example, the lesbian and gay, anti-racist and feminist movements can gain little political expression.

The result is not so much a democratic deficit, to be remedied over time, but a dangerous kind of democratic vacuum which is especially threatening at a time of growing economic insecurity for a large proportion of the population, who are therefore actively, and incoherently, seeking remedies but finding none within the existing political system. The far right in Western Europe has rallied its popular support under banners which invoke EC institutions as well as foreign workers as threats to the future.

The commitment which is common to the Western new left and those Eastern oppositionists who have remained outside the state – namely, the commitment to democratic civic movements as necessary though not sufficient agencies of social change – has a unique importance in filling the democratic vacuum and undermining popular support for the far right. Such movements have the power to create the social associations of daily life by which people gain both some power to shape their futures and a source of identity that is not defined by its hatred of others. The growth of such democratic civic associations, rooted amongst the most powerless and frustrated of society, will be a base from which the new authoritarianism and popular racism spreading across Europe could be countered. At present, however, the social base of democratic social and radical trade union movements is limited. There will need to be a concerted effort to extend that base from that of a minority counter-culture, to a political force for democracy and social security.

As with the peace and green movements of the early 1980s, this is more than 'single issue' campaign. Like them it involves a shared set of values and at least a vision of the principles of democratic control which would begin to answer popular frustration with the present trends of European politics. The politics of democratic social and trade union movements provides a basis. If they were to develop they would represent a new kind of left: in which a liberalism that had moved beyond individualism co-operated and contested with a form of socialism that no longer relied primarily on the nation state.

Notes

1 See the collection of Havel's opposition essays *Living in Truth* (London, 1986), especially 'The Power of the Powerless' and 'An Anatomy of Reticence'; Jaroslav Sabota's correspondance with E. P. Thompson in *Voices from Prague* (London, 1981); George Konrad's *Anti-Politics* (London, 1984).
2 I organized a weekend seminar together with the Transnational Institute in Amsterdam to explore this dialogue. A transcript has been published as *After the Wall: Social Movements and Democratic Politics in the New Europe* (TNI, 1991). Available from Frontline Books, 1 Newton Street, Piccadilly, Manchester 1, at £5.95.
3 This varies from country to country and is gradually changing, as people redis-cover the histories of their own countries – in which in most cases (Russia, Czechoslovakia and Hungary, for instance), such alternatives precariously existed – and as Westerners beyond the limited circles of neo-liberal think-tanks become involved in the processes of reconstruction.
4 Barbara Wootton, *Freedom Under Planning* (London, 1947), and Anthony Crosland, *The Future of Socialism*, revised edition (London, 1963).
5 'The Use of Knowledge in Society', in *Individualism and Economic Order* (London, 1949).
6 See chapter 2.
7 It was also the basis of an instrumental approach to nature: the natural world was treated as if it was made up of inanimate objects to be manipulated for human ends and unable to recoil with action of its own. See Ted Benton, *Natural Relations* (London, 1993), and forthcoming Kate Soper, *The Idea of Nature* (Oxford, 1994).
8 'The Use of Knowledge in Society', p. 80.
9 See the work of Sandra Harding, especially *The Science Question in Feminism* (New York, 1986) and *Discovering Reality: Feminist Perspectives on Epistemology, Meta-physics, Methodology and Philosophy of Science* (Dordrecht, Holland, 1983); Hilary Rose, 'Heart, Brain and Heart: A Feminist Epistemology for the Natural Sci-ences', in *Signs: Journal of Women in Culture and Society*, 9, no. 1; Donna Haraway, in Linda Nicholson (ed.) *Feminism/Post-Modernism* (London, 1990).

PART I

AN EASTERN CHALLENGE TO THE WESTERN LEFT

1

ENCOUNTERS IN THE NEW EUROPE

In recent years statesmen have not looked quite as in control as they once did. Lord Carrington, the erstwhile master of international diplomacy, appeared nonplussed by his Yugoslav mission. Mikhail Gorbachev, the arch-tactician, seemed bewildered at his loss of control of the Communist Party and in turn its loss of leverage on society. Off their guard, ruling institutions have also expressed unease. 'Historical change is happening in a way it was not meant to happen,' complained an American defence expert at NATO's headquarters.[1] During the Cold War everything seemed so predictable. Or at least, if something unpredictable happened – a student revolt, for example, or even a popular uprising – those in control had the ideological framework, and the power, to ensure that order would be restored. As 'Soviet inspired' on the one side of the Iron Curtain, 'engineered by the CIA' on the other, rebellion could be marginalized or crushed.

The rock-like certainties laid down at Yalta have been overwhelmed by the forces of the ocean, to use Shelley's metaphor for the power of the people. Shelley bids us not to fear the oceans' roar: he was welcoming its power to sweep away a corrupt and rotten ruling order. But in the years since 1989 the sounds have become distinctly threatening to the people who imagined they were free. For the people of Bosnia, Croatia and Serbia the aftermath of 1989 has been life-threatening, as leaders desperate to maintain or extend their power incite ethnic violence. In Hungary the aftermath has threatened newly-gained liberties, as the governing party fans popular nationalist sentiments into flames of xenophobia in an attempt to create cohesion in the midst of economic and social division. A new authoritarianism is establishing itself in Eastern Europe, using instruments of state power, from the army to the media, to arouse nationalist sentiments and establish control over societies breaking up unprotected from the forces of the international market.

Ugly noises are coming also from the West, from the prosperous streets of West Germany: the cries of Polish, Romanian or Turkish families as their houses are burnt or their children stabbed.[2] And from the political platforms of France, Austria and Germany, as the racist demagogy of Jean-Marie Le Pen, Jörg Haider and Franz Schönhuber turns migrant communities into scapegoats for economic and political insecurities whose causes lie outside national control.

Those who found 'the peak of the wave [of the European revolutions] so beautiful,' in Neal Ascherson's words, need to listen hard for hopeful sounds from beneath the swirling water. Sometimes they surface in the Western press – for example, when Jiri Dienstbier, the Foreign Minister in Czechoslovakia and leader of the social liberal minority, the Civic Movement,[3] publicly opposed the 'Lustration Law' introduced to ban any office holder under the Communist regime from office, and used to create a McCarthyite surge against anyone on the left, including some of those who led the opposition to the Communist regime;[4] or when the Helsinki Citizens' Assembly, founded in 1988 by Charter 77 and the European Campaign for Nuclear Disarmament, organized a peace caravan across the republics that once made up Yugoslavia, with participants from 14 different European countries (it ended in Sarajevo, with a human chain linking the mosque, the synogogue, the catholic and the orthodox churches). More usually, however, a Westerner must go and search out the people who are creating on the ground countervailing pressures to the sweeping force of xenophobia.

If such a Westerner has radical left-wing convictions she or he will be uneasy, perhaps unsettled, by the political language they hear, however critical they were of the old regimes. There are of course people in the East who speak a similar language to that of the Western new left: groups of left feminists, social ecologists, anarcho-syndicalists and libertarian socialists. Many are uncomfortable, however, with the word 'socialism', even though they would agree that they share social visions and values with those socialists involved in social movements in the West. Moreover, for the most part, they are too few to be considered at this stage a powerful force for change.[5] The historic parties of social democracy, revived often under the leadership of exiles returned after 1989, are not in a much stronger position, in spite of their political pedigree.[6] The old Communist Parties, however, purged in most cases of both their old leaderships and their old names, have been rather more successful, at least electorally.[7] There is convincing evidence at least from Hungary that large proportions of the population hold what are in effect social democratic economic values, or at least attitudes which value social security and economic egalitarianism. The association, however, of social democratic parties with Communism – whether because they actually were associated or because they echo its language and have not clarified their break – has restricted their appeal.[8] In most central and East European countries it has proved difficult for any significant section of the intelligentsia to develop a politics which articulates the underlying social priorities of a large proportion of the population, taking full account of the failures of command economics without accepting a neo-liberal economic framework.

Challenging encounters

The Western traveller will find other significant, though minority, allies in Eastern Europe against the new exclusivisms threatening to divide the continent. Their political mix is not easily labelled. They share similarly internationalist convictions to those of the Western new left and also like them place emphasis on public civic inititatives as agents of political change. At the same time, however, they support, with varying qualifications, policies for rapid marketization. They often express a commitment to a neo-liberal philosophy of the free market, if not to all its policy prescriptions.

First, however, some introductions.

Footsoldiers of the velvet revolution

Visit the offices of *Respekt* and *Revolver Revue* in Bolzanova Street, Prague, across the park from the main station recently renamed Wilsonovo Nádrazí – after the First World War American president. In the unlit, decaying grandeur of an art nouveau town mansion you will find, unannounced, the three rooms of this influential weekly magazine. It is a workers' co-op which first came together to run an information service during the 'velvet revolution'. Many of its 20 staff had become friends through playing in rock bands like the famous 'Plastic People' and 'DG 307', the musical equivalent of samizdat. Their bands are now amongst the best known in the country. And *Respekt* is advertised with style and neon lights on the subway. It sells around 75,000 copies a week.

The atmosphere in the office and the style of its occupants could have been transported from *Oz*, *Ink* or any of the publications which grew out of the Western 1968. Until, that is, you look a little closer at the posters: the patronizing stare of president Bush, without graffiti, next to the more familiar smirk of Mick Jagger. Or until the journalists talk approvingly about the monetarist economic programme of the Prime Minister, Vaclav Klaus. The comments of Martin Weiss, the economics editor, were characteristic: 'We want the reforms to be implemented swiftly. The market must be free to close down inefficient factories. Otherwise trade unions will push their own interest. The government should tell them their demands are wrong.' As Finance Minister in the first post-Communist government, Klaus had been quick off the mark with his economic programme, presenting it to the government in February 1991. This enabled him to outflank those like Voltr Komarek, the Deputy Prime Minister, who were arguing for a slower, more protectionist, more social democratic approach to the reforms, but who lacked a detailed programme demonstrating how their approach would work.[9]

The journalists at *Respekt* supported Klaus against Komarek but there was one fundamental issue on which many of them disagreed with Klaus and the neo-liberal right. At a Civic Forum conference in January 1991, when he was preparing the ground for his later move to turn the Forum into a neo-liberal political party, Klaus declared that 'civic movements are incompatible with a modern European state'.[10] Petr Janyska, *Respekt*'s political editor, believed the opposite: 'For us civic initiatives are vital to our new democracy. We have criticized Klaus for condemning them.' He added a further point of disagreement which provides a clue to the distinct character of these young people's espousal of neo-liberalism, quite different to the Prime Minister's interpretation of the same doctrine: 'Open government is important too.' Janyska insists that 'There is still too much cabinet-style, closed decision making.'[11]

For Klaus neo-liberalism is a technocratic model of how market economies best work and a set of monetarist prescriptions that flow from it.[12] In the eyes of many of the young footsoldiers of Prague's velvet revolution, by contrast, neo-liberalism is a set of moral and philosophical principles, stemming originally from the work of Frederick Hayek, whose writings were widely read by the opposition. But in their support for civic movements Petr Janyska and young people like him have associated neo-liberal principles with an implicitly radical notion of democracy which Hayek would find positively dangerous.

Yuppies or young democrats?

For a double-check on this unusual (to a Western ear) combination of radical social and cultural values with right-wing economics, take the night train to Budapest and visit the palatial offices, just off 'the heroes square', of FIDESZ, the Federation of Young Democrats. It is the third largest political party in

Hungary, with 22 MPs and a strong base in local government. The largest (and government) party is, in 1993, the Hungarian Democratic Forum (HDF), supported by the Independent Farmers' Party. Opposing this right-wing nationalist alliance is the SDS with 92 seats after the March 1990 elections; and FIDESZ. ('Opposing' is perhaps a rather strong word for the SDS, the social liberal party that in 1990 came to an arrangement with the HDF which it has now broken.) The iconoclasm of FIDESZ and its bold, imaginative tactics – a human chain either side and across the Danube against the Nagymaros Dam, poster campaigns satirizing the Communist hierarchs, independent womens' actions – made it a focus of youth opposition in the last months of the old regime, especially for students. By 1992 it was one rallying point for younger people disappointed with the conservative character of the new government.[13]

FIDESZ has become a professional political movement, inside and outside parliament. The lavish building it occupies used to belong to the old regime's council for supervising the church. It has now become something of an international youth centre. You might be ushered into the well-furnished offices of Andras Klein, a suave young man with a waistcoat and gentle American twang. He will proudly present their policy pamphlet with the familiar FIDESZ logo (an orange) on the front cover.

At the top of its list of aims is 'a rapid transformation to a free-market economy'. Moreover, they are sternly against groups, including workers' organizations, who press what they consider to be sectional interests against these reforms. They opposed, for instance, the taxi drivers striking in 1990 against sudden price rises. On the other hand, ecology is also a high priority: the campaign against the massive hydro-electric dam which the Kadar regime planned to build on the Hungarian–Czechoslovak border was their formative experience. They believe in equal opportunities and argue that economic institutions 'must be based on social solidarity and able to support enterprises weakened by economic competition'. Their espousal of the free market was not combined with the usual Cold War stance in which opposition to the Soviet Union became support for NATO and the foreign policy of the West. From their origins, FIDESZ have been openly against both military blocs and for a European unity in which the rights of national and ethnic minorities are guaranteed.[14]

FIDESZ declare proudly that their politics 'are an evolving hybrid' growing 'from the forces that gave rise to democracy in Eastern Europe'. A discussion with a group of their MPs in the square concrete block that used to be the headquarters of the old Communist Party and which is now the block for Hungarian MPs, reveals more of this hybrid character – increasingly a cause of division and debate. The issue of ecology illustrates it best. The hydroelectric Danube dam symbolized the old centralized planning system: 'If the government were the Pharos, the dam was their pyramid,' commented Clara Ungar, a FIDESZ economic spokeswoman and, in 1990, FIDESZ's candidate for Mayor of Budapest. Clara's Jewish parents at the end of the war were committed Communists, 'quite naturally, as the result of their situation,' Clara observed. Her own commitment to the free market, a natural commitment, she felt, given her circumstances, is the outcome of a lengthy process. This began with economics lectures from teachers who had tried to reform the system, to introduce enterprise autonomy, to stimulate markets, or in Clara's terms, 'to mend old clothes'. Observing the failure of half measures and influenced by the writings of Hayek, available in samizdat, she concluded that an 'entirely new suit of clothes was the only alternative'. But she was not 'a dogmatic Friedmanite'.

Zsusza Szaleni, a foreign affairs spokeswoman, interrupted: 'The libertarian economists have nothing useful to say about ecology or about peace. The libertarians base everything on individuals and private property but peace and ecology need social co-operation.' Zsusza took the issue of identifying the environmental and social costs of a project to develop her point: 'private businesses can't adequately assess these costs, it's beyond their scope. On the other hand, a government cannot run a business. A government can never run a business.' Her conclusion, drawing from their experiences fighting the Nagymaros Dam, put a lot of emphasis on local and environmental movements and citizens' groups. 'The government must respect their knowledge' she insisted, though without indicating the institutions through which a relationship with a more respectful government might work. 'The Danube Circle [the leading group in the anti-dam campaign before 1989] brought together all the different kinds of knowledge that were necessary to judge the consequences, but the government would not respond.' The HDF had altered the Communist Government's plans for the dam but its methods did not give any credence to the environmental movement.

FIDESZ's approach to the political process does not view political change as simply a matter for political parties. It is committed to campaigning outside parliament. 'We don't think that getting into government and taking hold of the state is enough to create democracy,' Clara asserted: 'We have to encourage self-organization built up from the communities.' This is the FIDESZ ideal; some might say it is rhetoric. Certainly it had become marginal to the concerns of FIDESZ's national leadership, though it was still the view of many of its supporters and local activists. For some people in FIDESZ, the commitment to civic movements was a necessary strategy specific to the circumstances of, effectively, a one-party state. Now that they can organize parliamentary political parties, they see no role for civic movements. Moreover, the vacuum in democratic and critical practice within the political institutions has tended to suck the energies of FIDESZ from the communities into the parliamentary and council chambers. There are now sharp divisions within FIDESZ in which those committed to turning the Alliance into a conventional, if youthful, parliamentary party, are dominant. They are determined and energetic in pursuing their parliamentary ambitions.

A new trade unionism?

There are other groups of people devoting themselves to self-organization: for example, the activists of the new independent trade unions. The strength and perspectives of these vary from country to country, as does the role they played in the democratic transformations. In what was Czechoslovakia, workers' strike committees formed almost overnight by factory supporters of the Civic Forum provided the revolution with the final support it needed. Jan Uhlír, a young worker activist in 1968, was a leader of a workers' occupation in one of Prague's largest factories, the CKD electrical factory. In the aftermath of 1968 indispensable technical skills had enabled him to retain his job. After lying low, he emerged again as leader of the strike committee twenty-one years later.

A welcoming character, not yet bureacratized by his new status as President of the new Metal Workers' Union, Jan Uhlír might invite you to join him on one of his visits to the CDK locomotive factory, with its own entrance to a suburban station on the Prague underground. The workers here were regarded traditionally by the Communist Party as the bodies on which the Party could always rely if they needed a 'spontaneous' demonstration. But during the 1989 revolution they had booed Communist Party Secretary Miroslav Stepán off the platform when he came on to win their 'spontaneous' support against the student-led revolt in Wenceslas Square. The man who stood next to Stepán as he mocked the students in the hope of winning the workers, was (in 1993) still the manager of CKD Locomotives.

The eight men and two women on the newly elected workers' committee are exploring ways of making use of privatization as a way of getting rid of this management and gaining some collective influence over the managment of the company. In this they are a group of workers after Jan Uhlír's own heart; a bit of a test case for his own thinking about privatization. He wants the Metal Workers' Union and local union committees to make use of privatization to gain an influence over management which they were never able to achieve under the Communists. (The new parliament also voted down modest proposals for legal rights for the participation of workers in the running of their enterprises.) Uhlír had his own plans for privatization: 'I am recommending that workers concentrate their coupons [distributed in the process of 'coupon privatization']¹⁵ into the buying of their own factory and that after privatization, they elect a committee which will represent them in the shareholding company.' It would seek to exert an influence on the management of the company directly to complement trade union bargaining. This and other strategies for workers gaining collective influence over the privatization process was, he believed, the best way to fight the corruption involved in privatization.¹⁶ Where did this approach put him on the political spectrum? He had clearly talked to Western trade unionists or leftists before: 'If I lived in Britain, I would most likely be a member of the left wing of the Labour party, but in Czechoslovakia I am a typical liberal like Mr Pithart [in 1991 the Prime Minister of the Czech Government] on the centre right. Our left is trying to keep the state totally in control. It is going up what on Darwin's theory would be a dead branch of evolution.' He used to share the left's belief in the state, 'But it was the degeneration of people at the top which made me believe that there has to be some form of competition: if it can't be the market then we, the workers, must do it. We must jeopardize the existence of the management. Until now incompetent managers have been going up and up.'

A challenge not to be evaded

My encounters with these people came after a long silence. It has been twenty years since my last sustained conversations with East Europeans on their home ground. They came as something of a shock to me: the kind of occasions that make you think on through the night and see things a little differently in the morning. They present a challenge that seems to be answerable, but when you try, it does not turn out to be so easy.

There are ways of evading this challenge but they only work in Western debate. One is the wishful 'I told you so'. It is the argument that free-market policies are producing social misery and unrest, and that this unrest will lead in the direction of social democratic regulation and intervention in the market, and/or attempts at workers' control and a re-awakening of interest in democratic socialism. The argument has a certain coherence, but again it does not take full account of the depth of people's rejection of practical measures with any explicit association with anything called 'socialism'.

Social misery and unrest certaintly exists. And it will grow. One of the most militant groups of workers in Poland is engineering workers in Warsaw. The economic policy of some of these workers is to get rid of the Jews who, they fantasize, are running business and the government. Another militant group of workers is miners in Slovakia; one of their first demands has been to be free of the Czechs. Not much sign here of a logic that leads from unrest to socialism. And this kind of consciousness is not exceptional. Even where there is evidence that values of social justice are widely shared, as Iván and Szonja Szelényi show to be the case in Hungary,[17] there is no party that has yet found a way of expressing them in a form that is free of association with the past, and therefore likely to win widespread support. In other words there is little at present in the public political culture of Eastern Europe to provide the links in the argument of Western socialists saying 'I told you so'.

The second evasion of the challenge, an evasion which also incorporates certain truths, is the 'we've never believed these regimes were genuinely socialist' argument. It is true and important publicly to recall that left-wing critics of the Communist states have a persistent and generally honourable record. From Rosa Luxemburg, Victor Serge, Alexandra Kollontai, Emma Goldman, Leon Trotsky, Ante Ciliga through to Ernest Mandel and Rudolf Bahro, they have been pointing out, from very different standpoints, how democracy is suppressed by a one-party system and how a self-interested bureacracy substituted itself for a working class. Kollontai questioned the 'ridiculously naive' belief increasingly shared by Bolshevik leaders 'that it is possible to bring about communism by bureacratic means', and argued for the development of the cultural qualities amongst the working class and peasantry that would make possible democratic forms of organizing production and distribution. Ante Ciliga, the Yugoslav Communist jailed in the USSR for five years in 1930, concluded that prison is 'the only place in Soviet Russia where people can express their feelings sincerely and openly'.[18]

Depending on when these different critics wrote, there have been historical moments when their arguments implied alternatives with some visible roots in social forces within Soviet society. These were times in other words, where some means, however fragile, towards making these alternatives a reality actually existed. The vision had a material reality which could register in people's experience – whether it was the remains of democratic life in the Soviets, the suppressed but nevertheless organized political tendencies in the Communist Party, initiatives by independent organizations of peasants and workers, or a reformist wing of the Communist leadership. The critics were never able to mobilize the power effectively to realize an alternative. But at least their criticisms, posed in terms of the contrast between actually existing socialism and the original objectives, and an alternative view of socialism had some grounds in the reality of the Soviet bloc. As the possibility of an alternative which could be meaningfully understood by Easterners as having some association with socialism diminished, the impact of critics writing within the theory and language of socialism declined. The fall of Gorbachev probably symbolized the final blow to the major influence of many such critics – even where their criticisms were directed at him as well as the old leadership.

This has importance for the theory and language with which the Western new left can answer the challenge posed by the pervasive, if contradictory, appeal of neo-liberalism. It means, I would argue, that although the elements of alternatives, even what many Westerners would perceive as socialist alternatives, are likely to develop in Eastern Europe – no doubt in most unexpected ways – they cannot necessarily be built on and generalized through existing theoretical frameworks of socialism. Rather, the Western new left needs, in dialogue with those movements in the East, to theorize these new social practices through a direct critique of the foundations of neo-liberalism, in particular the influential work of the Austrian economist and philosopher, Frederick Hayek. There then can be a regrounding of socialism, I would argue, in assumptions developed through such a critique.

Unlike arguments which take a socialist theoretical framework for granted, such a critique does have potential purchase on actual consciousness in the East. It has both a critical purchase because of the failure of neo-liberal economic prescriptions; and a constructive purchase on the belief amongst East European social liberals – quite inconsistent with neo-liberalism – in the importance of democratic 'civic initiatives' or 'civic movements'. This belief apparent for instance in the Czech Civic Movement, amongst some groups within FIDESZ and social liberals in Poland, involves a recognition of forms of purposeful, collective action that are supportive rather than undermining of individual happiness. It goes against the grain of the atomistic individualism that is a foundation stone of neo-liberalism.

The politics of East – West relations

An engagement with Hayek and the neo-liberal right is a useful intellectual exercise for the left, a way of sharpening its conceptual tools. But what bearing does it have on the struggles for democracy and social justice in Europe? A little local conflict in Hungary provides a clue to an answer.

On a Thursday night towards the end of September 1992, around 50,000 Hungarians joined a torchlight protest through the streets of Budapest. It was the biggest demonstration that the present government has faced. The organizers were a coalition, the Democratic Charter, of political parties of the left and the social liberals (including supporters of FIDESZ), different trade unionists and many writers and artists. What brought them together a year earlier to found the Democratic Charter was anxiety at 'the decline in democracy in the country and an upswing in nationalism and intolerance'. It was two developments in particular which brought them into the streets.

First, the government was engaging in an open attempt to achieve control over sensitive cultural institutions such as the radio, television and the school system. The social strains of growing unemployment, declining public services, widening inequalities and a processes of proletarianization (rather than the expected growth of the middle classes) have been facing the government party with problems of social cohesion and ideological control. The origins of the HDF are too contemporary and too socially restricted for it to have its own means for such ideological cohesion. It is consequently using the state to suppress critical debate and to instill nationalist values. Most notoriously, it tried to sack Gombar Csaba and Hankiss Ellenur, the heads of Radio and Television respectively. These people were not HDF party men, but they were supportive of its moves to marketize the economy and the government had approved their appointment. Their misdemeanour was that they encouraged open debate; they gave an airing to views critical of the government and they provided a secular framework for their programming, rather than promoting the HDF's particular nationalist conservatism.

The President, not a member of the HDF, took the unusual step of vetoing the move to sack them. Since then the HDF have attempted to mobilize popular pressure to reverse the veto. A front committee of the party, 'The Committee for Free Hungarian Information', organized a demonstration in support of the sacking of Gombar and Hankiss and 'against the denigration of the Hungarian spirit'. The Democratic Charter's demonstration was a reply to this action.

The rhetoric of the HDF seeks to equate opposition with defence of communism. Csurka István, in 1992 the deputy leader of the party and increasingly the spokesperson of a growing right-wing populism, added a further item to this propaganda equation: in a recent pamphlet he refers to the 'left-wing bloc which cannot be overwhelmed by anti-communist radicalism, and which, in the final instance, is trying to maintain the power structures in place since 1945. To this naturally belongs also the guaranteeing of Jewish influence, but the most important is the preservation of material positions and the inheritance of power.' The 50,000 marching in Budapest had come on the streets in protest against semi-official anti-Semitism (Joszef Antall, the party leader, did not explicitly condemn Csurka's remarks), as well as the authoritarian intervention in the press that Csurka was seeking to justify.

For the oppositionists against the previous regime, political developments are becoming depressingly familiar: 'The situation hasn't changed much,' said Istvan Rev, a Hungarian oppositionist (in 1992, advisor to the Free Democrat Mayor of Budapest) with a sad, exhausted look on his face; 'but now we have to fight against an authoritarian government which has the legitimacy of being democratically elected'. For the underground opposition (or in Hungary, the spa bath opposition: leading oppositionists made the renowned baths one of their meeting places), a channel of information and support through citizens' movements in the West was vital. But now that these people have won the right to vote between genuinely competing parties, to overthrow governments of whose actions they disapprove, is this co-operation of any importance to Central and East Europeans and to the future of Europe?

A statement by an HDF ideologue, Imre Konya, openly explaining the party's purpose in trying to sack the media chiefs, indicates that Western knowledge of and responses to developments in the East is a determining factor in the behaviour of the governing party of Hungary. He is quoted in a Hungarian daily paper, *Magyar Hirlap*:

> It was part of the government's political character that in the first period, confrontations should be avoided, in order that the country should appear in a favourable light to foreign eyes. Now, however, when the world's image of our country is unambiguous, when nobody any longer doubts the government's and the HDF's commitment to liberalism, democracy, press freedom, human rights and the market economy – in my view it is now possible to effect a root and branch transformation in the viewpoint and personnel of the Hungarian TV and Radio.

Western approval, once given, is literally a seal of approval, a licence. Jan Urban, a founder signature of Charter 77, election campaign organizer for Civic Forum and now an outspoken columnist on the liberal Czech newspaper *Lidové Noviny*, described to me the corruption taking place in the course of privatization. He documents it in his columns but the information never reaches the West, or at least is never sufficiently public to lead to a focusing of the seeing eye. Urban comments: 'Western governments have turned a blind eye, on the highly dubious grounds that the present government is the only alternative to chaos. We need partners in the West who will publicize the truth, as before.' The West's blind eye makes this licence permanent, unless unofficial eyes are alert and able to disseminate what they see.

A clear plea for co-operation from the East then, with those who stimulate a critical public in the West. It is also important that there is a flow of information and exposure about the West. For a lot of faith has been placed in what the West, especially the EC, will do for the East now that the people of these forgotten lands have overthrown the enemies of the West. It is a faith that weakens the impetus for self-government and creates a new kind of deference to authority.

The EC's response to the East: expectations and realities

In Central Europe, the EC has had a mirage effect. Like the blazing sun on the desert sand, the promises arising from the claims for the European 'free market' as they shone over the ruins of Communism created vivid pictures of European democracy. One of the first things that Vaclav Havel did when he became President of the Republic of Czechoslovakia was to speak in triumph and in supplication to the Council of Europe and the European Parliament. He warned that the EC should act to prevent a 'void of despair from being created [in Czechoslovakia] because instability exerts its influence and spreads from its original source. The EC has supported our efforts to establish a democracy, today you cannot be indifferent to what is happening in our country, if only for a question of your own survival'. Havel was thinking both of Czechoslovak entry to the EC and, in the meantime, access to its export markets.

The EC Commission and Council of Ministers, however, had a rather different view of their own survival and Eastern Europe's role in it. Judging by the negotiations over trade – eventually signed, late 1991, as the 'Europe Agreements' – the EC's main concern was to avoid giving Eastern Europe any openings where it had a limited competitive advantage, in particular textiles, agricultrural products, coal and steel.[19] The Central Europeans were wanting direct trading relation with the EC. Naively they believed that 'a free market' was an open market to those who wanted to sell. Ironically, the EC's European Bank of Reconstruction places very stringent conditions on its aid to Eastern Europe, particularly on the free movement of capital into these countries and the free movement of profits out. The advantage, it seems, of centralized market institutions is that they can set different rules for different purposes. A topsy-turvy sort of thing, this free market.

The new Central and Eastern governments of 1989 are desperately dependent on the West to facilitate the transition of their societies to some form of democracy. To establish the economic conditions for democracy they needed rapid and open access to Western markets, not only for immediate export growth but also to reassure Western investors, who would want to sell to the EC because Eastern markets are so miniscule. At the same time they needed a degree of protection closely related to reconstruction, instead of immediate exposure to the slicing winds of the world economy. This could have involved a degree of planning and public subsidy – through regional and local structures as much as national ones – at the same time as privatization, to build on the comparative advantages of the two approaches and identify likely. market niches. It would have involved enabling wages and social insurance to increase at the same time as prices were liberalized. They needed relaxation of the crippling debt burdens they had inherited from the governments against which they had fought – debts which were no fault of theirs. They needed support in establishing political structures of democracy, such as local and regional government, which would provide conditions for some of the planning (this time, of a pluralist kind) which reconstruction requires.

Such support would make the process of deciding on the content of economic restructuring at every level an opportunity to exercise newly-won political rights. They needed Western effort to assist the former Soviet Union's integration into the international system so that it could earn sufficient from exports to the West to import from Central and Eastern Europe. And they needed some commitment from the EC that their people and their states would become full members of the EC, and therefore gain more access to decisions which are anyway determining their fate.

Instead of a package like this (a modest version of the kind of support that Western Europe had from the United States after the Second World War), Central and Eastern European economies, already in crisis with the collapse of the Soviet market and the Comecon system of exchanges, received a prolonged sharp shock. The result, in those countries where the government accepted, sometimes sought, this medicine, has been a decimation of manufacturing, including private manufacturing; and turmoil in agriculture, especially amongst private and small co-operative agriculture.[20]

The consequences of Western austerity medicine on the ailing body of Eastern Europe have been intensified by its international environment: a global economy in severe recession. Unemployment is ravaging the people of these countries, sapping their self-confidence and morale – and reducing the likelihood of their democratic participation in the public life of their region or nation.[21] The character of Western aid does little to mitigate these corrosive economic conditions. The extent to which Central and East European countries have to service debts to the West could well cancel out the investment aid coming from West to East. Andre Gunder Frank reports that the annual flow of interest from the East on their total debt of £120 billion is between £10–15 billion. This sum is more than the entire capital of the European Bank of Reconstruction and Development.[22]

This approach has been justified in technical terms as the only scientific means to democracy. This also served to justify the means: that is, the strong-arm economic methods of the IMF. But there were and are other options by which the Central and Eastern economies could be integrated into the world economy. Instead of democratic consideration of these and other options, Western institutions, both US and EC, seem to have pursued the logic of the Cold War on the economic front. The governments of the East have been treated, rather like Germany after the Second World War, as countries without the capacity to take their own decisions, as societies whose fate is to be decided outside, by the victors of the war. In the process, Western elites are further denuding the already very stony ground of the economic soil that is necessary for democratic citizenship to flourish. Moreover, as the war in the former Yugoslavia tragically demonstrated and the growing migration of Easterners to the West gives continuing witness, the consequences cannot be curtained off from the rest of Europe.

Pan-European coalitions

In this context, more than mutual flows of information are necessary between democratic activists East and West. Pan-European political agencies – not necessarily parties, but movements and democratic networks; organizations, that is, able to mobilize many different kinds of power – are required, to exert pressure on Western institutions, to give platforms and legitimacy to the emerging Eastern opposition coalitions like Democratic Charter in Hungary.

Admittedly, for many of the Eastern democrats who think in terms of civic movements, especially those erstwhile oppositionists who now have parlia-mentary or municipal responsibilities, the commitment to building civic initiatives has been in the last two years low on their priorities. But in circumstances where powerful politicians are constructing new forms of au-thoritarianism based on a populist xenophobia, the minds of these democrats are concentrating once again on how to stimulate amongst their fellow citizens a critical consciousness, a capacity for public self-organization inde-pendent both of charismatic leaders and the state. These new struggles will need again to be supported by democratic social movements in the West.

The process of creating sustained co-operation East and West will be very much easier in physical and technical terms than in the pre-1989 days of clandestine meetings in private flats and evasion of secret police. But intellec-tually and politically, it will be more complex. There is agreement about the importance of defending democratic civic and political rights, but apparently a fundamental rift over the economic and institutional conditions which will underpin them. At the root of these disagreements are the doctrines of neo-liberalism and their widespread appeal amongst the political intelligentsia of Central and Eastern Europe. Those Westerners who become involved in a pan-European struggle for democracy and social justice must face the challenge presented by the influence of these ideas amongst the civic activists now regrouping for further efforts to establish genuine democracies.

Notes

1 Quoted in Alan Riding, 'Redoing Europe', *New York Times*, 15 April 1990.
2 Nearly 500 attacks on foreigners were recorded in the first nine months of 1991 alone. Since then right-wing attacks against foreigners have become a virtual everyday occurrence. So much so that German newspapers did not even bother to report the case of an 18-year-old Romanian who was clubbed to death in Rostock in March 1992. This was reported in *Newsweek* 27 April 1992. *Newsweek* also reports an Official for the Protection of the Constitution in Cologne conceding that 'The acceptance of the population for right-wing ideas is growing. The right-wing milieu hasn't grown much in size, but the militancy of these groups has grown explosively'. They further report that this Cologne agency estimates that there are some 4,200 active neo-Nazi skinheads in Germany and 'ten thousands' of supporters. Although the extreme right Republican Party won only just over 2% in the Federal elections in 1990, it has won over 5% in several *Lander*.
3 The Civic Movement broke away from the Civic Forum once Vaclav Klaus turned the Forum into a neo-liberal political party, the Civic Democratic Party.
4 See Zdenêk Kavan and Bernard Wheaton, *The Velvet Revolution: Czechoslovakia, 1988–1991* (Westview Press, 1992), pp. 179–82.
5 Their organization, publications and exact strength, like those of all political groups in Central and Eastern Europe, are in a state of flux. Details of their contemporary circumstances are available from Western organizations with which they have regular contact. These include the European Forum of Left Feminists, 83, Bartholemew Road, London NW 5 2AH; Helsinki Citizens' Assembly, Panska 7, Prague 1, Czech Republic; European Dialogue, 11, Goodwin St., London N4 3HQ; *Labour Focus on Eastern Europe*, 30, Bridge Street, Oxford OX2 OBA. See the directory at the end of this book.
6 The weaknesses of these parties, particularly in Poland, Hungary, the Czech Republic and Slovakia, is well documented by Jan Vermeersch in *The Working Paper Series* of the International Project, 'Transitions to Democracy in a World Perspective', no 1, December 1992.
    The slow progress of these parties surprised many commentators who presumed that the theoretical vacuum on the left, created by the moral, political

and economic débâcle of Communism, would quickly be filled by the social democratic parties. These parties were, after all, waiting patiently in the wings. As an example of this kind of commentary, see E. J. Dionne Jr, 'Communism's Fall is Good for Social Democracy', *International Herald Tribune*, 17 January 1990.

7   In the 1992 elections in what was Czechoslovakia, the Czech Communist Party – one of the few that did not change its name – gained 13 per cent of the vote and is the second largest party in the Czech parliament; the Party of the Democratic Left (the re-named Communist Party in Slovakia) is also second largest party in the Slovak parliament. In Hungary, the Hungarian Socialist Party, one of the successors to the Hungarian Socialist Workers' Party, won 10 per cent of the vote in the first free elections, twice the vote of the Hungarian Social Democratic Party. In the most recent Polish elections too, the old Communist Party polled well.

8   See 'Classes and Parties in Hungary', by Iván and Szonja Szelényi, *New Left Review*, 187, May/June 1991.

9   For an excellent analysis of recent developments in the former Czechoslovakia see Kavan and Wheaton, *The Velvet Revolution: Czecholsovakia 1988–1991*.

10 The party he formed later that year, the Civic Democratic Party, won over 30 per cent of the vote in the 1992 elections, while the Civic Movement, the party of Jiri Dienspier and Havel (had he been involved in party politics) did not even make the 5 per cent necessary to be represented in parliament

11 As it happens, one of Klaus's close collaborators, the Economics Minister, Dlouhy, spelt out the logic behind this closed decision making: 'An economic program is usually associated with the election cycle, that is with a political party or coalition. These parties do not usually submit such programs to the "working people" for widespread discussion. Their programs tend to be formulated by experts, and the elected government then simply implements them.' Quoted in Kavan and Wheaton, p. 163.

12 Klaus gained power politically by virtue of his technocratic financial expertise. Under the previous regime, although he was never a member of the Communist Party, he had a senior position in the Czech State Bank and then the Institute for Forecasting. He satisfied the popular craving to be governed by experts rather than ideological incompetents. He presented his reforms as the only technically valid solutions and expressed contempt for the amateurism of the previous dissidents – Havel, Dienspier etc. A source of his evident popularity is his ability to explain, on TV for instance, what is happening economically, and the case for his policies, to a population which is in a state of considerable confusion as to the real economic situation.

13 For useful socio-economic and political history of post-war politics in Hungary up to the end of 1989, see Nigel Swain, *Hungary: The Rise and Fall of Feasible Socialism* (London, 1992).

14 This probably reflects the influence of the independent peace movement which was formed in Budapest in 1982 against the militarism of Hungarian society

and which had contact with activists in the Western movement against cruise missiles.

15   Vaclav Klaus offered every Czechoslovak citizen the right to a certain number of privatization coupons – for a moderate sum and a wait in a long queue – which can be turned into shares. In this way he is trying to stimulate a share market, as well as to fulfil the vague expectations of ordinary citizens that they will make some material gain from privatization. See also chapter 2.

16   And according to Uhlír – with much chapter and verse: 'There is big corruption; especially amongst the present managers. For instance factory managers under-value the companies to persuade Westerners to buy them and leave them as managers.' There are all sorts of rumours: the deputy of the Civic Democratic Party obtained the ownership recently of the Czech book distribution company by somewhat mysterious means. Not surprisingly, the rumour is that he obtained this prize as a political favour. Klaus' governing party, the Civic Democratic Party, opposed the introduction of legislation requiring public figures to declare their interests.

17   Iván and Szonja Szelényi, 'Classes and Parties in Hungary', *New Left Review*, 187.

18   Quoted by Sheila Rowbotham in 'Clinging to the Dream', *Zeta Magazine*, June 1990.

19   The final agreements – after a walk out by the Poles, who declared their anger at the 'arrogance with which the EC is acting' – do include some concessions on textiles, coal and steel. But the deal on agriculture is that the EC is to directly subsidize Central European agricultural exports into the Commonwealth of Independent States and extract the quantity exported in this scheme from the quota allowed into the EC.

20   In Poland the businesses destroyed include many manufacturing enterprises that in microeconomic terms were efficient; the new private sector that is emerging is predominantly in retailing. Output in the early 1990s fell at between 23 and 27 per cent. The World Bank estimates that Polish output might recover by the second half of the 1990s. Others consider this over-optimistic. A senior advisor to the EC warns that the much celebrated 'J curve' evoked as scientific justification for the shock treatment may turn out to be an 'L curve'. A similar austerity plan proved completely unworkable in Yugoslavia and the IMF retreated in disarray. But its work had fatally undermined the already shaky authority of the Federal Government and helped to create the conditions in which ethnic and national aspirations led to war.

21   They have little or no unemployment insurance: the old guarantee of full (even if under-) employment made it unnecessary; the new situation of economic bankruptcy makes it impossible.

22   Moreover, the much-trumpeted reduction of the Polish debt by half is the *quid pro quo* for starting to pay interest on the remaining half after paying no interest on the whole debt. See 'Economic Ironies in Europe: A World Economic Interpretation of East – West European Politics' by Andre Gunder Frank, in the 'European Integration in Global Perspectives' issue of UNESCO's *International*

Social Science Journal, 131, February 1992. For a detailed analysis of the EC's relation to the East, see also Peter Gowan, 'The EC and its Eastern Neighbours', and Hugo Radice, 'Western Investment in Eastern Europe', in *Labour Focus on Eastern Europe*, issue 44, 1993.

PART II

AT THE HEART OF THE CHALLENGE

2

FREDERICK HAYEK AND THE SOCIAL-ENGINEERING STATE

Introduction

In December 1990, after a tense day negotiating with Renault and Volkswagen over the purchase of the Skoda vehicle manufacturer, a jewel in the Czech industrial crown, the Czech Minister of Privatization, Thomáš Jezek, described the influence of Frederick Hayek on his work: 'Hayek's influence works through my person. Hayek is a guarantee that we are going the right way.'[1] Ježek is no simple follower of fashion. He was a long-standing supporter of Charter 77, respected by those on its left for his principled resistance to the old regime. (The other driving force behind the privatization programme, the then Finance Minister Vaclav Klaus, who always prevaricated over Charter 77, never won this respect.) Jezek *believes* in Hayek's thought as providing the economic and philosophical foundation of a free society. He has translated all Hayek's major works and makes excited references to them as he describes his practical policies, assuming naturally that the listener will share his enthusiasm. At the time that Ježek was explaining Hayek's importance for the privatization programme, his translation of *The Road to Serfdom*, Hayek's most popular polemic against socialism, was in its third Czech edition.

Ježek's negotiations with two of the giant firms which dominate Europe's automobile industry – as part of the government's 'large privatization' programme – hardly illustrate the guiding hand of Hayek, who theorizes the market as the haphazard activities of millions of individual entrepreneurs. But the uniquely Czech 'coupon' privatization (applied to companies not fully privatized by the 'large' or 'small' privatization schemes) comes straight from a Hayekian recipe book, in its ingredients and instructions at any rate. When mixed with the real economy of foreign multi-nationals, sundry financial con men and the average person's lack of financial knowledge, the programme has turned out to be a rather different matter. The idea of coupon privatization was to provide every citizen with a book of coupons worth around $2,000 which they could register as shares in companies of their choice – or rather, their choice of what was available. For instance, Volkswagen, the victor in the negotiations over Skoda, vetoed the government's desire to sell 30 per cent of Skoda shares (Volkswagen had 70 per cent) to the public under the coupon system. VW feared that this would dilute its control.

In Ježek's idealistic plan, coupon privatization was to be a means of creating what Hayek called 'the catallaxy': the spontaneous relations of free economic exchange between individuals. Hayek argued that the catallaxy – in effect a theoretical term for the free market as an actual social structure – was the product of decades, even centuries, of evolution. From a Hayekian perspective, this evolution had been interrupted in Eastern Europe. Jezek saw himself as creating the conditions for history to begin where it left off in 1947.

The outcome of coupon privatization does not concern us here.[2] The point is merely to illustrate the considerable influence of this prolific economist-philosopher who, ten years ago, was considered a somewhat dated eccentric.

Hayekian themes in Eastern Europe

Such a direct attempt to translate Hayek's theory directly into precise government prescription is rare. Indeed, such an interventionist influence appears a little contradictory for the theorist of civilization by evolution rather than design. But certain Hayekian themes have been common cultural currency in Central and Eastern Europe in recent years; though without explicit recognition of their systematic, if contradictory, foundation.

Firstly, there is a powerful element of wishful nostalgia in much of the support for the 'free market' which echoes Hayek's theory of socialism – any kind of socialism – as a dangerous disruption of the 'spontaneous' order. The idea of the free market is associated in Eastern Europe with the notion of a return to a much idealized pre-Communist society.[3] Hayek believed in the resilience of the spontanous free-market order which, like a mountain spring suppressed by rocks, would pour out elsewhere. A similar belief now underlies the faith of many East Europeans that breaking the old state apparatus will release the pent-up energies of a spontaneous order which will create its own channels of development.[4]

The initial failure of the 'spontaneous order' to re-emerge as private enterprise has spurred increasingly radical moves to break up – rather than, for instance, attempt in some way to reform and democratize – the existing state, on the assumption that the spirit is there if only the rocks can be removed.[5]

Secondly, many people in Eastern Europe value the market for what they see as its lack of favour and discrimination, again echoing a Hayekian theme: the notion of the market as the essentially haphazard outcome of individual activity. There is sometimes a strong streak of fatalism about the hardship that the unregulated market is causing, even amongst those who suffer these hardships. Economic setbacks produced by the apparently impersonal forces of the market are more acceptable, at least initially, than those brought about by the conscious design of a single authority.

The relatively naive acceptance of the workings of these market forces – not as impersonal or haphazard as they look – is of course a reaction to the venal corruption of many of the people who ran the economy through the power of the state. So too is the way that the market is bestowed with magical powers. 'People here think that the market, like God's finger, will show immediately the current price, the equilibrium and will kick out the inefficient managers,' commented Vlado Benácek, an economics professor at Charles University, Prague, and himself an enthusiastic supporter of neo-liberal reforms. Again this echoes Hayek. Hayek 'marvels' at the workings of the market. 'If it were the result of deliberate human design . . . this mechanism would have been acclaimed as one of the greatest triumphs of the human mind.'[6]

Thirdly, amongst sections of the liberal intelligentsia there is a strong economic individualism, against not only the state but also other forms of collectivism – trade unions, municipal activity and so on. Here again they echo a fundamental Hayekian theme. It is as if their past experience of the state with its monoploy over virtually all collective action has led them to see a stark choice between individual and collective activity and, seeing the latter as associated with the past, to assume that the former provides the only true way forward. The civic movements in Czechoslovakia and Hungary in particular – collective organizations of a sort – were primarily moral movements, shared ways of expressing and protesting the truth. Except during the first years of Solidarity, civic movements in Central and Eastern Europe were not based on a possibility of social co-operation in organizing economic or social life.[7] Hayek, too, sees only a choice between economic arrangements in which planning is carried out by a 'single central authority', and those based on competition between individuals – that is, 'decentralized planning by many separate persons'. Social associations independent of the state play little role in his theory, except as would-be central authorities.[8]

It is not that Hayek's texts are being read in Eastern Europe like Mao's *Red Book*, but his concepts and themes are used to provide a moral and philosophical rationale to justify harsh economic policies. Moreover, these themes resonate with aspects of people's historical experience, including the final economic failures of the centralized economies. This is not only a response of the intelligentsia, though they have given it articulation. A population used to one ideology finds it natural, initially, to acquiesce in its equally ideological opposite, especially when it appears to offer a better life. 'People still look to a recipe for a shining future,' comments the columnist Jan Urban.[9] 'Many of us are privately sceptical; but there are few public forums through which to express this scepticism,' said a sociology student at the Central European University, expressing a view shared by most of a class of around 40. It is also the absence of tools with which to develop alternative directions that makes scepticism difficult. Critics are quickly branded 'Communists' because no third way has any credibility.

It is Hayek's philosophical arguments and the economic and political morality he derives from it, rather than his particular economic prescriptions, which underlie the influence of free-market ideas amongst liberal democratic activists. This means that many of the ideological tenets of neo-liberalism could well be resilient to the dismal failure of particular policies. The economic record of neo-liberalism in the West is regarded by many in the East through a rosy haze arising from moral and political rather than strictly economic judgements – reinforced in the past, no doubt, by the selective reporting of Radio Free Europe or Voice of America. The Thatcher and Reagan experiences are seen as success stories, and not just by rabid neo-liberals. Mr Jicinsky, the first post-Communist Vice-President of the Czecho–Slovak Federal Parliament, a 1968 reformer, ex-professor of jurisprudence, and no fool, described with approval how 'the Czech and Slovak public were greatly impressed by Mrs Thatcher; especially the way that she influenced the situation in Britain, overcoming stagnation and recession'.[10] He made this remark a month after Prime Minister Thatcher had been ignominiously pushed out of office, leaving Britain with the biggest trade deficit in its history. The historical record of neo-liberal economics, whether in Britain, the US or Chile, is not enough to prevent its influence from riding again, this time over the ruins of the Soviet bloc.

It is not enough practically and empirically to challenge the Hayekian nostrums that have permeated popular consciousness. Experience is already doing just that. But there is no inevitability that the questioning induced by harsh experience leads in the direction of a democratic and socially responsible alternative. On the contrary, the signs so far indicate the opposite, as disillusion combined with the absence of any legitimacy for the rule of law, leads to violent ethnic strife. Effective tools for developing such an alternative need to prove themselves against the intellectual roots of neo-liberalism's capacity to bounce back.

The cycle of Hayek's popularity

Hayek is the most resilient of neo-liberal thinkers, not only in his longevity or his prolific output,[11] but also in the strength of the intellectual foundations he gives to neo-liberal political economy. The cycle and geographical location of his popularity is striking.

The Road to Serfdom was rapturously recieved in the US on its publication in 1944, but in Western Europe the reception was cool.[12] During the social democratic consensus of the 1950s and 1960s Hayek was considered something of a political oddity. Seymour Martin Lipset describes a telling incident. In the fifties the CIA-funded Congress for Cultural Freedom[13] organized a 'world congress of intellectuals' on 'the Future of Freedom'. Labour politicians Hugh Gaitskell and Richard Crossman, conservative thinkers Raymond Aron and Bertrand de Jouvenal, and US opinion leaders such as Arthur Schlesinger Jr. were amongst a hand-picked gathering of 150 which met for a week in Milan in 1955. They found themselves in broad agreement. Conservatives were prepared to accept a moderate degree of state regulation; social democrats were prepared to accept a powerful private sector. According to Lipset, himself one of the American members of this world class of intellectuals, 'no one seemed to believe that it really made much difference which political party controlled the domestic policies of individual nations,' so long as they were against Russia. 'The only occasions in which debate grew warm,' Lipset remembers, 'were when someone served as a "surrogate Communist" by saying something which could be defined as being too favourable to Russia.' At the end of the Congress, however, a dissonant voice spoke up from the other end of the political spectrum. Frederick Hayek had remained silent until the final day. He then launched an attack on the delegates, according to Lipset's report, 'for preparing to bury freedom instead of saving it'. At that time, Lipset recalls, he was treated as somewhat eccentric.[14]

Twenty years after the Milan gathering, a Conservative Minister in Britain (Sir Keith Joseph) was to make *The Road to Serfdom* required reading for his civil servants. Prime Minister Thatcher spoke of Hayek reverentially as her guiding influence, and met him for several extended tutorials.[15]

The cycle of Hayek's popularity coincides, not surprisingly, with periods when state management of the economy in any form is either feared by powerful groups in society (as in the US just after the Second War); is associated with, and blamed for, a faltering of the economy (as was the case for an excessively mild form of industrial intervention in Britain); or when it patently fails to deliver the promised economic goods (as with the collapse of the command economies of the Soviet bloc). His polemics against state intervention were all encompassing: he saw moderate, Keynesian or social democratic forms as the thin end of the wedge of fascist or communist totalitarianism. This is the central argument of *The Road to Serfdom*.

The rise, fall and rise again of Hayek's influence, according to the successes and failures of economic state intervention, is revealing. The resilience of Hayek's rationale for the free market, in spite of its empirical vulnerability, indicates a deeper, philosophical foundation which the left has yet to dig up and critically inspect.

The practical, ephemeral and tacit character of much economic knowledge seems crucial to Hayek's theory. On this foundation he built his challenge to what he saw as the all-knowing social engineering states created by the left. (He is noticeably reticent about the social engineering of his own followers.) The power of his case ultimately does not lie with his own understanding of practical knowledge – this is flawed by a dogmatic individualism that blinds him to the social and potentially transformable character of economic knowledge. I would argue that the kernel of truth which gives his work such cyclical longevity is his critique of the positivistic, scientistic assumptions behind many forms of socialist or social reforming politics. Such an approach to knowledge underpins the confidence in the state as the prime, in some cases exclusive, agency of social justice. As long as the left has not developed a theory and practice of social transformation, regulation and co-operation which can take account of the practical and tacit character of social and economic knowledge, and therefore the limits on the knowledge of the state and party (the knowledge from above), then whenever the state regimes of the left fail to deliver the social justice they promise, neo-liberalism regains influence, and *The Road to Serfdom* comes out with a fresh cover.

It helps to understand Hayek's appeal to liberal intellectuals in the period of opposition and on a popular scale in the immediate aftermath of 1989, if one can envisage the political culture of 1920s Vienna in which he first developed his central themes, and if one can enter into the contests over the feasibility of socialism in which he was engaged throughout his life. A brief historical detour helps explain features of the resilience of his ideas: for instance, their comprehensive character, embracing philosophy, psychology, economics and constitutional politics; the politically and morally purposeful tone of much of his writing; and the fact that several of the issues which he debated with socialist theorists of his time were left unresolved.

Red Vienna and the making of a neo-liberal

It is ironic that a writer whose work stressed the unintended character of the social outcomes of individual behaviour should have an influence so close to his lifelong intention. His life's goals were formed in the highly politicized debates of 'Red Vienna' in the aftermath of the First World War, the downfall of the Austro-Hungarian Empire and the Bolshevik Revolution. Austrian liberalism was in disarray. Socialism was ascendant. So too was xenophobic nationalism. From an early age Hayek made the retrieval and renewal of free-market liberalism and the defeat of socialism the guiding animus of his intellectual work.

After military service, doctoral study and success in law and political science at the University of Vienna, then a year in New York, Frederick Hayek, aged 25, joined the *privatseminar* of Ludwig Mises, who earned his living not in the University but as Secretary of the Vienna Chamber of Commerce.[16] At this time Hayek was a moderate Fabian from a liberal academic and minor aristocratic background. Mises' polemic against the feasibility of a socialist economy, *Economic Calculation in the Socialist Commonwealth*, turned Hayek against any sustained state intervention in the market – other than to protect the workings of the market against particularistic interests. To share such an intellectual position immediately put Hayek in conflict with the predominant socialist/social democratic orthodoxy.

Following Mises he became an intellectual fighter.[17] He fought against state intervention not only in Austria, but also in London, to which Lionel Robbins invited him in the 1930s specifically to strengthen the neo-liberal resistance to Keynes. After the war he found a more peaceful and receptive base in the United States in Chicago.

The liberals in these debates, notably Mises and later Hayek, were influenced by a strong sense of a lost and valued world: the world of constitutional liberalism in the last half of the nineteenth century, whose leaders thought they could preside over an orderly dismantling of the Hapsburg Empire.[18] In historical terms, the intellectual project of Mises and Hayek was self-consciously to re-lay, in the disarray of the twentieth century, the intellectual tracks that would guide society back to the civilized order which ignorant, primitive social forces had disturbed. Early liberalism had, in Hayek's view, been insufficiently self-conscious of its achievements. It had released forces of working class militancy and xenophobic nationalism that it had no idea how to control.[19] Hayek's self-appointed task was to make free-market constitutional liberalism conscious of itself, and to put those genies back into the constitutional bottle.

The culture in which Hayek began his retrieval and renewal of liberalism had two especial advantages. Firstly, it encouraged intellectual debate of a kind that directly engaged with the main problems facing society. The Bohm-Bawerk Seminar, another of Vienna's famous *privatseminars*, was led by innovative figures independent of any single institution, who moved between academic, political and commercial life, bringing the preoccupations of each to the seminar. It included liberals such as Carl Menger, the founder of the Austrian school of economics, and Friedrich Weiser, as well as the liberal Bohm-Bawerk himself, who became a finance minister in the first government of the Austrian Republic. Joseph Schumpeter, the corporatist social democrat who served briefly as minister of finance, also joined the argument. Mises and Hayek faced strong antagonists in the socialist economists Otto Bauer, Karl Renner and Rudolf Hilferding. Bauer and Renner both later served in the Austrian Government, Renner as the first Chancellor of the provisional government of 1918 and Bauer as Foreign Minister and head of the Socialization Commission.[20]

Secondly, the intellectually and culturally pluralistic character of the *privatseminars* encouraged scholars to make confident use of the tools of many different intellectual disciplines to strengthen their case. Hayek's economic arguments, for instance, benefit from their foundation in an understanding, however flawed, of epistemology. The work of Carl Menger, founder of the Austrian School of economics and a major influence on Hayek, is exemplary in this use of a wide range of intellectual tools. His contribution was the subjectivist theory of value which became the school's distinctive position. He deployed ideas from history, psychology and philosophy to argue against the orthodoxies of the time, and asserted that the source of value – in his view, the central unifying principle of economics – was not any objective feature of a thing or its production, such as the amount of labour power it involved, but rather was individual subjective preference.[21] In other words, the only value which a good has, according to Menger, is its importance for an individual.[22]

The Austrian School's debate with socialism

Although Menger and the Austrian School developed their theory of value as an alternative to both Marxist and Ricardian labour theories, they did not initially attack the idea of socialism. Some were pragmatically in favour of a degree of social democratic/social liberal state intervention to influence trade, encourage certain sectors of business and remedy gross inequalities. After the war, however, the Russian revolution and the left-wing government of the Austrian Republic made the workings of a socialist economy a focus for forceful and practical debate.

Mises' attack on the possibility of a socialist economy was based on one central argument. All the same economic variables – consumer demand and resource scarcities, for instance – that guide resource use in a capitalist economy, he argued, must necessarily be taken account of under socialism. It was naive, he said, to expect money and prices to disappear for very long under socialism: as long as people have different preferences and as long as socialists aim to meet consumer desires, the allocation of consumer goods could only be adequately achieved by resorting to some system of money and prices. The infinite and constantly changing combinations of demand and resources could never be second guessed by a central planning system.

The most powerful socialist response, within the terms of the debate set by Mises, came from the Polish economists Oskar Lange and A. P. Lerner, together with the British socialist economist H. D. Dickinson. They did not seek to defend the labour theory of value as a basis for resource allocation. They took over the main assumptions of neoclassical, Marshallian economics, concerning the conditions for perfect competition: that is, perfect information, freedom of entry and exit, and the possibility of 'trial and error' in the determining of resource prices. They (Lange most consistently) developed a model in which a central planning board would administer factor prices of state owned enterprises in a way which, through the process of trial and error, imitated the capitalist market but without profit maximization. Lange was concerned to construct a model of a socialist economy able to do everything capitalism could do but also to fulfil social objectives which were beyond capitalism's capabilities. The planning board, in effect substituting for the market, would fix 'shadow' (because shadowing the market) prices of products such that the quantity supplied would equal the quantity demanded. Socialist managers, like capitalist managers, would be required to produce at the point where marginal cost was equal to this price. Yet marginal cost in such an economy would take social costs into account in the internal budget of the firm, whereas in a capitalist economy they would be treated as 'external' to the firm's economic calculations. This theory was developed just before the Second World War. The experience of the wartime economy reinforced widespread faith in the advantages of centralized administration, and the case for Lange's form of market socialism was, for most of the post-war period, widely accepted as coherent. The arguments of Mises and his protégé, Hayek, became marginal.[23]

Hayek's argument, going beyond Austrian School premises, fired salvos into this debate from a new, subversive angle: from an exploration of the very character of economic knowledge. Socialists and neo-classicists alike have ignored his arguments until recently. Most varieties of socialists in Europe could ignore them because in immediate post-war years history seemed more or less on their side. Neo-classicists were uninterested because an increasing preoccupation with econometric models had produced a lift-off from the real world; and so long as real-world economies were booming nobody tried to pull them back. Hayek's salvos lay in wait, unanswered.

Hayek's theory of knowledge

Hayek's central argument concerns the character of knowledge and of social order. His theory of knowledge states that because of the very nature of economic knowledge, no single brain, individual or collective (and he might now have added, computerized system), can know all the factors relevant to the economic decisions which they might take. Neither can a single authority effectively centralize the knowledge of individuals. The major part of economically relevant knowledge is, according to Hayek, 'knowledge of time and circumstance'. Often it is tacit – 'things one knows but cannot tell' – often ephemeral and always fallible. As a consequence, he argues, we enter the world socially blindfolded; we can never know the social consequences of our intended action. On this basis, we must understand social order and social development – in particular the development of private property and the market – as the unpredictable outcome of the activity of individuals. Its evolution is the result of unintended experiment. Any attempt to design or engineer a social outcome interferes in the natural processes of civilization. Such intervention is immoral and bound to have deleterious consequences.

The idealizing conclusions that Hayek draws from this about the 'free' character of actually existing capitalist markets have been well criticized on historical and empirical grounds, showing the element of conscious social construction involved in shaping the market institutions.[24] But an alternative understanding of knowledge and its social and economic production, distribution and utilization, has not been explicitly pitched against neo-liberal political and economic theory and used to ground the case for co-operative and democratic social and economic organization. The absence of such a challenge enables the case for the free market to gain a philosophical and moral appeal totally out of proportion to its economic and social viability.

The early Austrians rejected the assumption of perfect information in their work on value, concluding that knowledge of resource costs was so fallible that the subjective value of a good for the individual could be the only reliable indicator of value. They did not follow through the implications of this for understanding the workings of the economy as a whole. Hayek, moreover, did not just question the assumption of perfect information. He made the problem of information – or, more comprehensively, knowledge – *the* fundamental question of economics; a problem which arose from the very character of human knowledge:

> The peculiar character of the problem of a rational economic order is determined precisely by the fact that the knowledge of the circumstances of which we must make use never exist in concentrated or integrated form but solely as the dispersed bits of incomplete and frequently contradictory knowledge which all the separate individuals possess. The economic problem of society is thus not merely a problem of how to allocate 'given' resources . . . It is rather a problem of how to secure the best use of resources known to any of the members of society, for ends whose relative importance only these individuals know. Or, to put it briefly, it is a problem of the utilization of knowledge which is not given to anyone in its totality.[25]

Hayek turned the tables of the debate about socialism completely, criticizing the hidden rationalist assumptions of the neo-classicists as well as the active rationalism of the social engineers. He took the Austrian critique of these traditions to a deeper level than the original stress on a subjective determination of value. He thus strengthened the case for economic liberalism by defending it with a critique of the assumptions it had previously shared with state socialism and which had rendered it vulnerable to arguments framed – like Lange's – in rationalist terms.

The character of knowledge

Neo-classicists and social engineers alike, argued Hayek, were assuming a view of science which made the problem of knowledge deceptively simple. They viewed science according to the positivist model; that is, as the accumulation of laws describing empirical regularities. These laws provided the core of valid knowledge; all else was merely an approximation to such laws. Thus everyday knowledge was simply rough and ready scientific knowledge or pure speculation. On this basis, economically relevant knowledge could *in principle*, however unrealistic in practice, be available to all, as the neo-classical economists assumed. And certainly, if economic knowledge was a matter of codified generalizations and aggregations, then it could be centralized: there might be practical difficulties and problems of the measure in terms of which calculations could be made, but there was nothing about the character of the knowledge itself which would render it impossible to centralize.

Hayek questioned the idea of knowledge which underpinned this reforming zeal. In this he was influenced by Ernst Mach and his view of knowledge as sense data of experience unique to each individual. Later he was influenced by Michael Polanyi and his analysis of tacit knowledge, 'those things we know but cannot tell'. Hayek argued that scientific knowledge – which he saw as primarily a matter of classification of those facts, or sense data, that can be classified – is not all that there is to knowledge. He points to the 'body of very important but unorganized knowledge which cannot possibly be called scientific in the sense of knowledge of general rules: knowledge of the particular circumstances of time and place'. His paradigm is the knowledge of the entrepreneur: the shipper, for instance, 'who earns his living from using otherwise empty or half-filled journeys of tramp-steamers'; or 'the estate agent, whose whole knowledge is almost exclusively one of temporary opportunities'.[26] While the Austrian School before him also were giving an alternative view of value, price and equlibrium, his concern with knowledge opens up the question of how in fact prices are formed, what function they serve in the co-ordination of an economy, and what in practice are the processes favouring equilibrium. In his critique of the thought of his Austrian predecessors he argues that 'It is evident, however, that the values of the factors of production do not depend solely on the valuation of the consumers' goods, but also on the conditions of supply of the various factors of production'.[27] And vital knowledge of these is, he insists, uniquely individual.

Hayek then presents the choice for understanding or achieving equilibrium as being whether to bring all the dispersed information to a single central authority or 'to convey to individuals such additional knowledge as they need in order to dovetail their plans with those of others'. Since the character of knowledge makes the former option impossible, the problem becomes how best to implement the latter. Hayek's answer is an unregulated price mechanism, whose values would indicate the relative importance or 'marginal rates of substitution' of different products. On this basis, each scarce resource has a numerical index, a price 'which cannot be derived from the property possessed by that particular thing, but which reflects, or in which is condensed, its significance in view of the whole means–end structure'.

Crucial to Hayek's faith in the unregulated price mechanism as the means of economic co-ordination is the assumption that the information that the individual needs concerns simply the comparative cost of a commodity and nothing more. In an economy that has no democratic social regulation, this is in theory what price represents – though more often than not, in practice in modern capitalist economies it represents a series of strategic calculations by firms with considerable oligopolistic market power. Hayek assumes that the economic agent, consumer, entrepreneur or worker, does not need or want information about, for example, the conditions of workers or the consequences of the production process on the environment. It is on this narrow interpretation of economically relevant information that a price system is alleged to act, 'to co-ordinate the separate actions of different people . . . The whole system acts as one market, not because any of its members survey the whole field, but because their limited individual fields of vision sufficiently overlap so that through many intermediaries the relevant information is communicated to all'. He marvels at this system as a way of dispensing with the need of conscious control. It may not always be perfect, but because it has emerged without conscious human design it should not be tampered with, concludes Hayek, especially given the limited character of human knowledge.

Hayek concludes that the free market is a spontaneous product of civilization. He elides this claim of social theory into a moral case for the free market: as the product of accident rather than design, it favours no one and discriminates against no one. (Inequalities, presumably, are simply the haphazard outcomes of individual activity, which might be reversed on his model by a further round of the haphazard.) For Hayek, the role of the state must consequently be the very opposite of social engineering. Rather than improve or remedy the roughness of the market's justice, its role must be to protect the spontaneous order. Members of the highest body of state should be chosen with this protective, hands-off-and-keep-other-hands-off task in mind. Hayek allows for a lower assembly of regularly elected representatives, but this should be responsible simply for minimal taxation and the maintenance of basic infrastructure and social services.

According to Hayek's constitutional prescription there would be a higher body made up of male citizens of mature and expert judgement, preferably over 40 years of age, to guard the products of social evolution. They should be up for election every 15 years, so that they would not be susceptible to the kind of political pressures which might lead to tampering in the particular interest of a vociferous group. A military junta or well-protected Prime

Ministerial government have, it seems, been the nearest actual equivalents to this ideal arrangement.

Inconsistencies

There are two problems of consistency between the logical implications of Hayek's theory of the production and distribution of knowledge and his later political and economic prescriptions.[28] On the one hand, he sees all monopolies or attempts to concentrate power as a threat to the spontaneous order. The economic condition under which the spontaneous order can flourish is 'competition ... [which] means decentralized planning by separate persons'. He writes contemptuously of 'the half-way house between the two, about which many people talk but which few like when they see it ... [namely] the delegation of planning to organized industries, or in other words, monopolies'.[29]

The problem for his theory, however, is that monoplies have developed out of the capitalist market. In a sense, business monopolies or oligopolies could be understood as spontaneous developments of capitalist competition; yet they also become a source of power to carry out conscious, calculated economic projects affecting the rest of the economy. In this case, the spontaneous order carries in it the seeds of its own destruction. Or, one might argue that concentrations of economic wealth and power are the product of previous conscious attempts to direct the economic order. In both cases they become centres of all-knowing power, appropriating the knowledge of others – workers, consumers, competitors, sub-contractors – just as much as many a state institution. Either way, there is a case, on Hayek's own terms, for some kind of prohibitive state intervention. But his limitation on the scope of democracy and conscious public decision making means that he provides no basis for deciding which products of the spontaneous order could be interfered with.

Another way of putting this is that his criticisms of the abstractness of neoclassical equilibrium theory are incomplete. He points to features of the real world, in particular the character of human knowledge, to gain a closer understanding of *how* and under what conditions economies tend towards equilbrium, but he ignores real-life economic developments which raise the possibility of influencing *what kind* of equilibrium is arrived at. At one point in *The Constitution of Liberty* he does put forward his own personal view, arguing that the monopolies of business are somehow benign and certainly not as damaging as the monoplies of labour and the state. But this, from the point of view of his own theoretical system, is an arbitrary judgement, governed more by his animus against socialism than by logic.

He does express unease, however, as if aware of this monopolistic tension. What is really necessary, he argues at one point, is for everyone to be self-employed. Only then does everyone experience and understand the workings of the market and develop the capacities and moral ethics on which it depends: a willingness to take risk, an alertness to entrepreneurial opportunities, habits of thrift and self-discipline. The market, in his view, is the engine of self-education. He accepts that the giant monopolistic corporations create a problem in that their growth means a large population of employees relatively protected and therefore uninitiated into and disrespectful of the ways of the market – even favourable to socialism. He is not prepared, however, to follow a consistently liberal path of favouring legislation which disperses concentrations of wealth.

There is a further inconsistency, again concerning the organization of enterprises themselves. He states that the prime problem for economics is identifying the mechanisms for full utilization of the population's economic knowledge. His notion of the actual economically active population seems to be restricted to his ideal (the self-employed entrepreneur or the commercial agent), and not to include the reality of the significant section of the population engaged in wage labour. Indeed, none of his examples of economic activity – shippers and estate agents, for instance – indicates any concern with or knowledge of the social character of production itself. They are all taken from commerce. He appears to overlook a vast, frequently underutilized, source of tacit knowledge: the knowledge of waged workers.

This is a revealing omission: the basis of his theory is very narrow, or involves a fundamental contradiction. It can only be explained either by the fact that the spontaneous order at the back of his mind is made up of competing individual, commercial and economic agents; or by the implicit assumption argued by that other notorious twentieth-century Fred – Frederick Winslow Taylor – that all economically relevant knowledge implicit in the skill of the worker can be codified by management, and therefore does not exist independently of the entrepreneur. But this goes quite against Hayek's general approach to knowledge. If the state is unable to codify the knowledge of the entrepreneur because of the very character of human knowledge – not the nature of, for instance, social relations of power – then how can the entrepreneur adequately codify the knowledge of the workers?

Questioning of the organization of knowledge within production (that is, within the enterprise) raises serious problems for Hayek's reliance on price as *the* means of communication of economic information. The internal organization of the enterprise is constrained by the market and therefore by the workings of the price mechanism, but it involves economic relations other than those of price – discipline, supervision, training, various forms of co-operation – utilizing or failing to utilize tacit and experiential knowledge. Depending on the size and market power of the company, these can have a major influence on price. It raises the possibility of choices between different kinds of economic relations according to a variety of consciously chosen criteria, including whether or not they favour the utilization of practical knowledge – a possibility ruled out by Hayek's notion of a spontaneous order. Yet what if the spontaneous order produces forms of organization of production that seek to centralize knowledge, overriding the tacit or experiental knowledge of a section of the population? And what if this threat comes not from the state, the trade unions or some collective actor associated with socialism, but from the dominant actors in the capitalist market? Will the wise old men of Hayek's Upper House be prepared to intervene?

Underlying these particular inconsistencies or, more generously, 'tensions' in Hayek's theory, is a more fundamental contradiction: between the value he places on individual liberty and human agency on the one hand, and his theory of evolution and the value this leads him to place on social order on the other. His denial of some direct, even if incomplete, connection between human intention and social outcome, and his contention that the outcome of human activity is entirely haphazard, in effect make accident the main mechanism of social evolution. Democracy and social choice become redundant. On this basis, social evolution is very little different from natural evolution. The only difference in fact is that humans, or at least mature wise male members of the human race protected from the vulgar pressures of the people, can discover the trends of evolution and make society conscious of them in order to safeguard them. In effect, therefore, Hayek's arguments lead him, in spite of his libertarian starting-point, to favour order and tradition over human agency. His bizarre constitutional proposals are not the eccentricities of an old man, they reflect the final priorities of his theoretical system. And they guide the political practice of his disciples.

The authoritarianism of the philosopher of freedom

Thus on close inspection we find a social phliosophy which in its own inner priorities – not simply its uses or abuses by particular politicians – leads in quite the opposite direction to the initial hopes which the young democracts at *Respekt* or in FIDESZ projected on to the idea of the 'free market'. Where they hoped for a society in which individual and collaborative creativity could shape economic life, we find Hayek's free-market model provides for only the semblance of individual creativity.

Where they have come out of their private exiles hoping for a sphere of public activity, independent of the state and not necessarily entirely within the market – what they call 'civil society' – Hayek would push them back into a private domain where they are out of temptation of social projects or design.

Where they looked forward to participating in a pluralistic politics to debate and decide the future direction of Hungary or the Czech and Slovak Republics, Hayek would take the question out of their hands and into a special Chamber of older men who know better, leaving democratically elected representatives to debate tax percentages and the state of the drains.

The individualism of Hayek's theory of knowledge

The crucial assumption that leads Hayek into these contradictions is his treatment of knowledge as an individual attribute, rather than as a social product. He regards it as almost a physical characteristic, as if the mind and body were one and the individual's knowledge what they atomistically and uniquely experienced. He extols the price mechanism because it makes possible 'not only a division of labour but also a co-ordinated utilization of resources based on equally divided knowledge'.[30] Knowledge could only be seen as equally divided in this a priori way if it was understood as a given feature of an individual's existence.

He is more explicit about this sense of an experiential limit on an individual's knowledge when he justifies his thought against what he sees as the rationalist individualism of John Stuart Mill – whom he lumps together with French writers, such as the Encyclopedists and Rousseau, who acknowledge no limit on human rationality. He asserts that there is an

indisputable fact which nobody can hope to alter and which by itself is a sufficient basis for the conclusions which the individualist philosophers drew. This is the *constitutional* limitations of man's knowledge and interests, the fact that he cannot know more than a tiny part of the whole of society and that therefore all that can enter into his motives are the immediate effects which his actions will have in the sphere that he knows. All the possible differences in men's moral attitudes amount to little, so far as their significance for social organization is concerned, compared with the fact that all man's mind can effectively comprehend are the facts of *the narrow circle of which he is the centre.* [Emphasis mine.][31]

What is significant about this statement is not its recognition of limits on human reason but the dogmatically experiential and therefore individual nature of these limits, closing off possibilities (rightly) of total rationality and complete knowledge but also (wrongly) of social action to share information and extend the knowledge of individuals through associating for that purpose.

This dogmatically individualistic assumption is crucial to the conclusion which he draws from the fallible character of knowledge: that we enter the world socially blindfolded. For Hayek, as I have already shown, the nature of human knowledge is such that not only can we not know the social consequences of our action with certainty, but we cannot even approximate such knowledge through combining with others, thereby cutting a hole in the blindfold and ensuring our actions come nearer to achieving their goal. For Hayek, on the contrary, the social structures we create, we create entirely unintentionally. The assumption that knowledge is an individual attribute thus is essential to his conclusion that social order is the 'haphazard outcome of our individual activity'; and to the implication that accidents rather than conscious social projects are the legitimate mechanisms of social evolution, the grist to the mill of trial and error.

If knowledge is understood as a social product, the foundation of Hayek's case for the free market begins to crumble. For if knowledge is a social product then it can be socially transformed through people taking action – co-operating, sharing, combining knowledge – to overcome the limits on the knowledge that they individually possess. Empirical evidence bears this out even in the private market, Hayek's paradigm case of order created in spite of every individual's blindfold predicament. Consider two politically and economically quite different cases where social organizations have been created successfully by economic and political actors, specifically to share information, extend their knowledge of their economic environment and thereby come nearer to achieving their economic goals. In Japan, for example, leading companies and the state have created and now sustain a central economic networking institution for the economic elite, a part of the Ministry of Industry and Technology (MITI) which facilitates the sharing of plans, information on international markets, and areas of mutual interest, such as labour relations and aspects of technological development. Participants in this process have created additional informal networks which further share information and skill. These dense knowledge networks amongst the elite of the Japanese economy have undoubtedly been a vital ingredient in the competitive success of the Japanese economy. But no one could call them spontaneous. They have certainly brought many unintended benefits to Japanese corporate management and the state (and no doubt contributed to the corrupt nature of Japanese politics), but there is no doubt that intentions to intervene in the market in a particular way have driven the process.

The second very different example comes from Italy: the flourishing textile industry in Modena near Bologna. There, entrepreneurs in small businesses and co-operatives (rather close in some ways to Hayek's self-employed ideal), have clubbed together, instead of relying only on their own individual sense data and alertness, to set up a Textile Centre to gather knowledge about textile technology and trends in the international market. The Centre then shares this information with all those who affiliate to it. Again, here is a conscious and successful attempt to overcome the limits of individual experience and gain a fuller picture of the economic environment in order to compete more successfully in it. There is no presumption to be all-knowing. But there is a determination to share and combine the insights of individual experience, in order to meet shared goals.

Epistemologists and philosophers of science – most notably another Austrian, Ludwig Wittgenstein – long ago convincingly challenged the individualist view of knowledge, owed to Mach, which forms the foundation of Hayek's theory.[32] Philosophical notions face many socially determined lags, and whether an idea is confirmed in people's daily experience is an important factor. For instance, long after Galileo had proved to the satisfaction of the scientific community that the earth moves round the sun, the opposite idea – an idea so apparently consistent with everyday experience – continued to dominate common sense. In societies like those of Central and Eastern Europe, where the majority of people have had little option but to live a form of private exile, participating knowledgeably in only a small circle of friends, Hayek's individualistic understanding of knowledge did not grate against day-to-day experience, did not appear unreasonable, and does not prove a sticking point in the appeal of his whole social philosophy. These circumstances are changing.

The very different experiences in the West, of which Japan and Italy provide examples, explain why even as neo-liberal economic prescriptions spread in the 1980s, Hayek's wider philosophy has not caught on. Support for neo-liberal economics from the Western economic elite – notably measures of market de-regulation – are more a function of the internationalization of capital than of Hayek's philosophy of the free market. Britain, where economics in the seventies and early eighties was notably ideological, was unusual for the West. In some respects it was more similar to later developments in the

East, in that Hayek provided the conceptual framework used to sell monetarist economics as a moral and ideological crusade.

The democratization of knowledge

Evidence of considerable social variation in the organization of knowledge, and of purposeful action to transform the existing production and distribution of knowledge, does not validate a positivistic view of knowledge as in principle always codifiable and centralizable. Rather, it indicates the need for a theory of social knowledge that absorbs Hayek's essential insight into the continuing flow of uncodified and often uncodifiable knowledge but rejects his dogmatic assumption that this knowledge is constitutionally and irredeemably individual.

Recognition of the social character of knowledge implies that, depending on its distribution and organization, people can through social co-operation increase their understanding of the social consequences of their actions, even though they can never know these consequences in every detail for certain. This in turn implies that people purposefully can influence society with some (albeit limited) knowledge of the outcome, and that this knowledge can always be improved upon. Any particular social arrangement (for example, the organization of the economic market) thus becomes not the haphazard outcome of individual activity, but an outcome whose relation to the intentions of the human actors involved must be open to empirical inquiry. It could be the more or less intended outcome, depending on how comprehensive is the understanding of the actors and the extent of their sources of power to act.

An understanding of knowledge which recognizes its socially variable conditions of production and distribution also makes possible an alternative theory of social evolution as radically distinct from natural evolution, but yet not presupposing a designing, directing mind or collectivity. It would involve a recognition that social evolution is the outcome of attempts by people rationally, if never perfectly rationally, to construct/design social projects which are then the subject of trial and error. This understanding enables one to consider a social order in a way which recognizes the distinct role, for good or ill, of purposeful human agency and creativity.

This provides a basis for questioning what institutional framework market relations should operate, and of what values and mechanisms should regulate these relations. In other words, we move the private market from the realm of the sacred – God's finger, as the Czech economist describes popular conceptions of the market – to the profane: particular historically shaped and historically transformable institutions.

We can also separate the ideal of socialism from presumptions, implicit or explict, of an all-knowing political agent or set of institutions, and open up the possibility of forms of social regulation and control which utilize practical knowledge and recognize its fallibility. The all-knowing state, however formally democratic, has been a powerful fantasy at the back of many a socialist mind. The assumption that all the knowledge necessary to a socialist transformation of society can be codified, turned into an overview of society and draw upon in a single, more or less democratic process, underlies the reforming and revolutionary ambitions, respectively, of Fabianism and its latter-day practitioners, and Leninism in its various forms. The debates within and between these political traditions have been over how much of society the state should control or what kind of a state should do the controlling; for example how decisions should be made at every level of the planning process. But they have all shared the belief in the possibility, indeed desirability, of a single process of economic and social planning in those spheres where state intervention is deemed necessary. The idea of 'autonomy' or horizontal 'network' forms of co-ordination has not been part of their vocabulary. Moreover, common to their conceptions of the party, whether parliamentary or Bolshevik, is the notion of a leadership that knows and interprets the laws of social development and, whether through a form of political Taylorism or through formal democratic debate, is able to distil and centralize the knowledge of the membership.[33]

Since 1968 these conceptions have in practice, though not sufficiently in theory, been challenged. Much of the practice of the social movements which emerged during and after 1968 – the student, feminist, peace, ecological and other more community-based movements – along with workers' organizations activated by the collapse of the boom, produced a cumulative popular challenge to all-knowing forms of socialism. At the same time many of them shared the original egalitarian and democratic values of socialism. One of the features which much of this practice (though by no means all) has in common is the practical assertion of an alternative view of knowledge, both to that which underpins the free-market right and that which gave state socialist experiments their sense of certainty. An alternative view of knowledge is essential, as the resilience of the ideas of Hayek illustrates, to an alternative view of economic organization, state administration and political agency. William Morris describes men and women as 'the ever-baffled and ever-resurgent agents of an unmastered history'. This provides an appropriate description of the sense of purpose, qualified by a spirit of self-conscious experimentation, of the new left.

Notes

1   Interview with the author.

2   See Bernard Wheaton and Zdenek Kavan *The Velvet Revolution; Czechoslovakia 1988–1991* (Oxford, 1992), pp. 157–8.

3   These are somewhat inaccurate given that in Central Europe, in Czechoslovakia, for instance before the Second World War, there were periods of social democratic government, strong trade unions and a large co-operative sector.

4   Mrs Thatcher provides a particularly vivid illustration of this belief, learned from the same Austrian guru. She believed that by withdrawing the state from the economy she was releasing a suppressed 'spirit of enterprise' which would then drive the economy to new heights of prosperity. For a moment she was worried: 'I held my breath. Had the spirit of enterprise survived? I was immensely relieved when I found that it had,' she said in 1986.

5   Except, for example, in Poland, where popular resistance has forced the government to weigh the advantages of releasing a spirit whose existence has still to be proved, against those of responding to social forces whose existence in the streets and factories was very real.

6   See F. Hayek, 'The Use of Knowledge in Society', in *Individualism and Economic Order* (London, 1949), p. 87.

7   Perhaps this is one reason why these movements so quickly dispersed after being used as vehicles for achieving power.

8   See 'The Use of Knowledge in Society'.

9   Interview with author, October 1991.

10   Interview with the author.

11   The scope, range and sheer volume of Hayek's work is vast, spanning more than six decades, involving virtually every discipline within the humanities and consisting of 34 books authored or edited, 25 pamphlets, and 235 articles, up to 1984. He was still writing before his death in March 1992.

12   Including, in the US, serialization in *The Readers' Digest*.

13   For details on the CIA's role and purpose in setting up the Congress for Cultural Freedom, see *The CIA: A Forgotten History*, by William Blum (London, 1986).

14   See Seymour Martin Lipset, *Political Man* (London, 1960), pp. 403–5.

15   An indication of the influence of Hayek is the way that Ian Gilmour, a leading Conservative critic of Margaret Thatcher in his critical account of the Thatcher Governments, refers to the ideas of Hayek whenever he is in fact criticizing the policies of Mrs Thatcher. In the Conservative circles for which he was writing, the association was sufficiently close for such a code to be effective.

16   Philosophers, economists, historians and sociologists met twice a month in Mises' office for discussion with important men from the business and banking community. Sometimes, with the help of the US-based Rockefeller Foundation, an international scholar or political leader might also participate.

17   Another participant in the Mises seminar, Fritz Machlup, conveys the combative character of Hayek's intellectual mentor in these years:

> Mises fought interventionism while almost everybody was in favour of some government action against the 'evil' consequences of laissez-faire. Mises fought inflationism while a large majority of people were convinced that only a courageous expansion of money, credit and governmental budgets could secure prosperity, full employment and economic growth. Mises fought socialism in all its forms, while most intellectuals had written off capitalism as a decaying system to be replaced either peacefully or by revolution, by socialism or by communism. Mises fought coercive egalitarianism while every 'high-minded citizen' thought that social justice required redistribution of wealth and/or income. Mises fought government supported trade unionism, while progressive professors of political science represented increasing power of labour unions as an essential ingredient of democracy.

Machlup adds that 'Hayek became the most forceful exponent and defender of the economic and political views of Von Mises.' See 'Ludwig Von Mises: The Academic Scholar Who Would Not Compromise', *Wirtschaftspolitische Blatter*, 28, 4 (1981), pp. 6–13; quoted in 'Origins of Market Fetishism', by Kari Polanyi-Levitt and Marguerite Medell, *Monthly Review*, June 1989.

18   Even in private, the *privatseminars'* debates were electrified by a sense of the impending downfall of an old order, and therefore an awareness of strange dangers and unaccustomed possibilities. 'Those who were most sensitive to all this because so ambiguously poised between civilization and anti-Semitism, between privilege and ignominious rejection were the intellectual Jews, along with the old patrician families, a stratum of cultivated bureaucrats and the elite of the Social Democratic Workers Party.' Ernst Fischer, the Hegelian philosopher, here describe exactly the mixed social strata from which the Von Mises seminar drew its participants. See *Opposing Man* (New York, 1974).

19   Carl Schorske, in his classic evocation of fin-de-siècle Vienna, captures the way the Austrian Liberals' every move produced its opposite with his description of the cultural dissonances surrounding the disintegration of the Austro-Hungarian empire: 'A German nationalism articulated against aristocratic cosmopolitans was answered by Slavic patriots clamouring for autonomy. When the liberals soft-pedalled their Germanism in the interest of the multi-national state, they were branded as traitors to nationalism by an anti-liberal petite bourgeoisie. Laissez-faire, devised to free the economy from the fetters of the past, called forth the Marxist revolutionaries of the future.' See Karl Schorske, *Fin-de-Siècle Vienna, Politics and Culture* (London, 1961).

20   The socialization programme proposed by Bauer and Schumpeter in effect made the debates of the *privatseminar* public. It was this programme which provoked Mises' public polemic against the possibility of socialism.

21   This subjectivist theory of value was in opposition to classical economic theory, which understood value as governed by past resource costs, with varying interpretations and understandings of the relative importance of the resources of labour, capital, land and raw materials. Neo-classical economic theory developing from the work of Alfred Marshall, notably his *Principles of Economic Theory* (London, 1920), understood value as jointly determined by physical costs and utility (a more abstract subjectivity than that proposed by Menger). Therefore, according to Marshall, there has to be some means of allocating limited resources amongst an infinite variety of wants.

22   'Value is the importance that individual goods or quantities of goods attain for us because we are conscious of being dependent on command of them for the satisfaction of our needs' (Menger's *The Principles of Economics*, introduced by Frederick Hayek, first published in 1871). Individuals should therefore be able to rank all goods and services in terms of their own set of personal preferences. This subjective understanding of value became the basic premiss of the Austrian School. Prices are established by economic actors making valuations of goods and services and calculating how best to spend their incomes according to their preferences. Price according to Menger is merely 'a symptom of an economic equilibrium between the economies of individuals'. (For a useful summary of Menger's work see *The New Palgarve Dictionary of Economics*, eds Eatwell, Milgate and Newman (London, 1987).)

23   For useful summaries of 'the calculation debate' see Karen Vaughn, 'Economic Calculation Under Socialism: The Austrian Contribution', *Economic Inquiry*, (1980), pp. 535–54; Don Lavoie, *Rivalry and Central Planning*, (Cambridge, 1985); and also, from a critical socialist point of view, Robin Blackburn, 'Fin-de-Siècle: Socialism after the Crash', in *After the Fall*, ed. Robin Blackburn (London, 1991); Andrew Gamble, 'Capitalism or Barbarism: The Austrian Critique of Socialism', *Socialist Register*, 1985/6.

24   See particularly writers building on the work of Karl Polanyi – especially *The Great Transformation* (London, 1944) – for instance, G. Hodgson, *Economics and Institutions* (Cambridge, 1988).

25   'The Use of Knowledge in Society', in *Individualism and Economic Order* (London, 1949; first publ. 1945), pp. 77–8.

26   'The Use of Knowledge in Society', p. 80.

27   'The Use of Knowledge in Society'.

28   The latter are set out most fully in *The Constitution of Liberty* (London, 1960).

29   Hayek, 'The Use of Knowledge in Society', p. 79.

30   'The Use of Knowledge in Society', p. 88.

31   *Individualism and Economic Order*, p. 14.

32   Ludwig Wittgenstein, *Philosophical Investigations* (Oxford, 1963).

33   This is documented very clearly as far as Lenin is concerned by Carmen Claudin-Urondo, in *Lenin and the Cultural Revolution* (Sussex, 1977).

In the course of my work on Hayek I had several very helpful discussions with Mary Falmer, then a graduate and teacher at Sussex University. She died tragically, and avoidably, in spring 1993. I want to record my gratitude and respect for her work on Haye. I hope that even though it is unfinished, it will be published.

3

TRANSFORMATION FROM BELOW

Introduction

Many possibilities and openings were glimpsed in 1968. Many different themes can be read back into this moment when the institutions of the Cold War were rejected by those who were supposed, gratefully, to inherit and eventually lead them. But it also was a moment when the shapes of alternatives were not in focus. The importance of some of the themes influential in this revolt has only become clear in subsequent years. New ideas and practices in the production, organization and character of knowledge is one of these. Some of the movements that developed after 1968 have questioned existing forms of knowledge more self-consciously: in particular, the women's movement, the ecology movement and the networks of radical technologists and shop-floor activists who have had an influence in West European trade union movements.

A questioning of the kinds of knowledge that underpinned the hierarchies and routines of university life and its relation to the state, industry and the military, was a powerful theme in the student revolt. Their demands for a significant say for students in the devising of courses, for instance, challenged the implicit presumptions about whose knowledge mattered in public decision making; their attempts to include in their courses topics of immediate political urgency raised questions about what kinds of knowledge could be counted as valid. Their innovatory forms of organization and expression – teach-ins, workshops, the dissolving of the platform speaker into meetings in the round, co-operative working instead of hierachies – all now quite commonplace, were the first public challenge to the values and methods implicit in the dominant organization of knowledge.[1]

Angelo Quattrochi captures the experience of increasingly standardized education from which this questioning arose, in his description of the 'Mouvement du 22 Mars', a prime mover in the 'events' in the classrooms and then the factories of Paris. The Mouvement was the creation, he says, of 'Students with frail hands and troubled minds. Students . . . in the university-factory where they give answers but don't ask questions'.

Their minds are policed by discipline, patrolled by examinations. Their hearts frozen by authority. Their state within the state mimes the society from which they are insulated. And yet, they do not own and they do not belong. . . . Their university mimes society, mimes the factory. They threaten its functioning, using gaily and daringly the shreds of learning handed down to them. They reconstruct patiently in the silence of their rooms the pieces of the puzzle which needs them obedient and well behaved, respectful to their grave and grievous masters and mindless to the outside world. And yet the tools they are handed, however blunted by their majestic keepers, spell irreverence and reveal traps, false doors, distorting mirrors, barriers, closed gates. At the very end of the long dusty roads: injustice.[2]

The history of social movement politics from 1968, the differences and disjunctures as well as the continuities, has yet to be written – it is probably too heterogeneous to be encompassed in one work.[3] For my purposes, I will simply trace what I percieve as a recurring critical theme: the questioning and overturning of the character and organization of what counted as valid knowledge and hence as the exclusive legitimate source of authority.

Out of critique grew innovation and the practical assertion of alternatives: in particular the assertion, in whatever initially *ad hoc* ways, of the validity of experiential knowledge, not simply as a source of empirical instances, or falsifications, of a general law; but as clues, signposts and stimuli to deeper understanding and theoretical innovation. Combined with this was an attempt to demystify theoretical knowledge and to advocate a pluralistic approach to its development. These themes run through the activity, ideas and forms of organization of the student and worker rebellions of the late 1960s and early 1970s, the women's liberation movement and sexual emancipation movements that emerged in the mid 1970s, the radical workers' organizations that persisted in many countries, albeit in minority positions, through to the 1980s, the socially conscious ecology movement that developed in the late 1970s, and the peace movement of the early 1980s. Their distinctive approaches to the character and social organization of knowledge was part of what made these movements 'new'.

Their eclectic, egalitarian and, above all, social approach to knowledge lay behind a sceptical approach both towards the state, including the promise of a socialist state, and to the party as the prime or exclusive agencies of change. Their confidence in the possibility that valid sources of knowledge could come from experiences of the inside of oppression and exploitation led many in these movements to believe strongly, sometimes blindly, in their own personal and collective power to change the world. Their newness lay in part in the fact that, unlike many movements since the winning of the universal franchise, they did not see their role primarily as a means of putting pressure on parliament. Indeed, in the majority of West European countries their distinct historical identity is as movements created by the first generation to have grown to adulthood after a sustained experience of majority governments led by parties claiming to represent working-class people. All the new democratic movements and the radicalized trade union movement wanted changes that could not be achieved simply through pressing for more of what these governments had, at their best, provided.[4]

Characteristics

The movements that exploded across Western Europe, amongst workers as well as amongst students, were unusual in that they were not about bread or even immediate material conditions. The student rebellion was a lot more than a protest against student overcrowding and disaffection from mass teaching. The factory-like features of the campuses of the late 1960s were symbolic of a wider predicament.

Neither can the revolts be understood simply as an explosion of the frustrated expectations of the first generation who never knew the hardship of war and had all the benefits of a welfare state and a booming economy. This and the apparent lack of economic uncertainty about their future undoubtedly help to explain the self-confidence with which the student movement aspired to change the world. It does not, however, fully characterize the extensive involvement of young workers, nor the indirect reverberations that 1968 had amongst other, less privileged social groups, throughout the seventies and early eighties.

A clue to the special significance of the rebellions that began in the late sixties is that wherever they emerged they were a challenge to arbitrary and unaccountable forms of authority: to managements imposing the discipline of the assembly line; to the deans, principals and university administrators who stood by rules that had lost all practical function beyond protecting the position of those already in power; to trade union bureaucracies that had lost any sensitivity to the demands of their members; to parts of the welfare state that many of its users came to experience more as forms of control than providers of care; to the stifling conventions of polite culture as well as the incorrigible claims of scientistic technocracy.

A common feature of these authorities was their appropriation of knowledge: their claim to know what was good for the students; to determine the place of the worker in the production process; to lay down the best interests of women; to presume the power to control material life – the economy, technology and nature. The movements that challenged these authorities contributed to a complex process that from diverse economic, cultural and political angles shook the methods of governing, public and private, associated with the post-war institutions.

The institutions of the post-war consensus

Many analysts seeking to understand the conditions for capitalist stability in post-war years, (notably 1945–73) and to gain clues about its breakdown, theorized the predominant features of the economic and political institutions and their interrelationships as 'Fordist'. There is widespread agreement on the characteristics of influential tendencies in the organization of production, consumption and the state that originated with F. W. Taylor and Henry Ford in the 1920s, and spread in part through Ford's business success. But the influence of these tendencies was historically and geographically extremely uneven. There is considerable disagreement about how widely applicable the theorization of Fordism is.

On the side of production, Fordism involved a dramatic move away from the craft-based patterns of industrial development of the late nineteenth century. With Henry Ford came standardization. Under the system he established first at the River Rouge car factory in Detroit, products were standardized; this in turn required that the parts and tasks of production were also standardized: for a mass-produced run of cars, the same headlight could be fitted to the same car body in an identical manner. With standardized tasks came the possibility of mechanization with special purpose machines for mass production. The tasks involved in working the machines were subjected to Frederick Winslow Taylor's 'scientific management'.

Any skill that was absolutely necessary to a particular task was codified by management, and each task broken into component parts so that unskilled manual workers could be instructed in exactly what to do. This made possible a highly productive assembly line system in which the product flowed past the worker who did his or her task according to the instructions. Such a production system involved high initial or fixed costs, though running or variable costs were low. There was therefore a constant drive for volume. For such a production system to be profitable there had to be mass consumption of standardized goods. The pressure to achieve these conditions in turn influenced the development of an infrastructure favourable to large scale private consumption, most notably in the US in the 1920s and 1930s: a predominance of road transport over public, collectivized transport. The need for mass consumption further generated a massive expansion of advertising as Fordism reached its peak across the consumer durable industries in the late forties and fifties.

In the US Roosevelt's New Deal, and in Western Europe Keynesian demand management and the welfare state, helped to sustain the conditions for mass consumption and production. These are understood therefore as central features of the Fordist settlement. A further dimension of this settlement concerned labour: the costs of fixed capital and the assembly line conditions for high productivity put a premium on management control over production. Whenever and wherever Fordism was introduced, there followed strikes and more individualist but, for the discipline of the assembly line, equally disruptive forms of labour resistence. After a time, a more or less explicit bargain was struck: high wages in exchange for management control.

Put schematically, the theory has an overly neat, almost functionalist feel to it. But it identifies one powerful tendency in a period of stability that was the product of contradictory and lagged historical processes. It is not a substitute for detailed historical study. Moreover, it has few predictive powers concerning the character of the order, orders or absence of order that will follow Fordism.[5]

A full-scale engagement with the debates on this attempt to understand the underlying social order of post-war capitalist nations is beyond the scope of this book. There is one corollary, however, which is important for the argument of this book: the distinctive assumptions concerning knowledge built into the Tayloristic methods of management that have been so vital to the economic success of Ford and Fordism.[6]

Fordism, Taylorism and the knowledge of centralized management

Commentators on Fordism have focused on its technological conditions (assembly line, standardized production) and the macro-economic and political requirements – mass consumption and the publicly funded provision of a healthy, literate labour force. Underlying these features of production and consumption is a methodology and an understanding of knowledge, laid out most systematically by F. W. Taylor in the 1890s and 1900s, but elaborated in practice in private and public organizations for the following half century.

At the centre of this methodology is the thesis that the practical knowledge developed by workers in the course of their labour is such that there is no insurmountable obstacle to its codification and hence centralization: 'Every single act of the workman can be reduced to a science', Taylor asserts in *The Principles of Scientific Management*.[7] In fact he defines scientific knowledge in the sphere of management in such a way that: 'the development of a science . . . involves the establishment of many rules, laws and formulae which replace the judgement of the individual workman'. Moreover, he believes not only that all practical knowledge of any economic relevance can be centralized, but that it is vastly more efficient so to do; so much so that he can boast of his system that 'the workman is told minutely just what he is to do and how he is to do it; *any improvement which he makes upon the orders given him is fatal to success'*.[8] The basis on which Taylor believes management is able to give the worker these instructions is that management has assumed the burden of 'gathering together all the traditional knowledge which in the past has been possessed by the workman and then classifying, tabulating and reducing this knowledge to rules, laws and formulae'.[9] These rules justify a precise division of tasks so that the effective execution of each task does not depend on any particular characteristics of the individual worker.

These rules also provide a 'scientific' and therefore supposedly neutral technical basis for rigid hierarchies of power and authority: 'Thus all the planning done [in the past] by the workman must be done by the management in accordance with the laws of science. It is also clear that in most cases, one type of man is needed to plan ahead and an entirely different type to execute.'[10] On this basis production targets could be met, it was presumed, with mechanistic certainty and reliability.

Taylor himself did not invent the assembly-line whose success in the auto industry was to give his methods their global and historical influence. But his ideas inspired Henry Ford to give mechanized reality to the precise division of labour and machine-like workmanship that his science inspired. This partnership was not surprising, for the aim of his science and his definition of efficiency were totally at one with the Fordist drive for quantity: 'The greatest prosperity,' he argued, 'exists only when that individual has reached his highest state of efficiency, that is when turning out his largest daily output'.[11]

The economic success of Taylorism, reflected in the spectacular output of the US auto industry throughout the 1920s and early 1930s, laid the bases for its influence in the management of public institutions as well as private; state socialist societies as well as capitalist ones.[12] The principles adopted by Henry Ford to centralize the knowledge of the factory worker were seized upon by Vladimir Lenin to centralize the knowledge of economic actors in whole industrial sectors. Lenin praised Taylorism as a set of neutral principles of productive and administrative efficiency; they became inscribed in the methodology of Soviet administration in every social sphere.[13] In Britain, Fabian notions of planning and Morrison's model of the public corporation both drew heavily on Taylor in their measures of efficiency and their centralizing methods of administration. And in the development of social services, the idea of the standard product was put to social democratic purpose, in building a welfare state to provide a universal service to meet basic needs.

The underlying priorities of the time, on both sides of the Cold War, were particularly open to turning management and public administration into a science. The first decades of the post-war period were a time when output and basic provision came before self-development, creative skill and special needs, and when the idea of democracy, West as well as East, had no trace of a developmental character. It had become a passive, periodic choice between political elites. Moreover, the decades of Taylorism's greatest influence coincided with the period when confidence in the conquering powers of science over the forces of nature and society was at its height.

The confidence that science/knowledge would show the way reached its political apotheosis in the West in the early to mid 1960s, with the technocratic confidence surrounding both the Wilson government in Britain and the Kennedy regime in the United States. The French Fifth Republic, with its *dirigiste* form of government and powerful monopolies, and in spite of some archaic aspects (not entirely absent in Harold Wilson's Britain), had become a less glamourous but much emulated model of modern technocratic capitalism. In the East a related faith, focused on the command economy, reached its zenith in the mobilization of Soviet resources to defeat the Nazis in 1944 and complete the country's industrialization. With good reason, the memory of this achievement has been a powerful influence.

Significantly, history dealt blows to the confidence of the ruling elites on both sides of the Iron Curtain in quick succession. In the East, the sources were Krushchev's revelations of the crimes of Stalin, followed by the repressed uprisings of Hungary, Poland and then, 12 years later, Czechoslovakia; in the West it was Vietnam, and the defeat by a peasant army and campus revolts of the technologically mightiest army in the world.

The information generation

The students and workers of 1968 were the products of Taylorism at the height of its extension to the universities: the final enclaves of a more pluralistic sphere of society which had in prewar years enjoyed a certain autonomy from the imperatives and models of production. With the massive expansion of higher education and an increasing routinization of what had been an elite education, students were experiencing for the first time the rigours of Taylorian methods just as these methods were beginning to break down in the wider world – whether the world of the shop floor, where absenteeism was rampant and unofficial strikes mounting in intensity, or the world of international relations, where a 'scientifically' managed army was being defeated by a peasant guerrilla army (albeit a guerrilla army using the arms of Taylorist planned factories in the USSR).[14]

The students were the first generation of mass university education: the first generation not destined to become the cadre of a ruling elite; and the first generation most of whom were not themselves the sons and daughters of this elite. Many of them in effect were being trained as information workers to handle the codified knowledge that was becoming central to the running of production and the economy, and to the administration of an expanding public sector. The destiny of the majority of them was to participate in the production process and the daily organization of public institutions as people who could handle information, manipulate knowledge and deploy language, like previous generations handled coal, manipulated metal, deployed a machine tool. The generation trained for this society would be the first generation to use computers with the habitual familiarity with which previous generations came to use cars.[15]

Social and economic organization has always implicitly involved the use of information. But by the late sixties as production, even within a single company, depended increasingly on the efficient flows of a system of units and inputs, Western state administration too became increasingly a matter of systems of co-ordination. The result of both these developments was that the organization of information, the utilization of knowledge and the development of skill became central economic issues in themselves. People had to be trained in the use of information, or trained to apply their other skills in a context where flows of explicit information were becoming increasingly important.

The increase in student numbers was one sign of a change in their social destiny. The numbers of students going through French higher education, for instance, had expanded from 170,000 in 1960 to 600,000 by 1968, too many by far to find even petty ruling status.

Other signs lay in the increasingly technocratic character of education. As knowledge, its gathering, processing, classification, distribution and utilization, became a driving force of the economy, or at least a necessary mediating link in the process by which all other economic factors realized their economic value, the content of courses became increasingly instrumental. New divisions were imposed between disciplines; students were required to specialize before their own studies and development led them to choose; external careers had to be specified before students had any inner sense of finding themselves; exams, with their absurdly narrow measures of success, became overwhelmingly important. Liberal aspirations to rounded education appeared subversive by comparison. The demand to be 'whole', to exercise the imagination – 'all power to the imagination' as the graffiti proclaimed – was politically explosive.

At the same time these students were gaining an inside view of this emerging industrial and political culture. As they were trained in its working they lost any awe that the wider public had of the technology that it valued. A distinctive feature of the student movement of the late 1960s and early 1970s was the active involvement of scientists using their inside experience to expose the inhuman ways in which technological advances were being used: in chemical warfare in Vietnam, in psychological torture of prisoners in Northern Ireland.[16] Their work through international networks shook the scientistic culture of neutrality and forced political debate not only about the uses of technological innovation (a debate with a long tradition), but also on the direction of innovation and the content of technology. As this work developed, it was not anti-science – after all, it was led by scientists who continued to make social use of their researches. But it rejected the dominant claims that were made for the progressive and infallible character of the Western tradition of science.[17] It helped to tear away the veil of scientific certainty and technological invincibility surrounding both sides of the Cold War.

Reverberations

The spontaneous demands and tactics of the student movement had reflected its opposite: to the instrumental, codified knowledge of the authorities the students counterposed imagination, values, wholeness and experience. Against hierarchical administration, the students pitched their own forms of direct democracy. However, these forms, invented to suit the needs of the moment, were often generalized in a way which supposed that society was simple and homogeneous.

The student challenge to orthodox definitions of knowledge and authority affected a whole generation, and significant minorities in generations that followed. In the process, through trial and many errors, the search for and experimentation with new forms of organization produced more complex notions of democracy and pitched wider sources of knowledge against the monopoly of the state expert or corporate manager.

The student movement's challenge to the claims of neutral, scientific expertise by those with economic, cultural and social authority, helped to stimulate – for the most part, unintentionally – the founding of the women's liberation movement, with its own definitions of knowledge and need. In questioning the incorrigible basis of scientific advance, and stressing the values and political choices involved in technological change, the radical students prepared the way for the eco-socialist criticisms of Keynesian theories of growth and public investment.

The challenge of the late sixties generation to the legitimacy of those in power is closely associated with their immense confidence in themselves as the subjects rather than objects of historical change. The extraordinary political energy of these years demonstrated in a concentrated way the power that people potentially have to dissolve constraining structures which in 'normal life' they passively reproduce. It encouraged a reliance on self-organization and direct action, and with this a pooling of their own knowledge, extension of it by direct contact with potential allies with different vantage points, rather than acceptance of an acknowledged authority. It produced a dialectic (if that is not too pretentious a word for a somewhat chaotic spiral) between action and knowledge: collective action revealing things not previously known, that in turn help to focus further action. This sense that anything is possible has been tempered by defeat, but the experience contributed to the development of traditions of direct action which have continued through the dramatic actions of the anti-nuclear movement in Germany, the factory occupations throughout Scotland and the North of England in the early 1970s, through numerous local symbolic actions like the tree hugging of the green movement in Sweden, to the internationally famous camp of the women at Greenham. It has also inspired a more gradualist and more sustained form of direct action: a stress on acting immediately to bring about some change, however limited, against oppressive circumstances; change which ortho-dox political strategies would postpone until the achievement of a socialist government.

This radical gradualism has produced many new institutions and ways of living, though their sustainability has depended, ironically, on social democracy – the very political strategy they were often initiated against. These institutions (women's centres of various kinds, innovations in health care, extensions of adult education, radical cultural centres and more) depend, in good part, on the availability of public resources, even if they radically transform how these resources are managed. As social democratic governments have been weakened from the right, and by changed international economic relations, these institutions have had to devise new strategies for survival.

Social movements have both multiplied and diverged in many different ways since 1968. But I want to argue that many of their activities have in common is an implicit political methodology opposed to the social engineering methodology that more or less dominated the political institutions of the Cold War. This revolt has not led in a single direction, even in practice. There are broadly two, not entirely separate, directions. One still involves a vision of social transformation, a different kind of society; the other is more particularistic, more limited in scope, asserting a particular identity, bringing about transformations for one group, like a radical extension of trade unionism to the interests of particular oppressed groups. The two directions are not totally separate but they are distinct. My focus will tend to be on the former. In this chapter and the next, I will sketch how in their practical rebellion against dominant forms of authority and the appropriation of knowledge the new movements have developed the tools for a democratization of knowledge. In Part III I will explore how these tools are being applied in practice by analysing exemplary initiatives in public management, economic resistence and political organization.

Democratizing knowledge; democratizing the state

At their most coherent the ideas and practice of recent democratic social movements could be described as holding out a practice and emerging theory of 'differentiated democracy', combining participative democratic practice in the everyday workings of social and economic life with formal representative democracy to set objectives and frameworks. I will point to the way that this implicit vision of democracy arises in practice out of challenges by social movement activists in Western Europe to the positivistic principles of administration – expressed most clearly by F. W. Taylor – of the post-war state and corporate institutions.

Rarely did the activists of 1968 systematically express their rebellion in terms of an explicit theory of knowledge and method of social understanding. Their methodology was implicit. Moreover their radicalization against existing state and corporate institutions had brought them up against forms of scientific and hence political reasoning shared by the dominant socialist traditions, both Leninist and social democratic. Pragmatically, the new movements created their own ways of organizing based on their own experiences of sources of knowledge and skill ignored by existing managerial methods, and on previously subordinate anti-postivistic traditions.

In some countries these traditions were articulated in a highly self-consciousness, theoretical manner. This was the case, for instance, in Germany with the Frankfurt School.[18] In Britain such traditions took a more applied form, drawing on unorthodox understandings of knowledge and science in the writing of history, in cultural criticism and in the practice of adult education. The work of E. P. Thompson and Raymond Williams has been most influential in this arena. Although their concerns and histories are in many ways very different, it is significant that they share an enthusiasm for adult education: an area of activity in England, Scotland and Wales were a distinct cultural approach has thrived, subversive of positivistic orthodoxies. Edward Thompson gives a sensitive description of its strengths and its pitfalls in a lecture published as a pamphlet entitled *Education and Experience*.[19] It is a profoundly egalitarian tradition. It goes beyond what Thompson calls 'the political claims of *égalité*' and challenges cultural subordination too. In adult education, this implied a recognition of the importance of the experience that the adult student brings to the course: 'This experience modifies, sometimes subtly and sometimes more radically, the entire educational process: it influences teaching methods, the selection and maturation of tutors, the syllabus: it may even disclose weak places in received academic disciplines and lead on to the elaboration of new areas of study.'[20] In politics, this cultural revolution meant an end to paternalism, a goal of the Painite tradition associated with the French revolution, but marginalized as the leadership of the labour movement sought to gain status and position on the terms of the existing deferential culture. It seems that reformers from the upper and middle classes have always found it more easy to advocate political and economic programmes of equality suffrage than they have to shed the cultural attitudes of superiority. Yet so long as the political claims of *égalité* are not followed up by the development of popular self-confidence, then the impulse to self-government withers.

Essential to such an egalitarian culture, and hence a thoroughgoing democracy, is a mutuality of intellect and experience. A problem within the work-

ing-class movement, in England at least, has been a counter-position of the
two, often in reaction to the class-ridden character of educated culture. The
obvious common response to this has often been anti-intellectualism, whether
in the form of a reckless militancy or a complacent sentimentalism.
Thompson and Williams tried instead, both by practical personal example
and in their writing, to illustrate and explore a creative dialectic between
experience and theory, intellect and feeling. The focus of Thompson's 1968
lecture, which is exemplary of this dialectic, was education. Thompson concludes the lecture (addressed mainly to other educationalists) by arguing that
'the universities need the abrasion of different worlds of experience in which
ideas are brought to the test of life'. The movements which emerged after
1968 began to bring this dialectic into the practice of politics. They were not
free of debilitating counterpositions, at times producing extreme forms of
both antihumanist theoreticism and populist anti-intellectualism. But in
many of their lasting initiatives, as I will show in subsequent chapters, they
faced state and party institutions with the same abrasion that Thompson
advocated for the universities. And in doing so, in Britain at least, they have
been influenced directly and indirectly by practical traditions of cultural,
political and economic democracy, sustained by writer–agitators like
Thompson and Williams.[21]

Knowledge and the foundations of the women's movement

The early women's movement was perhaps more explicit and practical than
any other in its challenge to conventional approaches to knowledge. In the
first phase of the women's movement, in the absence of any relevant core of
scientific knowledge of the conventional kind – based on laws that summa-
rized empirical regularities or generalizations – women started by sharing and
reflecting on their own experiences in ways which would enable us to see
where and how to take action. We called this 'consciousness-raising'. Historically, the reality and impact of consciousness-raising was uneven. The implications of experience were not self-evident. And where consciousness-raising
sanctified experience in an exclusive manner, counterposing it to theory,
rather than valuing it as a complementary source of understanding, then
consciousness-raising groups could stifle dissent and produce a false homoge-
neity, often followed by painful fragmentation. Looking back, however, with
the benefit of lessons learnt, I think it is possible to identify several distinctive
approaches to knowledge which came out of this process. They represent
elements of an alternative to the positivistic conceptions of knowledge that

underpin the state institutions on which women depend but with which they are daily in struggle. At the same time they provide a basis, against Hayek, for collective, transformative action of a knowing but not all-knowing kind.[22]

Firstly, out of the consciousness-raising process developed a recognition of knowledge which is implicit in previously unrecognized or under-valued skills. From this arose, for example, an extended analysis of housework and child rearing as skilled and socially valuable work which needs to be treated as part of the public sphere. A recognition of tacit knowledge was also the basis of a major criticism of the health and maternity services – and eventually the whole range of public services – for treating its patients as ignorant and passive.[23] This generated initiatives for greater responsiveness to women's own knowledge, curiosity and desire to have some control over their bodies; that is, for a notion of expertise involving greater interaction between professionals and 'lay' patients, users and clients.

A second challenge to conventional notions of expertise is the insistence by many feminists that emotion can be productively combined with reason in the extension of knowledge. Women came to consciousness-raising with ambiguous feelings, about each other, about motherhood, about their sexuality, about waged work, about the left, about men. Far from emotion being in practice opposed to reason, a hindrance to the discovery of publically useful knowledge, it was a stimulus to curiousity, a driving force to search into one's feelings, or someone else's, in order to understand something previously unknown, or only partly known, and to investigate further.

A third result of much consciousness-raising was a recognition of the fallibility of knowledge as an effect of unconscious motives or unknown conditions, which are only revealed through breaking out of old patterns of behaviour or being willing to confront uncomfortable facts.

A fourth feature of the approach to knowledge common to many women's liberation groups was an attempt to understand underlying social processes; a dissatisfaction with the conventional explanatory methods of subsuming the problem to be explained under a generalization. Feminists writing about the aims of consciousness raising, describe the intention of discovering 'what is really going on' behind the surface of daily experience; of 'getting to the roots of women's oppression'. They refer to a sense of the interconnectedness of apparently discreet experiences: to a need to understand 'the whole gamut of women's situation'. Conventional explanatory methods seemed too superficial for this task; generalizations based on empirical regularities seemed simply to redescribe the problem, rather than get to its entangled roots. The limitations of legislative measures, such as equal pay and equal opportunity legislation, are indicative of the inadequacy of these analytic tools.

A final, distinct feature of the early women's movements' approach to knowledge was that at the same time as 'getting to the roots' of their oppression (to reality out there, as it were), they self-consciously explored their own collusion in this oppression. They were constantly alert to the connections between transformation of self and transformation of social structures. This had two kinds of consequences for their activity. Firstly it led feminists to treat culture seriously as a complex of structures with material consequences. For instance, feminists placed much emphasis on the values taught and practised in nurseries and child care centres. Public provision in itself did not mean that their children would be cared for in a democratic, co-operative and egalitarian culture. The struggle over who controlled the character of the provision became as important as the provision itself. Feminists have also placed a high political priority on creating the infrastructure of a lasting alternative culture: feminist publishers, magazines, theatre groups, bands, cafés, centres and so on.

Our self-consciousness as women, about the way that we in part reproduced the structures of our own oppression (and not as mere dupes or 'carriers', but as active agents who had certain, however limited, capacities to transform these structures), produced a stress on activism. We were impatient of resolutionary politics of parliamentary parties, even if we were sceptical of much of what claimed to be revolutionary politics. Our understanding of structures and of how they were reproduced and could be transformed meant we tended towards, or perhaps invented, a radical gradualism – radical in the sense that we were highly critical of the existing state and placed little reliance on its ability to meet our demands; gradualist in the sense that we mobilized whatever resources we could, to achieve in the present whatever changes we could in the direction of our long-term goals. An illustration of this approach comes from the experiences of the GLC Women's Committee. Throughout the 1970s, in the absence of adequate child care, women in London as in many other West European towns had created an impressive range of projects for their own and other children, of an egalitarian and democratic kind; so much so that when the GLC Women's Committee moved to provide a major childcare programme, there was already the basis for it in the communities of London. In one year the Women's Committee spent £3.5 million on over 400 childcare projects.

This is in some ways an idealized summary. No one women's group would necessarily arrive at these conclusions and strategies. But it summarizes those features of the women's liberation movement's approach to knowledge which are innovative and which illustrate the ways in which the social movements have a richer understanding of non-codified forms of knowledge and its potential to be shared and made public; an understanding which provided a starting-point for their particular kinds of challenge to the social engineering state.

Much of the practice of all the new movements and the trade union organizations which they influenced reflects the same implicit challenge to a positivistic mentality of science as the women's movement, stressing to different degrees the importance of tacit knowledge, of the developmental and fallible character of knowledge, of feelings and emotion as a stimulus to knowledge rather than an entirely contrary human attribute, of the search through a pluralistic approach to theory for underlying structures. At the same time they share a sense of the self as agent of transformation.

The movements' challenge

As I hope I have shown, the political legacy of positivism was transmitted most influentially via Taylorism. The best way of highlighting the distinctive challenge posed to this legacy by movement practice is to identify those aspects of the predominant methods of state and private corporate institutions that bear the mark of Taylorism and positivism more generally, and then to contrast these with principles drawn from movement practice. For the present, I will make broad assertions, deepening my arguments in later chapters.

Taylorian principles of management are based on a restrictive conception of knowledge in which the only valid knowledge is scientific; all else is an incomplete version of science or is pure speculation/superstition. The implication of course is that those with scientific knowledge know best and the ordinary person is ignorant. This had many practical effects, for example, in the running of the welfare state, and the treatment of the users of services as passive clients/victims with nothing to contribute to the process of diagnosis or service improvement; similarly, front-line workers were expected merely to implement the orders of experts from above.

Against this, rather along the lines of the consciousness-raising of the women's movement, the workers' movement in their campaigns on health and safety, and the green movement in their early warnings of environmental damage, asserted the importance of forms of knowledge that are generally unacknowledged in public policy making. These forms include everyday knowledge embedded in feelings and skills that should be taken account of along with the professional medical and educational knowledge, for example; or historical knowledge gleaned from personal memory or biographical evidence which could, say, contain insights for the development of a locality unavailable to the professional town planner. These radical movements have concerned themselves with the social conditions that favour the development and transformation of this knowledge, in a way that previously dominant social democratic and Leninist traditions did not.

At their best these movements, or projects arising from the movements, have tried to organize their own policy making processes in a way which explicitly takes account of the everyday knowledge and skills of their base. Thus their organizations are based on an autonomy and diversity of initiative and debate that is common to projects influenced by any of the movements: workshop style discussion, rotation of leaderships positions, the creation of horizontal networks, reflect this concern to tap forms of knowledge outside the orthodox notion of science. Where they aim for unity, their notion is, in practice, a complex and differentiated kind of unity. Such co-ordination is rare, except for where groups have united around a particular cause: trade unionists, feminsists and other left-wing activists uniting against anti-choice legislation on abortion; just about every radical campaigning group uniting with the miners in Britain in 1984–5; the united action against Cruise Missiles across Europe. There has been little experience of anything beyond informal interconnections; the movements have proved better at autonomous initiatives than any sustained form of unity. In chapter 7 I analyse how in some countries they have had an influence on new left parties which gives them a somewhat unstable political expression.

Consider also the dominant approach to the development of science. It is an approach which stresses the cumulative, linear character of scientific knowledge, and which tends to mask theoretical innovation and exaggerate consensus. It resists pluralism and lateral experiment; produces a cautiousness and conservativism in policy research, and little encourages alternative sources or research.[24] All this was apparent not only in most state administrations but also to varying degrees in Social Democratic, Labour and Communist Parties which, in the 1950s and 1960s, were reinforcing structures based on hierarchies and responding rigidly and paranoically to challenges from outside the circulating political elite. It was also a feature of the larger, most established private corporations, particularly in Britain and the US, until recession caused shakeups and internal competition. Against this, the social movements posed, in their practice, an experimental pluralism. On the rare occasions when the social movements have had political influence they have voiced critical views of technology and science: the Science Shops in Holland, Technology Networks in London and Sheffield, the campaign in Italy for 150 paid hours off work for education. Within the movements this heterodox understanding of forms of knowledge has encouraged a plurality of centres (not necessarily to their political advantage) and publication of research, debate and theoretical work.

A further feature of the engineering state is its instrumental form of reasoning. Such reasoning has two politically significant features. (1) It posits a purely external relationship between ends and means. Ends are given by politicians and means prescribed by technocrats. One implication of this is that there is no conception of self-activity by those who will benefit from the change. (2) A further implication is that the policy making and implementing institutions of the state are presented as neutral, as if the means chosen do not favour one group over another.

Instrumental reason has an exclusive focus on the external, billiard-ball-like relations between social variables, as if one social variable will have a simple causal effect on another (for example: the idea that public subsidy for private companies produces industrial expansion; or that redistributive taxation and welfare provision eliminates poverty). Such an approach ignores the internally structured and differentiated nature of every social 'variable'. Depending on the power relations within private companies, for instance, public subsidies have been wasted; and inequalities of gender within working-class families has meant that blanket redistributive policies have not significantly improved the economic position of women.

Inherent in instrumental reason is a belief in the overwhelming power of a rationality based on empirical evidence. Against this form of empirical rationalism the social movements, in much of their practice, have shown a sober assessment of the limits of human reason. Feminists have pointed to the power of unconscious motives, which rational argument cannot easily reveal or acts of will transform; radical shop stewards highlighted the tacit practical knowledge of skilled workers, reflected in what they do and make but not easily put into words; Greens insist on the damage to the environment that is the likely unintended consequence of many of our daily habits of consumption; the peace movement warns of unknown and unknowable conditions which could trigger off a nuclear war.

Against the conventional separation of end and means, the post 1968 social movements tried to exemplify in the process of change the values underlying their political goals; to prefigure the ends in the process of achieving them. At times this has led to a disastrous oblivion to the constraints of untransformed structures. At its most effective, however, it illustrates a novel political recognition of both the way in which we ourselves reproduce, and therefore could potentially transform, social structures; *and* of how many of these structures endure independently of us and require complex and sustained alliances to transform.

Post 1968 movements have also demonstrated in their practice a common resistence to the practical consequences of the social democratic state's focus on external or quantitative aspects of social institutions, and its purely instrumental treatment of their internal relations. The early movements' confrontations, with the administrators of state provisions were almost entirely precipitated by issues of quality and democratization. When financial cuts hit these services, from the 1973 oil crisis onwards, such movements had a difficult and sometimes impossible path to tread: defending public resources but demanding a transformation in the way that they are managed. On the unusual and brief occasions that the left social movements has had a taste of power, most notably in the Greater London Council and Sheffield City Council, it has tried, with only limited success, to break down the state's internal hierarchies; to establish direct and responsive relations with service users; and to introduce democratic ways of measuring and controlling the standards of services that focus on quality, range and access as much as quantity.

The political lag

These social movements were not the first to challenge positivistic understandings of knowledge. For some time positivism in social science had been seriously under question in Western philosophical circles, in the work of Karl Popper, Imre Lakatos, and Thomas Kuhn for instance.[25] In the relatively stable, not to say frozen circumstances of the Cold War, however, there was a long lag before such questioning could uproot the foundations that positivism had given to public policy institutions. Its notions of science as cumulative rather than characterized by periodic breaks and revolutions; of knowledge only as general laws describing constant regularities; of a sharp distinction between fact and values and therefore between ends and means; and an exclusive focus on external relations between 'variables', as if less visible internal differentiation did not exist: these were entrenched in powerful public and private institutions. The weight of the military – centrally planned and controlled, West as well as East – further reinforced the lag between revolutions taking place in the philosophy of social science and the methodology and practice of public policy.[26] It was the students of 1968 who explosively exposed the disparity. They were unable themselves, though, to overcome it.

Ironically, these movements unintentionally stimulated forms of capitalist modernization that, in the absence of a coherent new left, were exploited by the neo-liberal right in its dismantling of the welfare state, and by a new generation of productivity-oriented management in its use of information technology to reorganize the process of consumption.

Modern corporate management is sometimes credited with initiating the move away from Fordism, and is understood by many to be the originator of concepts of 'flexibility', 'decentralization', 'networking' and other terms which are now familiar buzz-words of up-to-date forms of organization.[27] In fact the 'post-Fordist' forms of organization in industry – for example in the Fiat factories of Northern Italy and the auto industry round Paris – arose in significant part from a managerial rethink forced by workers breaking the bond of the Fordist bargain (more wages for more effort) and refusing to submit themselves to the boredom and stress of constant repetition of minutely fragmented tasks.[28] Similarly the shakeup of the public administration of education – including in some countries attempts at its marketization – has been an attempt to train an intellectual workforce in spite of student rejection of the educational assembly line.

As the term 'post-Fordism' implies, the alternative to Fordism is an open question. It is being answered by those with the power to shape organizations to suit their purposes. It includes the adaptation of Fordism to the new international markets. In industry corporate management have been highly successful in combining flexibility in production with centralized control over finance. 'Post-Fordism' is consequently identified with those who have had the power to determine what came after Ford. The early rebellions from below, including many of their less convenient insights for those in power, are forgotten. Moreover, parts of the left sometimes end up defending Fordist political forms simply because their rejection has become associated with the right.[29]

More than stories

One problem behind this weakness of the new left is that the social movements' alternative to the predominant rationalities of state and corporation tend only to be found in stories. Stories do not always travel well across cultures or historical periods. There are limits of stamina in the number of times wandering exiles can tell the story of the GLC's economic policy, the

Foreigners Committee of the Red–Green coalition in Frankfurt, the technology policies of the metal workers' union in Germany. And there are limits to the tolerance amongst listeners. Theorization of such experiences would enable lessons to be shared: so long, that is, as it is a theorization which does not subsume the particular but is attentive to its complexity, allowing new questions to enter the debate as the theorization spreads. But here we come up against a stange paradox. The new left, with their origins in intellectual contestation, produced an unprecedented amount of theoretical work for a generation in revolt. Yet the theorization of their own emerging practice is significantly underdeveloped compared to their theoretical critique of capitalist and actually existing socialist societies. Why is this? What does it indicate about the theoretical legacies on which they drew? And what are the lessons for belated but urgent attempts to theorize before politically induced amnesia sets in?

Notes

1   I am not the first writer who has analysed the 1968 student movement and the movements stirred up by its wake in terms of their approaches to knowledge. Ron Eyerman and Andrew Jamison have written an excellent analysis, primarily of the environmental movement, which sees the 'cognitive praxis' of a social movement as decisive in its ability to transform society. They focus on the post 1968 movements of which they see the contemporary environmental as an integral part. But they also apply their conceptual framework convincingly to the nineteenth-century social movements – the Owenites in England, for instance; the followers of Proudhon and Cabet in France – showing how their innovative practices popularized and elaborated new scientific, experimental approaches to society. See *Social Movements: A Cogntivive Approach* (Oxford, 1991).

2   From Angelo Quattrocchi and Tom Nairn, *The Beginning of the End*, (London, 1968).

3   There is an extensive literature on 1968 itself, including semi-autobiographical accounts like that of Tariq Ali, *1968 and After, Inside the Revolution* (London, 1978); a study through oral history: Ronnie Fraser et al., *1968, A Student Generation in Revolt* (London, 1988); a study in contemporary history such as David Caute's *The Year of the Barricades* (London, 1968); analytic studies such as G. Katsiaficas, *The Imagination of the New/Left: A Global Analysis of 1968* (Boston, 1987); Gianni Statera, *Death of a Utopia: The Development and Decline of Student Movements in Europe* (New York, 1975).

4   This bears some similarity to R. Inglehart's characterization of these movements as 'post-materialist', because of their concern more with improving the quality

of life than material security. See R. Inglehart, *The Silent Revolution* (1977). But it is misleading to imply that the concerns of these movements are not in certain respects as materialist as pre-war movements: that the womens movement's demands for child care, its initiatives to set up battered women's centre, for instance, are not as material as the unemployed workers' movement. Moreover, the kind of economic prosperity and security in West European economies which gave the post-materialist argument a certain validity has not been sustained. Extreme poverty and insecurity co-exist in the West with considerable affluence. Many of the activities of recent movements are concerned with the causes and consequences of such inequality (the spread of feminists organizing with low-paid women workers – see chapter 3; the anti-racist movements across Europe).

The differences with many older progressive movements which flows from my analysis is that they do not look to government alone or even primarily to resolve their problem, to engineer, as it were, a solution. Moreover, even where they look to government or demand material resources, they are concerned with the democratic quality of social relations in the administration of these material resources. If it is necessary to characterize these movements as 'post' anything, 'post-social-engineering' would be the term which would flow, rather clumsily, from my analysis.

Other writers who have identified distinctive features of recent movements include Claus Offe, who stresses the way that they have extended and redefined the boundaries of institutional politics; (See C. Offe, 'Challenging the Boundaries of Institutional Politics: Social Movements since the Sixties', in ed. C. S. Maier *Changing Boundaries of the Political* (Cambridge, 1987) and 'New Social Movements: Changing Boundaries of the Political', in *Social Research* 52); Alberto Melucci, who stresses the radicalism of the movements in transforming the organization of everyday lives and creating in effect an often hidden but nevertheless subversive counter-culture (see A. Melucci, 'Ten Hypotheses for the Analysis of New Movements', in ed. D. Pinto, *Contemporary Italian Sociology* (Cambridge, 1981) and 'the Symbolic Challenge of Contemporary Movements', *Social Research* 1985); and Jean Cohen, who analyses the new movements as creating new political identities pressing non-negotiable demands (Jean Cohen, *Class and Civil Society: The Limits of Marxian Critical Theory* (Oxford, 1983) and with A. Arato, 'Social Movements, Civil Society, and the Problem of Sovereignty', *Praxis International* 4, no. 3).

5 The most succinct summary is Robin Murray's article 'Fordism and Post-Fordism', in *New Times*, eds Stuart Hall and Martin Jaques (London, 1989); see also Murray's analysis of the impact of Fordism on the post-revolutionary methods of Lenin and the administrative institutions of the Soviet Union: 'Fordism and Socialist Development', a working paper available from the Institute for Development Studies, Sussex University, Brighton. Jamie Peck and Adam Tickell have written a critical summary of the literature and provided an

extensive bibliography – not only on Fordism but also on the regulationist approach to capitalist restructuring – which have been particularly influential in studies of the decline of Fordism and the supposed emergence of 'Post-Fordism' in its various forms: 'Accumulation, Regulation and the Geographies of Post-Fordism: Missing Links in Regulationist Research', in *Progress in Human Geography*, 16, 2 (1992). In her *Imaginary War* (Oxford, 1990), Mary Kaldor put Fordism in a wider political context by discussing it as part of the making of Atlanticism and how it was sustained by and helped to sustain the Cold War.

6   Frederick Taylor set out his influential principles in *Principles of Scientific Management* (New York, 1911).

7   Taylor, *Principles of Scientific Management*, p. 34.

8   F. W. Taylor, *The Art of Cutting Metals* (New York, 1906); emphasis mine.

9   Taylor, *The Art of Cutting Metals*.

10 Taylor, *The Art of Cutting Metals*, p. 38.

11 Taylor, *The Art of Cutting Metals*. For critical discussions of Taylorism see Mike Cooley, *Architect or Bee* (London, 1987); Alfred Sohn-Rethel, *Intellectual and Manual Labour* (London, 1978).

12 By 1929 the US produced over 2.9 million motor vehicles, compared with 211,000 in France, 182,000 in Britain and 117,000 in Germany.

13 See Robin Murray, 'Fordism and Socialist Development'.

14 Perhaps this conjuncture of process helps to explain the extraordinary, and extraordinarily short-lived alliance of workers in the auto factories of Western Europe and the students of its major cities.

15 See *Student Power*, eds R. Blackburn and A. Cockburn (London, 1968); U. Bergmann, R. Dutschke, W. Lefevre and B. Rabehl, *Rebellion der Studenten oder die Neue Opposition* (Frankfurt, 1968); D. and G. Cohn-Bendit, *Obsolete Communism: The Left Wing Alternative* (London, 1968); *Le Mouvement de Mai ou le Communism Utopique* (Paris, 1968).

16 For documentation, especially on Northern Ireland, see for instance P. Ackroyd, K. Margolis, J. Rosenhead and A. Shallice, *The Technology of Political Control* (London, 1975).

17 See for instance Hilary and Steven Rose, 'The Radicalization of Science', *Socialist Register*, 1972; *The Political Economy of Science* (London, 1976).

18 Marcuse was particularly influential. See his *One Dimensional Man* (London, 1964), and *An Essay in Liberation* (London, 1969).

19 E. P. Thompson, *Education and Experience*, the Fifth Mansbridge Memorial Lecture (Leeds University Press, 1968).

20 Thompson, *Education and Experience*, p. 1.

21 Kate Soper has written a very perceptive analysis of E. P. Thompson's 'socialist humanism' as expressed in his political essays and pamphlets, his work as a historian and his notable theoretical and polemical engagement with Louis Althusser. See Thompson's *Poverty of Theory and Other Essays* (London, 1978) and *Troubled Pleasures* (London, 1990). For Raymond Williams, see Neil Belton,

Francis Mulhern and Jenny Taylor, *What I Came to Say* (London, 1989). For interesting references to disagreements and common themes between Thompson and Williams, see *Politics and Letters: Interviews with 'New Left Review'* (London, 1979). See also Perry Anderson, *Arguments Within English Marxism* (London, 1980).

22　For duscussion of the theory and practice of consciousness raising in the women's liberation movement, see Hester Eisenstein, *Contemporary Feminist Thought* (Boston, 1984); Sheila Rowbotham, *The Past is Before Us* (London, 1989); Jo Freeman, *The Tyranny of Structurelessness* (London, 1984); Kathie Sarachild, 'Consciousness Raising: A Radical Weapon', in *Feminist Revolution Redstockings* (Boston, 1971).

23　See Lesley Doyal, *The Political Economy of Health* (London, 1979); Ann Oakley, *Social Support and Motherhood* (Oxford, 1992).

24　There is an important distinction between a notion of experiments designed to confirm a general law (a notion characteristic of a postivistic view of science), and experiments designed to explore and deepen theoretical hypotheses. For further discussion of this see R. Bhaskar, *A Realist Theory of Science* (Brighton, 1972).

25　Karl Popper, *The Logic of Scientific Discovery* (London, 1959); Imre Lakatos, 'Falsifications and the Methodology of Scientific Research Programmes', in *Criticism and the Growth of Scientific Knowledge*. eds Lakatos and A. Musgrove (Cambridge, 1967); Thomas Kuhn, *The Structure of Scientific Revolution*, 2nd edn (Chicago, 1970).

26　See Mary Kaldor's *Imaginary War* for a description of the effects of the military on the character of the Cold War state in the West.

27　See for example Geoff Mulgan, 'The Power of the Weak', in *New Times*, eds Stuart Hall and Martin Jacques (London, 1989).

28　Hilary Partridge, *Management Strategies Towards Labour in Fiat* (PhD thesis, Durham University), covers the period from the early 1950s to the early 1980s. See also a Working Paper on the Communist Party and the trade unions in Italy from the early 1970s, published by the European Policy Research Unit, Department of Government, Manchester University.

29　For the debate about the character of Fordism and post-Fordism, see Robin Murray, 'Fordism and Post-Fordism', and 'Benetton Britain: The New Economic Order', in *New Times*, eds Hall and Jacques.

4

THE THEORY AND POLITICS OF KNOWLEDGE

Introduction

In the late sixties activists in new movements were unselfconsciously eclectic in the theoretical traditions on which they drew. For example, Daniel Cohn Bendit, a leader of the French student movement in 1968 and a member of the critically minded anarchist grouping *Noir et Rouge*, defined himself as an anarchist 'negatively' by his rejection of dogmatism. He did not completely reject Marx, any more than he accepted Bakunin. When he was pressed to define his position, he placed himself in the general stream of 'council communism'.[1] Sheila Rowbotham, who was active in the British New Left and a founder in 1970 of the Women's Liberation Movement, described the reading of the New Left in the sixties: 'Unselfconsciously we read Kropotkin and Bakunin as well as Marx, Ghandhi and G. D. H. Cole, Camus, Sartre and Emma Goldman. We bought *Anarchy* as well as *Peace News*, *Sanity*, *Tribune* and *Labour Weekly*.'[2]

Although anarchistic themes have been and continue to be influential on the radical movements of the last twenty years or so, criss-crossing with various feminist and ecological traditions, Marxism of various forms has been the most persistently and pervasively influential tradition. Exploring the precise character of its influence provides the clues to the undertheorization of the movements' political innovations and to how these innovations might now be best understood and spread.

The new social movements have always had an uneasy and eclectic relation with Marxism, reflected in the variety of engagements with it to be found amongst movement activists. On the one hand, an impetus of these movements' rebellions was a rejection of the models offered by both sides of the Cold War: a rejection of both Second International and Soviet Marxism and their attendant reductionism and economism was for the majority almost automatic, if not thoroughly thought through. On the other hand, in their practical break from the shallow complacency of the post-war consensus they needed critical concepts to understand the Vietnam War, the factory drudgery that existed alongside the exotic promises of a consumer culture, the state repression and cultural standardization. The extent and form in which Marxism was a source of such concepts varied from country to country, depending on pre-existing left traditions. In countries like Germany, France and Britain where there was a well established Marxist tradition critical and independent of official communism, it was a widespread cultural and intellectual influence among many activists whether or not they were members of any Marxist organization.

The influence of Marxism

Looking back it is possible to distinguish two distinct influences of Marxism, one positive, the other negative. The Marxism which had developed in opposition to Soviet orthodoxy – especially through the Frankfurt School but also work like that of Isaac Deutscher,[3] in a non-sectarian Trotskyist tradition, or like André Gorz,[4] who applied a creative materialism to contemporary capitalism and the strategic problems of labour's resistance – this Marxism provided a necessary framework for developing critical explanatory concepts and theories.

The creative development of Marxism as a source of analytic tools and research agenda for explanatory social theory, however, was not paralleled by equivalent development of Marxist theories of political agency.

The underlying problem is that Western Marxism of the post-war period – critical theory along with the earlier more revolutionary writings of Lukács and other anti-Stalinist Western Marxists – was concerned to understand the conditions of the defeat of the revolutionary project. This led to a concern with consciousness and culture, which became central to their continuing contribution to critical social theory. With little prospect of socialist change in post-Yalta Europe, they had little motive, however, to address problems of agency and organization.

The case of the critical theory of the Frankfurt School illustrates these limitations best, because of all schools of Western Marxism it probably has had the greatest influence on the new movements.

Critical theory

The influence of critical theory on the emerging social movements of the late 1960s – especially the student movements of Germany, Britain and the US – enabled these movements, which in many respects were unorthodox, to establish a creative association with Marxism. Critical theory provided the stimulating force for application of Marxist concepts of imperialism, exploitation and the class nature of the state, combined with concepts from non-Marxist theorists (Freud and Weber, for example) to analyse bureacracy, authoritarianism, information technology and sexual repression: concerns well beyond Marxism but at the centres of the new movements' interests.

Although critical theory was influential on these matters of substance, it also resonated with the movements' philosophy of action. Critical theory's insistence, against the laws of capitalist crisis predicted by orthodox Marxism, that 'history is made' by 'the situated conduct of partially knowing subjects',[5] accorded with the social movements' emphasis on ideological and cultural critique and their initially self-confident sense of themselves as agents of social change.

Habermas' notions of 'the life-world' and communicative action, which he argues need protection from colonization by the political and economic systems, provides a powerful theory of the cultural influence of the new social movements and legitimates their role as a counter culture. And there are significant parts of the social movements who do indeed see themselves in this role. There are others, though, who desire to transform the existing economic and political systems. Habermas sees these latter phenomena as unavoidable products of modernization against which the social movements can at best protect some public space for undistorted communicative action. Rather than treat culture, economy and polity as varying parts of interconnected social relations – as in effect did activists in the new movements, moving with relative ease from university actions to organizing with workers in the factories – he treats them almost as different kinds of phenomena. Political and economic systems he sees as 'thing-like constraints on communicative action', and analyses them as if they were inanimate objects, in effect reverting to a positivist method. In this sense, the second generation critical theorists, most notably Habermas, unintentionally follow economistic Marxists in underestimating the cultural and subjective dimensions of political and economic power, inspite of the importance they give to culture as a separate sphere.[6]

In this way, contemporary critical theory could not provide a guide to political agency that accorded with the aspirations and sense of possibility typical of the activists of the 1970s and, in a different way, the 1980s. Moreover, Habermas' sharp demarcation of the economic system and 'the lifeworld' could not account for the workers' radical resistance to the disciplines of this system. Indeed, the critical theorists dismissed the workers' movement as a spent and incorporated force. Yet it was these simultaneous explosions of revolt, in the factories and in the universities, sharing many critical values, whatever their positive alternatives, which led the politically conscious amongst both to want more specific guides to political action.

Marxism as a theory of political agency

In spite of the weaknesses of Western Marxism as a guide to action, activists were drawn to it by the critical content of its tools for understanding contemporary reality. Partly as a result they frequently, if only temporarily, joined Marxist (Trotskyist or Maoist) groups or parties. The main function of these organizations prior to 1968 had been to guard the flame of revolutionary Marxism, as Tom Nairn puts it, 'in a world that would not catch fire'.[7] They had to varying degrees become incredibly conservative not only in terms of their style and routine – these in many cases were intelligently altered – but more fundamentally in terms of their central concepts of organization. Even where they had opened themselves to innovative theoretical traditions (for instance, organizations such as the International Socialists in Britain, which drew on the libertarian Marxism of Rosa Luxemburg, Hal Draper and others), this openness did not extend to taking sustained risks with their own organizations.

Werner Hülsberg, a historian of the German Greens, describes the paradoxes of this Leninist phase through which significant parts of the new left passed in their search for new forms of organization (in Germany the predominant form was Maoist): 'These non-human parties, with their Stalinist organizational forms, turned young people into political automa-tons and failed totally to break out of their isolation. These organizations were not a continuation of the Extra-Parliamentary Opposition (the '68 inspired movement in Germany) but a break with it. Self-organization, love of life, spontaneity, and enlightenment were replaced by zombie-like obedience, discipline, asceticism . . . which the intelligent among them couldn't take for long.'[8] And indeed many of those who went briefly to the Maoists later joined anti-nuclear 'citizens' initiatives' in founding Die Grünen, which was created explicitly and proudly on principles of 'base democracy', almost the polar opposite of the kinds of 'democratic centralism' to be found on the sectarian left (some would say that grass roots or base democracy, however, has been implemented in an equally rigid manner).

The problem was that the Leninist parties or groups that emerged out of the shadows with the first popular challenge to Cold War politics were steeped in a methodology which was itself the object of the revolt. These revolutionary organizations could provide a banner for younger movements struggling against US imperialism, against poverty, injustice and exploitation and for a period many people worked through these organizations for these causes. But the activists in these movements interrogated and rejected those who claimed superior, overarching knowledge. They soon found that Leninist organizations tended to make just such a claim, grounding it in somewhat teleological interpretations of Marxism. After brief and often exhausting attempts to make these organizations capable of learning from new movements, activists wandered off, some into new political projects, including explorations of non-Leninist forms of radical political organization, others into creating spaces in their job or community for political change, or into subversive cultural ventures; others became disillusioned with the possibilities of political and economic change, and contributed to a 'life-world' that was being increasingly absorbed into the existing economic system.[9] It is revealing that, across Western Europe, wherever these organizations had roots in the new movements (Britain and Italy in particular) it was feminist activists who broke open the contradiction between the encrusted methodology of warmed-up Leninism and the emerging political culture of the new movements. Feminism and then black militancy were profound challenges to the ideology of social engineering.

Here is evidence of another lag in the impact of questioning of conventional theories of knowledge. Recent developments in the philosophy of knowledge and the emerging forms of left political practice to be found amongst movement activists tended to emphasize the experimental interaction of theory and experience. Yet the organizations of the Leninist left, despite protestations to the contrary, ended up safeguarding theoretical truths rather than taking the risk of learning from novel political initiatives. I would suggest two explanations of the lag. The first is a matter of political environment and the second of theoretical tools.

Marxist politics: its political environment

The influence of latter-day Leninism, with an ultimate priority on preserving the Bolshevik tradition, however that is interpreted, has been strongest in those political environments where the radical left has felt most strongly the fear of betrayal. The more their political environment has bound them as the dependent, subordinate partners of governmental parties of the left, the more this fear has constricted their political imagination. In Britain and France, where the political system made it difficult for the new left to sustain its own political expression, and construct experimentally its own relation to a social base, the influence of a more or less petrified Leninism was at its height. In Britain social movements have produced a dense undergrowth of projects and campaigns, and concerted onslaughts have occasionally been mounted on the methods of the all-knowing sects. But without political representation these alternative groups find it difficult to accumulate the experience and refine the theory necessary for a political identity of their own.

Where the new left face an electoral system that allows for a greater plurality of representation, and the possibility of an independent political identity, there has been a pragmatic process of developing new political parties or radicalizing ones led by an earlier 'new' left out of splits with social democratic or Communist parties. In these circumstances – most common in Northern Europe – there has been a greater confidence on the radical left about embarking on new organizational and political experiments without fear of diverging from some sharp, thin line of political correctness. The German Greens, the purest 'new party', developed the most explicitly new institutions of 'base or grass root democracy'.[10] The Dutch Green Left, creating a new left party out of a merger of three older parties – one radical liberal, one pacificist socialist and the third Communist – has also created new kinds of political institutions so that, for instance, the majority of its active supporters, who see themselves as involved primarily in movement activities rather than the party itself, can nevertheless contribute to the work of the party without being sucked away from movement activity into a party apparatus. New left parties in Denmark and Norway, which grew out of pre-1968 splits in Communist and Social Democratic Parties, have more gradually adapted their parliamentary methods in response to the pressure and innovations of the new movements. In Italy most successfully, there has been the phenomenon of Euro-Communism, which has been responsive to the agendas set by the social movements – especially feminism and ecology – but not always to their radically transformative goal and extra-parliamentary methods. Methodologically, Euro-Communism represented a rejection of the official Leninist concept of a single party monopoly in favour of party political pluralism and the more or less conventional model of a parliamentary party. In this, however, party professionals would still be the prime source of party policy and direction. They would simply be more willing to form alliances, and do deals with professionals from other parties.[11]

Marxist politics: its theoretical tools

The problem of theoretical tools seems to be this. In much of his writings Marx implied a theory of knowledge in which the tacit and particular insights of experience play an important role. Consciousness, according to Marx, develops through experience of a changing and contradictory society. His notion of experience and social being is an active one in which people are interpreting and debating their reactions to events; thus ideas and culture are part of practical experience. It is in practice, he argues, that the working class 'are in a position to achieve a complete and no longer restricted self-activity, which consists in the appropriation of a totality of productive forces and in the development of a totality of capacities entailed by this'.[12] However, he never translated such general notions into principles of political agency. At the time, this might have been wise. He looked upon parties and political organization as essentially practical instruments, temporary and necessarily flexible.

On this basis, Lenin's form of party might have been treated historically as a particular kind of political instrument appropriate for a distinct historical moment. Instead, with the authority of the Russian revolution behind it, it became a model which distorted and hardened under Stalin into an international strait-jacket for part of the European left.[13] Its establishment as a rigid model was aided by the fact that even if its origins were pragmatic, it was argued for in a manner that gave it foundations of reinforced concrete. Lenin asserts that 'class consciousness can be brought to the workers *only from without*, that is, only from outside the sphere of relations between workers and employers'.[14] This was primarily a polemical critique of the idea that the consciousness developed through trade union struggles either already is, or could spontaneously become, political class consciousness. It is a rejection of the assumption that workers will spontaneously and through the struggle of the workplace develop an understanding and connection with struggles for democracy and social justice in spheres beyond the factory. Lenin went on to argue that only the party, the laboratory and the transmission belt of revolutionary political science, could interpret the wider society to the workers in a way which would generate this political consciousness: only a disciplined party of professional revolutionaries could unite workers' struggles with those of other subordinate social groups to create the power to overthrow the state.[15]

Lenin did not write his tracts as part of a doctrine for all time. His writings are rather the developing, sometimes self-contradictory, thoughts of a political leader reacting to events, with an acute sense of the opportunities for fundamental transformation and the need for strategic intelligence to grasp them. Whatever the appropriateness of his theory of the revolutionary party to the circumstances of twentieth-century Russia,[16] it became hardened into the presumption of an all-knowing organization, unable to acknowledge the need to learn from the practical and cultural insights of working-class and social movements that had a political life and history of their own. Hallowed by 1917, it became embalmed in the thinking, often only half consciously, amongst many parts of the radical left.

Few of the social movement activists who joined or associated with Marxist organizations profoundly believed Lenin's theory of consciousness, at least with its Kautskian emphasis. They were more attracted by the different emphasis which Mao and Trotsky place on popular self-activity and cultural revolution. But although Trotsky and Mao at different times demonstrated a real understanding of the creative capacities of working people, both clung tightly to notions of political leadership and organization which took it for granted that those with scientific knowledge, understood in theoretical terms – in terms of knowing the overview – would set the direction and control the process of cultural revolution/self-activity. Their latter-day followers (even those who demonstrate considerable organizational creativity, like the International Socialists since the 1970s, later the Socialist Workers' Party) took a similar course. Judging by the accounts of members and ex-members, their procedures did involve some notion of learning from struggle and from working-class experience. The problem was that they believed all this practical knowledge must be absorbed through a central process and then a single 'line' arrived at to which every branch and member were bound. Moreover, the line was usually all-encompassing, or at any rate quickly became so if a section of the party (such as women, gays, lesbians, blacks), initially allowed autonomy, took serious initiatives of their own. A genuine recognition of practical knowledge, of both tacit and ephemeral kinds, and a commitment to its expression would require spheres of autonomy co-ordinated within a framework of shared goals. Without the autonomy by which groups of members (or individuals) can act on their experience, a component of knowledge is lost, repressed or appropriated in a fragmented, partial way by the leadership.[17]

Rosa Luxemburg was one of the few Marxist writers and activists from the early twentieth-century years of working-class militancy and revolutionary insurgency who directly challenged Lenin's political methods. She argued that these methods were leading the Bolsheviks to drain genuine power from the soviets to be concentrated in the Party's Central Committee. Her definition of socialist democracy was one in which the working class ruled by means of 'the most active, unlimited partcipation of the mass of the people, of unlimited democracy . . . This democracy must be the work of the class and not of a little leading minority in the name of class – that is, it must proceed step by step out of the active participation of the masses: it must be under their direct influence, subjected to the control of complete public activity: it must arise out of the growing political training of the mass of people.'[18]

Moreover, Luxemburg did not share Kautsky's and Lenin's belief in the superior knowledge of the party leadership: 'Let us speak plainly, historically, the errors committed by a truly revolutionary movement are infinitely more truthful than the infallibility of the cleverest Central Committee.'[19] The problem, however, is how such a participative approach can be translated into sustainable organizational forms in periods and places where there is no revolutionary movement but instead constant, everyday struggles that only indirectly pertain to state power. Rosa Luxemburg did not live to confront this problem, and the legacy of Lenin and the Russian Revolution proved overpowering, even in 1968. The leadership of the post-war Marxist groups who revived Luxemburg's ideas were not willing to take the risks, including risks for their own leadership, that implementing them would have entailed. The imperative of safeguarding the theoretical truths won the day.[20]

Post-modernism and its critics

In countries where no new party of the social movement left had emerged (Britain, France and the US, for example), post-modern theories expressing the fragmented character of contemporary cultural and political life became especially influential – though they have been influential throughout the West. There are many ways in which post-modernism, with its characteristic concern for the symbolic, has been in close accord with the activities of the social movements and has helped them gain a reflective self-consciousness.

'Post-modernism' has become too embracing a term to be very useful. It has been applied both to theorists concerned with the relation of the symbolic to extra-symbolic reality (who would be more accurately described as 'cultural materialists'), as well as those who consider the symbolic or discursive to constitute reality. In both cases, however, the concern to scrutinize cultural forms expresses the impulse of the social movements to take apart the soothing consensus of post-war social democracy. The women's movement, for instance following the US black civil rights movement, challenged universalizing concepts of 'citizenship' and 'human rights', showing how these hid from view both inequalities and differences which excluded social groups from access to power. Similarly, in the green movement, critical scientists and technologists together with community activists subverted the modernist commitment to technological 'progress', revealing values and implicit choices embedded in this apparently neutral notion. Post-modernism has also raised the problem of 'totalitarianism' in 'totalizing' theories, reflecting a tendency within the social movements to favour a pragmatic, piecemeal approach to theory. Furthermore, it echoes and theorizes the social movements' concern with language; like them it has drawn attention to the role of language in creating our social and cultural life rather than simply reflecting a reality 'out there'. Post-modernism, however, describes the emergent qualities of the culture out of which the social movements developed, rather than a theorization of the movements themselves. This was a culture which produced neo-liberalism as well as libertarian socialism, Richard Branson and Virgin Records as well as Tom Robinson and Rock Against Racism.[21]

What post-modernists who deny extra-discursive reality cannot express about the social movements, is their purposeful collective effort aimed at transforming structures that exist independently of their activities. They are unable to understand what makes Rock Against Racism different in its purposes and its consequences from Richard Branson and Virgin records.

The women's, anti-racist, green and peace movements, for instance, are not simply concerned with changing discourse; their concern with language is part of an effort to achieve greater public truthfulness about the institutions which materially constrain people's lives. Their emergence and continued existence presupposes that the only way to overcome this oppression is for these victims to become active subjects transforming relationships which they would otherwise tend to reproduce. The debate and argument in the social movements about how to do this is not just a series of diverse solipsistic statements, it presumes common reference points against which stategies for change can at least be tested in practice – something that most post-modernism would deny. Post-modernism has been more influential after the setbacks faced by the social movements in the late 1970s. Geographically it is most influential in France, where the early social movements were at their stongest (in 1968), and yet where they suffered the severest defeat. It is perhaps more of a theory for *ex-members* of social movements, loyal to the culture of which these movements have been a part, but disillusioned with the frustrating efforts of bringing about social change.

Many such people would nevertheless identify with the left and feel politically hostile to neo-liberalism. Yet in this their instincts are stemming from a more universalistic culture than post-modernists can offer. For post-modernism itself does not, I would argue, provide adequate tools to answer the radical right. To be fair, post-modern writers do not claim this as an aim. However, there are those on the left who dress their politics in post-modern garb as if it helped to make the left popular or convincing in a culture influenced by the radical right. In fact, on their own, the tools of post-modernism produce only a more volatile version of the radical right. For like Hayek, post-modernism cuts the connection between human intention and social outcome. While for the radical right the incompleteness of our knowledge means that society is the outcome of the blindfold and therefore haphazard activities of the individual, for the post-modern theorist, society is an equally haphazard plethora of solpsistic statements of various sorts. The only significent difference is that while the neo-liberal is interested in social order, the post-modernist celebrates chaos. Where the right's dilemma is to explain the social order which pertains despite the haphazard outcomes of individual activity, the post-modern dilemma is to identify the criteria for the value judgements without which even their own activities would be impossible. The radical right resolve their dilemma through what they argue are the moral and political outcomes of social evolution, to be protected by the state against all particularistic protest. The post-modernists resolve their problem by various forms of narcissism, ethno-centrism and relativism. Both devalue the processes of democracy.

Critical realists: underlabourers for the new left?

A distinctive intellectual undercurrent in the whirlpools of the late sixties and early seventies was an intense interest, especially in Britain, in anti-positivist thinking in the philosophy of science. It was an intellectual revolution stirred by the unlikely figures of Karl Popper in his role as philosopher of science and author of *The Logic of Scientific Discovery* (as distinct from his role as Cold War polemicist and author of *The Open Society and Its Enemies*, for which he is more well known), and the later Wittgenstein, whose philosophical debut in the 1920s was as a leading logical positivist, applying the principles of mechanical engineering to the understanding of society.[22] Popper challenged conventional assumptions of the linear, cumulative character of scientific development. Wittgenstein stressed the social character of language and meaning and consequently our knowledge of the world, undermining the individualism that flowed from empiricist notions of knowledge as the atomistic absorption of sense data. These challenges were taken up by Imre Lakatos, Paul Feyerabend and Thomas Kuhn.[23] Kuhn demonstrated the character of science as a social institution that was, like any other social product, subject to the exercise of power. Kuhn argued that, typically, science alternated between periods of 'normal' science during which aspiring scientists (not nature) were tested on the basis of the dominant paradigm; and periods of revolutionary science, during which the paradigm suffered such an accumulation of anomalies that rival groups, or more often just a new generation of scientists, generated a new paradigm, around which the scientific community eventually cohered for another round of normal science. Lakatos tried to synthesize the insights of Popper on the one hand (that science could be rational) and Kuhn on the other (that science is by fits rational and irrational). He elaborated a methodology by which research programmes could be judged according to whether they were progressive or degenerating – thus knowledge could be cumulative but still fallible. Feyerabend points out that science develops through the existence, at any period of time, of a plurality of competing scientific theories, and argues for much more individual choice for the scientist. He took this insight to extreme irrationalistic and relativist conclusions. By the late sixties monistic and deductivist notions of science were under severe attack.

One approach to an alternative was emerging out of the linguistic philosophy of J. L. Austin, who developed a dimension of Wittgenstein's stress on the social character of language and the contextual character of meaning. Austin's method was to analyse everyday language and its presuppositions.[24] More often than not this turned philosophy into a trivial pursuit. Linguistic philosophy did, however, take the development of philosophy out of the realms of a debate that was spiralling away, not only from the world but also from the ways in which humans sought to describe and understand the world. Although much linguistic philosophy got lost in the minutiae of everyday speech, it also stimulated two breakthroughs.

The first was to explore the actual practice of scientific reasoning. In the course of such investigations, Rom Harré and Mary Hesse took even further the critique of deductive and instrumental reasoning of the sceptics mentioned above, showing the importance in science of models, analogies and a whole range of non-linear forms of reasoning. They also demonstrated the value-laden character of scientific knowledge. The second breakthrough was P. F. Strawson's attempt to start from everyday language but to probe further, asking what must be the case for speech activity to be possible.[25] This transcendental method of argument originated with Kant, who asked what must be the case for experience to be possible. It led from reflection on the use of language, whether in everyday life or science, to considering what the world must be like for language to be used and science undertaken. Critical realists later developed this line of reasoning into a radical break from the anthropocentric thesis that being can always be analysed in terms of statements about our knowledge of being, and therefore philosophy can concern itself exclusively with human knowledge of the world, rather than of the character of the world itself.[26] They developed the term to transcendental argument and asked what must the world be like for philosophy, science, social activities in general and human emancipation to be possible?

Surprisingly, perhaps, all these developments, from Popper and Wittgenstein to Strawson, turned out to be vital resource for a generation of young British social scientists radicalized by 1968. They were faced in their academic work as well as in their politics with practical, empirical problems: how to understand economic underdevelopment; how to explain the continued subordination of women in liberal capitalist societies; how to understand and transform the stasis of British society. With these questions in mind, it did not take long to become frustrated with what the shelves of conventional sociological and economic studies had to offer. Threads of critical and Marxist theory, and especially history, existed in British culture, but they were too sparse to weave a rich tradition. Continental Marxism began to be available in translation in the late sixties, and provided another resource.[27] But in many ways that Marxism was engaged in its own internal debates; only here and there – Althusser's 'On Contradiction and Overdetermination', Marcuse's *One Dimensional Man* and Habermas' *Knowledge and Human Interests*, for instance – did it provide tools for radical empirical analysis and the means of transformation.

This paucity of easily available critical tools led social scientists such as Roy Bhaskar, William Outhwaite, Andrew Collier, Ted Benton, and later Mary Kaldor, Michèle Barrett and many more – none of whom started their work as philosophers – to explore systematically questions of method and, in the latter cases, to apply them to problems of empirical analysis. In some instances their frustration with existing theories of the problem with which they started led them to reconsider the very basis of scientific knowledge. They were all sympathetic to Marxism as the framework for a research programme, but not satisfied with its present form. So a second impetus was self-consciously to reconstruct tools of materialist analysis. Roy Bhaskar's work is the most systematic implementation of these two projects. He began his philosophical journey as an economist concerned with problems of underdevelopment and the relevance of orthodox economic theory to them; the apparent irrelevance of the latter to the issue of explaining and overcoming third-world poverty posed a problem which his writing has set itself to answer. William Outhwaite has developed some of Bhaskar's ideas, also drawing selectively on some of the insights of critical theory. Others have developed and applied these ideas in relation to ecology, feminism, and the military. There now exists a distinct intellectual school of 'critical realists' whose work, significantly, is based to a large extent outside the academy and applies itself to political and social problems of the day.

The conceptual tools they have developed make it easy to overcome the lag between the collapse of positivistic understandings of knowledge and science in philosophical circles and the persistence of these methods in state, party and economic organization. Concepts alone, however, can never achieve institutional change. It is the way they harmonize with and help to clarify the practice of the movements with whom they share their origins, that gives them this potential potency.

The social production of knowledge

An intellectual outcome of the 1968 revolts against the ruling military and industrial institutions of the Cold War was scepticism of all claims to social neutrality, especially those of science and technology. This led to a widespread reflection on the social context both of particular theories and of the production and distribution of scientific understanding itself. This focus on the social production of knowledge was the starting point of critical realism. Whereas other philosophies of science analyse the language of science or seek to reconstruct science according to some ideal type, critical realists looked at science as a form of social production. The transcendental question that critical realists ask is, what must the world be like for experimental activity and the distinctive activities of scientific production to be possible?

Knowledge and being

The process of answering this question led them to insights that parallel those implicit in the practice of the social movements. In a sense this is to be anticipated, in that social movements seeking to transform society without any precise recipe are themselves engaged in a continuing process of experimental activity, the focus of these critical philosophers' concern. But critical realists have conducted a philosophical investigation which helps us to ground some of the insights implicit in movement practice, and to make use of them.

I have argued that one of the main insights of the movements is their recognition of the importance of many different kinds of knowledge – tacit, experiential, theoretical – for a full understanding of a problem or phenomena. In its most radical form critical realism argues that there exist several levels of being, or reality. It shows how experimental activity in social science presupposes the existence of social structures or mechanisms which generate or produce more or less directly observable phenomena. These structures and mechanisms are not themselves necessarily directly observable – though in some cases they can be. They need to be discovered, through experimentation, through investigation following various clues and with empirical controls of different sorts. Already this implies the likelihood of different kinds of knowledge: the existence of different forms of being requires different kinds of knowing if these distinct levels are to be understood. Knowledge, for instance, of the effects of structures or mechanisms can be gained through direct experience or clues to their effects through more indirect experience. On the other hand, knowledge of the structures themselves is best gained through the construction of and experimentation with theoretical hypotheses on the basis of knowledge of past and present effects.

This approach to ontology grounds a critical Marxist insight (though not exclusive to Marxism) influential in the radicalism of all the social movements; an insight that identified levels of reality beneath and behind the world of phenomenal, directly observable events (and meanings), but without denying the reality and real consequences of these appearances. In natural science, the atomic structures – and behind them their electronic configurations – which produce the observable phenomena of matter would be an example of such mechanisms. In social science, where closed, laboratory, conditions are absent, and where the understandings of the agents of structures and the social position and perspective of the social scientist are all in some way involved, an example might be the mechanisms of domestic, cultural and economic subordination which produce the position of women as objects of display. Women's representation as sex objects itself has a reality with cultural effects, which reinforce deeper, not necessarily observable, mechanisms of oppression. In understanding a problem, therefore (or, to put it in political terms, in developing a strategy for change), critical realism implies the need both to take into account people's own perceptions of their circumstances and to draw on other evidence and hypotheses to explore, where possible, with the people concerned, causal mechanisms at work of which these people might not be aware, because, for example, of the existence of unacknowledged conditions or unconscious motivation.

In this way the critical realists justify the social movements' attention to language, culture and the expression of distinct identities but they understand these as related to underlying structures of power. Unlike post-modernism, therefore, they can sustain philosophically the presumption of most social movement activists, of a real world independent of their knowledge of it – the object of their efforts of transformation. But in contrast to many forms of positivism, critical realists make this presumption in a way that does not reduce this reality to one structure or one level of reality.

A differentiated world

This theorization of the differentiated as well as structured nature of reality provides a foundation for the emphasis of many movement activists on organizing autonomously and at the same time forming alliances on particular issues and/or converging, conditionally, in support of a political party. This political practice presupposes a plurality of different structures. Some of these are seen as in internal and hierarchical relations with each other – though this is a matter for empirical research and experiment.

The value the social movements place on the shared interrogation of their everyday knowledge arises from a sense of themselves as the agents of social change. Knowledge and action are inextricably bound up. Critical realism provides a grounding for this in its rejection of the conventional positivist assumption that facts and values are entirely separate and its demonstration of the value-laden character of our knowledge of the world. This is daily illustrated in the way that we reproduce or transform social institutions. New knowledge about the consequences of our passive acquiescence in these institutions can lead people to take transformative action in their own lives.

This leads to critical realism's 'transformational model of social activity'. The model suggests that social structures exist by virtue of the individuals who reproduce or potentially transform them. Such a theory implies – contrary to the positivist, determinist model – that the reproduction and transformation of society depends on actors' understandings of the relationships and structures in which they participate. This transformational model extends critical theory's recognition of the importance of the meanings people give to their own action, to the recognition of the importance of subjective consciousness in material structures of economic and political power. It takes us out of critical theory's fatalism concerning these structures without leading to voluntarism.

In the early days of social movements, the energies newly released by the discovery of collective power encouraged an initial voluntarism both of the individual and the collective. Critical realism guards against this in its analysis by directing our attention to social relations – as Marx did in his substantive work – rather than either atomistic individuals or supraindividual collectivities, as the explanatory key to understanding social trends and events. Without an understanding of social relations mediating individual behaviour and the reproduction or transformation of social structures, the left tends to lurch from voluntaristic Jacobinism to deterministic structuralism, depending on whether 'the masses' are quiescent or in revolt. Critical realists show how the nature of social structures depend upon social relations, between capital and labour, ministers and civil servants, parents and children.[28] Consequently, although it is the activity of these people which transforms or reproduces these relations, nevertheless the relations into which people enter exist before the indivuduals who enter them. This 'relational view' accords well with the distinctive character of the new left: on the one hand it emerged, from 1956 onwards, as a reaction to the bureaucratic collectivisms of Labour and the Soviet Union, and at the same time it was sickened by the hyped-up individualism of the consumer boom. Its implicit model of society posits relatively enduring but transformable relations between individuals, rather than either as the sum of individual action (dogmatic individualism) or as supra-individual wholes (bureaucratic collectivism).

Knowledge as a social product

How might these conceptual tools help the social movement left clarify the wider implications of its practical alternative to the free-market right?

I showed in chapter 2 how Hayek presents us with a choice between an open and a closed prison. His individualistic understanding of knowledge leads him to an overly restricted choice between fallibility and false claims to omniscience. This implies the political choice between the rough justice of the free market, understood as the haphazard outcome of individual activity, and the central planning of a party that claims to know your every interest. At the root of this hopeless choice is the way that Hayek's view of knowledge breaks the connection between human intention and social outcome, making accident rather than human creativity the mechanism of evolution. Much of the more politically conscious activists of recent social movements hold out the elements of an alternative. But Hayek's choice has theoretical staying power, in spite of practice which points in alternative directions. Critical realism helps us theoretically to justify, learn from and disseminate the alternative practice. In particular, it does so by providing the tools to theorize the practical insights of movement activists into the varied, social character of knowledge.

Knowledge, like language, is not a physical or natural attribute of individuals. According to critical realism it must therefore be an attribute of individuals by reason of their social character, their participation, active or passive, in relations with others within inherited structures. And if it is social it will have historical and relational aspects, to varying degrees. This means that the content, distribution and structure of any particular area of knowledge pre-exist any individual. An individual is born into a heritage of knowledge. But how that knowledge and its organization are reproduced or transformed depends on the individuals who in any way participate in it, whether passively or actively.

If we combine this understanding of knowledge as a social structure with Hayek's initial insight into the fallible, dispersed and ephemeral character of knowledge, we arrive at a conclusion quite contrary to Hayek's. People will mobilize whatever resources they can, including co-operation with others, or the control of others, to overcome the limits of their knowledge and thereby come closer to achieving their purposes. This is one factor explaining why, for instance, the market does not and probably never has worked in the way that Hayek envisages. Ever since markets began, producers and sellers have used whatever resources at their disposal to gather to themselves the knowledge that enables them to influence the market to their benefit. And the different ways that market economies have developed is evidence that they (employers, trade unions, governments) have had some success. The outcome is rarely exactly as they hoped. But on the other hand, where they have had power, including extensive knowledge or means of controlling knowledge, their purposes have undoubtedly been a direct influence on the evolution of market institutions.

Similarly the individuals creating the networks of social movement organization are gathering the knowledge they need from different vantage points in order to understand the social mechanisms at work and take action to influence, spike or reverse them. In the cases of the women's, peace and green movements there has been some success. The historical distinctiveness, indicated here, of the social movements of recent years is a politics of knowledge which has broken from both a confidence in scientific reason as providing the complete social map for political intervention. But the deep and varied limits they recognize on reason does not, in their view, break the link, however tenuous, between their intentions and the social outcome of their intended actions. Much of their practice indicates a belief in the possibility, through social organization, of extending and combining fragmented knowledge to gain not 'a complete picture', but rather a better understanding of the social mechanisms at work, so as to direct their efforts in order that their intentions might be more efficiently fulfilled.

Knowledge and democracy: some implications

Where does this approach leave solutions to the problem of social order? It eliminates as empirically impossible both order through the accidents of a naturalistic model of social evolution and order through centralized design (even the authoritarian regimes of the Soviet bloc were not able to control society as they intended). Furthermore, if, contrary to the accident theory of social evolution, the mechanism of social evolution is the conscious, purposeful projects of groups and individuals changing their social environment by trial and error, then the question arises of procedure and criteria for a just and ordered framework within which these projects can be undertaken. Processes of democratic public judgement thus once more enter the equation, potentially at every level of society, after Hayek's attempt to replace them with the elite processes of discovering and protecting supposed laws of evolution and civilization.

But 'Democracy' cannot be brought triumphantly centre stage, as if its character is not significantly altered by a new approach to knowledge. As a means of government its forms are unavoidably, if usually invisibly, underpinned by presumptions concerning what workings of the economy, polity and social order can and cannot be known, in what way and by whom. It is apparent retrospectively that the different institutional arrangements that claim to be 'government by the people' have been and continue to be influenced implicitly by a range of beliefs about the knowledge and capacities of different sections of the people and by views on whether and how this knowledge should be mobilized. Tom Paine made the need for a form of government which awakened human capacities that normally lie unutilized, central to his polemic for representative government and the political rights that should go with it:

> It appears to general observation, that revolutions create genius and talents; but those events do no more than bring them forward. There is existing in man, a mass of sense lying in a dormant state, and which unless something excites it to action, will descend with him, in that condition, to the grave. As it is to the advantage of society that the whole of its faculties should be employed, the construction of government ought to be such as to bring forward, by quiet and

regular operation, all that extent of capacity which never fails to appear in revolution.[29]

Once representative democracy was achieved, however, its forms were determined by representatives of labour, and by political leaders with less generous views of 'ordinary' human capacities, and greatly influenced by the social engineering philosophies which came to dominate the left. Beatrice Webb's belief, for instance, that 'the average sensual man can describe his problem but is unable to prescribe a solution' no doubt influenced the British Labour Party's acceptance of, more accurately deference to, the expertise of senior civil servants, to the exclusion of opening government departments up to the expertise in Labour's own ranks. And Beatrice Webb openly expressed an assumption widely shared by socialist intellectuals and Labour leaders alike.[30]

A view of knowledge which, by contrast, validates theoretical, experimental, tacit and social dimensions, has radical implications for the character of democracy. The innovative democratic forms of recent movements rebelling against authorities claiming omniscience illustrate some of these.

Innovations can take place both in the forms of democracy, emphasizing processes of participatory self-government, and in extending the levels of society at which questions of democracy are considered relevant. Democracy, for these new movements, is a matter for the institutions of everyday life: the institutions of work, welfare and community, as well as for those of state. As the projects of these movements have had to metamorphose to survive – in the face of market pressures or state austerity and/or repression – or as they have reflected on how to spread their networks or generalize from their particular experiences, they have experimented with new forms of non-market social and economic co-ordination. And they have explored forms of regualtion independent of but in wary partnership with sympathetic elected political authorities. In some countries, mainly at a local or regional levels, they have forged precarious new forms of representation, through which new left parties seek to represent not only individual voters but also movements capable of changing social institutions independently of the state.

Finally, in the context of the re-ordering and suppressing of traditional forms of popular soverignty that is taking place as the private market dominates Europe-wide decisions, the new movements are pressing principles of subsidiarity: insisting on decision making at the lowest appropriate level from the standpoint not of the private market but of social, ecological, and democratic needs. The next section of this book will explore the pattern of 'differentiated democracy' which can be glimpsed in the messy and uneven experience of the movement left.

From movements to institutions

Social movement politics have come a long way since the students of 1968 demanded 'wholeness' and what they imagined would be the immediate transparency of direct democracy throughout society. From De Gaulle's victory in the elections of late May 1968 through to the defeat of the miners' strike in Britain and the failure of the West German Greens to win representation in the Bundestag, the social movement left has had considerable experience of defeat and loss. At various times they have been dismissed as a youthful phase, either literally or in political terms, which will pass. The some social implication is that they will mature and provide fresh blood for existing social democratic parties. And undoubtedly some social movement activists have joined such parties. Usually, however, they have taken their social movement politics with them: like the feminists who campaigned successfully for quotas for the representation of women on leading SPD committees, or the black militants who have been demanding recognition of their rights to autonomous organization in the Labour Party. Sometimes they have withdrawn, recognizing a dead end. Most significantly, however, their distinctive politics has lived on and developed through a variety of initiatives and projects. Most of the latter are institutionalized to some extent, sometimes through public funding, through needing to survive in a market environment, or as a competitor in the electoral process. But in becoming institutions, with varying relations to movement style organizations, they illustrate in the West practical possibilities for a new kind of left, more able to respond to what are seen as the failures of socialism in the East. Often participants in this left are unconscious of the wider significance of these innovations. They are realistic in their modesty since these innovations are incomplete and cannot be presented as a coherent alternative. More often than not they are embedded in practice. But they are worth investigating because they provide tried and partially tested tools for such an alternative.

Notes

1 *Magazine Littéraire*, 8 May 1968.
2 Sheila Rowbotham, in *Beyond the Fragments*, by Sheila Rowbotham, Lynne Segal and Hilary Wainwright (London, 1981).
3 I. Deutscher, *The Prophet Armed: Trotsky, 1879–1921* (London, 1954); *The*

Prophet Unarmed: Trotsky, 1921–1929 (London, 1959); *The Prophet Outcast: Trotsky, 1929–40* (London, 1963); *Stalin: A Political Biography*, revised edn (London, 1966).

4   See for example André Gorz, *Strategy for Labour* (Boston, 1968).

5   Quoted in William Outhwaite, *New Philosophies of Social Science* (London, 1987) – along with his Jürgen Habermas (Cambridge, 1994), the most relevant exegesis of critical theory for the arguments of this book.

6   In an important sense, Habermas, with his dualistic view of culture and material systems, has not followed through the original promise of the Frankfurt School. The first generation of critical theorists – Horkheimer, Adorno and Marcuse, for instance – were concerned with investigating the relation of culture, consciousness and unconsciousness to the material structures of everyday life, with a view to social transformation, about which, however, they became increasingly pessimistic. See Paul Connerton, *Tragedy of Enlightenment* (Cambridge, 1980).

7   Tom Nairn, *The Beginning of the End* (London, 1968), p. 129.

8   Werner Hülsberg, *The German Greens* (London, 1988), p. 51.

9   As Habermas was to argue in *Theory of Communicative Action*, vols I and II (Cambridge, 1987).

10 For an explanation of this idea see Werner Hülsberg, *The German Greens* (London, 1988); and *Green Politics*, by Charlene Spretnak and Fritjof Capra (London, 1985).

11 See chapter 7 for a detailed analysis of the methodological differences between the new parties influenced by the social movement left and the traditional parties of the left.

12 Marx and Engels, *The German Ideology*, in *Collected Works*, vol. 5 (London, 1965), p. 87. Marx's concept of 'praxis' expressed this understanding of the importance of practical knowledge. See the entry on 'Praxis' by Gajo Petrović in *A Dictionary of Marxist Thought*, ed. Tom Bottomore (Oxford, 1983).

13 A process traced by Fernando Claudin in *The Communist Movement* (London, 1977).

14 *Collected Works* (London, 1965), p. 422.

15 For a full explanation of Lenin's political thought see M. Liebman, *Leninism Under Lenin* (London, 1975); also E. Mandel, 'The Leninist Theory of Organization', in *Revolution and Class Struggle: A Reader in Marxist Politics*, ed. R. Blackburn (London, 1977).

16 See Sam Farber, *Before Stalinism* (London, 1991) on the debates within the Bolshevik party before Lenin's death. He suggests that in spite of the flaws of Leninism, it would be wrong to see the brutal authoritarianism of Stalin as somehow inscribed within it, an unavoidable consequence of the revolution that Lenin led. See also Rosa Luxemburg, *Rosa Luxemburg Speaks*, ed. M. A. Waters (New York, 1970).

17 For a critical history of the International Socialists, through which many of the radical left in Britain passed in the 1970s, see Martin Shaw, 'The Making of a

Party', *Socialist Register*, 1978.

18 Rosa Luxemburg, *The Russian Revolution and Leninism or Marxism* (Michigan, 1961), pp. 76–8.

19 Luxemburg, p. 15.

20 I have in mind here the experiences of the SWP in Britain, Lotta Continua and Avante Guardia Operia in Italy, and Lutte Ouvrière in France. For the material on the history of the far left in Italy, see Paul Ginsborg, *A History of Contemporary Italy* (London, 1990).

21 See David Harvey, *The Condition of Postmodernity* (Oxford, 1990); Kate Soper, in *A Meeting of Minds* (London, 1991), and 'Postmodernism and its Discontents', *Feminist Review*, 39 (a special issue entitled 'Shifting Territories: Feminism and Europe'). See also R. Braidotti, *Patterns of Dissonance* (Cambridge, 1991). The distinction between those post-modern theorists who, whatever they avow, undertake analyses of the material or extra-discursive aspects of social reality, and those who are completely unconcerned with the material dimension of life, is illustrated by on the one hand the early work of Foucault (*The Archaeology of Knowledge* (London, 1962)), and on the other hand the stance of a Baudrillard – treating such phenomena as the Gulf War exclusively as a media event (see C. Norris, *Intellectuals and the War* (London, 1991)). For a thorough discussion of the changes in Foucault's work, see H. Dreyfus and P. Rabinow, *Michel Foucault* (Hemel Hempstead, 1982).

22 K. Popper, *the Logic of Scientific Discovery* (London, 1959). L. Wittgenstein, *Tractatus Logico-Philosophicus* (London, 1961).

23 T. S. Kuhn, *The Structure of Scientific Revolutions*, 2nd edn (Chicago, 1970); I. Lakatos, 'The Rationality of Scientific Research Programmes', *Criticism and the Growth of Scientific Knowledge* (Cambridge, 1967); P. Feyerabend, *Against Method* (London, 1975). See R. Bhaskar, *Reclaiming Reality*, chapter 3 (London, 1988) for a full discussion.

24 See for example J. L. Austin, *Philosophical Papers* (Oxford, 1962).

25 See especially P. F. Strawson, *Individuals* (London, 1951).

26 See Bhaskar, *A Realist Theory of Science* (Sussex, 1978).

27 Mainly through *New Left Review* and New Left Books (now Verso).

28 See for instance Bhaskar, *Reclaiming Reality*.

29 *The Rights of Man*, in *The Thomas Paine Reader* (London, 1987), p. 277.

30 See Fred Whitmore, 'British Socialism and Democracy in Retrospect', in *Socialism and Democracy*, eds Sean Sayers and David McLellan (London, 1991).

PART III

NEW KINDS OF KNOWLEDGE FOR
NEW FORMS OF DEMOCRACY

5

FROM SOCIAL MOVEMENT TO
SELF-MANAGEMENT: A CASE
STUDY FROM THE WOMEN'S
MOVEMENT

Introduction

A scruffy-looking leaflet was pressed into my hands. 'A women's meeting in the East, want to come?' asked Lydia Hollenburg, a Green Party parliamentary spokeswoman in West Berlin (this was January 1990). We arranged to meet at the 'ZK Building', the old Zentrales Kommittee building of the East German Communist Party, where, strange though it seemed, the 'independent association of women' would meet.

To get my bearings I went first to 'the House of Democracy', where many of the opposition movements in what was East Berlin have their offices: Democracy Now, the Green Party, the independent women's movement. The man at the reception gave me what seemed like precise instructions to the women's meeting: 'Karl Marx Platz, Kirche, grosse building.' But like much of the centre of what was East Berlin, the combination of Bismarckian grandeur and Stalinist gigantism makes you feel like a bewildered matchstick. There were at least two churches and several official buildings. The ZK building turned out to be the one that looked most like a morgue.

My first expectations had been of an informal meeting, but as I mounted the steps of this concrete bunker I feared I might face the ranks of the Democratic Women's Alliance (the Communist Party's women's organization) under a new name. First impressions were contradictory: a vast conference hall; fixed seats; hundreds of women, holding up yellow voting cards.

The women themselves were mostly young, in jeans or long skirts, hippieish earrings, berets, scarves; talking and laughing and managing to concentrate all at the same time. Much like the women one would have seen at founding meetings of the women's movement in the West. As I soon discovered, this *was* the founding meeting of an autonomous women's movement, just two months after the breaching of the Berlin Wall. The idea had been launched in early December by feminist actresses, authors, church groups and reformist women in the then SED (Communist Party). Nearly 2,000 women had first come together at a women's festival. Now they had to consolidate. This was the 'Gründungskongress' to agree a constitution, a programme and candidates for the first post-transformation elections on 18 March 1990. The women's movement was to stand in coalition with the Green Party.

Here were around 700 women representing a rough 7,000 others in 80 or so groups across the country. Since early December 1989 they had been represented on the 'Roundtables' responsible for national and regional government. They had blockaded the entrance to the national Roundtable meeting, only letting participants enter on the promise of support for their representation. Where had such an organized movement sprung from so quickly? Petr Wuinerlil, one of the organizers, had been involved in an opposition women's group for nearly eight years. She works for the Protestant church. 'Most of the women's groups worked under the church's roof. It was the only possible solution because there were no public spaces for us.'

The few individual women involved in the wider opposition movements, like New Forum, had not found their needs represented. This was another impetus to form an autonomous women's movement. Leipzig women had walked out of New Forum *en bloc* earlier in January. The Indendent Women's Association has public space now but official institutions are even less responsive to women's needs than in the days of the Roundtables. (B. Einhorn's *Cinderella Goes to Market* (London, 1993) is the most comprehensive study of the position of women in Eastern Europe since 1989, and of women's organizations in these countries.)

Democratic social movements like this East German women's movement have been growing in varying degrees out of the shadows of Central and Eastern European politics, both before 1989 and since. In East Germany, the women's movement was especially well developed. The East German Protestant Church had provided a unique degree of protection. The initial strength of citizens' movements in the winter months of 1989 – at least in Czechoslovakia, East Germany and, in a more complex way, Poland and Hungary – was sometimes misinterpreted by Westerners, myself included, as indicating the basis for continuing social movements similar to those in the

West. In fact, the citizens' movements in the East were first and foremost a concerted public expression of moral and political protest. With the exception of Solidarity they had little history, or possibility, of organization to meet immediate economic and social needs. It is this latter activity which has given movements in the West, in particular the trade union and women's movements, their resilience independent of political parties. Movements in the East broke up into numerous political parties, leaving few activists committed to public activity in the wider society. Whether in the form of the trade union movement, with its roots in the nineteenth century, or the women's movement of the last twenty years, movements in the West have been able to organize to achieve material transformations in the present as well as hold out visions for the future. Moreover, these movements, whether or not they were concerned with economic issues, could create extensive infrastructures, employing staff, producing newspapers, establishing a material base for their activities. In the Soviet bloc there was little or no space for either of these ways of putting down roots into the material life of society.

One of the legacies of this feature of recent social movements in the West (the women's movement and ethnic minority organizations especially) has been democratic institutions organized to meet a social need on a self-managed, non-profit basis. Though they started, often in the 1970s, as voluntary organizations run on a shoe-string, the more successful campaigned for and obtained some public funding. Without losing their self-managed character they became accountable for their standards and framework, usually to the municipal or, where it exists, regional government.

Centres for battered women and rape crisis centres are clear examples of this trend. Other examples include centres for the unemployed and for harassed ethnic groups, organizations responding to the needs of the low paid and homeworkers, groups concerned with hazards at work or with new technologies – organizations managed by a combination of trade union and community representatives and sympathetic experts. Yet others have directly economic functions combined with social and environmental objectives: a variety of co-operatives and community enterprises and increasingly sophisticated community federations of commercial and social projects, for whom public funding was a source of initial capital. In many cases the day-to-day autonomy of these projects is based not only on a contract with the source of state funding but also on the fact that their funding comes from a plurality of sources: commercial revenue, grants from philanthropic trusts, as well as a variety of local, regional, national and EC-level state bodies. There are also some cases where local and regional government staff, influenced by or active in recent radical movements, have applied ideas of participatory democracy and self-management to the running of local government itself. They have worked with other local government workers and with users of local services to develop, for instance, a genuine decentralization of services.

The absence of any opportunity for such autonomous public activity to grow in the East helps explain why Hayek's dogma, that the only alternative to totalitarianism is the free market, has had such a widespread moral and ideological appeal – even if in practice, people are pursuing an eclectic mix of principles. As overblown free-market prescriptions ostentatiously fail, a social vacuum is growing and looks increasingly likely to be filled by nationalism. The experiences of Western movements in creating public but non-state institutions cannot provide simple models for people in the East. The historical conditions both of state and of the emerging civil society are so different. But the previous chapter makes it possible to generalize some principles from the innovations and the errors of movements in the West. These could feed the political imagination in the East.

'Bringing forward all that extent of capacity . . .'

In this chapter, I intend to explore the workings of these principles through a detailed case study of a public service – an adult education college – that was founded in the late 1970s by the women's movement in Gothenburg in northern Sweden. Such a study is an exploration of what it would mean to organize a part of government (a public service) so that, in Paine's words, it 'can bring forward, by quiet and regular operation, all that extent of capacity which never fails to appear in revolution.' The feminists founding the Women's High School in Gothenburg were in effect creating the day-to-day means by which the capacities that they discovered in themselves in the revolutionary days of the women's liberation movement, could be brought forward amongst working-class and immigrant women who had not been directly part of that movement.

The case study explores the consequences for democracy of a recognition that knowledge has a valid experiential, practical dimension combining with a theoretical, generalizing one. The study shows how this recognition implies that for democracy to be effective, the processes – formal as well as informal – by which decisions are *implemented* (that is, the details of managing an organization) must be democratic, as much as the way in which overall policy decisions are made. The forms that democracy take at these different levels are likely to vary. However, any notion of democracy based exclusively on the formally democratic procedure for electing representatives and deciding between competing programmes and policies, is far too narrow. It allows only for the expression of opinions. It ignores the exercise of capacities whose contribution cannot necessarily be formally articulated. The democracy of doing must complement the democracy of deciding. This I will argue is one of the practical meanings of the radical movements' idea of 'participatory democracy'.

On the other hand, the case study which follows also illustrates how the (frequently informal) 'democracy of doing' depends ultimately for its sustainability over time on a framework of formal decision-making procedures. Such a framework needs explicitly to recognize the conflicting interests involved in a project and to enable them to negotiate openly.

The case study illustrates innovative democratic mechanisms for the socialization of knowledge. It also illustrates how sustaining these innovations depends on material conditions of economic equality and security, a core of shared values, and a culture which generates self-confidence.

The study illustrates a further feature of an approach to democracy based on an understanding of the fallible yet socially transformable character of human knowledge: this is, the importance of a built-in process of experiment and shared reflection on the common project. This space for experiment and reflection requires considerable material security. It is not easy for an organization to have relaxed discussion when the pressure of government policy is such that the local authority is unlikely to renew its grant. But where possible this principle has been part of the culture of the public activites inspired by recent movements. For this reason, their political practice has ideally been developmental, and is able to overcome unanticipated problems: each new initiative also is an experiment leading to the formalization, elaboration and amendment of the original principles.

Democratic administration in practice: a case study from Sweden

The feminists who founded the Women's Folk High School in the port of Gothenburg were certaintly reconsidering their principles when I first met them in February 1990. It was five years since the school's foundation. They were experiencing a certain loss of the energy that had sprung from an influential and high profile women's movement and from their own political and personal awakening. This 100 strong women's adult education college with 24 staff – responsible for teaching, the nursery and administration – teaching a wide range of language, handicraft and a variety of academic courses, is an ambitious and generally successful example of the new kind of autonomously managed public institution which the women's movements have stimulated. I visited it just when the staff were re-evaluating the school's basic structures: notably the School Board and its relation to the teachers.

I wanted to explore, through a practical example, how the women's movements' approach to knowledge and skill influences its innovations in democracy. I hoped to confront in practice some of the difficulties in applying the ideas and culture of the movement to the running of a public institution. Finally, since the women's movement provides many examples of attempts to manage public resources in new ways, I thought that a study of one of these would help to assess the wider applicability of feminist ideas to democratic alternatives to neo-liberalism.

The Gothenburg Women's School

A patchwork tree of knowledge, a brown velvet trunk branching out into leaves and fruit in shades of green and red silk, hangs in the entrance hall. It demonstrates, in Swedish style, a pride in female crafts turned to a feminist cause. It symbolizes the school's purposes and origins. At the top of the tree is an embroidered picture of the 'Kuinnohus': the Women's House and focus throughout the 1970s for the Gothenburg Women's Liberation Movement.

It was at meetings in the Women's House that the idea of the school began to take shape. This was the mid-1970s. By 1979, the Women's House was holding 20 evening classes. These were the inspiration for the core courses at the school. These courses are symbolized by the fruit on the embroidered tree. Pink silk letters on a green background covered with women's faces of all colours, spells out 'Kurs For Invandrar Kvinnor': courses (mainly in languages) for immigrant women. A leafy branch carries white satin letters announcing the mathematics and other basic courses which would give women a recognized education certificate. Then there are pictures symbolizing courses overtly associated with social change: 'Freds-kurs' (peace studies) and 'ecologie projekt' (ecology projects).

These courses met a need which public provision failed to satisfy. Some women came to the courses at the Women's House because the curriculum was specifically designed for women and the atmosphere was supportive. For others the courses offered new chances of self-development and the possibility of training in an area of technology not normally considered appropriate to women – involving metalwork or construction, for example.

The number of feminists involved in teaching the early classes at the 'women's house' grew. The intensity of their commitment grew too: 'We said to each other "why can't we do this full-time?"' Stina Sundberg, at 24 one of a younger generation of feminists who joined the original core, remembers. 'We could see the need for a school that would become an institution, and I really mean an institution that will be there for years after I am dead and everyone presently working there is dead.'[1]

Maybe it is too early to tell, especially when the influence of neo-liberal economics on public spending, even in Sweden, is threatening to marginalize the position of all Folk High Schools. But they have certainly created an institution which *could* last, if the external environment was favourable.[2]

Even by conventional standards, the school is a quite a success story: over five years it has grown steadily, with only one or two major upsets. The number of full-time students has grown to 100. Its annual budget is now around £1 million. The students are positive in their judgements of the school. A growing number of women's organizations are getting involved in its short courses. It is highly respected, though not fully understood, within Folk High School and other educational circles. As an institution founded and run by feminists, it has also established new democratic structures influenced by, but developed significantly beyond, the ideas of the early women's liberation movement.

New structures at work

The Gothenburg women built their forms of self-management within conditions laid down by the government's Education Board responsible for the funding of Folk High Schools. The Folk High Schools are a rare example in Sweden, the land of state administration, of a publicly funded provision that is autonomously managed. These adult colleges were started by the Farmers' movement in the nineteenth century; the temperance movement then took up the idea and, finally, the labour movement ensured that the principle was carried over into social democratic Sweden. They are owned and part-funded by these movements themselves, by regional and local government. They also receive a minority of their funding from national government through the Educational Board. This Board requires that the constitution of the school include rules: in particular, a single head teacher and a board of named individuals (not just representatives of organizations). The bottom line for the Gothenburg women, on the other hand, did not depend on the formal structures in themselves but on whether these structures were sufficiently spacious to enable the women to put their values into practice. 'We said we wanted a flat structure,' said Eva Warburg, expressing one of the women's fundamental values, 'and that means sharing responsibility for caring for the school.'

An intimate democracy: sharing responsibility and power

The ideal of 'sharing responsibility for caring for the school' was essential to each of the women's personal views of the school's founding principles: it was both the common commitment and the basis for the success of the project. It meant that democracy was both a public and a personal matter. Stina Sindberg described the importance of an inner sense of responsibility: 'It is a process in which you cannot step aside – you've always got to do something about the problem at hand. This is an intimate process of trying to figure how democracy should work. It also affects your own feelings, and the way you think. And this gives you the possibility of building democracy elsewhere.'

If responsibility for an institution's cohesion and overall effectiveness lay with some people and not others, such an arrangement would introduce by the back door some of the very inequalities which the women's movement was committed to eradicate – including tendencies to appropriate rather than share information. Responsibility always in the end demands or takes its own reward. Unaccountable hierarchies of power, the appropriation of information and selective responsibility reinforce each other: a flat power structure and the sharing of knowledge would not last if responsibility only lay with a few. On the other hand, the spreading of responsibility could not be just a moral imperative, it needed to be anchored in the organization of the school's day-to-day work.

The headmistress problem

The first problem in achieving this spread of power, information and re-sponsibility was the concept of a 'headmistress'. The Gothenburg women did not object to one teacher being formally the head: the person who signed letters and cheques, and where appropriate spoke for and represented the school. What they rejected was the idea of one person having overall re-sponsibility for the school. Rotation of such a job between the teachers did not, they believed, solve the problem. Their objection was not simply to the concentration of power and information in the hands of a particular person. They objected to the very idea of a structure with a single focus of responsibility. It tends to centralize the view of the whole, fragmenting the majority's understanding of the school's overall workings and reducing their potential contribution and influence. For example, it encourages, among other side-effects, a certain deference to a higher authority. Consequently it tends to limit both the creative development of the whole and the self-fulfilment of each member. The women visited other Folk High Schools and observed that democratic styles (consultation, accessibility) of exercising this responsibility did not alter the tendency toward a single or very select focus of responsibility.

The women decided that one of them should be formal 'head teacher' for two years at a time. She receives the FHSK head teacher salary because of the extra bureacratic burden that she shoulders. But she works with two other women on an otherwise equal basis, sharing out the responsibility for the basic care of the school: the budget; negotiations with government; developmental issues, such as teacher retraining and study leave; the promotion of the school among new constituencies. The school's Teachers' Council sets up small groups to work with a headmistress on one of these areas. One of the headmistresses normally becomes the next 'head teacher' and the third is the woman who has just done her stint. All three women are meant to have the time to continue some teaching and take their turn at cleaning and routine work in the office.

For the regular educational work of the school, the Headmistress Group would be accountable to the 'Lararrad', the Teachers' Council. On strategic, financial and developmental work, the Headmistress and the Teachers' Council are accountable to the School Board. The teachers meet every week for a whole afternoon. They decide the division of labour and the work of the Headmistress Group, and they set up specific working groups and choose the annual replacement of the Headmistress Group. It is also the place where problems are supposed to be shared, and support and (normally) constructive criticism exchanged. Different teachers chair and take minutes at each meeting.

Skills, servicing and the division of labour

(i)   School staff

Every member of staff is urged to play some part in the teaching, including the three women whose main responsibility is the bookkeeping and the administration of the office. There is also a general rule that every teacher does several hours work a week, in the office, answering telephone inquiries and other tasks that require no specialized skill.

Behind this negation of traditional divisions of labour lies the belief that shared responsibility requires a sufficient glimpse of the inside of each other's responsibilities to understand the constraints and priorities with which everyone works. It is not that everyone could know everything, but rather, as Lena Greenwood, who did the bookkeeping and taught English, put it, that they know enough 'to have respect for each other's working conditions and frames, and to make it normal to share problems on the assumption that people know what, practically, you are talking about'.

The conscious effort to understand each other's 'frames' is important because the teaching process unavoidably separates the staff from each other. The 17 teachers are scattered accross six class rooms in two buildings; they sit mainly with the students at lunch and coffee. The brief moments that they are in the staff room are normally moments of individual preparation or recovery. Several courses do involve two or three staff – but on the whole the teaching is left to the individual teacher, who becomes deeply involved with the work of her group. Co-operation in the running of the school has had to be consciously worked for; the values nurtured by the practicalities of teaching tend to favour pedagogic specialism and enthusiasm, unavoidably drawing the teacher away from the more co-operative values needed to run the school.

(ii) Nursery staff

For the nursery workers, a third small wheel in the mechanisms of the school, cohesion is not such a problem. Six trained nursery teachers provide child care and pre-school teaching for the children of all those who work or study at the school. Their work process makes for a far more intense kind of co-operation than does the work organization of the school teachers. In the compact nursery area, upstairs from the school, with its two play rooms and kitchen/eating room, the staff literally work together all day. They meet together early in the morning before the rest of the school arrives, and over toast and coffee, they plan the day, discuss the children and prepare the tools of their unpredictable trade. The rest of the day they help each other teach, entertain and discipline 20 children of varying ages and linguistic backgrounds. Running the nursery and working in the nursery are virtually synonomous. The administrative division of labour is primitive: one woman is responsible for the budget, another two represent the nursery on the Board, another one on the Course Council.

(iii)   Students: a room of their own

The students, like the teachers, the headmistresses and the nursery teachers, have their own democratic groups through which to influence both the matters which concern them directly and the general running of the school. The students' home base is their course group. Each course group has a room they can treat as their own. They care for it, from the necessities like changing the light bulbs, to special effects like candles to give the room a cosy glow in the dark winter afternoons. Here they hold a weekly meeting, talking first between themselves and then with the course teacher. They put to her requests, sometimes demands, and work out course projects and plan for the coming weeks. Here too they elect their representative to the Course Council, hear her report back from previous meetings, work out with her their ideas on the items coming up at the next meeting, and put forward their own items of Course Council business. In this way, and through occasional school assemblies on major items of controversy and importance, the students have a real influence: 'I think it's very important that everyone has influence; that everyone has this feeling of power. I think we do,' said Britt Grandin, a student on the Women's Studies course, which had just put successfuly a list of demands to their teacher about how they wanted the course to be reorganized.

This process is also part of their education in the possibilities of democracy. Rita describes the way she learnt of these possibilities: 'It was strange in the beginning to find that you could change things. It's difficult to find the words in meetings. You're not used to that freedom and so at first you can't take it. It takes time and discussion, discussion in your class. You begin to see yourself in a new way.'

A *democracy – direct and indirect*

The mechanism through which all three of the separate wheels of the school connect is the fortnightly 'Kursrad' – the Course Council. At this meeting – like the Teachers' Council, serviced by a different pre-elected chairwoman and minute-taker each time – representatives of every part of the school (one headmistress, two teachers, two nursery teachers, and two students) discuss and decide on matters of common concern. Usually issues for discussion are snags in daily organization of the school which the group responsible cannot resolve. Take the first meeting of the spring term, for instance. The group responsible for the food reported that money was running out because some people were eating but not paying. Posters exhorting payment had not solved the problem. A special assembly of the whole school would be called. How can the Course Council help? Another issue was opening hours for the nursery for mothers on a particular course; then there was a discussion of visiting speakers; and of use of the school by other women's organisations ...

The distinction between the scope of the Teachers' Council and the scope of the Course Council is important – though taken for granted and rarely remarked upon. The Teachers' Council has the final say on the school's specifically educational work. The Course Council, on the other hand, deals with those issues which concern the staff and students as equal members of the same institution: food, cleaning, visiting speakers, use of the building and so on.

Wider responsibilities

The school's democratic constitution was not only a matter of Councils, course groups, and all the rest of the self-managing activities going on in the schools' long, low buildings in Nordostoost Passegen. Its founding statutes imply that the school should be a means of furthering the aims of the women's movement. Stina Sundberg's description of her encounter with the Swedish government officials at the final hurdle, illustrates a strong sense both of acting on behalf of something wider than themselves and of having a social legitimacy independent of, though cautiously acknowledged by, the state. 'We were asking for a total income of 7 million kroner [just under £1 million],' she tells the story with a gleam of mischievous superiority in her eyes; 'there I was, a 24-year-old, facing middle-aged officials from the Department of Education, the Department of Employment and the Home Office. The man from the Home Office turned to me and said: "Have you any money?" [Folk High School Foundations are supposed to put in a small amount of money themselves] We had no money at that time, but I knew that we had the support of many, many women and that together we could find it. So I looked him in the eye and said "Yes"'.

Stina saw herself acting neither as a future employee of the state nor as part of a private partnership, but as a part of a social movement, the women's movement. Similarly, the school is neither a direct arm of the state nor is it governed by the private market. Its connection to the wider society is through its integration with the varied and diffuse networks of the women's movement and through an ultimate accountability to local and national government for meeting certain requirements in exchange for its public funding.

Institutionally, this connection is maintained and in theory guaranteed through the School's Board.

The Board and the women's movement

In the Folk High School Legislation, the School Board is the steward of the school's finances and, legally, the employer of the school's staff. The Women's School Foundation Trust – that is, the members of the Gothenburg Women's Liberation Movement who established the school – created the Board and, except for those elected from different parts of the school, appointed its first members. 'Our aim was that it should be a mixture of what's going on in the school, what's going on in society and what's going on in the political groupings in Sweden,' explained Lilian. The first task of the Board was 'to maintain a continued connection with the activities of the women's movement and to ensure that the school developed its courses to respond to changes in the women's movement'.

Everyone on the board, though present formally as an individual, is accountable for carrying out certain responsibilities. Some are responsibile for making present on the board the concerns of the three groups (teachers, nursery staff, students) making up the school; others have been appointed to the Board because of external involvements and a commitment to use these contacts in the interests of the school. This latter group are not formally representative, it is true, except in the sense of representing the Foundation Trust's perception of the new constituencies of the women's movement, so they are not under the direct pressure of being externally accountable. But they are accountable to the Board to bring to the school the concerns and interests of wider groups of women with whom they are involved. By the 'women's movement' the founding women meant women's groups wherever they are, factory or hospital, childcare centre or political party. Their aim was to create the kind of institution which could constantly change, and encouraging change is central to the aims of the school. At the centre of the school's embroidered tree of knowledge is a white satin question-mark on a dark red fruit. A symbol of future changes they cannot predict.

These are the structures, then, like the wheels of a mechanical watch: different sizes, different purposes, separate to a degree but within a framework that brings them together. To an extent they make each other move, to an extent they depend on each other. But why do they all continue to whir round so productively? Have there been times when they have slowed down, or when wheels have turned into pyramids with the old familiar hierarchy emerging?

The values of autonomy

The structures work partly because of the culture and values of the school. The school's most fundamental principle, one of its *defining* principles, is that it is a school run by women for women. Men can visit but they cannot participate in the work of the school. This is not the outcome of a belief in separatism; it stems from a belief that women's autonomy from men is necessary to challenge male power. 'We should have a room of our own so long as we face oppression in this society,' says Eva.

Autonomy is the basic democratic ideal of self-determination, on the basis of which a variety of relations with others (in this instance, men) might be chosen. And so with the school. Many staff and students are active in political parties, trade unions and other mixed organizations. But the purpose of the school is to develop women's capacity for autonomy; for independent choices about their lives.

'You don't feel the same way as with men,' said Rita, who works with men in her community on a youth club committee. 'With just women you have more freedom to be whatever you are, because you don't have to defend yourself.' The problem for her was not that she wanted to impress men, or that she found herself deferring to men; it was more straightforward: 'The problem is that you are afraid of not being respected as a person; you have to think out how to make them listen to what you say. In the main they don't.' She added that 'they don't think consciously, "this is a woman speaking, she can't do anything". It is something accumulated, built in to the culture.' The school's commitment to women was a commitment to reverse this and similar processes of devaluation, and to do so in a way which associates self-development with respect for other women and solidarity with other people silenced in different ways. The results show in students' comments about the culture of the school. 'You are considered as important; in the past you didn't count,' says Mary, who came to the school from a narcotic addiction centre, and this term is responsible for the economics of the school meals, making sure everyone pays for their meals and proposing remedial action when they do not. She also represents her course group on the Course Council. 'You learn to listen to others and respect other women' commented a Turkish woman, learning Swedish. 'You have to feel responsible for your studies. The group is very important. If I didn't work the group wouldn't exist,' said Rita, who used to work in a state nursery.

Clearly there are several senses to the idea of 'women's values'. The values apparent to any visitor to the Women's High School are certaintly women-centred, in that they have come out of an institution committed to women's autonomy, but there is no notion of feminist truth dictating their shape. The founders of this school consciously chose to create a school that would enable women to gain the courage to make their own choices in the world as it is, including the choice to organize to change it. The values expressed in the daily life of the Gothenburg School are both the fruits and the sustenance of autonomy: a process in which women have been able to decide what aspects of their past identity they want to hold on to and what they want to cast off; what new values, borrowed from sympathetic traditions or generalized from direct experience, might guide their lives; how they might use what they've held on to in accordance with new priorities.

There is a pleasure sharing atmosphere about the place: delicious food; cake for tea; an attractive room for a smoke; a well stocked, comfortably furnished library; a light clean building whose walls are covered with an extraordinary range of pictures and posters from all over the world. If Virgina Woolf were able to visit the school she would judge such comfortable living to be itself a sign of victory.[3] These women have held on to a certain domesticity but applied it generously and collectively to a wider purpose. Housework and cooking is collectively done, on a course group rota – and in the process turned sometimes into classes on agri-business and environmental economics.

The women draw on values from elsewhere to weave their own. The teachers found the pedogogic tradition of the Folk High Schools, with its stress on 'developing a critical sense, independence and a capacity for co-operation', and its aim of 'increasing the student's awareness of his or her own circumstances and those of the world at large', a helpful one for their feminist objectives. Some of the teachers had not seen the political signifi-cance of this pedagogic approach before. 'I'd always taught that way, but I'd never really connected it with my politics – the politics I was involved in was simply concerned with fulfilling a goal quickly and efficently; it was like a kind of machinery,' Lilian remembered. Feminism led her not only to see her teaching in a new light but also to improvise on the Folk High School methods to meet the needs of adult women. A similar process of borrowing from older radical traditions goes on when a course makes an international visit, for example to India, and establishes lasting inter-national ties.

Women-centred values, then, are a complex and contradictory thing: a product of a variety of histories to be shaped by contemporary organization.[4] They cannot be read off from the social category of women, even women together in a consciously feminist institution. At the Women's School they are being renegotiated and reinterpreted constantly by women with different histories and material circumstances.

The organization and culture of the school thus both appear to have a strong base on which the women are able creatively to improvise. At the time of my visit, however (I spent a week there,teaching and observing, in 1990), the organization had not proved quite strong enough. Or to be more precise: its logic and appropriateness proved strong, but key elements of it, especially the role of the Board, were not sufficiently formalized and deeply enough internalized, by the teachers or the Board members, to override the taken-for-granted ways of working that had been built up from the early days of informal collaboration in the women's movement.

Informal structures breakdown

A shortage of funds half-way through 1989 meant that the school had to reduce its wage bill by the equivalent of two teachers. In the end two of the newer women left. The episode ended in muddle and unhappiness, 'with people going away for the summer holidays not really knowing what was going to happen when they returned'. A term later, at the beginning of 1990, the structures making up the school had still not fully re-engaged.

In effect what had happened is that the Teachers' Council, led by the older founding women, instinctively took responsibility for the decisions – without any objection from the Board, who were formally responsible. Looking back, the chairwoman of the Board, Anna Moffat Spak, believed that if the Board had taken its distinct strategic role seriously it could have have found a happier solution. The Teachers' Council was too engrossed in the daily running of the school to arrive at a wise decision over a funding crisis. And in taking responsibility it created conflicts of interest within itself which might never have arisen on the Board.

The problem was the informal way in which teachers and Board members had treated the Board during the first years of the school. It brought together women from many different experiences and fed ideas and contacts into the work of the school, but in practical terms was little more than a support committee for the teachers.

The founding group of teachers had accepted in principle the need for the Board. But their own identity was so closely tied to the women's movement that, virtually without thinking, they denied to themselves the existence of an institution, involving representatives of all the different groups in the school, more able, through its very formality, to consider transparently all the different perspectives and sources of information on a problem affecting everyone, and hence to judge the overall needs of the school. When I asked teachers who had recently joined the school to whom they were accountable, by whom they were employed, they said after a few moments reflection: 'the women's movement'. The older women would frequently say: 'ourselves'. For them the notion of the Board as representing women's interests beyond the women who actually ran the school, and as potentially able to see the school differently, was not a live consideration, even though formally the Board was set up with this potential built into its constitution.

In effect the founding women transferred subconsciously the approach typical of the early days of the women's movement, united by its sense of self-discovery, to circumstances where conflicting interests over limited resources were at stake and damaging inequalities of power incipient. In fact, the delicate mechanisms which the founding women had themselves evolved to resist such inequalities rest on an acknowledgement of points of unavoidable potential conflict of interest or vantage point. They involve the creation of open structures that bring these areas into a democratic negotiation. The redundancy crisis revealed that there was insufficient self-consciousness and formality about the essential features of these mechanisms; they had evolved pragmatically, adapting the existing Folk High School structures, without everyone being aware of the importance and detail of the whole. There was rarely any rediscussion of the processes. The structures were taken for granted. The reasons for them were not made explicit either to new recruits or by way of a reminder and re-evaluation to the older members, until the festering redundancy crisis forced the discussion into the open.

The experience of the school thus points to some of the problems as well as the strengths of the women's movement's ways of organizing and approaches to knowledge in the practical instance of building an institution. The organizational approach inherited from the early women's movement tended towards a rather undifferentiated communalism, an insufficient recognition of complexity arising from distinct and sometimes conflicting interests between women who have other interests in common. Associated with these problems of organization in the women's movement has been an approach to knowledge which sometimes slipped from recognizing the validity of practical, experiential knowledge to sanctifying, and simplifying, subjective experience. The presumption 'I experience therefore I know' denies the possibility that a problem might be experienced in different ways from varying positions, generating several distinct contributions to knowledge; and that for a full understanding, these different contributions would need to be compared, debated and synthesized. Organizationally the former approach militates against the pluralistic and sometimes formal structures necessary to bring different sources of knowledge together to achieve a solution that best satisfies common interests in an institution or project.

The founders of the Gothenburg School had made many leaps beyond the early optimism of the women's movement towards informal 'structure-lessness'. As teachers and in most cases socialists, their respect for the knowledge that comes from practical experience did not lead them consciously to privilege their own. The carefully thought out structures of the school were a product of the learning which went on throughout the women's movement as women percieved in their own organizations unacknowledged and unequal structures existing alongside a pervasive myth of structureless. By the time they came to plan the school, the Gothenburg women – like women setting up similar, if more modest, projects all over Western Europe and North America – had already begun consciously to invent clear visible structures appropriate to the purpose at hand. The argument was no longer beteen 'looseness' and 'stucture', but over what kind of structure, including options that provided for a certain 'looseness'.

Formalizing the differences

The crisis at the school took the learning process one step further – after day-long discussions and a weekend away. The formalization which they were already working towards in their structures required, the crisis taught them, an explicit recognition of differentiation, as well as of integration. Differentiation of function; differentiation in the time that individual women could give to the school; differentiation in women's histories, especially their involvement in the women's movement. And the value of these distinct experiences were recognized as potentially valuable sources of different and sometimes conflicting perspectives on a shared institution, differently understood.

Practical recognition of these differences and more explicit definitions of the formal structure through which they could be negotiated and debated has, it seems, given the school a stronger unity.

Here is a case of an autonomously managed institution meeting a proven social need, funded by national and, mainly, municipal government, and accountable to these elected bodies for its standards and basic structure. It provides a particularly clear example of the importance of autonomy within a negotiated framework, for a process of democratic management to develop in which everybody's knowledge is utilized and developed to the full. This is being achieved in Gothenburg not only because of the School's educational purpose, but because of its structure and its culture. What is more, the 'everybody' consists of women, many of them working-class women, immigrant women, previously unemployed women, whose knowledge and capacities are usually the least utilized of all. What are the conditions for this and how widely applicable are these conditions?

Democracy embedded in daily activity

The women who founded the school developed its structures on the assumption that a participative democracy was essential to the effectiveness of the school. This explains why democracy is built into the work of the school, through the Course Groups, the Nursery Workers, and the Teachers' Council, and through the requirement that all staff do some teaching and take their turn in the office and the kitchen. In these ways the democratic process draws on women's everyday, often tacit knowledge expressed through joint work. This is a resource which the structures purely for formal decision making (the School Council and Assembly) could not directly tap. This day-to-day participation in the running of the school, closely tied to its essential work – as distinct from relying only on a formal democratic decision-making process going on at several steps removed – is an application, more or less conscious, of the women's movement's recognition of knowledge embedded in people's daily exercise of their skills. The Gothenburg women created democratic structures which are similarly embedded in what people do. They did this because their commitment to democracy was not simply as a political virtue but as a way of drawing on and developing the capacities of everyone to build a school which would fulfil ambitious educational goals.

The politics of self-confidence

Similarly the Gothenburg School is influenced by the women's movement's attempts to combine the emotional with the intellectual and cognitive aspects of life. The democracy of the school has a strong cultural component to it. The term 'emotion' has the wrong connotations; it is almost anti-democratic in its associations, but the democracy in the school is not exclusively rationalistic. Students and staff expressed feelings about their involvement with the school: feelings of self-affirmation, confidence and personal and shared power. Much conventional male-dominated public life, whether business or politics, also depends on such feelings, but felt by men as a result of their private relations with women. Thus it could be argued that emotion and reason are already combined in the dominant culture, but exclusively privately, and consequently in a way that is invisible from the perspective of public life.

Virginia Woolf makes the point in a literary form. She talks in *A Room of One's Own* about the way that women give men confidence in their public roles; men do not reciprocate. Yet as she puts it, 'Without self-confidence we are as babes in the cradle'. 'Women have served all these centuries,' she continues,

> as looking-glasses possessing the magic and delicious power of reflecting the figure of man at twice its natural size. Without that power probably the earth would still be swamp and jungle. The glories of all our wars would be unknown. We should still be scratching the outlines of deer on the remains of mutton bones and bartering flints for sheep skins or whatever simple ornament took our unsophisticated taste. Supermen and Fingers of Destiny would never have existed. The Czar and the Kaiser would never have worn crowns or lost them. Whatever may be their use in civilized societies, mirrors are essential to all violent and heroic action.[5]

Virginia Woolf is describing a process which explains why women's participation in public institutions, even relatively democratic ones, does not automatically increase when economic divisions and dependencies are weakened. These experiences of the school and other feminist projects or feminist caucuses or groups within mixed organizations indicates that women's participation in public institutions is only established if another condition is met. The experience demonstrates that there also needs to be a conscious cultural challenge demonstrating an alternative culture that gives positive value to women's public actions. In other words, there is at the School a cultural, emotional resource from which the women involved benefit. It is a vital condition, along with the material conditions of economic independence, and publically provided child care, for the development of women's capacities and their full expression in the democratic organization of the school.

Two-way mirrors are clearly in operation in the school. On the one hand, as one student said, 'You are considered as important; whereas where I worked in the past you didn't count'. On the other hand, as another student said, 'you learn to listen to others and respect other women'. With teachers trying to set the example, the women give each other confidence. But from the point of view of understanding the connections between such a culture and democracy, it is important to recognize the *public* context of such affirmation. The absence of the one-way demands of male-dominated culture, and the flourishing of mutually supportive friendships among women, is clearly important in this process. But the school's culture of shared power and mutual respect, for example, could not be achieved simply by a reversal of the private process described by Virginia Woolf.[6] There are several other public processes at work.

First, there is the teaching process through which teachers work consciously with a variety of methods to reconstruct severely battered egos. Then, most importantly for the argument of this book, there is everybody's experience of public freedom, through the sharing of power. 'I think it is very important that everyone has influence; that everyone has this feeling of power. I think we do,' was how one student described it. And remember how another student described the way such influence changed her: 'It was strange at the beginning to find that you could change things. You're not used to that freedom and so at first you can't take it. . . . You begin to see yourself in a new way.' These students are describing a process of self-creation, affirmation and identity through their involvement in the public activities of the school. The conditions described by Woolf, however, involve men gaining private satisfaction, private reaffirmation, from women, for their public feats. The reversal of this, through the provision of such confirmation by men for women, or women for other women, would be no bad thing, and certaintly goes on at the school. But what is also a distinctive feature of the school is the fact that the students gain confirmation and satisfaction in good part through their contributions to the public processes of the school's self-government.

What matters, then, is the interaction of a co-operative civic culture with a participatory power structure. To reinforce the point, consider the weakness of each of these on its own. A counter culture that simply supports women as they mount the ladders of a closed and hierarchical (and consequently competitive) power structure will eventually dry up. It is a scarce resource if it is not constantly reproduced and enriched through women co-operating in a participative structure. The experience of women's groups in Social Democratic Parties, lacking a larger, strongly participative women's movement bears this out. Women nearing the top of the ladder in these parties will tend to demand of their friends, male and female – as a result of the imperatives of concentrated power – the one-way mirror which eventually renders those friends subordinate. On the other hand, a participatory power structure set in a traditional masculine confirming political culture will not elicit sustained popular participation, especially from women, and in the end will transform itself back into the traditional mould. Neither will such a power structure be able to improvise and adapt in response to new challenges. The large numbers of co-operatives and collectives which, over time, have slunk back into conventional procedures, whatever the disguise, bear witness to this.

The importance to a democracy which aspires to the full utilization of everyone's capacities, of a public culture nurturing self-confidence, has special implications for any subordinate group or class: blacks, the working class, the unemployed. Many organizations amongst these groups have had as part of their purpose the creation of a sense of collective pride. The problem until now has been that such public self-confidence has mainly existed amongst men and in part at the expense of women's energies.

Other influences of the distinct approach to knowledge and capacity developed within the women's movement were visible in more pragmatic aspects of the school's organization. A recognition of the fallibility of their knowledge produced structures which could encourage flexibility. Where decisions only affected a specific group, that group had the autonomy to decide in its own way, experiment, change its mind. The Course Council and School Assembly stuck very strictly to issues which affected the running of the school as a whole and could not be resolved in bi-lateral discussions between specific groups. Even then it only took decisions when it was strictly necessary to have a collective agreement. There was a certain creative anarchy about, for instance, decorating the school. A group of women would put up a sculpture or a picture, it would stay until people got tired of it, and another informal group would experiment. Where collective decisions were unnecessary they would not be taken. The Course Council, partly because of its rotating membership – another concession to fallibility – had no desire to extend its remit beyond the issues brought to it from constituent groups.

The desire 'to get to the roots' of women's oppression through consciousness raising was evident in the school's approach to its own problems. No superficial generalizations would satisfy the teachers or the Board members when trying to resolve the crisis after the redundancies. Usually, the resort to such an approach produced arguments for surrender to conventional forms of management: a strong head teacher minimizes the effects of crises, would be the traditional answer. Many a radical experiment, lacking a radical approach to knowledge, including knowledge of itself, has succumbed to this kind of argument. And at times of exhaustion and despair, the women sometimes felt this would be a relief. They could then just get on with their particular teaching speciality and forget about everything else. The problems they were facing in January 1990 were indeed the result of eliminating traditional structures of authority. There *was* a sense in which it would be easier to return to them, easier in comparison with the uncertainty they are facing in creating new structures of their own – easier, but going backwards. The conventional hierarchies were after all one of the sources of frustration they had first identified in the early days of the women's movement. So they persevered, talking and analysing, drawing in people from outside who used the school or who had always supported it. In effect they applied their early 'consciousness raising' search for the roots of the problem to their own structures to understand the mechanisms at work and at fault, and to innovate further.

Finally, the awareness, common in the women's movement, of the way that the structures of oppression were reproduced and potentially transformed, has produced an intense sense of shared responsibility for the school's organization. The collective institution mattered, it had to be cared for, but the collective was not seen as a thing apart from the relations between individuals who were therefore responsible for its problems and its achievements. This sense that the structures and their failings were a result of their own decisions, or at least could be changed or reproduced by them, acted as a pressure for an honest approach to difficulties. There was no point in blaming or ganging up: it would all end with everyone having to resolve the problem. This relational view produced a distinctive approach to power: as something that could be shared, that could have many sources in producing and practising a common purpose.

The feminist imagination

Innovations of the kind discussed in this chapter are not exclusively feminist; neither are the conditions for popular participation that the experiences of the women's movement can help us identify exclusive to women. Herbert Marcuse once remarked that the social experiences of women made them especially able to envisage alternatives to capitalism. He was not implying that this was a capacity inherent in femininity, or that it was necessarily, at all times and in all circumstances, a capacity exclusive to women. He was suggesting that the social experiences of women, of being treated as marginal by the competitive wage economy and by the official political culture, of seeing the underside of power, of materially unrewarded care for others, meant that when they stood up against this subordination, the alternatives they dreamed of could be very radical.

Vital to this radicalism, I would argue, is the approach to knowledge which many feminists developed in order to make sense of their subordination, and to identify sources of power for change.

The nature of women's subordinate position not only within conventional politics but also in the radical left, led feminists to dig further than male socialists or liberals to find the roots of their powerlessness beyond oppression of class or cultural prejudice. Although their is no single feminist view of democratic organization or of the state – and plenty of examples of feminists acting in an extremely undemocratic manner – feminism as a movement has been the most sustained pressure in the West for extending and deepening democracy.

A particular stimulus for women to press for measures that extend democracy, including material conditions for its sustenance, has been their own vested interest in changing structures from which they had been effectively excluded. Moreover, by the late 1960s, after a major expansion of higher education from which many women (albeit in low proportion to men) had benefitted, more women had the self-confidence and expectations to define their own objectives and demand a share of power. The women's movement, especially in the West, is in an historically rare position: the majority of its activists combine the position of being part of the intelligentsia, with the tools and confidence for public critical reasoning, *and* being themselves part of an oppressed group. The radicalization expressed by the modern women's movement was therefore not simply an intellectual commitment to change, as with many of the male students active in 1968, but also an emotional and material need for tranformation of their own circumstances, circumstances they had come to understand as social and political rather than purely personal. Consequently, feminists were not satisfied with either the methods of social democratic left, with their habit of packing problems into a briefcase with assurances that the matter would be dealt with in due course; or with the imperative of the revolutionary left to postpone discussion of practical solutions until after the struggle/revolution.

My choice of the experiences of the women's movement as a lens through which to scrutinize a public institution in its 'quiet and regular operation', and the manner in which it can bring forward all the capacity which never fails to appear in moments of upheaval and transformation, is therefore not an arbitary one. Radical public-sector trade unionists, tenants' organizations, black people's organizations and more, have all created examples or campaigned for models of democratic management. But the practice of the women's movement – the lessons to be drawn from its difficulties as well as the inspiration from its successes – has been the most sustained practical influence on recent attempts at new forms of democratic management. The influence stems partly from the existence of many working examples. It also arises from the diaspora of the movement: it has dispersed as a nationally and internationally organized force, but feminists have taken their ways of organizing and their attitudes to the state with them into specifically feminist inspired projects in other movements – the peace and green movements, and parts of the trade union movement and parties of the left.

In and against the state

A distinctive feature of the modern women's movement is lasting initiatives which have their origins in urgent attempts to make immediate improvements in women's circumstances. More often than not these have involved struggling to change women's relationship to the state.

Like the student movement of the late 1960s, the early women's movement was in revolt against the state. In so many of a women's encounters with the state, whether at the Social Security Office, the hospital, the school or the social services, the state was the warder seeing to her needs – sometimes kindly sometimes rude, but never willing to tolerate any wayward assertion of a woman's own definition of her desires. Yet as women built up some collective power to break out, to organize a nursery, to set up rooms of their own, or to establish classes for their further self-education, they found themselves turning to the state for resources. Increasingly, especially as the economic recession of the mid-1970s led to cutbacks in social spending accross Western Europe, feminists found themselves facing a dilemma.

They needed the social provision, they wanted it to meet needs they had never before made public, but they could not trust the existing ways in which these resources were managed. Fortunately, however, they had built up considerable public self-organization. In Northern European countries with a developed welfare state, this had two sides. On the one hand, it involved experience of limited provision of self-help in health, education, child care, distribution of food, provision of advice and so on. On the other hand, it involved experience, sometimes as state workers, sometimes as users, of where there were spaces or cracks in state organization and control, which they might occupy and open up; and of where they had allies in the wider community with whom to do so. They had accumulated this experience through trial and error, but all the time holding on to the insights gained through their initial encounters with the state. The feminists who had been active in the 1970s approached the state in the 1980s from a position of determined independence, from which many new feminist activists took their cue.

Normally such self-managed services have developed where no service whatsoever existed before: rape crisis centres, women's health clinics, centres for battered women. Or, like the Gothenburg Women's Folk High School, they may be an extension, specifically for women, of an existing provision. Occasionally self-management of public resources has developed within an established service, usually as a result of some conflict with senior management or a supportive political administration. These are rare circumstances where the workers and users of a service or part of a service have established autonomy in their daily conditions and operations on a co-operative rather than hierarchical basis, but are ultimately accountable to the elected politicians.[7]

The wider relevance

Of what wider relevance to problems of a democratic society are the insights into the conditions for democratic self-management gained through exploration of this Swedish feminist experience, emerging as it has out of a rare combination of circumstances? However unusual the circumstances, it is nevertheless a living counter-example to Hayek's choice between either an all-knowing power imposing a social design against the grain of evolution, or abiding by the supposedly haphazard outomes of individual activity. Here is a social mechanism in which women gain sufficient understanding from conscious communication and sharing of knowledge, both structured and informal, and in which they can develop a common sense of purpose and knowledge as to the social direction in which they going. Yet there is no one overview. From any angle the structures are transparent.

This is only a feature of the internal workings of an institution, a philosophical free marketeer might answer back; maybe Hayek had a blindspot with regard to this, but his analysis of the two choices facing humanity certainly applies to the wider social and economic environment. There is indeed a school of thought on the left which, following John Stuart Mill, holds that the free market is the only economic environment consistent with self-management. No clear alternative at this wider societal level can be read from the Swedish experience; but before moving on directly to apply the understanding of knowledge developed in earlier chapters to the problem of economic co-ordination, it is worth noting what in fact the economic environment of this remarkable school actually is. There is no doubt that, up to now, it has been unusually favourable, with the long established Folk High Schools providing a rare tradition of autonomously managed social provision funded by the state; the possibility of public support from several levels of state administration; the development of a relatively cohesive women's movement with a strong socialist feminist bias; and with the rare combination of the radical educational skills developed, over decades, with the innovatory boldness of the women's movement's approach to organization. But what, in terms of principles that could be generalized, are the essential elements that these circumstances produced?

I would point to three: a contract with the state which involves public funding in exchange for meeting standards agreed by a democratic parliament; a regulated market; and the information gathering networks of the women's movement.

Fundamental to both the school's material survival and the autonomy of its self-management was a contract with the state on terms set out by legislation on Folk High Schools. One partner in the contract was constituted by the initiative and limited resources of the women's movement. But here is a case where autonomy and the creativity, innovation and self-government that it allows, did not, contrary to neo-liberalism's presumption, depend on private property or complete independence from the state. Second, vital to identifying the character of the needs the school should fulfil and to influencing the school's ability to do so, were the more or less organized networks of the women's movement feeding into the increasingly formalized decision-making institutions of the school. Third, there were the pressures of the market, expressing demand for the service the school could offer. Prices (i.e. school fees) were not set primarily by this market; assessments of the likely needs and circumstances of the potential uses of the school and the availability of government grants were the main factors. To be successful the school did have to attract demand; the market was not irrelevant therefore to the dynamics of the school, though it was not based on individual purchasing.

On what kind of economic environments – the forms of economic coordination and the character of property relations – does self-management and the full utilization of the knowledge of those working in and using an institution or enterprise thrive? It remains to be shown that the approach to knowledge developed in Part II contributes towards criteria for economic coordination, just as it has contributed towards criteria for democratic self-management.

Notes

1 Quotations from women at the Gothenburg Women's Folk High School are from interviews with the author unless otherwise specified.
2 For analysis of the changes in the Swedish economy, including the cutting of welfare spending – first carried out by the Social Democratic Government in October 1990 – see R. Taylor, 'End to old go-it-alone illusions', *Financial Times*

29 October 1990; Janos Pontussen, 'The Crisis of Swedish Social Democracy', unpublished paper for the Centre for Social Theory and Comparative History, University of California, Los Angeles, April 1991; Steven Kelman, 'Swedish model on a diet', *Guardian*, 7 August 1991.

3 On her return to London after a visit to Oxford, Virginia Woolf muses on the differences between the circumstances of the men's and the women's colleges at Oxford: 'Why did men drink wine and the women water? Why was one sex so prosperous and the other so poor? What effect has poverty on fiction? What conditions are necessary for the creation of a work of art?' Virginia Woolf, *A Room of One's Own* (London, 1977).

4 See Sheila Rowbotham, 'What do Women Want? Women-Centred Values and the World As It Is', in *Feminist Review* 20 (1985) for a more general discussion of this approach to the issue of women's values.

5 Woolf, *A Room of One's Own*.

6 See also the sociological work of Anna Jónasdottir, for example *Love Power and Political Interests* (1991). For detailed descriptions of international feminist campaigns and projects involving democratic management of public resources, see the Association of Community Works, *Women in Collective Action* (London, 1982); E. Haavio-Mannila, Drude Dahlerup et al. (eds) *Unfinished Democracy: Women in Nordic Politics* (Oxford, 1985); Sophie Watson (ed.) *Playing the State: Australian Feminist Interventions* (London, 1990); chapter 9 of Sheila Rowbotham, *The Past is Before Us* (London, 1989). For descriptions of a variety of trade union and community initiatives over the management of public services and difficulties they now face, see Dexter Whitfield, *The Welfare State* (London, 1992).

7 For a very coherent presentation of this see David Prytchitko, 'Hayekian socialism', *Marxism and Worker Control; The Essential Tension* (New York, 1992).

6

FROM GRASS-ROOTS ORGANIZING TO NEW ECONOMIC NETWORKS

Introduction

At a small informal seminar on 'Privatization and Economic Democracy' during Spring 1991 in the new class rooms of the Central European University in Prague, a fascinating dialogue took place between two old friends. On the one hand, there was the veteran advisor to Solidarity in its early struggles in the shipyards of Gdansk, Tadeusz Kowalik, with his extraordinarily expressive face, almost rubbery in its mobility. Engaging him with a courteous wit was the urbane Jerzy Osiatinski, also a long-time oppositionist, more recently the Minister of Planning in the Mazowecki Government – and now, in 1992, Finance Minister in Lech Walesa's latest government. In the 1950s they had worked in the same room, one on a biography of Oscar Lange, the other of Michael Kalecki. They knew each other well and could argue from diametrically opposed positions without animosity. The spring weekend in Prague was just such an occasion. Their very different post-Communist hopes had failed. Neither Osiatinski's belief that a modified shock therapy, accompanying an opening of the economy to the West and leading to a variant of Keynesianism, nor Kowalik's hopes for a regulated market based on self-managed enterprises, had much purchase on present Polish realities. They were open to consideration of alternative strategies, while defending vehemently their distinctive and increasingly divergent principles.

Afterwards, in one of Prague's cellar cafes, I asked Kowalik what values he and Osiatinski used to have in common. It was clearly more than old friendship that kept them arguing. After a long pause and much movement of expression, Kowalik replied: 'the values of John Stuart Mill'. One quotation from Mill's *Principles of Political Economy* summed up what he meant:

> The form of association, however, which if mankind continue to improve, must be expected in the end to predominate, is not that which can exist between a capitalist as chief, and work-people without a voice in the management, but the association of the labourers themselves on terms of equality, collectively owning the capital with which they carry on their operations, and working under managers elected and removable by themselves. . . .
>
> But while I agree and sympathize with Socialists in this practical portion of their aims, I utterly dissent from the most conspicuous and vehement part of their teaching, their declamations against competition. With moral conceptions in many respects far ahead of the existing arrangements of society, they have in general very confused and erroneous notions of its actual working, and one of the greatest errors, as I conceive, is to charge upon competition all the economic evils which at present exist. They forget that wherever competition is not, monopoly is, and that monopoly, in all its forms is the taxation of the industrious for the support of indolence, if not plunder.

For Westerners who have witnessed how monopoly and oligopoly emerge out of the unrestrained competitive struggle, and have experienced a spectrum of more and less democratic forms of state intervention, this faith in the self-evident, spontaneous democratic virtues of competition does not have much bearing on the world as it is. In Eastern Europe, however, this combination of opposition to state monopoly – both the old state and increasingly the new – and an enthusiasm for some form of self-management finds an echo amongst critical trade unionists and intellectuals. Without a sympathetic state, however, there has been little sustained experience of self-management to fuel this enthusiasm, and many, like Jerzy Osiatinski, have been become disillusioned and come to consider self-management to be impractical.

Aspirations for self-management

For many of those interested in some form of self-management, 'the state' (or in effect, the party) was management, and frequently a management for whom they had nothing but contempt. At first privatization seemed to them an opportunity to rid themselves of such management and, they hoped, have more say themselves in the running of the enterprise. Opinions vary, but the view is now widespread in Central and Eastern Europe, that privatization is being introduced with methods more typical of a command economy than a democracy.. 'The minister sees privatization as the opposite of nationalization and thinks he can introduce it in the same way,' says Jan Uhlir, President of the Czech Metalworkers' Union, commenting in 1991 on the privatization programme of Václav Klaus, at that time the powerful Minister of Finance.

Some trade unionists are satisfied simply to achieve what they consider to be genuine collective bargaining: 'Workers owning their plant is a concept from 1917 – we don't want that anymore. We want clarity on who owns a plant – somebody we can negotiate with,' declared Sergei Chramov, a spokesman of SOZPROV, a trade union federation founded in 1989 in Russia linking independent trade unions from the mines, mechanical engineering and transport.[1]

There are other trade unionists, however, who believe that workers should have a strong say in management. The aspiration does not come from 1917 but from their own experience: 'We've seen the short-sightedness of our managers for so long; they are not able to see far enough beyond producing the machines we produce now,' declared Ladislav Binko, the chairman of the new workers' committee at the CDK locomotive factory on the outskirts of Prague. They feel collectively responsible, as a workers' committee, for the future of the factory. They are exploring ways of buying it themselves by getting fellow workers to invest their 'coupons' in the factory and then going to the bank for further support, using the machinery as collateral.[2] They believe that workers should have the right to choose between different forms of ownership, collective, state or private, and between different managers. All sorts of schemes for worker ownership and control are being aired.

The intellectual and political context in which Ladislav Binko and the CDK committee are working offers only stark and idealized alternatives for the wider economic environment: the market or the state. The existing state is discredited. There have been few forums for discussing alternative, more democratic and more economically and socially effective forms of public control over economic relations, both domestic and international.

This is partly a result of the efforts by those in positions of political and cultural power in most of the former Soviet bloc to limit the boundaries of legitimate debate. ' I'm attacked for being a Communist, just for suggesting that the government should have an industrial policy,' exclaimed a frustrated junior Minister in the former Czechoslovak Ministry for Economic Affairs; someone who, in the West, would be considered a moderate Keynesian. Any kind of state intervention is viewed as second best, a retreat to the old methods that is likely to presage further economic failure. The only basis on which public intervention in the economy has become legitimate is when it is sanctified by nationalism. Various forms of economic nationalism, involving varying degrees of privatization, are now the dominant alternatives to the opening of the East to the pressures of the Western market and a short sharp shock. The Czech republic has recovered from this shock with a desire to continue with the treatment. Other countries are stumbling along with equally short-sighted notions that national protection and domestic devotion to national productivity can solve their chronic economic crises.

International circumstances are unfavourable for any solution to the crises of the Eastern economies. But there is no doubt that significant public involvement, of a new kind, is necessary. It is disastrous for such interrelated economies to attempt to understand this in nationalist terms. Moreover, the conservative character of nationalism means that the old state institutions of the domestic economy are used uncritically. There are small minorities arguing for an alternative approach. The party of Tadeusz Kowalik is a supporter: Solidarity Praxi, for instance, argues for regional economic co-operation between the economies of Central and Eastern Europe as they make their way in the international market. This would be combined with selective forms of protection and positive public industrial policies. Such an approach requires public institutions able to take precise action. And this requires a degree of inside and often ephemeral knowledge not normally available to state bodies. The issue then is what kind of mechanisms could make possible public intervention in the economy to improve people's living standards, consciously utilizing the practical, experiential knowledge to which free marketeers claim only the individual private entrepreneur has access.

Self-management and economic regulation

This returns us to the need to scrutinize the model classically set out by John Stuart Mill and developed more recently by David Prychitko:[3] the combination of workers' self-management and the market. The importance of this view for the argument of this book is this: that the widespread implicit challenge, 'on the ground', to the presumption that the private entrepreneur has all the appropriate economic knowledge to revive the economy and must therefore be allowed a free hand, is a pragmatic belief in the knowledge and capacity for self-management of many of the recently elected factory committees. In itself, it does not provide an economic strategy, but it is an approach in dissonance with both the old orthodoxy and the new. Its starting point is appropriate: with those in these collapsing economies who have the practical knowledge about production.

Does the thesis of the social character of economic knowledge that I argued against Hayek, provide any clues as to mechanisms of co-ordination in an economy based on workers' self-management of the enterprise? Mill's view of knowledge and of the formation of individual capacities for knowledge was very different to that of Hayek. Mill's developmental and educational view of democracy implies a recognition of the social character of knowledge in the sense of an individual's knowledge being shaped to a significant extent by social institutions. This understanding gave Mill's liberalism very different foundations to that of Hayek. Indeed, Hayek argues, along with others more sympathetic to Mill's position,[4] that in driving his view of democracy to its logical conclusion, in the second edition of *The Principles of Political Economy*, Mill ended up arguing for socialism.[5]

Mill, like Hayek, warned against the possibility of an overbearing, despotic state if the market were regulated. He was also, however, against any political and economic system which deprives individuals of a 'potential voice in their own destiny', on the grounds that this undermines the basis of human dignity. For Mill, 'the highest and harmonious expansion of individual capacities' depends on peoples' active involvement in determining the conditions of their existence. Moreover, Mill believed that when people participate in the resolution of social problems affecting themselves or a wider collectivity, energies are unleashed which enhance the likelihood of imaginative solutions and successful strategies. Participation in social and public life undercuts passivity and increases general prosperity 'in proportion to the amount and variety of the personal energies enlisted in promoting it'.[6] What a contrast to Hayek's notion that ' all man's mind can effectively comprehend are the facts of the narrow circle of which he is the centre'.[7]

Mill's developmental view of individual capacities does not, however, lead him on to a radically distinct view of the knowledge problem involved in economic co-ordination. His case for the market is mainly a case against economic monopoly, for both political and economic reasons. Competition is, in his view, necessary for innovation and therefore economic progress. His justification of the market was essentially based on the importance of competition and therefore economic pluralism. Whatever the adequacy of his analysis in his own day, in present circumstances, where the threat of monopoly comes not only from the state but also from concentrations of economic power produced by the private market, a new question is posed for anyone who shares Mill's belief in workers' self-management and in an egalitarian pluralism. The question is whether there are mechanisms of economic co-ordination and regulation which allow an element of competition between self-managed enterprises, and which at the same time promote social and environmental goals arising from society-wide democratic processes in economic affairs. Or, putting it negatively, can both market pressures and the rampant enterprise egoism that historically has tended to undermine the practice of self-management be contained other than exclusively through the state – and hence ineffectively, given the state's inadequate knowledge? How would such non-state social mechanisms require the support and resources of a democratic state? What would such a state need to be like to provide the appropriate support?

The social organization of economic knowledge

Studies of the workings of actually existing market economies and of the practices of the institutions and economic agents which shape them indicate that the way that knowledge is distributed and organized is central to the way that existing economic arrangements reproduce themselves.[8] The social distribution and organization of economic knowledge is being discovered as a vital economic variable. For some time there has been a recognition of the role of informal networks, social connections and, more recently, of inter-enterprise systems of direct co-ordination.[9] This is acknowledgement, in the reproduction of a capitalist economy, of social relations that are neither market nor plan, neither the haphazard outcome of individual activity nor the design of an all-knowing central authority. The importance of many of these informal institutions lies above all in their role in sharing knowledge, in making established economic actors more knowing and consequently more powerful. In this chapter I want to argue that central to a variety of trade union and community based challenges to the present economic order are efforts to democratize and socialize economic knowledge. I will argue further that they illustrate the emergence of means of socializing the market through mechanisms embedded in independent democratic associations sharing practical knowledge, rather than the state – though these mechanisms, to be sustained, would need the support of the state institutions. This alliance between public institutions and independent associations would in turn lead to a process of democratising the former and making them more responsive.

Over the last twenty years or so a distinct feature of radical workplace and local organizing has been the creation – initially *ad hoc* but in many cases increasingly formally organized – of popularly based networks, especially on an international or at least continental scale, where no adequate means exists of political co-ordination on the left. Trade union committees, health and safety projects, initiatives for socially responsible fair trade, lesbian and gay movements, women's and other campaigning groups with a common interest, have found ways of associating without losing their autonomy. One of the prime purposes of making the connections, in the course of a variety of immediate practical tasks, has been to gather, share and accumulate knowledge which makes resistence more effective in reaching its target. To achieve this over a sustained period they have sometimes been supported by local or regional governments or, more recently, the EC; otherwise they have obtained funding from trade unions, sympathetic foundations and Church organizations.

Dimensions to making knowledge democratic

The extent to which these groups are self-conscious about the politics and economics of knowledge varies. Five different dimensions to the democratization of economic knowledge stand out. Taking them seriously would imply major economic and political changes, of which I give some indication.

Firstly, there are the attempts to make the otherwise invisible knowledge of subordinated groups a legitimate, valued part of public culture and policy making. Examples of this would be the sustained efforts of groups active over low pay and homeworking amongst women; health and safety and environmental hazards; working conditions in industries predominantly employing ethnic minorities and foreign workers, making public inside information and proposals for action ignored by mainstream politics. For this kind of knowledge to be built into policy making, there would need to be some statutory rights for organizations representing these groups to have input into the policy making and implementing process; some statutory power or state support would need to be given to these organizations if they are to be effective.

Secondly, popularly based organizations engage in processes of intelligence gathering about the decisions and trends shaping a community or workforce's future. In this way they can gain a view of the wider context of a particular decision and – in the absence of any adequate action by government – plan effective action from below. For trade unionists, resisting the rundown of their factories, or for communities threatened by speculative property development, this has been a matter of challenging directly the private concentration of knowledge. They have used their (albeit subordinate) insider position to glean fragments of information. Through their networks with insiders at other points in the institution and with informed outsiders, they then piece this information together to gain the knowledge from which they have been excluded. Use of this knowledge in bargaining and campaigning strategy can have the effect of transforming such groups from ignorant outsiders snapping at the coat tails of the decision-makers (as the latter disappear into their secret meetings), into influential actors. They may not be physically present at the meetings, but their knowledge can so accurately guide their action and mobilize their power toward the points of bureaucratic vulnerability or division that they become a major consideration in every decision. The well-known examples in Britain include the shop stewards' committees on the Upper Clyde in 1971, the Lucas Aerospace shop stewards in the mid 1970s and, in the community, the Coin Street Action Group in Waterloo in the 1980s and the many local campaigns for alternatives to the government's development of the London Docklands from the late seventies to the early nineties.

An extension of this dimension of the democratization of knowledge is the gathering of knowledge not only to shadow the management of a single corporation or public institution, but to track the market and institutional linkages in the whole chain of production, distribution and consumption. Such a tracking process, usually carried out over a long period of time as the need and opportunity arises for contacts across the chain, gives the organizations concerned a map of points of potential leverage and an indication of the alliances necessary to take effective action. A well-developed network of this kind exists across the chocolate producing and retailing chain. From peasants working on the cocoa plantations in Brazil to women on the assembly line of Mars and Cadbury in Slough and Birmingham, there is a well organized, well informed forum for joint campaigns and solidarity action. Amongst the issues on which it has won some limited victories are the use in Brazil of pesticides that endanger the plantation workers' health and the quality of the local environment; and support for plantation workers' action for a very modest improvement in their wages.[10]

A third dimension of the democratization of economic knowledge has been the struggle to get built into economic decision-making processes a full recognition of the tacit knowledge of production and need that is embedded in workers' daily exercise of skill. This has been a prolonged guerrilla struggle both in factories and in the delivery of public services, against managers and management systems that cannot cope with uncertainty and consider protection of their prerogatives to be their first priority.

In one sense this struggle, in effect against the legacy of Taylorist management methods, has been won: the ability to 'tap the gold in the worker's mind', as one Japanese consultant put it, is the new criterion of good management. The struggle has increasingly revolved around the power relations and the terms on which workers' knowledge is appropriated or shared. Is the gold tapped outside any bargaining process, to be used in production plans determined entirely by management, with outcomes that might well undermine the worker's security or conditions? Or is it gathered initially through the workers' own organizations to be the basis of plans and proposals which are negotiated over by the different, conflicting interests?

In Britain especially, but also in other countries whose governments are privatizing the public services, there is a fourth dimension to the effort to socialize knowledge: the defence of co-operative, non-market relations within a public service and of the daily exchange of essential knowledge and skills that this encourages. One of the consequences, unpredicted by the privatizers, of introducing internal markets within the health service, and pitching departments and hospitals into financial competition with one another, has been the breakup of vital channels of communication based on trust and co-operation through which knowledge was exchanged whose benefits could never be costed, measured or accounted for in market terms. This was knowledge which could not be exchanged other than through relations of co-operation. These policies, rationalized by Hayek, end up destroying the means of fully utilizing the practical, ephemeral knowledge that Hayek so valued in his shipping and estate agents and whose maximum utilization he was so keen to achieve. The problem of knowledge was unlikely to be at the fore of policy makers' minds, but even if it had been the individualism of their philosophic foundations would have blocked them from recognizing the importance of practical knowledge that could only be harnessed through social co-operation rather than competition.

This particular struggle over public services is at the present time a defensive one, but it has led people to become more aware of the practical importance of the co-operative social connections through which knowledge is, often informally, shared. The experience has also highlighted some of the conditions – including the dominance of non-commercial social efficiency criteria – necessary to achieve this co-operation.

Grass-roots economic networks: experiences and conditions for success

In this chapter I will highlight three kinds of experience in which these attempts to change the distribution of economic knowledge are apparent. They all indicate the importance for the achievement of a democratic and socially just economy, of popularly based networks for sharing economic knowledge.

Even where the scope for economic self-government is severely restricted by overbearing concentrations of economic power, there are people sharing and developing knowledge along the chain of production of a commodity – from the mines or plantations of the raw material to the factories producing the final good – or across the factories and homes involved in the final manufacturing process. I will take as cases the experience which emerged from one of the most organized sectors of workers – car workers; and the experience of the least organized, or rather those most isolated by their work – homeworkers.[11]

Such networks frequently are associated with local and regional organizations which have taken on a monitoring and campaigning function with regard to, for example, low pay, the environment, health and safety or technology and working hours.[12] These non-state public organizations, managed by trade union and community organizations, employing research and campaign workers, with some state or foundation funding, are an increasingly common phenomenon in Western Europe. At present they are usually in conflict with both national governments and national and multi-national employers. However, if political parties adopting their goals were to come to office, they could become intermediate but partially independent bodies vital to effective social regulation. They have access to inside information from the standpoint, and with the involvement, of the people who the regulation is intended to benefit.

I also will describe examples of democratically organized networks of workers, scientists, consumers and users challenging the present directions of technological change and, often from within the heart of the design process, devising alternatives. Their work illustrates choices implicitly made in the development of technology. Moreover their organizations – for instance, trade union initiated Technology Innovation Centres in Germany, Technology Networks in London – have enabled forms of tacit knowledge that the existing market has by-passed or blocked, to gain practical expression and effect, leading to commercially and socially viable innovations.

Finally, I will point to different kinds of attempts to socialize the market for consumer goods: whether through organizations which inform consumers of the environmental hazards of certain products, or the conditions of labour in their production; or through producers researching and sharing research into their markets to reduce the haphazard element in their operations. Again, these campaigning networks are usually connected with non-state organizations[13] which, if political parties with similar aims gained power, could feed vital pragmatic knowledge into local, regional or national institutions for guiding public investment and loan policy, implementing price controls or consumer goods standards.[14]

The politics of economic networks

In themselves, these networks do not provide a ready made alternative economic mechanism. They have been formed primarily as networks of resistance or, in the case of networks of co-operatives and centres of technological innovation, they exist only in the nooks and crannies of the capitalist edifice. Where they lack the support of some public institution or independent foundation they have a very precarious existence, but for the argument in this book they are important because they illustrate the possibility of social relations which democratize economic knowledge across enterprises, between consumers and producers, between the state and the inside of the labour process. They also point to the kinds of alliances by which people without private capital could gain greater power over their economic destiny.

These networks can only have a lasting impact if they are in an alliance with parties in government that are carrying out programmes of economic redistribution at international, national and local levels. Democratic networks can only be effective means of utilizing the economic knowledge of the population under conditions where there are no major concentrations of inaccessible economic knowledge (these are, invariably, the corollary of concentrated wealth that is not democratically controlled).

The socialist–feminist economist Diane Elson has sketched out in a bold and helpful manner the kind of public institutions which, with the networks of voluntary organizations, could achieve a socialized market in which enterprises had considerable autonomy but within a framework of price regulation, wage policy, and availability of finance. These macro-economic factors would be decided politically and implemented through the knowledge gathered by publically supported grass-roots networks.[15] Elson's is a useful model, which can take account of the practical and social character of knowledge argued for in this book, and which provides a focus for future debate. A summary of it follows later in this chapter.

There is little direct experience from which to identify how the partnership between state and non-state public economic networks might operate. Indeed, I would argue that contemporary organizations of economic resistance and co-operation are a result of the failure of traditional parties of the left to achieve economic justice and democracy commensurate with their achievements in the provision of basic welfare. This failure has occurred in the face of the high expectations and self-confidence of the first generations benefiting from secondary (and in many cases higher) education, a long economic boom and a welfare state.

The failure stems not so much from social democratic betrayal as from inherent limitations on the economic transformations of which the nation state is capable when the most powerful economic forces at large in it are internationally organized.[16] Most of the networks described in this chapter are international. They have sought to exert some social pressures against commercial ones on an international level, where the nation state is of limited use. On the other hand, these networks are weak without political support at whatever level they can get it. The examples described in this chapter tend to have taken a pragmatic view of political representation. They tend to seek material support and public legitimacy through elected politicians at every level. As well as acting to socialize the market, they also (and consequently) seek in practice to democratize parts of the state, or at least to make it responsive to the initiatives and knowledge of those outside the political system. In the final section of this chapter I draw from a limited regional experience – in London, where a section of the left sympathetic to social movements had a brief taste of power – to explore the strategies that such a process of democratization might take.

1   Networks across the transnationals

In the mid 1970s an active network of trade unionists from Britain, West Germany, Holland, Italy and Brazil came together out of frustration with the powerlessness and inertia of both national governments and national trade union structures in the face of the steady globalization of major corporations. The first priority of these trade unionists had been to gather information, partly from one other and partly through the work of committed researchers. They wanted to build up their knowledge of what their company was planning and what developments in the industry would shape its options, as well as to compare wages and conditions.

At the same time, ex-students of the 1968 generation, self-conscious of their own privilege, were testing out forms of political engagement which brought them into a practical relationship with working-class organizations.

Across Western Europe a new kind of research got under way in which small numbers of academics worked closely with local trade unionists to investigate the activities of the transnationals. Independently of each other, but evidence of a common intellectual culture, projects sprang up: Counter Information Service (CIS) in London, producing 'counter' company reports on Rio Tinto Zinc, GEC, British Leyland (focusing especially on their interests in South Africa); SOMO (The Foundation for Research into Multinationals) in Amsterdam; work on Seimens based in the University of Constanz; in Italy, committed researchers worked closely with the FLM, the metal workers union. The commitments of this generation of critical intellectuals to the needs and struggles of the Third World, led them way beyond the conventional agendas of the official trade union movement to the conditions of workers in the Third World plants of Western corporations. Active workplace trade unionists were responsive. They were concerned enough to initiate campaigns, for instance, against the low wages that their company paid in South Africa, and to collaborate with the independent researchers, helping with their investigations and distributing the results on the shop floor.

In 1974 an influential book came out of the Institute for Policy Studies (IPS) in Washington: *Global Reach*, by Richard Barnet, documented the enormous hidden power of the new transnational corporations. As information spread about their power, the way this power distorted development and subverted what little democracy existed, these corporations became the object of widespread moral outrage. Churches became interested, most notably the World Council of Churches, which was strongly influenced by theologians radicalized by the extremes of wealth and poverty in Latin America and by the US government's support for dictatorships. In the late seventies a group of people coming from all these various networks – Bhaskar Vashee from CIS and then the Transnational Institute, the European Associate of the IPS; Marcus Arriga the Brazilian director of the World Council of Churches' 'Participation in Development' programme; Gerd Junne from Constanz University and several others – convened a Western-Europe-wide conference of engaged researchers and trade union activists. This led to the founding of TIE, the Transnational Information Exchange, and one of the beginnings of a new hybrid form of organizing peculiarly suited to tracking and countering the sprawling arrogance of multinational capital.

More recently, in the 1980s, the international forums built up by TIE, with a transnational core of strategically minded shop stewards, provided a vital opportunity for shop floor trade unionists to size up shifts in managements strategies, and to devise and co-ordinate their responses. After a period of serious defeats across Western Europe, these shop stewards are seeking once more to get at least one step ahead. Conferences on 'Toyotism' in Barcelona; on new management techniques in Sao Paulo, hosted by the militant CUT, the general workers' union of Brazil; on the components industry in Wolverhampton, bringing together workers in the car components industry with workers in car assembly; of workers from across General Motors' global reach: all are evidence of this.[17]

Now their discussions are moving more confidently on to questions of positive strategy for the industry. Here they have an advantage on management as a result of social movements, notably the green movement, outside the workplace. The impact of this movement, with its criticisms of a society dominated by the car and aeroplane, has put the leading companies of the car industry as well as the electricity generating industry on to the defensive. The next auto industry workers' conference will be on 'the car and society'. One of the organizers is Willi Horst, who used to work at Mercedes Benz and then as an MP for the German Greens. 'We earn our living making cars but we live in communities that are being destroyed by the cars: at this conference we will discuss how the industry could change and public transport expand so that at the end of the day car workers still have a livelihood and a socially acceptable job.'

Trade unionists in the Ford Motor company were particularly active in developing not only an information exchange and solidarity network but also an international mechanism for policy making. The aim was to formulate policies which would then influence national bargaining and campaigning strategies. In a sense the relative strategic sophistication of Ford shop stewards was shaped by the vanguard character of the challenge they faced from their own management. The Ford motor company had been in the forefront of reorganizing its management structures on a continental and then global level. By the mid-1970s it was well-placed to respond to an intensification of international competition by selectively cutting its workforce and playing the world market to maximize its competitive advantage. It had no long-term commitment to basing production in any one country, although it was heavily dependent on certain national markets, including Britain. The reaction of national governments has been mainly to offer financial incentives to the company to locate on their soil, a policy whose benefits, if any, are only short-term. While national trade union officials in the late 1970s and early 1980s, were still fumbling in their confusion, hoping that a sympathetic Government could bring to bear the necessary pressure to make Ford build British, Spanish, German or whatever national trade movement they represented, active trade unionists from Spain, Britain, Portugal, Germany and Belgium created the 'Ford International Combine'. As with the work of TIE, the purpose of the Ford Combine – which had an informal association with TIE's auto-industry work – was to share the localized knowledge of workers in particular plants and, with the help of research into the wider trends in the industry, to enable all those involved to gain an overview (in effect an underview) of the decisions affecting their futures.

This gave each group of workers separately in their own plant and together through the shop steward Combine a basis for more effective, more accurately targeted action. It also illustrated a new approach to economic strategy.

International organization between shop floor, office and laboratory workers provides a basis for developing policies derived from an international knowledge. (And it is crucial that it is at this workplace level, the level of inside knowledge rather than the level of regional or national trade union officials, that the organization takes place.) The policies might be executed at a number of different points in the company's empire, but for once they would be based on extensive inside knowledge. Without a policy forum fed by this kind of knowledge, government policy has no more than a hit and miss character. It is hitting not so much a moving target but a target enmeshed in a complex of relationships that enable it both to disguise its strategic needs and vulnerabilities and to escape or take compensatory action in reaction against the government. An example of disguise is government bargaining power over coporate inward investment. With detailed inside knowledge and monitoring, government could estimate the importance of a particular investment for a company's plans and therefore calculate when and how to push a hard bargain. Without this information the company can give the impression that it is doing government a favour, and make few concessions to a government's employment and regional policies, or other social and economic objectives. An example of the corporation's ability to escape government restrictions is import controls. These have been a form of government intervention popular with socialist politicians seeking to exert control over multinational capital. However, as a main policy, they can simply displace the problem elsewhere, causing unemployment in a country whose government is less protectionist.

An alternative has been suggested by Ford workers at Dagenham as a result of their experience with 'the Combine'. Steve Riley, now the convenor at Dagenham and a member of the executive of the T&GWU, explained: 'Workers in Britain and in other countries, through international ties and links, would co-operate together in terms of planning "unit build" [the number of cars built per worker] and have an agreement on it and also on the level of cars they are producing and where they are going.' Governments and unions could then use their respective sources of bargaining power to negotiate this policy with Ford (governments applying pressure on issues associated with markets, and unions on those corresponding to the supply of labour). Obviously it presupposes a high degree of international solidarity, and that sympathetic governments will simultaneously be in power. But policies agreed internationally by the workers involved are not only more effective in controlling transnationals, they are also more likely to enable traditions of international solidarity to put down real roots in different nations and regions.

As an organization the Ford Combine's initiatives only rarely had official trade union support, and even more rarely, political support.[18] It was not a lasting force. It did however illustrate the possibility of a new approach to industrial strategy, avoiding both the unwarranted presumptions of over-arching knowledge – and the blind, over-confident bumbling – of government planners, and the naive optimism that market forces will arrive at an adequate solution. In this approach, workers organizations behave a little like tugboat crews, with all their experiential knowledge of harbour conditions, guiding the state, rather like a large tanker, towards where it could intervene with effect.

The tugboats need to be organized and their day-to-day knowledge self-consciously deepened and combined with other theoretical forms of knowledge. Moreover, their authority needs to be recognized by the elected and executive institutions of the state. Auto workers have been amongst the best organized section of workers in the growth industries of the post-war period. In an industry which concentrates large numbers of workers in one place, where they share very similar conditions and where every stage in the production process is highly interdependant, this is not surprising.[19] Initially it was a fairly homogeneous workforce to organize – white male, full-time, concentrated in particular locations.

2 Organizing the knowledge of the 'unorganized'

Such well organized groups of workers might well be able to sustain a practical partnership with a democratic and responsive state in the face of unaccountable economic power. But, one might equally argue, there are many workers – part-time, temporary, small-enterprise, home or outworkers for instance – who surely need the state to act for them. Their needs are so obvious (material security) that politicians or state professionals can presume to know the solutions. Homeworkers (that is, people working for their employers from home on temporary casual contracts), because they are literally 'on call' for the company, experience perhaps the most extreme conditions militating against a process of sharing knowledge. The idea of them organizing to assert their needs and gain leverage over their circumstances, let alone lay the basis of new economic relations, seems quite utopian. If ever there was a case for social engineering or benevolent paternalism, it is for the protection of these, mainly women workers.

Homework, moreover, is seen in conventional economics as insignificant or anachronistic in the new international division of labour. At first sight, the idea of women in their kitchens (with children playing or bawling in the backyard) machining parts of smart dresses that will sell under fashionable labels on the shopping malls of the West, seems more like a picture from the Third World, bound to fade away with economic development. In fact, it is an increasingly common scene in the cities of Italy and Britain and in different industries in Holland, Germany and France – 'Third World labour in the mainstream of First World production', as Swasti Mitter puts it.[20]

The numbers of homeworkers are growing, as is the industrial spread of their employment. As a feudal baron needs his serfs to sustain his wealth and his power in the face of an uncertain balance of military power, but is reluctant to bear the cost of caring for them, so the modern corporation needs to be surrounded by homeworkers to provide flexibility of supply in the face of an uncertain market. For such companies, responsibility for these workers undermines their attraction.

For nearly a hundred years, since the German Social Democrat Eduard Bernstein introduced protective legislation for homeworkers, interventionist state policies have assumed homework to be a survival from more primitive phases of industrial development. The predominant assumption was that a welfare state, with an interventionist bias and a well organized labour movement, would eventually lead to its elimination and the establishment of high waged factory work as the universal feature of a modern economy. At first, in the last decade of the nineteenth century, the state's approach was positively hostile to homework, seeing it as a 'disease' whose conditions could infect the rest of society. Legislation just before World War One and again after the Second World War, however, was infused by a sense of obligation to the poor. Some important gains were made in terms of minimum rates and conditions. Yet these turned out to be inadequate solutions, mainly because there had been no effort to investigate directly, or provide a platform for, the needs identified by homeworkers themselves.[21]

Even in the early years of the century, homeworkers had been active in the campaigns of Sylvia Pankhurst, which linked the case for women's suffrage to women's economic and social circumstances. The rise of feminism in the 1970s, often converging with grass-roots forms of community and trade union organizing, again enabled the voices of homeworkers themselves to be heard. The joint efforts of feminist activists and militant homeworkers produced an impressive range of organizations: Homeworker's Support Centres in Italy and Holland; Women's Employment Projects and Outwork Campaigns in different parts of Britain. A European and international network now meets to share inside information about the workings of companies (like a London clothing firm that cuts cloth in London for machining by homeworkers in Cyprus to be returned for sale in London) to compare and criticize their respective governments' policies and to formulate their own strategies. Sometimes they hear of inspiring examples in homeworkers' own organizations. These spread like wildfire through networks eager for models of development. The Self-Employed Women's Association (SEWA) in India is a recent example like this. You cannot open a newsletter or report on homeworking without hearing about this extraordinarily hybrid organization – a veritable one-person band in terms of the range of functions carried out by one organization. It was set up as a women's trade union and organizes women pieceworkers, homeworkers, street vendors, craft workers and contract cleaners. At first it used traditional negotiating methods, but as the women became more knowledgeable and creative in addressing their needs it adopted more flexible forms of organizing, including co-operatives, a women's bank and educational courses.[22]

To go from supposedly passive victims to economic actors struggling for greater economic self-determiniation involved a new kind of alliance between researchers, politicians and workers, organized in quite unconventional ways. The traditional homogenizing concepts of industrial policy makers, like 'the clothing sector', combined with the conventional assumption that 'labour' was defined by its location in the workplace, would have led to a simple alliance with the clothing trade unions (in Britain, the Taylor and Garment Workers' Union). But investigations into the nature of the industry, including the work carried out in privately knitting arms of jerseys, sewing buttons and zips and stitching gloves, quickly led to a realization that alliances with the real insiders in the industry, and the insiders with a vested interest in changes, would be much more complex. Sixty per cent of the work of the Cypriot clothing industry in North London, for instance, is done by homeworkers. Investigation of the full extent of homeworking is itself a process of economic networking. Because of its casual and unregulated character, statistics do not exist. The trades unions in London had considered it to be outside their sphere of influence. Implicitly, many officials took the position that all work should be done in the workplace and by an act of wishful thinking struck it from their thoughts. This was convenient for them, but not for the women for whom homework was the only chance of an income.

Vital to the success of the homeworkers' networks has been an extensive well-connected gang of feminist networkers – busybodies some might say – concerned with the problems of women workers and conscious of the limits of formal trade union organizations. They felt it was their business, whether they were based in a union, a community organization or carrying out research in a polytechnic, to follow the threads of women's problems, however many administrative and organizational boundaries they had to cross.[23]

Resistance and the seeds of alternatives

What is revealing about the auto workers' international combines and the homeworkers' organizations is the way that the organizations and networks initiated for self defence proved to be an impetus, however fragile, for attempts to exert control over the market in pursuit of a positive economic policy.

Fundamental to this is a process of sharing and combining knowledge, with varying degrees of self-consciousness about the process. Sometimes the workers concerned are very conscious of the importance of knowledge and the need for researchers to complement but not to appropriate the knowledge of the worker. They are often working with researchers who can put their knowledge into a wider, macroecomic context or can formulate hypotheses to help make sense of their collective knowledge and test these hypotheses with experiential knowledge. A list of demands produced by homeworkers in London included demands on researchers and academics 'to recognize the need to work as part of community based projects; to ensure that the results of their work are made available to homeworkers' organizations; to continue to keep in touch with the projects and homeworkers with which they work.'

These associations of workers and researchers, however, have little access themselves to all the sources of knowledge required to bring about change – let alone material and political sources of power. The incompletenes of their knowledge stems partly from the speed of economic change, the ephemeral character of much economic knowledge and the infinite amount of tacit knowledge that remains private. But the incompleteness also stems from certain structural features of the position of labour.

3   Socializing technical knowledge and the means to innovate

One such limit is an incomplete knowledge of the majority of workers of available or possibly available technological options. Unless they are high-level designers with access to international technological developments, workers' knowledge is more or less limited to the technology of the place where they work. This means that when management introduces new forms of technology they have little sense of what alternative might be preferred, given their distinct priorities to those of management; or when management is slow to innovate they have little idea of what might be the best innovations to push for and no means themselves to innovate. The structural position of particular groups of workers means that their knowledge of technology is often bounded by the options chosen by management. The only way out is access to sources of technical knowledge exchanged outside the work context and built up from many expert sources.

The power of tacit knowledge

Throughout the late 1960s and 1970s an increasing number of technical and design workers joined trade unions, especially in engineering and computer technology. An important minority amongst these white-collar trade unionists were ex-science and technology students radicalized by the experiences of the Vietnam War and the various waves of the peace movement ever since. The experience driving the majority of these workers to the union consisted of very similar problems: the job insecurity, low rate of increase in wages, lack of say in their pension fund, which had led the majority of shop floor workers to join unions decades ago. The pressures of mass production in an increasingly competitive market had steadily eroded the privileged status of the design engineer; computer-controlled technology was both the final leveller and a new source of collective bargaining power. These newcomers did not just provide higher dues for head office: many of them also acted as a yeast in the trade union dough just at a time when it was needed.

In bringing their understanding of technology over to the side of labour, they provided for white-collar manufacturing trade unions (or trade unions that organize white-collar and blue-collar workers as one) a source of self-confidence that management offensives were in danger of destroying. A significant minority of these technical trade unionists questioned the idea of an inevitable march of technological progress in line with which trade unionists must inevitably fall. Firstly, they challenged the particular uses of technology in chemical warfare and in the atomic bomb. Then the social costs of management's new technologies came under scrutiny: the stress they induced, the accidents which they caused. Finally, designers and shop floor workers in the heat of the technological revolution began to uncover the choices and values involved in the design and innovation process itself.

Across Western Europe, a minority of scientists and technologists worked with trade unions and community groups to change the social uses and context of science: Science Shops in Holland, the Utopia Project in Sweden, the British Society for Responsibility in Science.

In 1975, the alternative corporate plan of the Lucas Aerospace workers concentrated these different challenges in one vivid, high-profile initiative. Shop stewards in this company in the forefront of defence technology decided that traditional industrial tactics (strikes, occupations and so on) were leading nowhere, and moreover were difficult to maintain when workers could see no positive outcome. In the hope of bargaining support from the newly elected Labour government, the Lucas shop stewards drew up an imaginative plan, during two years of discussion and experimentation in Lucas factories across Britain, of socially useful products on which their supposedly 'redundant' skills and energies could be employed.[24] The Lucas plan was just one initiative, and in itself cannot carry too great a burden for the case for an alternative approach to technology. Its significance lies in what its fame and influence indicates about wider social trends. It would not have had the influence it had if it had not expressed many shared aspirations. And indeed, wherever trade union bargaining remained strong – West Germany, Holland, Sweden, parts of Italian industry – other workers and engaged intellectuals creatively applied many of its principles, and made them their own.

In the late 1970s and early 1980s the German Metal Workers' Union created conversion committees in most of the major German arms factories. More recently they have established Innovation Centres in major towns, for trade unionists to gain advice about strategies in the face of new technologies, and analysis in the case of chemicals or machinery which threaten the health and safety of the workers or the community. More ambitiously, these centres generate ideas for diversification plans in the case of closure or redundancy.

A paradox of the Lucas Aerospace workers' plan is that it symbolized a potential that existed throughout the better organized parts of the labour movement in Europe in the 1970s, yet explicit plans and proposals from labour have been the exception rather than the rule. The explanation for the paradox is that trade unionists make calculations before spending their scarce spare energies: there has to be some credible chance of success. In the case of the Lucas Aerospace stewards – cautious, prudent trade unionists in the majority – it was the commitment of support from newly-elected Labour Minister for Industry, Tony Benn.[25] Without some prospect of government pressure on the company, the Lucas stewards had little hope even of serious negotiations, let alone success, and they would never have taken the initiative which they did. Their potential for developing alternatives would (as for the majority of active trade unionists) have remained dormant. Such political support was rare, and indeed support from the Department of Industry for the Lucas workers did not survive Tony Benn's removal to the Department of Energy. In Sweden and West Germany it was occasionally forthcoming from regional or municipal government, and in Italy and West Germany, again, from the powerful metal workers' unions.

Incomplete though these politicaly supported trade union initiatives were, their occasional appearance represented a major political and, implicitly, analytical shift. In this, these often thwarted initiatives left a significant legacy. Their implicit political shift was away from relying on the state as the sole, or even prime, executor of a socially responsible industrial policy, and in the direction of some kind of partnership between workplace trade unions, workers' self-managed or co-operative enterprises and a responsive state.

In London in the early 1980s, with the radical administration of the GLC, the mere fact of whole-hearted political support for popular initiatives to create jobs, matching skills with needs, was important for releasing some of the creative potential of active trade unionists. GLC support in terms of really effective bargaining power with management was a bit of a chimera – its powers were so insignificant.[26] But even the prospect of public backing stimulated workers in a large brewing company in Tower Hamlets, in a bookbinding company in Southall, in a heavy engineering company in Acton, in the furniture industry in East London and (with representatives of the community) in the Royal Docks – all faced with the loss of jobs – to campaign for detailed alternatives. Sometimes these figured alternative products, sometimes new ways of organizing production, new markets or new skills and training for labour.[27]

Beyond the workplace: need and innovation

Alternative bargaining strategies of this kind were about more than saving jobs. The prospect of living on the dole was the initial stimulus but it was combined frequently with horror at the wastage of skill and energy when so many needs went unmet. Workers' proposals frequently tried explicitly to identify the kind of needs which they could be meeting with new marketing strategies and/or a new relationship with the public sector as a consumer. These initiatives, however, were predominantly producer-led – with the exception of a few originating from inner city communities under threat from speculative property development.

Conventionally, there are two alternatives: market-led or state-led. Implicitly most of the workers pressing these alternatives rejected the idea of there being one solution dictated by the market. They were not in any abstract sense 'anti-market' – the brewery workers' proposals were full of ideas for reaching new markets. Rather, they were challenging their company's acceptance of the limits of its markets. They were pointing to ideas that would mean a change in the company's relation to its external economic environment. This might involve the state, for example, in changing its public purchasing or in providing funding to independently managed enterprises. But these popularly based alternatives were also rejecting the state itself as the appropriate diviner of need and stimulus to innovation. State dominated alternatives would not draw on the tacit everyday knowledge which these workplace trade union and community organizations found in their own experiences they had been able to release. Neither could the existing private market.

The GLC and its investment quango, the Greater London Enterprise Board (GLEB), experimented with a possible mechanism to bring about a variety of different kinds of direct contact between producers, users, inventors and scientists in the process of innovation. Mike Cooley, one of the designers/ authors of the Lucas Aerospace alternative plan, supervised the experiment. They created six 'technology networks' criss-crossing London. Three focused on specific topics: the London Energy and Environment Network (LEEN), the London Transport Network (LTN) and the London Innovation Network. Three were based in geographical areas: North London, South London and East London. These networks aimed to connect users: for example, tenants with problems of dampness and condensation in the case of LEEN, or disabled people at present unable to use public transport in the case of LTN, and workers e.g. direct labour unions or bus unions, technologists, scientists and inventors. Most of the networks were based in or near polytechnics, with access to the poly's technical facilities and support from its staff. Through their connection with GLEB – which provided their initial funding – the 'technets' were associated with facilities for production. Several innovations stimulated through the networks were actually produced by GLEB supported co-operatives or part GLEB-owned firms.

Here was a glimpse of a possible new stimulus to innovation and a means of follow through. Needs were matched with ingenuity and productive capability, but this was achieved neither through a plan laid down from above nor through the happenstance of an unregulated market. Rather, a process of matching took place through a network consciously set up by institutions and groups of people – including the local authority – with different kinds of knowledge, practical and theoretical, of the needs going unmet and the resources unused. They organized and funded it with this purpose in mind, yet without presuming they could predict or should lay down exactly how the matching took place. The character of tacit skill was understood: innovations were supported on the basis that they worked and close colleagues could see their potential – rather than because the inventor spelt out his or her case on paper. The networks had an autonomy (within certain criteria that governed their funding) which was crucial to their role in a process of innovation. The launching of the innovation did not depend on the luck of access to private capital.

4   Organizing around consumption

Consumption itself is another sphere where democratically organized networks sharing economic knowledge have emerged counter to the atomizing
pressures of the private market.

Activists in the new social movements have not generally theorized their
approach to the market.[28] Their initiatives, campaigns and culture bear
witness to a distinctive, if complex, view. The generation of 1968 were the
children of the boom as well as of social engineering states. They imbibed and
reacted against a smug, self-satisfied culture of consumerism, in part a celebration after the scarcities of war, in part the creation of new, standardized,
life-styles with the new consumer goods coming off the expanded assembly
lines of mass production. 'Little boxes, little boxes,' sang Tom Lehrer in a
stinging satire of middle and aspiring working-class life in the 1950s, 'all
made out of ticky tacky, all just the same. There's a blue one, there's a red one,
and a yellow and orange one . . . and they all look just the same.' Their
rebellion was at different moments a cultural desire for a source of hope
beyond more commodities, something more than money could buy. It was
also a social perception that many acute social needs were not expressed
through the cash nexus – nor responded to by the state. At the same time
their life-styles reflected a market reality: the possibility of new, more specialized markets. The boutiques, craft shops and street selling that thrived in
every centre of student revolt – from Telegraph Avenue, Berkeley to
Kreuzberg, West Berlin – provided ideal niche markets for the enterprising
co-operative or conventional entrepreneur.

Driving their rebellion towards a belief that there was nothing spontaneous about existing market arrangements, was cumulative evidence of major
corporations exercising power to shape and organize the market.[29] The role of
advertising, the increasing concentration of company ownership, the
oligopolistic power of the successful company, and the close, secret links
between corporations and government, all pointed to a complex of institutions that were the creation not of a single conspiracy but certainly of the
conscious exercise of power. Claims for the competitive free market spontaneously maximizing the happiness of the majority lost their ability to convince
and to justify. The creation of counter power to intervene consciously and
collectively in the power relations of the market became fair game. Throughout the 1970s, feminists organized campaigns against the stereotypes of
women that cavort in front of us on the advertising hoardings. Consumer
organizing became an instrument of political pressure with the boycotting of
South African oranges, and of Barclays Bank for its treatment of its black

South African employees. Influenced by the impact of these campaigns, environmentalists have exposed the damaging effects of aerosol sprays and other environmental hazards, beer drinkers campaigned successfully against the big breweries and their attempts in Britain to tie pubs to their tasteless mass-produced beer. The idea of collective consumer action has spread to campaigns of pressure against, for instance, Dutch and British clothing companies, for their super-exploitation of women in the Philippines, India and Malaysia. The 'Clean Clothes Campaign' based in Amsterdam mobilises to put pressure on big retail stores to get them to accept responsibility for the conditions under which the clothes they sell are produced, across the whole chain of subcontracting from the principal suppliers to the homeworkers.

The most ambitious initiative to transform the present organization of the market is originally TWIN, the Third World Information Network, and TWIN Trading. These two projects, founded with start-up funding from the GLC in 1985, come from many of the same traditions as the consumer campaigns, especially those concerned with economic conditions in Third World countries. They themselves, however, are companies which act directly to improve the economic position of the local producer by helping them to help themselves. They provide information, technical support, marketing and other help to enble these producers to co-operate together as appropriate, do without middlemen and, as a consortium or co-operative, trade independently. They are part of the International Federation for Alternative Trade which was founded in 1989. IFAT's member organizations in 1989 had a turnover of over US$200 million; their present turnover is US$300 million, which is an indication of the importance and the growth of efforts to achieve a more socialized market, through co-operatively organized networks exchanging information and practical assistance.[30]

All these movements and more indicate that contrary to the assumption of neo-classical and neo-liberal economics alike – and their pervasive ideological influence – people, even when consuming, do not see themselves simply as consumers weighing up price against preference or marginal utility. They have distinct interests as consumers but they see themselves also as trade unionists, and/or citizens with an interest in the social and environmental conditions of a commodity's production.

What are the presuppositions and the practical implications of these campaigns and networks? Firstly there is a presupposition that people should be socially accountable in their use of financial, human and natural resources. Secondly there is a recognition of the interconnectedness of consumption, production and other conditions of daily life – the quality of the environment, the culture, relations between the sexes, for instance – and a belief in the need to know and take some responsibility for the character of these interdependencies. Marx's notion of commodity fetishism, of the way that under capitalist market relations the exchange of commodities distorts these social interdependencies, echoes the contradictory experience of a society where, for example, car ownership and the apparent freedom purchased by the buying of a car is an everyday aspiration and yet the conditions of the car worker are the most mind-enslaving drudgery. Finally, the direction of the social movements' attempts to overcome these forms of alienation was not to look primarily to the state as either the only vehicle for social accountability nor as the only means of knowing or acting on the interdependencies of the economy.

5　Networks and economic and political power

Economic co-operation and the sharing of knowledge and discovery does not just happen. As we have seen, the channels for it have to be consciously organized. Perhaps the most distinctive economic idea that social movement practice has, often unknowingly, contributed to the development of a democratic economics is the idea of an openly organized network between economic equals.

Many of those directly involved know well the economic significance of their activity, but just as childcare is frequently not recognized as work, so grass-roots organizing about the conditions and character of production is not recognized as economics. Yet the associations of trade unionists and researchers across the auto-industry and other sectors, the international campaigns of homeworkers, the 'Technets', science shops, I.G. Metall Innovation Centres and other grass-roots centres for technology transfer and advice, and the International Federation for Alternative Trade are all organizing from within economic relations. Whether it be production, the processes of innovation, the channels of trade, they are changing or creating the economic relations in which they participate even as they organize.

There's nothing necessarily democratic or egalitarian about networks. The term 'network' sounds and is in itself more or less socially and politically neutral. Modern business theory sees 'information rich' networks as a key to market success.[31] In one sense there is nothing new about networks as an ingredient in business success. What after all were old boys' networks, the gentlemen's clubs of London, the free masonry of local government, police and business exchanging information in the steam baths? Good contacts and 'on the spot sources' of business intelligence have always been the invisible hands behind a successful business. Entrepreneurs have always created social networks to gain the knowledge to exert greater control over their environment.[32]

Networks have been an unacknowledged economic variable until recently, because neither the neo-classical nor Hayekian framework could comprehend such a sociological and informal factor in industrial performance and economic growth. The neo-classicists, who presumed perfect information, had little place in their theory for real-life entrepreneurs with their imperfect knowledge and their 'uneconomic' means of overcoming their ignorance. The Hayekians got closer to actual entrepreneurs but closed their eyes when these acted as social rather than atomistic animals and sought to extend the knowledge and increase their chances of realizing their purposes.[33]

What can we draw from recent experiences about the distinctiveness of the economic networking produced by the social movements and the parts of the trade union movement that they have influenced? The networks involve a division of tasks but a minimum of hierarchy. Their knowledge, mutual trust and consequent power depends on their autonomy from those who dominate economic decisions; it is fed by their roots amongst those with the everyday knowledge and skill to implement or to resist these decisions. In the most effective networks, this everyday knowledge is combined with theoretical knowledge based on researching wider trends. Moreover the networking process is normally the everyday activity of formally open and democratic organizations which have regular elections for the people responsible for maintaining the direction and infrastructure of the network.

Private businessmen, by contrast, are involved in discreet networking rather than public industrial policies with their risks of democracy, publicity and raised expectations amongst the workforce. Strict albeit unwritten codes of secrecy and limited entry are the characteristics of networking of the ruling economic elite.

Not only are popularly based democratic networks distinct in their methods of working from those which lubricate the ruling elite, they also play a very different kind of economic role. Within an economy based in major part on private wealth, in which it is broadly assumed that so long as companies act legally, they are acting in society's best interests, the networks which informally connect the main economic actors merely help each one steer their own business through an uncertain and predatory terrain. The knowledge gleaned through the informal networks of this elite merely feed into existing centres of corporate decision making. The exchange of information which goes on between the financiers, industrialists, retailers and civil servants of capitalist economies, either through the informal system of clubland in

Britain or the state supported networks of the Japanese Ministry for Industry and Technology (MITI), is subservient to each company's profit maximization. It is an aid to private competitive success, making each competitor more knowledgeable about the economic environment and therefore enabling each company to plan more effectively for the future. By contrast the networks created by radical trade unionists and social movement organizers are gathering knowledge of social needs to press them against the priorities of corporate accumulation, or to demand and guide state action.

The networks described in this chapter contain the potential to feed a knowledge of social needs and social costs and also an extensive practical know-how into mechanisms for regulating the market. Indeed, if they are to have any lasting effect, popularly based networks exchanging information and socializing knowledge of needs and resources, have ultimately to feed into or be part of economically or politically powerful institutions.

At present they feed mostly into oppositional economic institutions such as trade unions, considerably increasing their effectiveness; or into local or regional attempts to support alternative economic strategies. But thinking ahead and imagining their positive role in an economy based on self-management, their role would be as a necessary complement to public institutions of co-ordination and regulation.

Institutions for a socialized market: a possible model

Diane Elson proposes the principles that should guide the development of such institutions. Firstly, measures should be taken to overcome antagonisms between buyers and sellers both in the labour market and the consumer goods market. Crucial to her proposals for the labour market is a basic income so that people are not forced for survival to sell their labour power. Rather they would be able to exercise genuine choice about where they worked.

As far as the consumer goods market is concerned, some form of market and price mechanism is essential to her model, but just as the labour market is considerably civilized by the provision of a basic income, so the market would be socialized through a public process of price formation, in which social and environmental considerations would be central. This would be achieved by public bodies, including publically funded consumer unions, that shared information about prices, wages, conditions and environmental consequences of production. This would put buyers and sellers on a more equal footing and ensure that individual units considered the implications of their decisions for others, as well as for themselves.

The structure of property rights underpinning this model would be worker-managed public enterprises supervised by public regulators, international, national and regional, who would enforce democratically agreed norms for the utilization of public assets. Enterprises would normally be expected to be self-financing. If they fail to break even, the regulators would be responsible for restructuring and providing transitional finance. These public financial bodies would also be responsible for ensuring, through regular social audits, that enterprises complied with social legislation regarding work and the environment and standard of goods that firms imported.

This model involves an extensive regulatory system. However the workings of this would not rely exclusively or even primarily on the state. Crucial to its function is inside information plus knowledge of the needs of consumers and workers. This knowledge would be gathered by the kind of organizations discussed in this chapter. These organizations would, if they met certain democratically agreed criteria, gain the support of public institutions for the role they would play in what would in effect be a decentralized, interactive planning system.

Such economic and political relationships seem far from present-day economic reality. This reality, however, is not stable. Whatever stability exists in the West has been achieved through an artificial depression of the popular expectations engendered by several generations' experience of the universal franchise, the expansion of social provision (especially education) and the economic prosperity long boom. A cultural spirit that has broken from deference and aspires increasingly to self-government, is not an easy genie to put back in the bottle. Yet the pressures that it put on public spending and on profit margins meant that it had irrevocably burst the confines of a Keynesian mixed economy. A simple return to this model, even on an EC-wide level, though undoubtedly beneficial in the short run, especially if its scope was extended to the East, would only lead to a further cycle of inflation and unemployment. The only other alternative to the unstable and increasingly authoritarian maintenance of economic discipline through high unemployment and 'strong' government is to enable the desire for self-government to be realized in economic life. Only genuine economic democracy could possibly create the conditions for the economic self-discipline necessary to avoid inflation without unemployment. One should add ecological self-displine too, for economic self-government has egocentric tendencies, even if the ego is a collective one, unless there are sensitive regulators rooted in educative voluntary social organizations. It is in this context that Diane Elson's proposals, and also the related ones of, for instance, Pat Devine, Alain Lipietz and Michael Barratt-Brown, are worth practical consideration.[34]

In the meantime, the democratic economic networks essential to such alternatives need infrastructures if they are to spread. The networking of the elite has infrastructure in plenty. Traditionally it depended on the clubs, the family connections, the country houses, the cohesion of class interest; today the networking of modern business depends on an infrastructure of wealth, political power, communication and media, and overriding common interest.

An invisible feature of much of the work of popularly based networks is their dependence on the support work of a minority of organizers whose job it is to keep the contact going – who could almost be seen as professional 'networkers', like the five or six TIE staff across the globe, the various full-time workers for homeworkers campaigns, the 'Technets' core staff. They organize horizontally, making maximum use of information technologies.[35] They raise their funds from a variety of sources: radical churches, local authorities, charitable trusts, trade unions, individual subscriptions. But in the absence of sustained political support, they remain precarious.

If these grass-roots mechanisms for socializing economic knowledge are to have any chance of becoming a lasting basis for an alternative way of organizing the economy, they need political allies: to provide immediate infrastructure; to consider and campaign for the kind of institutions of a democratic state and a socialized market that would utilize the practical economic knowledge that democratic networks accumulate; and to collaborate on strategies for breaking up the present private and corporate concentrations of economic power so that workers' self-management becomes a possibility. I will draw on two frequently analysed experiences to illustrate the limits and possibilities of horizontal forms of economic co-ordination, the conditions under which they thrive, and the pressures on them to revert to antagonistic competition.

6   Non-state public bodies and the state

(i)   Modena and Mondragón

The organized networks of textile producers round Modena in the North Italian region of Emilia Romagna illustrate some features of a formally and relatively democratically organized and publically supported (by the regional government) network for the purpose of openly sharing knowledge of the market, in this instance, between producers. I want simply to highlight features of this particular North Italian experience which illustrate the potential for such horizontally organized networks for socializing economic knowledge. It does not provide in every respect an ideal model; nor indeed does what has been referred to as the 'Third Italy' represent a single model.[36] The networks around Modena developed for economic reasons but their character was shaped by a strong co-operative tradition that had been long established in the region's agricultural production and was carried over into industry. Related to this regional tradition, the indigenous roots of the Italian Communist Party have always been strong, amongst the business community as well as within the trade unions (there is extensive overlap between the two). The Modena textile producers' network clearly is not a case influenced by the social movement left. But it has provided, sometimes in a rather idealized form, an inspiration to socialist economists searching for strategies beyond the dichotomy of market and plan.

The Modena experience certainly does not provide any kind of ideal type. For instance, there is a growing inequality emerging between producers which is undermining the mechanisms for sharing knowledge of the market – mechanisms that presuppose a certain equality of circumstance between entrepreneurs – and leading to more conventional forms of competition. Local trade unionists complain of entrepreneurs, especially some of the larger ones, seeking to weaken collective bargaining and a PCI-influenced tradition of obligation to their workers. But there are distinctive and innovative elements of the situation that are relevant to my case for ways of socializing knowledge of the market. (I would argue that stronger forms of regional state intervention are necessary to protect and sustain these positive distinctive features.) I can best highlight these features by drawing a contrast between Modena and the other Italian success story: Benetton.[37] There are similarities between the two, in that both are engaged in specialized production for niche markets in fashion, much of their production uses computer controlled machinery to produce short runs economically and they use computerized distribution systems which link them to retail outlets and thereby avoid the need to produce for stock, 'just in case' a product is reordered. Because of these technical and market similarities these two experiences, which are very different in terms of social organization, often get lumped together as part of a single, homogeneous trend towards 'flexible specialization'. Interestingly, both have their origins in homeworking.

Benetton is commercially a traditional capitalist firm, centralizing marketing knowledge, finance and production targets. But it decentralizes production itself to small workshops – who often decentralize further to clusters of homeworkers. The relationships beyond the small workshop are co-ordinated from above, from the Benetton head office, a palatial villa outside Venice. This is where the design, marketing and financial activities of Benetton are concentrated. And from here, the Benetton siblings are now executing their latest campaign to Benettonize the USA, then on to Moscow.[38]

By contrast, the small companies in Modena, near Bologna, Emilia Romagna, have developed a horizontal system of co-ordination and co-operation. They share on a local basis the design, marketing, and financial facilities which Benetton concentrates at the centre. The small towns of Emilia Romagna have shown that the multinational corporation is not the only institution which could gather that knowledge. The success of the small (there are few enterprises with more than 20 employees) partnerships and co-ops which produce fashion knitwear in Carpi and the other towns in Modena, shows that there is another, co-operative way of gathering and using knowledge of the market.

Historically evolved models cannot be transported from one context to another but the principles underpinning a vital institution in Emilia Romagna do have a wider relevance. The CITER (Centro Informazione Tessile dell' Emilia Romagna) is supported by subscriptions from all the local businesses. It also obtains some financial and research support from the regional government. Its first task is to investigate the market. It employs researchers who attend the leading European fashion shows, talk to buyers of major stores, try to divine cultural trends and then report back to *all* the affiliated businesses, together. Moreover CITER has an extensive data base of designs with which companies can devise their own distinctive designs. The crucial principle is that all the information which in conventional capitalist companies is secret – commercial secrecy being an essential ingredient of corporate competitive success – is shared. It is as if CITER see the market as an indicator of taste which they both co-operate on a local basis and compete internationally to provide for.

There are certain traditions of co-operation amongst small employers everywhere but it is usually exclusively at the expense of labour. In the London's clothing, furniture and footwear industries, for instance, employers seek to cut labour costs almost to the bone. The idea of common services to increase design capacity and improve knowledge of niche markets would seem a bit academic to most of them. In this case, the only people in the industry with a vested interest in new, more co-operative strategies for competition are a minority of strategically minded trade unionists.[39] In Emilia Romagna too employers' cost cutting is sometimes a problem, but entrepreneurs face a strong union and are often themselves of Communist sympathies – interviewing the secretary of the major small business association in the region, the CNA, in Modena, was a little like visiting a Communist committee room outside an election campaign.

Finally, a vital lesson from the Modena example is the importance of a structure of property that does not allow the dominance of particular and private power over the power stemming from social co-operation. Political action is already needed to protect the present co-operative arrangements around CITER from the centrifugal consequences of larger predatory firms developing without a vested interest in the shared knowledge that CITER can provide.

Another apparently very particular regional economy whose wider significance is, clearer within the perspective of this book is Mondragón in the Basque country. Like the forms of industry-wide co-operation in Regio Emilia, the relative success of its co-operative structure owes something to a regionally-rooted culture that placed a strong value on labour and on the community. As in the enterprises of Carpi, Mondragón's co-operatives within an industry gather information about their market collaboratively and share financial, research and other facilities. Moreover, there is a strong emphasis on developing, utilizing and sharing the skill and knowledge of the co-operators: 'It is necessary to socialize knowledge in order to democratize power because in fact knowledge is power,' said Father José María Arizmendiarrieta, the founder of the school from which the Mondragón co-operatives began. Theoretical and practical knowledge are both valued and drawn upon: 'We have recognized that theory is necessary, yes, but it is not sufficient: we build the road as we travel.'

In Mondragón, this understanding of the economic importance of socialized knowledge is underpinned by social, co-operative property relations and by stringent measures against enterprises growing beyond a certain size. Both these mitigate against the emergence of economic inequality and hence antagonistic competition, atomization of decision making, secrecy and economic opacity. The culture and social mechanisms that have grown on this egalitarian basis seek not only to reproduce co-operative values but seek all the time, quite self-consciously, to preserve 'equilibrio' – that is, a balance between the particular needs of an enterprise and the needs and goals of the wider community. Success on the international market is one of their goals – and indeed a condition for their survival – but it does not override considerations of employment, education and democratic communication.

The Mondragón co-operatives have continuing problems, including industrial conflict in the mid-1970s and the constant threat of unemployment in the 1980s. But there is a self-conscious process of evaluation in operation both in the co-operatives, in the co-operatives' groups, in the all-important bank, the Caja Laboral, and in the recently established Co-operative Council. If complacency or egoism set in at one level, there are plenty of counterbalancing mechanisms bringing social priorities to bear. The economic success of the co-operatives alone ensures that they merit attention. In terms of employment they have grown from 23 workers in one co-operative in 1956, to 19,500 in more than one hundred co-operatives and supporting organizations. Throughout that time, a period which included years of deep recession as well as years of international boom, only 3 out of 103 co-operatives closed down.

There are some insightful studies of Mondragón, most notably *Making Mondragón: The Growth and Dynamics of the Worker Cooperative Complex* by William and Kathleen Whyte; and there are evangelists for particular principles of the co-operatives (Robert Oakeshott of Job Ownership Ltd was an early enthusiast, drawing attention to the financial stake that each co-operator has in the co-operatives).[40] But until recently, this case has been of marginal interest, even to people concerned with industrial policy and regional development. Its extraordinary situation as an economically democratic enclave in Franco's Spain is one explanation for its isolation. Another is that in terms of mainstream economic debates shaped by the Cold War, its non-state, non-private nature was incomprehensible. Commentators explained it away with references to the genius of its founder, José María, or the unique character of Basque culture. Now there is wider debate about what can be learnt from reflecting on its workings. The notion of forms of democratic economic co-ordination that rely neither on the market nor on the state, though interacting with both, and the principle of incentives that balance the individual with the social are being explored more seriously as the exclusively state route to social justice has come to a dead end, and increasing numbers of people have found the road to the free market a terrible disappointment. Moreover, the Basque government is giving significant support to Mondragón and experienced members of the co-operative are playing a leading role in giving the government economic advice.

(ii)   The role of a democratic state: a local experience

Down by the River Thames across the road from Waterloo Station are the attractive houses with gardens, shops and workshops. This is the Coin Street Development: a micro network of co-ops and community groups supported by the Coin Street Community Trust. If City-based developers had had their way it would now be swish but half empty office blocks, and the people of Coin Street would be living in windswept housing estates in outer London, away from their friends, torn from what had become a community. Since the early 1970s the Coin Street Action Group had fought with every conceivable weapon to save their inner city village. On their own they would have been defeated: they had the ideas and the public support in their own area, but no wider political platform or legal political power. With the election in 1982, however, of a sympathetic GLC, whose Councillors included activists with a long history of involvement in campaigns against property speculation, they had some useful allies. The GLC used its planning powers to keep out the property developers. It then provided financial and expert support for the local community organizations, working through the Coin Street Action Group and Coin Street Community Builders.

Here is a modest and small-scale illustration of the kind of political support required to create the conditions for the full driving force of co-operative networks. As with most of the experiences reported in this book, Coin Street offers no complete model but its history indicates important features of such political support. On the one hand, it has to involve preventa-tive action against centres of unaccountable economic power. This is the tanker role for which the knowledgeable tugboats – the Coin Street Commu-nity Action Group – have to prepare the way, and guide the direction. It is a role for which a political party has to win a democratic mandate. It is a role in which the party does not presume that it can rely on its formal control over an administration (in this case municipal) to direct economic institutions to meeting social needs. Rather, it uses its control over the political administra-tion to provide support to democratic organizations able to mobilize the knowledge and skills of local people. The first kind of support that such a political authority can provide is financial support, on the basis of the values and goals with which the party won political office. Secondly, it uses what powers it has negatively, to break up or restrain and weaken unaccountable centres of power, whether financial, industrial or property-owning.

For a regional or municipal authority, let alone a national or continental state, to play this kind of economic role a radical transformation of their existing organization would be required. In particular it would require break-ing from the integuments of the networks of the past; networks between departments of industry and corporate bosses, between transport departments and lobbies for private transport, between environment departments and private property interests which build into the state a vested interest and inertia against the preventative, restrictive action on the economically power-ful. On the other hand, it would need structural change to be open, responsive and accessible to democratic organizations gathering practical knowledge. Such an openness could not be achieved as part of a public relations exercise. The import of this chapter is that various forms of practical knowledge, reachable only through non-state public organizations, have an essential economic contribution of their own. They are able to gather, democratize and share forms of knowledge for which no state body can substitute, whether in production, technology, marketing or trade.

Movements and the state: the London experience

Throughout this chapter, when referring to examples of a new kind of partnership between popular economic networks and a political authority, I have found myself, against my inclination, referring to British examples drawn from the experience of the GLC. I have searched Western Europe for other examples. On issues of ecological conservation, the rights of foreign workers, and the welfare needs of women there are illustrations from Copenhagen, Frankfurt, West Berlin and many smaller towns of campaigning movements in a sustained alliance with new left political parties who are sharing power with social democracy. On issues of political economy as a whole, however, the conversation always returns to the GLC; activists on the continent are interested in hearing of this experience. When they have held any political office, invariably as subordinate partners in a coalition, they have rarely been allowed near economic policy.[41]

By a series of unique political opportunities[42] a radical political administration came to office in London between 1982 and 1986 and *had* to develop a partnership with the networks of the social movement and trade union activists if it intended to carry out effectively its radical manifesto. The new left – or, more accurately, Labour politicians – influenced by and open to the politics of the new movements as well as the left of the trade union movement, won a power struggle inside the near moribund London Labour Party and led what was in effect a coalition (within one party) administration of the GLC.[43]

As a redistributive administration of both the richest and the poorest parts of one of the most populous capital cities of Europe, Ken Livingstone's Greater London Council was an unusual case of being 'state-like' in its resources, its high profile and its democratic legitimacy, but lacking any statutory powers for intervening in the economy. It either had to ride market forces, tossing a few subsidies here and there gaining merely a few palliatives from private developers, and reneging on its election commitments, or it had to make common cause with those with inside economic knowledge and a collective self-interest in its policies for saving inner cities communities and jobs, opening up training and job possibilities for black people and women and strengthening trade union organization. Some reflection on this experiment, acknowledging its limitations, therefore provides lessons for the potential role of government at different levels, in the economic co-ordination of an economy based on self-management.[44]

Grinning cheekily across the river Thames at the most right-wing government in Britain since the 1930s, Ken Livingstone's administration of the GLC was the most left-wing government of the capital city in post-war years. For local government its resources were considerable: its revenue budget was £800 million a year. It had limited and indirect powers over transport and, in its association with the Inner London Education Authority, education; it had control over strategic planning and major public facilities for recreation.[45] And it was itself an employer of 22,000 people. Relative to the economic problems facing Londoners – in parts of the East End of London as many as one in four of the labour force population were unemployed – and to the power of those with a vested interest in the economy remaining more or less as it is, these resources were trivial. They were certainly hopelessly inadequate on their own to have any significant impact on London's ailing economy.

The importance of these resources and powers was that they were too small to give any sane politician, however ardent a social engineer, the illusion that the GLC could solve the problems of the London economy. But they were significant enough to give others the confidence, platform and some of the material wherewithal to take action themselves. Many things could, and have been, said about the GLC,[46] but for my argument the vital lessons lie in how this state institution began to be changed, mainly as a result of pressure from outside, to utilize the practical knowledge of Londoners to implement and elaborate the policies on which Labour was elected to office.

The left-wing councillors leading the GLC had an acute sense of the limits of the knowledge that could be centralized through themselves and the officers of County Hall. The political outlook of several of them had been formed through grass-roots campaigns amongst women, in threatened communities, in the trade unions. Statistical details on employment in London, on the use of buildings, road congestion, on use of the underground, on noise levels, were stored in abundance in the GLC's excellent Research Library: expert teams had accumulated this kind of knowledge conscientiously over the years. But the expectations engendered by the new GLC and its political openness in meeting them required another kind of knowledge. Women's groups, ethnic minorities, local shop stewards' committees, disabled people, community action groups, lesbians and gay men were all pressing their cases on to the new councillors. Where in County Hall was there any knowledge of these needs? It committed itself to saving jobs, and to supporting the proposals of workers and communities to do so. Which department in County Hall was holding discussions with these groups?[47] It committed itself to standing up to the plans of the transnational corporations which dominate London's economy. But would the management of these corporations share information on their plans with the GLC? It was committed to improving its own services to Londoners. But who had detailed knowledge of what Londoners felt about these services and how they might be improved? There was no chance of procrastinating on these commitments. There were plenty of organizations, of varying degrees of formality, whose expectations were excited by these promises and who presumed the right to request resources and a platform for their activities.

Out of this combination of political commitments from elected politicians and pressure from groups of Londoners, the GLC developed mechanisms in an *ad hoc* way which made public and sometimes effective a wealth of practical knowledge ignored by the market and the conventional state alike. The knowledge of subordinate groups of their needs and possible remedies; the knowledge of workers and consumers that is embedded in skills and daily experience; the strategic intelligence pieced together to anticipate management secret plans or the consequence of market changes: these kinds of knowledge were brought into public policy making through a combination of the following means.

First was an expansion of the GLC's grant-giving strategy beyond funding youth and community facilities, to funding groups working for social and economic change. This was a vital and innovative part of the GLC's strategy for encouraging initiatives based on local knowledge, organized independently of the state but in a partnership with it. Some of the most effective grant aiding was in response to popular resistance to imposed job loss or privatization: the campaign of the National Communication Union against the privatization of British Telecom; the campaign of Ford workers against the closure of the Dagenham foundry. Or it might be a response to a more diffuse discontent: for example, that of transport workers wanting to explore the consequences for them and their passengers of One Person Operated buses, or the anxieties of construction workers facing the run-down of Direct Labour Organizations and wanting to develop a strategy. Sometimes the GLC would be asked to support a major joint initiative by a well-established workers' or community organization, such as a meeting of Ford workers worldwide organized with Ford shop steward committees, or the alternative plan for jobs and the environment drawn up by the Campaign Against the Airport and the Newham Forum in Docklands. Through funding such organizations as the GLC gave public recognition to the importance of local knowledge and, so long as the organizations' aims were compatible with those with which the GLC was elected, it gave what political clout it could to make this knowledge effective. In this way it delegated and indirectly extended its power. In doing so it accepted a degree of uncertainty; it could not control the exact way the funds were used. The funding was conditional on broad guidelines of policy and principle, but the organizations were autonomous in how they worked.[48]

Second, in several cases, these autonomous groups and movements elected representatives on to council committees (the case of the women's committee) or groups advising council committee (in the case of planning and ethnic minorities), so that they were not simply receiving money at arm's length, but were feeding back their ideas and experiences into the wider policy making process.

Third, the GLC's Industry and Employment Committee provided resources for workers and community leaders and activists to have the time to educate and inform themselves sufficiently to be able to turn their own knowledge and skill into the basis for alternative policies. The information and skill of planning, of gaining an overview, identifying the trends, and calculating the costs and benefits have always been the monopoly of managements, whether industrial management or government. As the difficulties for hard-pressed trade union representatives or community activists of breaking this monopoly became apparent, the GLC spent an increasing amount of resources on enabling such people to have the time, access to research, and experienced help to become 'popular planners'.

The process of letting go of the traditional social-engineering presumption that social transformation is carried out primarily through the state was not easy. The traditions from whence the GLC came were among the best traditions of social engineering and the legacy is difficult to rework, especially when entrenched in a long-established hierarchy and division of labour. Where the GLC failed to use its resources, however, to activate those with the inside knowledge of production or of social needs, little or nothing was done or major mistakes were made. For example, several of the investments by GLEB, made without paying close attention to the insights of workers and shop floor supervisors with regard to the character of their management and the most effective way to organize the factory, proved to be unwise.[49]

But the kind of partnership with democratic civic organizations that this requires can be contradictory and difficult. On the one hand there are divisions within and between popular organizations; there are considerable variations in organized strength; there are the problems of retaining an autonomous base, the source of the organizations' distinctive knowledge, at the same time as working in partnership with a part of the state; and there are the distinct interests of the politicians and public officials. These are not irresolvable. The importance of practical knowledge and the possibility of socializing it implies that these questions concerning the social mechanisms for making knowledge public and effective are a central part of economics. In this sense I am sympathetic to Hayek's assertion that 'the utilization of knowledge not given to anyone in its totality' is central to the economic problem of society, and also to his criticism of the turn towards an econometrics which treats the question of knowledge as unproblematic.[50] Still, by insisting that the price mechanism is the only means for gaining access to popular knowledge, Hayek distracts attention away from the empirical questions concerning the organization of knowledge, almost as soon as he has drawn our attention to their importance.

Conclusion: self-management, markets and the knowledge problem

Does this discussion of the possibilities of socializing practical economic knowledge take us beyond John Stuart Mill? Does it provide any glimpses of means of economic co-ordination which might protect self-managed enterprises from the predatory pressures of an unregulated market without crushing them under the benevolent or paranoid impulses of a central state?

As I noted at the beginning of this chapter, Mill does not directly address the knowledge problem of economic co-ordination. His main case for the market rests on his arguments for competition and pluralism. But he and his present-day followers imply that the only form of co-ordination compatible with pluralism is the more or less free market, thereby implicitly denying any other non-market form of economic co-ordination that could transform both market and state, making the market a more co-operative mechanism and state institutions more responsive to popular needs. Since economic co-ordination does rest, ultimately, on the way in which economic knowledge is organized, one could say that when it comes to economic co-ordination – in contrast to enterprise management – Mill adopts, rather implicitly, an approach to the knowledge problem similar to Hayek's. He presumes that the unregulated price mechanism is the only way in which individuals or groupings of individuals know of each other's economic activites. The only other model of co-ordination for Mill is a dovetailing from above, through the state.

A recent book makes the case for worker self-management combined with an unregulated market in a way which combines a Marxian (and morally Millsian) analysis of the enterprise with a Hayekian analysis of the problem of economic co-ordination.[51] David Prychitko's case stems from what he sees as an essential tension in Marxism between the decentralizing, libertarian impulse which arises from Marx's analysis of alienation and exploitation, and the centralizing logic of Marx's critique of the commodity fetishism produced by the market. In arguing for the overthrow of commodity relations and the transparency of the social relations of economic life, production, and consumption, Marx, Prychitko argues, was in effect advocating a command economy which, because of the complexity of economic life and the ephemeral, practical character of economic knowledge, had an inbuilt logic – contrary to Marx's own values – towards authoritarian rule by experts.

This powerful argument expresses the core of many a liberal's rejection of socialism. It identifies accurately a tension in Marx. It is only resolvable with an understanding of knowledge which leads to a very different interpretation of the aspiration to transparency that is central to Marx's vision. The conventional Marxist interpretation, though not explicitly proposed by Marx, views transparency in terms of the idea of a single political process. The debate between different Marxist traditions is then about the democracy of this process.

There is another interpretation of transparency, however, which rejects both a conventional Marxist and a Hayekian view of economic knowledge. Transparency could be achieved through *accessibility* rather than the permanent possibility (which turns out in reality to be an impossible or authoritarian fantasy) of a total picture. A condition for the possibility of transparency in the sense of the accessiblity and availablity of knowledge, would be the elimination of inequalities of power and wealth by which knowledge might be appropriated rather than shared.

This implies an understanding of knowledge, in this instance economic knowledge, as socially produced and socially variable – and transformable in the character of its distribution and organization. And if knowledge is socially produced and socially transformable then there is always scope for democratizing and socializing economic knowledge, in pursuit of social objectives in the process of economic co-ordination. In other words, popular self-management need not stop at the workplace door, only to give way to the haphazard pressures of the market or the imperatives of the state. Organized democratic networks, supported by the state and the self-managed enterprises, can investigate the expressions of taste and demand indicated by market trends, can gather knowledge of social needs, and environmental costs, and share tacit skills in ways which turn relations of economics – including those of buying and selling – into transparent relations between people.

Such a possibility, however, depends on the existence of political agencies that enable the economic knowledge culled from organizing on the inside and the underside of production and the market to be expressed, valued and represented.

Notes

1 By the sound of them, they will negotiate hard: 'Our task,' announces Sergei Chramov, 'is to make our labour as expensive as possible. When foreign companies want to dismiss workers, we will try to organize them and defend them'.

2 They are nervous about this though, especially since the countries that provided their main markets (what was the Soviet Union, Iran and Syria) are actually or potentially politically so unstable. They admit that 'people are more concerned about the fact that they might be fired than that they are potential shareholders'. They feel there should be some social safety net. But they can see that that is not enough: 'we need new jobs to be created'.

3 See David Prychitko, *Marxism and Self-Management, Essential Tension* (New York, 1992).

4 In an article on the Italian political philosopher, Norberto Bobbio, *New Left Review 170*, Perry Anderson describes how after the completion of the revised edition of *Principles of Political Economy* in 1849, rewritten in response to the 1848 uprisings across the capitals of Europe, Mill always regarded himself as a liberal and a socialist. Anderson quotes Mill's *Autobiography*: 'The social problem of the future we now considered to be how to unite the greatest individual liberty of action with a common ownership in raw materials of the globe, and an equal participation of all in the benefits of combined labour.'

5 Hayek wrote a book about J. S. Mill's marriage to Harriet Taylor, based on their correspondance. Its main purpose was to explore her influence (a socialistic influence, Hayek suspected) on the *Principles of Political Economy*. The correspondance indicates an intellectual partnership but does not prove that Mill had been seduced from the true way of liberalism, i.e. the liberalism of Frederick von Hayek. See *John Stuart Mill and Harriet Taylor: Their Freindship and Subsequent Marriage* (London, 1951).

6 See *Considerations on Representative Government* (London, 1861), pp. 207–8, 277–9.

7 F. A. Hayek, 'Individualism: True and False', in *Individualism and Economic Order* (London, 1949).

8 See for instance G. Hodgson, *Economics and Institutions* (Oxford, 1988); and L. M. Lachmann, *The Market as an Economic Process* (Oxford, 1986).

9 Co-ordination for example of Research and Development, product development, production scheduling: a co-ordination process made easier by electronics technology. See R. Kaplinsky, 'Electronics-based Automation Techniques and the Onset of Systemofacture', *World Development*, 13, 3 (1985). Also A. Sayer, 'New

Developments in Manufacturing: The Just-in-time System', *Capital and Class*, 30 (1986).

10   See *The Global Chocolate Factory*, published by the Transnational Information Exchange, the International Food Union and the Dutch Food Workers' Union. (Available from TIE, Paulus Potterstraat 20, 1071 DA Amsterdam, The Netherlands).

11   The work of these networks could be seen as in effect preparing them for self-management if and when these concentrations of economic power are broken up – through self implosion (cf. the Maxwell empire), state action or some unpredictable combinations.

12   In Britain these include the various regional Low Pay Units, Hazards Centres and some Trade Union and Community Resources Centres and Centres for the Unemployed.

13   In Britain, organisations which have organised such action on consumption include 'Women Working World Wide' and 'Friends of the Earth'.

14   See Diane Elson, 'The Socialisation of the Market', in *New Left Review* 190, for ideas about decentralized forms of price setting and control.

15   See Diane Elson in *NLR* 190, and also 'Socialising the Market: Breaking the Circuit of Capital', in *Socialism and the Market*, ed. Justin Schwartz (London, 1993).

16   For a timely guard against sweeping statements about globalization see a most useful analysis of both the trends towards internationalization and the limits on this process, for example in labour markets: 'Global but Leaderless? The New Capitalist Order', in *Socialist Register* (1992).

17   See copies of the regular TIE Newsletter. I should add that these discussions are no 'freebies' for the activists who attend. TIE managed to raise funds, for example from the World Council of Churches, to contribute to fares, but participants have to get their shop stewards' committee to pay the rest or cover it themselves. Very often they have had to contribute from their own pockets.

18   By 1984, the Combine did manage to draw national officials behind them. Together they obtained the support of municipal authorities in London and Liverpool to gain a wider audience and a political platform for the kind of policies they had developed through their international discussions. They organized an international conference of Ford workers' representatives across the globe and a well-publicized public inquiry into Ford's investment strategy. But they were a victim of their own success. They lost control over the follow-up and further international initiatives have been slow to get off the ground.

19   This does not mean that unionization was easy. In the 1930s it took considerable courage to start a union in the British midlands or northern Italy. Motors were a strategic sector of the economy, however, and once militants broke through, the union hierarchy saw it was in their interests to devote considerable resources to maintaining union strength.

20   See Swasti Mitter, *New Technology and the Rise of Manufacturing Homework: A Case*

Study in the UK Clothing Industry (1984).

21 See Sheila Rowbotham, *Flexible Production and Women's Casualised Labour; Strategic Approaches to Homework.* A Paper for the Working Group on Economic and Social Cohesion.

22 An impressive history of SEWA and analysis of its considerable importance has been written by Kalinia Rose, entitled *Where Women Are Leaders: The SEWA Movement in India* (London, 1992). SEWA produce their own bulletin: *We, the Self-Employed*, available from Self-Employed Women's Association, Ahmedabad 380017, India. For further history, analysis and description of the contemporary position of homeworkers and their organizations, see S. Rowbotham, *Homeworkers Worldwide* (London, 1993). See also *Dignity and Daily Bread: New Forms of Economic Organizing Among Poor Women in the Third World and the First* (London and New York, 1993).

23 A visible result of this work in London in the early 1980s was a city-wide conference of homeworkers groups, sympathetic trade unions and the Greater London Council. For the first time in decades, homeworkers had a public voice.

The conference provided a platform for a wide range of ideas overlooked by the benevolent, protective state. To some extent the participants took the achievements of this state for granted and put their emphasis on how poor women could achieve more self-determination in their lives by improving access to levers of choice and control. Their demands were addressed to many different organizations: to trade unions to include homeworkers' wages and conditions in all agreements, to work with community organizations to promote the interests of homeworkers and to reorganize their structures so as to make them more accessible to home workers. They had an even longer list of demands to local authorities, and to the Labour Party nationally. Then they spelt out how women's groups and community groups could help homeworkers become better organized. Their needs here were, first, the extension of homeworkers networks across the country and internationally so that all the threads of homeworking could be tracked. Second, they wanted an enrichment of the options in their own localities beyond pressure and propaganda to include the co-operative approach best pioneered by SEWA.

24 For the story and the ideas that inspired it told by one of the leading activists see Mike Cooley, *Architect or Bee?* (London, 1987); and for a detailed narrative based on interviews with most of the participants see Hilary Wainwright and Dave Elliott, *The Lucas Plan; A New Trade unionism in the Making* (London, 1982).

25 Tony Benn was sympathetic to radical initiatives from below to shake up the industrial and political establishment. He had been considerably radicalized by both his previous experiences as Minister for Technology in an earlier Labour Government, and by witnessing the occupations and work-ins of trade unionists resisting the first repercussions of the recession.

26 See page 179 of this chapter.

27 See Theresa Hayter's chapter in *A Taste of Power: The Politics of Local Economics*, eds M. MacIntosh and H. Wainwright (London, 1987).

28 Though Diane Elson's article in *New Left Review* 190 on 'The Socialization of the Market' is a major step in this direction, building especially on the concern of the women's movement with the reproduction of labour power, a process which is vitally affected by the way that consumption is organized.

29 A particularly influential book was Vance Packard's *The Hidden Persuaders* (latest edn, London, 1981).

30 TWIN and TWIN Trading produce a regular newsletter on alternative trade and technology. It is available from TWIN Ltd., 4th floor, 5–11 Worship Street, London EC2A 2BH.

31 For a summary of this literature see *Markets, Hierarchies and Networks*, ed. Grahame Thompson (London, 1991).

32 In a world of less and less rule – governed economic activity, the networks of the rich and powerful seem to be more essential than ever to the preservation of their interests.

33 As market and resource limits on mass production have pushed the competitive frontiers to design and identifying specialized market niches; skill, knowledge and information have come to figure more clearly as variables in the equations of economic success. Networks between designers and universities and the creative 'synergy' of science parks are positively recommended. Normally down-to-earth business journals wax lyrical about the benefits of intellectual cafe life where the brains, business and science supposedly gather.

The problems of adapting to the economic realities following the oil crisis and to the new competitive pressures of a rapidly restructuring world market, have led to a very up-market kind of networking: between the government, banks and business managment, drawing on the expertise of technologists. The Japanese Ministry of Industry and Technology provides the model.

34 See Pat Devine, *Democracy and Economic Planning* (Cambridge, 1988); Alain Lipietz, *Towards a New Economic Order* (Cambridge, 1992); Michael Barratt-Brown, *European Union: Fortress or Democracy* (Nottingham, 1991). See also the proposals of Hans Breitenbach, Tom Burden and David Coates in *Features of a Viable Socialism* (Hertfordshire, 1990).

35 Michael Barratt-Brown has an extended discussion of the concept of 'networkers' in *European Union*.

36 There is an extensive literature on 'the Third Italy'. See Sebastiano Brusco, 'The Emilian Model', *Cambridge Journal of Economics*, 6, pp. 167–84; 'Small Firms and Industrial Districts: The Experience of Italy', in *New Firms and Regional Development in Europe*, eds D. Keeble and E. Wever; Fergus Murray, 'Flexible Specialisation in the "Third Italy"', *Race and Class*, 33, 1987; Michael Best, *The New Competition: Institutions of Industrial Restructuring*, chapter 7 (Cambridge, 1990).

37 The contrast is between their methods of economic co-ordination and utilization of knowledge. There are likely to be close connections between enterprises in

Carpi and Benetton: no doubt enterprises in Carpi sometimes carry out sub-contract work for Benetton. And some of the larger firms in the Modena area aspire to be like Benetton.

38 See Kenneth Labich, 'Benetton Takes On the World', *Fortune*, 13 June 1983.

39 See *Beneath the Veneer*, which documents the ideas of shop stewards from FTAT (the trade union of Furniture and Allied Trades), published by the GLC's Popular Planning Unit (London, 1986). Available from the Centre for Local Economic Strategies, Alberton House, St Mary's Parsonage, Manchester M3 2WJ. The GLC's industrial strategy, *The London Industrial Strategy*, should be available from the same address.

40 New York, 1988. See also H. Thomas and Chris Logan, *Mondragón: An Economic Analysis* (London, 1982), and *We Build the Road as We Travel* (Philadelphia, 1991). Articles include 'Mondragón: Spain's Oasis of Democracy', *Observer*, 21 January 1973. K. Bradley and A. Gelb, 'Motivation and Control of the Mondragón Experiment', *British Journal of Industrial Relations*, 19 (1981); 'The Replicability and Sustainability of the Mondragón Experiment', *British Journal of Industrial Relations*, 20 (1982); 'The Basque Workers' Co-operatives', *Industrial Relations Journal*, 10 (1979).

41 In London the situation was in a sense politically misleading. The left's control of a regional Labour Party, the London Labour Party, gave it a taste of admin-istrative power before it had mass popular support. In effect it was in a coalition with right-of-centre and social democrats, but it was in the leadership of this coalition; whereas in Denmark, West Germany and Norway, new left parties have won a sufficient number of votes on their own terms to be in municipal coalitions with social democracy, but not enough to be laying down the direc-tion of the coalition.

42 The peculiarities of Labour politics in Britain, however, mean that although the left is in a permanantly subordinate position nationally, on a local level it can, with astute wheeling and dealing, end up with municipal office. This was how new left activists-turned-Labour-Councillors ended up running the administra-tion of London from 1981 until London-wide government was abolished by Mrs Thatcher in 1986.

43 It later won popular support, partly through policies such as cutting fares on London's buses and underground, through its open style and by being cast as the underdog in the face of Thatcher's successful attempt to close it down.

44 In a certain sense, these experiences of the new forms of economic regulation and co-ordination are not very much more developed than in the East. Elements of them – the various civic economic organizations and a relatively democratic local state – of course, have very much stronger roots. But as economic institu-tions they are undeveloped, with a few notable exceptions. The problem is that while in the East state domination of the economy has been a material fact, in the West the *idea* of the domination of the economy by a democratic state has policed the mental universe of the left, stifling the imagination of more complex

forms of popular soverignty over the economy.

45 These gave it another kind of leverage on the economy – though conventional economists rarely thought of these public service activities as part of the economy.

46 See Ken Livingstone's *If Voting Changed Anything, They Would Abolish It* (London, 1987) for the story of how the left gained office, what it did with it and how the Government abolished the GLC. See *A Taste of Power; the Politics of Local Economics*, for more details of the experience of the GLC's economic policy.

47 The GLC Research Library did in fact keep an impressive store of publications from community groups, but until the new administration came in their was little history of collaboration with these groups on economic and planning matters.

48 This autonomy might sometimes involve biting the hand that fed them. 'If it had gone into a second term, the GLC would have had a hard time,' remarked Mandy Cook, who worked on grants for the Industry and Employment Department, 'because it would have faced challenges from groups of people who had developed the confidence and had the time to look at things clearly'.

49 See chapters 6 and 8 of *A Taste of Power*.

50 Hayek, 'The Use of Knowledge in Society', in *Individualism and Economic Order* (London, 1949), p. 78.

51 See David Prychitko, *Marxism and Workers Self-management, The Essential Tension* (New York, 1992).

7

POLITICAL PARTIES OF
A NEW KIND?

Introduction

Earlier chapters have demonstrated the importance of a new approach to social
and economic knowledge: one that values and seeks to share its practical
dimension while seeking to democratize its theoretical dimension. The last
two chapters have illustrated the way in which innovative forms of democratic
association, originating in the movements of the late sixties, seventies and
eighties, provided collective means of utilizing knowledge stemming from
experience. Their experiments illustrated the importance of these new forms
of organization, autonomous, though not entirely separate, from both state
and market. But we also observed that non-state forms of public action need
a supportive and independent relationship to political power if they are to be
effective agents of economic and social change. For instance, the Gothenburg
school would have been extremely difficult, if not impossible, without the
economic and political conditions of social democratic Sweden; on the other
hand, we saw in chapter 6 the weakness of networks of economic resistence
that lacked political allies.

The problem is establishing a relationship in which political representatives respect the distinct sources of power and knowledge of democratic
movements. Although circumstances were very different, as were the character of 'the movements', activists in social movements in the West and the
oppositionists who led the civic movements in the East shared a mixture of
contempt and hostility towards professional politicians and political parties.
In the early 1980s especially, with the growth of a pan-European movement
(or perhaps more accurately, network) for peace and democracy, the writings
of East European intellectuals on anti-politics struck a chord with the politi-

cally homeless Western new left. Movement activists on both sides of the Iron Curtain were searching in practice and in their imagination for forms of organization through which to create a source of political power that was grounded in individual integrity. For a very brief period, the popular movements that led the transformations in Czechoslovakia (Obcanske Forum: 'Civic Forum') and in East Germany (Neues Forum: 'New Forum') particularly appeared as if they might provide a model.[1] Many of the leaders of these movements believed they were creating a new form of politics: anti-politics seemed to be becoming a political force with its own groundsprings of power. Indeed, so strongly did the advocates of anti-politics believe that through these movements they were creating a new political form, that they resisted pressures either to turn or break up these movements into political parties.

Paradoxically, these advocates of a democratic civil society were defeated by the absence of such associations. For without a strong base of voluntary public organizations working for democratic transformations, the civic movements that arose to overthrow repressive one-party regimes quickly succumbed to the conventional Western model of parliamentary parties whose all-consuming priority is electoral politics. As they clung on to the movements, working hard to preserve their unity, others were organizing the political parties which reduced the advocates of 'movement politics' to a rump in both the Czech Republic and Slovakia, and a small minority in what was East Germany.[2]

The movement politicians were in a contradictory position. At the same time as being deeply suspicious of political parties, and fervent advocates of social change through a reinvented democratic civil society, they wanted some form of pluralist parliamentary politics. Unsurprisingly, they had little notion of the possible relationship between the two. At the opening session of the Helsinki Citizens' Assembly in October 1990, Vaclav Havel, one of best-known writers on anti-politics, illustrated but did not resolve the problem. On the one hand he reiterated the theme of much of his writing as a playwright and boiler-stoker before 1989: 'true social impact resides in the strength of the word of truth, in a person's courage to call things by their true names, regardless of consequences.' Speaking the truth could be done without parties, indeed was more likely to be done without parties. On the one hand he accepted that since entering, in his words, 'the world of high politics', he was becoming a 'technologist of power'. He defended this on the grounds that it was in the interests, he believed, of building 'a new, different, truly democratic system'. 'Simply,' he explained, 'a person in the world of high politics is forced to manoeuvre, to take acount of various conflicting interests, of various ambitions, of the balance of power represented by different groupings. Such a person is forced to behave diplomatically. Simply, we are now in a different arena.' Later on, however, he stated starkly that 'It is possible to pursue what we perhaps imprecisely called "non-political politics" . . . it is possible to do this even when you hold power. This I firmly believe and stand behind'.[3]

Havel's language in this speech (vivid and specific when describing the 'world of high politics', uncharacteristically vague when describing the democratic politics of civic movements) betrayed the fact that there was little positive connection between the two kinds of politics in the Czech and Slovak Republics after the euphoria of the revolution was over. The problem of the relationship remained unresolved. The question of whether there are alternative technologies of power to that which governs the existing machinery of state has hardly been asked.

It would be smug, though, to imply that there was a clear model in the West of what such a positive connection might look like. The predominant historical models of relations between politics and civic movements are those between Labour and Communist Parties and the working class organized through the trade unions. In both the parties of Second International and the Third International, the movements, predominantly the trade union movement, were quite explicitly subordinate to the leadership or representation of the political parties.

Recent social movements in the West have been trying to achieve more equal relationships between themselves and sympathetic political representatives; at times the movements have insisted that political representatives are nothing more than 'voices'. Their orientation towards the parliamentary system is different from that of movement activists in the East. The movements in the East grew up perforce outside the one-party political system. They saw parliamentary democracy as one of their aims. The movements in the West organized their base camps outside the parliamentary political system, through choice, because parliament had proved an ineffective instrument of democratic decisions. Ironically, the lessons of experience have brought the views of these two groups closer.

Eastern oppositionists tended to rush headlong into parliament, realizing belatedly that an active civil society would not be born overnight: it needed mid-wives working overtime. Western movement activists, on the other hand, found that they needed political representation and, if possible, access to office. They wanted this access, however, but on the strength of their extra-parliamentary base. The problem for social movements in the West has been one of establishing the kind of relationship by which political representation amplifies and legitimates collective social and economic action, rather than substitutes for it, causing gradual asphyxiation.

Movements and different kinds of parties

For the last twenty-five years or so, social movements in Western Europe have been serious rivals to the traditional parties of the left – Social Democratic, Labourist and Communist; not rivals which play the same game, competing within common rules, but rivals playing a more engrossing game on an adjoining field, sometimes with flair, sometimes in chaos, sometimes taunting the players over the fence, sometimes making a tactical alliance. It is a more fundamental rivalry than the electoral competition created by the parties, like the Greens in Germany or the Green Left in the Netherlands, which explicitly support the social movements. What seems to have been going on in Western Europe is an underlying rivalry of political method rather than simply of political parties.

The rivalry shows up, for instance, in surveys of the populations of several West European countries since 1945, measuring peoples' interest in politics and both their participation in unconventional (non-party) political activity and their membership and activism in political parties. While interest in politics and participation in unconventional activity, such as petitions and campaigns, showed an underlying rise, active membership of the traditional political parties of the left (and the right) declined over the last twenty-five years – with one or two fluctuations in between.[4] The ebb, especially of youth, away from the traditional parties has not been followed by an equivalent flow towards membership of (as distinct from electoral support for) new parties more directly reflecting social movement politics. (A distinctive feature of these new left parties is a low membership compared with the extent of electoral support – and probably the extent of the non-party activism of these voters. In Germany, the Netherlands, Denmark and Norway the voter – member ratio of, respectively, the Greens, the Green Left, the Socialist People's Party and the Left Socialists is lower than that of the main established parties of the left and the right.[5])

The social movements of the last twenty-five years, and the fragmented projects and campaigns they have spawned – with all their limitations – have challenged the monopoly claimed by traditional left parties on the leadership of social and economic change.[6] Women running rape crisis centres, squatters campaigning for homes, trade unionists striking for a shorter working week, peace activists camping around a military base, have not spurned support from political parties (they frequently lobby for political allies), but they believe they are *already* engaged in a project of social transformation. Moreover, in being so, often they see themselves as acting as politically as they might within a political party – though often with more immediate effect. Movement activists are also wary of allowing the new parties which champion their cause electorally to establish a monopoly. They see a sympathetic political party as potentially supporting a dynamic of political change of which they themselves are a vital motor.

When the euphoria lifts and the power structures adjust

Self-confidence amongst persistent social movement activists, however, has been combined increasingly with a political realism. There have been moments when it seemed as if the social movements could sweep all before them. It is euphoric to nearly win, or at least to feel part of a near victory, especially if one starts off alone and ends up part of a movement. At times the very creation of a movement can soften the perception of defeat. But the point about defeat, however close, is that the successful enemy learns, regroups, retools and prepares to fight another day, or even to absorb conflict. In France the Gaullists survived 1968 to modernize the centralized French state; in Germany, the education system recovered from the challenge of the student movement by adapting and absorbing selectively some of its less subversive demands; in Italy, Fiat survived the 'hot autumn' of 1969 and its repercussions throughout the 1970s to organize production so that it was less vulnerable to workers' actions. Just as construction technology develops after earthquakes to make buildings at once stronger and more flexible, so the state and private corporations of post-war Western Europe learnt from the rebellions of the late 1960s and from the oil crisis of 1973, to build into their organizations a new flexibility, at the same time as strengthening their centralized capacity to control a complex whole. They even plagiarized the language of the social movements in the process – from 'loose structures' through 'networks' and 'circles' to 'sharing leadership'.

Sometimes the movements have overestimated the importance of success in one sphere and at one moment. The Conservative Party in Britain and the Republican right in the US recovered, at least politically if not economically, from defeat at the hands of the miners and (in the US) in Vietnam, with new weapons of attack – especially the freeing of government from the management of social provision and industrial support. The result of these processes, aided by information technology, is a more co-ordinated, more globally interconnected, more sophisticated capitalist ruling order. It is not an order without contradictions, however: notably of recurring recession and competition between new transnational regional economic blocs.

Social movement politics, shaped by its roots in circumstances of expansion, social provision, and popular political self-confidence, took a battering under the new strategies of industry and state across Western Europe in the late 1970s and in the 1980s. A background of growing unemployment, especially in Britain, Italy and France, sapped an earlier self-confidence to attempt the impossible. There were self-inflicted failures too.[5] On many fronts there seemed to be a retreat from the public battlefield: education and industry were no longer permanently the sites of dramatic struggle. Nonetheless, the German metalworkers' strike of 1984, the strike of British miners in 1985 and the militancy of public sector workers in France – all manifesting demands and forms of organizing influenced by the innovations of the 1970s – indicated that the war had not been won, even if the terrain was more of the employers' choosing. On directly political issues – nuclear power, the deployment of missiles and, more recently, anti-racism, for example – movement networks created over the previous decade have provided the infrastructure of powerful mass mobilizations on an international scale.

The strengths of the social movements, rather like a guerrilla army, stem from the fact that, mostly, they aim to act with the people on the ground. In general their campaigning and organizing is based closer to the majority of people's daily lives than the episodic electoral populism of the traditional political parties of the left. However, just as a guerrilla army faces a centralized and powerful enemy, so with the social movements and the parties which support them. Their base and the source of power is local (that is, where people live, work and socialise); but these movements can only achieve their goals if they are able to mobilize and exert this localized strength against corporations and unaccountable political bureaucracies whose power is national, and increasingly international. Moreover, several of the goals themselves – economic equality, ecological safety and sustainability, and the provision for social need among them – require democratic decision making with binding national and international authority.[8]

When the movements first emerged, a certain amount of centralization and cohesion occurred spontaneously. The first discovery of the power of self-organization and the revelations that action brings of the interrelatedness of different problems produced a burst of energy. Newly radicalized activists busily made connections, went to conferences, produced newsletters and created in effect an alternative political culture. More exceptionally, this became the basis for alternative political institutions. In most major European cities (Kreuzburg in Berlin, Staatsliedenburt in Amsterdam, and so on) the cultural products of this are still there, strengthened sometimes by the self-reliant cultures of black or other minority communities, commercialized somewhat, as a means of survival. But on the whole, these cultural oases have been marginal and subordinate except where they have had a political voice and a wider national and international cultural expression or organized network.

Sporadically, movement projects and organizations produce regular publications through which to co-ordinate and interconnect their activities. Activists establish centres of various kinds which give the movement left a lasting physical presence and informal cohesion. The more organized and far-sighted are assiduously creating international networks using communications technology to the fullest that their resources will allow.[9] But rarely have movement activists devoted much attention to how to create lasting forums and connecting mechanisms between movements.

Instead, they have either remained disparate, as in France; or found an occasional focus in a local or national left within the major working class party, as in Britain; or, where the electoral system is favourable to minorities, they have looked to the possibility of direct political representation as a stimulus to some kind of precarious unity.

The public competition for state control, however chimeral or displaced from the real sources of power this struggle might be, is, in a modern capitalist society, an immensely powerful concentrating force. Social activities that are not pulled into some relation to state institutions or lulled into acquiescence with the consensus by which it is governed, can be easily marginalized. Extra-parliamentary movements and struggles can occasionally break through by a mighty, concerted effort. But their power to do so depends on the extraordinary activity of thousands of people breaking the routines of their everyday lives. With livelihoods to earn and dependents to care for, it is difficult to keep up the pace and intensity of the kind of mobilization which hits the headlines and forces an issue into public debate. State apparatuses and conventional political parties do not have this problem. They earn their livelihoods from political power and office.

Recent movements of the left have found that a sustained public presence, itself vital for keeping their networks and projects alive, requires the focus, the public platform and the resources – which can be gained in most West European parliamentary democracies through representation in national, regional and local assemblies. Evidence for this can be seen in the creation of new parties directly from extra-parliamentary movements (the German

Greens are the most notable example of this), the concerted influence on existing parties of the radical left (developments in Norway, Denmark and Holland illustrate this), and the creative use of occasional opportunities for local power (as in the case of the GLC in the early 1980s).

The problem has been how to ensure that these representatives act in the service of the movements, their supposed masters who are usually very much weaker than then they, the ostensible political servants backed by the resources of the state. But at least there is a tension, a two-way relationship. The party does not have a monopoly over the agency of transformation.[10]

With varying degrees of explicit commitment those parties created or powerfully influenced by recent movements on the left have in common a modesty – at least in theory – about their own role in the process of social transformation. This is underpinned by a scepticism about how much a parliamentary victory on its own can achieve. That is, the self-defined purpose of these parties tends to be to use the state institutions over which they have some control to enable or support independent citizens' action, rather than to act as if radical change can be brought about exclusively or even primarily from within the legislature.[11]

There are notable examples of attempts, fraught with problems, to use control over state institutions to strengthen the self-organization of groups facing problems which that state institution is incapable on its own of resolving. The most publicized include the Women's and Ethnic Minority Committees of the Greater London Council and the Foreigners' Committee of the city government of Frankfurt (established by Danny Cohn-Bendit). In other cases, such as Copenhagen and West Berlin, radical left parties in coalitions or responsible for particular departments have achieved similar effects, though not the same public impact, by working with social movements projects as their main means of formulating and implementing policies. This movement representation symbolizes a recognition that parties operating through the state do not have the inside knowledge and power to bring about the transformations to which they are committed. Neither can parties adequately represent that knowledge and the social driving forces which lie behind it.

This partnership between political parties and autonomous movements has many problems, some of which this chapter will discuss. The most obvious is the way that it can degenerate into either a corporatist relationship in which the state's embrace undermines the autonomy of the movement and makes them part of a single political body, or into a zero-sum particularism in which groups simply push sectional interests regardless of wider democratically agreed policies.[12] The importance of the partnership for the argument of this book is that, especially at a local or regional level, it provides a means by which the practical knowledge shared and accumulated by people to define and find solutions to their needs, influences the exercise of political power. It is a relationship between two distinct sources of power and knowledge, one based in society, the other within the state. Corporatism tends to refer to a situation where a social group pursues its interests through becoming a part of the state.

The new parties

i)   The German Greens

In March 1979, at a school hall near Frankfurt, 500 delegates from an ideologically dissonant range of organizations founded what was to become the first party created to serve the political purposes of the post 1968 citizens' movements: the 'Further Political Association' (FPA) – the Greens. There was no question that the various supporting organizations or movements should give up, delegating their work to 'The Party' as an organization able to encompass the totality of their vision. On the contrary, the idea was, as the title suggests, an association for limited purposes: an election campaign for a nuclear-free Europe and a decentralized 'Europe of the regions'. At the same time, other social movement and extra-parliamentary organizations were making similar electoral alliances for City and Land elections: conveying the minimal character of their political purpose with specifically electoral titles like Alternative List or Multicolored List.

In January of the following year these various alliances came together in Karlsruhe for the first constitutional convention of the Green Party, Die Grunen. The idea – it seemed so straightforward at the time – was to create 'a parliamentary voice for the social movements'. Movements, most dramatically the anti-nuclear movement, had won massive popular support only to have their demands completely ignored in the Bundestag and Länder, as if they counted for nothing.

The SPD-FDP Federal government not only used its parliamentary position to marginalize the anti-nuclear movement; its Chancellor, Helmut Schmidt, put intense and successful pressure on the DGB, the West German Trade Union Organization, to withdraw its support for a moratorium on new nuclear power stations. As part of a clampdown on the internal opposition that had flourished under Willy Brandt's somewhat more tolerant, progressive Chancellorship, the SPD leadership passed 'the muzzle decree', which required that every publication of Jusos, the increasingly radical youth movement of the SPD, had to be agreed by the party leadership.

The political steel wall which SPD coalitions – from 1966–9 with the CDU, as well as 1974–82 under Schmidt – erected against extra-parliamentary protest led a wide political range of movements to believe that a new party was the only chance of their demands gaining even a presence within the elected assemblies of the FRG. And many believed that a national, electorally legitimated voice was the only way for the left to break out of the isolation and sense of powerlessness which had bred the desperate though calculated political violence of Baader Meinhof. From the mid 1950s until the electoral competition from the Greens made itself felt by 1985 (with the partial exception of Brandt's rule), the SPD had become a more closed, more fiercely anti-communist, more fervently cold-war party than any social democratic party in Western Europe. The SPD Mayor of West Berlin reflected this culture at its most hysterical in his comments on the Ausserparlamentarische Opposition (APO, extra-parliamentary opposition) to the 1968 Party congress: 'You should see these characters. You should look them closely in the face, then you will know, their interest is to destroy our free political order.'[13]

Against this wall of political paranoia pushing back anything that disturbed the consensus, a momentum of unity developed amongst the disenfranchised. The people who met in Frankfurt and then again in Karlsruhe espoused many different political beliefs. A small minority were right-wing conservationists, who soon realized that the Greens were not an appropriate mouthpiece. The majority came to feel the need for a political voice after periods of varying lengths, talking, shouting, sometimes screaming into the political void as activists in the anti-authoritarian student movement, feminist, peace and ecology movements of the previous ten years or so. A significant minority had also been involved in the K-Gruppen, various Maoist influenced marxist groups, inside and outside the SPD. Ironically, Schmidt's leadership of the government and of his party had unwittingly welded together a unique political force, which later as an electoral competitor was to give the SPD a far more effective push to the left than the internal opposition which he so ruthlessly sought to suppress.

Apart from the initial conservative wing of the Greens, there was significant agreement on values and vision. From the start, Die Grunen was anti-capitalist. It was not an orthodox anti-capitalism. It was driven by a belief that capitalism's unrestrained growth entails the exploitation of exhaustible resources (for which future generations will have to pay), as well as fostering exploitation of people's need to sell their capacity to work. This represented a development of the early student movement questioning of the capitalist/

corporate state, into an explicit rejection of any notion that technological advance represented social and economic progress. This was an important break from the assumption, which under the influence of Soviet Marxism had become orthodoxy on parts of the left, that productive forces were the driving force of progress.[14]

The first disagreements, hardening into a paralysing factional struggle, were over questions of strategy: the role of the party's parliamentary representatives and whether or not the party should join coalitions with the SPD. At the same time, however, between 1979 and the Green's unexpected electoral breakthrough in 1983, the need for a public political presence, a voice, was so overwhelming that questions concerning the positioning of the voice, who it spoke to, its relation to other voices and so on, were left to the future.[15]

A balance sheet of the twelve years of Die Grünen can only be an interim one. On the one hand their electoral presence until German unification had undoubtedly helped to turn the SPD from being the most conservative social democratic party in Europe to the one most responsive, on paper, to the policies of the social movements. It adopted policies against nuclear weapons and power, and took on board much of the ecological and feminist agenda of the Greens. It remained broadly corporatist on economic and industrial policy rather than bending to the monetary orthodoxy sweeping through the rest of the Second International. This modest shift to the left, however, has not been tested in government.[16] Chancellor Kohl was able to orchestrate the process of unification in a manner which strengthened the conservative, nationalist sentiments amongst German people. He did so at a speed which left both the SPD and the Greens almost speechless.

Just when the need for the continued pressure of the Greens was demonstrated, their own future at a Federal level was dramatically weakened by their indecisiveness over unification. The sudden moves towards unification caught them looking in at least three different directions. Scepticism about unification, however, need not have been such a negative factor. Over half the German people also felt confused and ambiguous about the repercussions of Kohl's unification. But the Federal Greens seemed too preoccupied by internal battles even to offer a political transit point for voters with sound reasons for scepticism.

As the cold war stance of the SPD had thawed so the external pressure on the social movements to unify dissolved, and strategic and tactical divisons within the Greens became an apparently permanent blockage to the party's development. The shock of losing all their West German seats in the Bundestag in the first post-war all-German elections (they lost their seats under the 5 per cent rule, because their vote was 4.9 per cent), however, has led to a new sobriety towards factionalism, made easier (some would argue) by the departure both of those who were most insistently against any coalition ever, and those most hostile to any form of socialism. In Land and city elections in 1991 the Greens have done relatively well. In the Länder of Hesse and Lower Saxony, for example, they have won over 8 per cent of the vote and are in coalition with the SPD, in Bremen with the FDP and SDP, while in the city of Munich they formed a new coalition with the SPD. This regional strength indicates that the Party has roots which give it the stability from which it might resolve its difficulties as a Federal party.

ii) The Danish Socialist People's Party

Parties which provide a political voice for recent social movements have also been the product of an earlier breakaway from a traditional left party. So it was with the Socialist People's Party (Socialistisk Folkeparti, SF) in Denmark.[17] This began as a majority breakaway from the Danish Communist Party. The split was over the Soviet Union's repression of the Hungarian uprising, and then Soviet antagonism towards Tito's Yugoslavia. But these disagreements led the breakaway party to reject also the political methods of Soviet Communist Parties: notably democratic centralism and the assumption that the Communist Party alone can lead the way to socialism. They threw out too the CP's narrowly workerist definition of social forces, with an interest in socialist transformation. And they rooted out the underlying philosophy of a deterministic, scientistic, teleological view of socialism.

This was in 1959 and 1960. In Denmark, as elsewhere in Western Europe, reactions to 1956 and debates about Yugoslavia laid many of the intellectual foundations of the new left. But at that stage, movements for radical transformation, autonomous of political parties, were thin on the ground. The new party programme of the Danish SF talked vaguely about support for the trade unions and working-class struggles, but in its first decade the party was first and foremost a parliamentary party, albeit a radical one. Its prime strategy for socialist transformation was building the bargaining power for a coalition with the Social Democrats – and this meant parliamentary bargaining power. When it did enter coalition in 1967, it found that it lacked the bargaining power to defend the inflation-linked indexing of pensions and social security payments. A part of its membership formed a breakaway, called the Left Socialists, which went on to win six seats and on some issues acted as an electoral pull on the party to move to the left. Many of its members have since returned to the SF and it is no longer represented in the parliament.

Throughout the early and mid seventies, activists from the social movements (the women's and anti-nuclear movements in particular) and a radical minority in the trade unions joined both parties; though the Socialist People's Party with 11 per cent of the vote and an open and democratic structure was the greater draw (the Left Socialists organized, more or less, on a Leninist model). This new generation of activists made use of the SF's openness to bring about a process of further democratization. They transformed the party's relationship to the political system, pulling its activity towards the social movements, opening up direct channels of communication between these movements and the party and winning a commitment to 40 per cent women on every party committee. In the process they replaced almost all the old leadership, including Omann, Chairman of the party from 1968–74, who left with several others and later joined the Social Democrats. The new, mainly social movement or ex-social movement activists have created a party which has had considerable electoral success and retains close, although mainly informal, links with the campaigns and projects of the social and radical trade union movements.

The new attitude of the party towards coalition was to continue to aim for coalition but only on equal terms. They were not thinking so much of parliamentary parity but an equality which they believe can only be achieved if they work closely with 'basic or grass-roots movements' including radical trade unionists – 'not to embrace them like the old Communists did', warned Gert Pedersen, Chairman of the party from 1974 until 1990 and himself an ex-member of the Danish Communists. The balance in the party's activities depended of course on the strength of the movements: the height of work with the movements nationally was with the anti-nuclear and peace movements. But in Denmark's municipalities, where the ecology and women's movements are a lively part of daily life, these movements are also, through co-operation with the SF, guiding the decisions of the municipality. The SF holds the balance of power or is part of a 'red' (SF and Social Democrat) coalition in two thirds of Denmark's municipal councils. Its share of the vote at the last local elections was 11 per cent – 4 per cent more than at the last general election.

The effectiveness of the SF in combining a practical parliamentary and municipal strategy with sustained support for militant extra-parliamentary movements has been helped by the fact that, unlike the Italian Communist Party, which did not fully break organizationally from Moscow (or from democratic centralism) until the 1970s, they have not felt guilty and vulnerable to pressures to make themselves respectable and legitimate. This is a pressure which leads, judging from the experience of the Italian and British

Communist Parties, to the overhwelming predominance of parliamentary concerns and conventions. The early and complete break of the SF's founding members has given them the freedom to be radically left without constantly have to prove they are not tools of Moscow.

The Danish Socialist People's Party still tends in practice to be dominated by its parliamentary group, in spite of its commitments to the movements and its procedures for avoiding this dominance. A new leader was recently elected – 40-year-old Holger Nielson – after a gruellingly democratic election campaign in which he and his opponent spoke before every party branch across the country. Holger, radicalized as a student in 1968, but an MP since 1980, replaces Gert Pedersen, a founding father of the party and first and foremost a socialist parliamentarian, though very open to the ideas of the new movements. The party is probably open now to pressure for a shift in emphasis towards efforts at change through trade unions and extra-parliamentary action. But established political routines, backed by the sigificant resources provided by the state do not easily dissolve. Moreover there is at present little sustained extra-parliamentary pressure.

iii)   The Dutch Green Left

A third variant in the process of parties emerging to express the politics of the social movements is the amalgamation of several left parties, which through common involvement with the new movements find their political ideas converging. The Dutch Green Left is a good example. In the spring of 1989, the Radical Political Party (PPR) the Pacifist–Socialist Party (PSP), the Communist Party of the Netherlands (CPN) and the Evangelical People's Party (EVP) formed a common front. Under the Green Left banner it won more seats (6 rather than 3), together with a campaign that had greater national impact than their separate efforts. Moreover, activists new to any of the existing parties began to join; and in fact one of the new MPs, Paul Rosenmöller, a radical dockers' leader from Rotterdam, was not a member of any party. Similarly, another leading candidate was chosen for her work organizing immigrants; she was not a party member. Unaffiliated social movement activists were also represented on the board of the Green Left. As Wil Evers, editor of *Green Left* put it, 'The impetus for the Green Left came from the social movements.'[18]

The parties which now make up the Green Left recognized the consequences of the movements for the development of their own theory and action as a political party. As they merged their different organizations, they sought consciously to build an organization which was based on the fact, as Joost

Lagendijk, International Secretary of the Dutch Green Left, observes, 'that most party members and future members are also active in a variety of social movements and campaigns with very practical objectives and would only want occasionally to be heavily involved in the party.' The Green Left's policy making consciously aims to draw on the knowledge accumulated in social movement campaigns and research projects. In the process, they have succeeded in creating forums for discussion and joint action across the social movements which have benefitted the movements as well as the party.

Of the three parties, the German Greens, the SF and the Dutch Green Left, the Green Left has been most self-conscious about negotiating formal relationships with social movements organizations. One reason is that social movement organizations in Holland are, like all voluntary organizations in this country, more institutionalized than anywhere else. Many of them, especially those concerned with social welfare and minority rights, receive financial support from municipal councils – a tendency strengthened by the Green Left's growing influence at a municipal level. Moreover, some of them have become accustomed to negotiations with political parties through constant attempts to draw them into state commissions which produce worthy reports but rarely have practical results. (It is interesting that neither the peace movement nor the anti-nuclear movement, both targetting issues at the heart of the state's power, are welcomed into this paternal embrace. The militant anti-apartheid movement which developed in Holland in the 1980s was also kept outside the commissions of the Dutch state.)

Joost Lagendijk gives another, more internal reason for the Left Greens' conscious efforts to establish regular working relations with the social movements: 'Because all of us were giving up old party habits and interests we had to think through every step carefully; and we've been able to learn from the mistakes of the German Greens.' Joost has attended several conference of Die Grunen, and as International Secretary has been able to observe the growing pains of new left and new green parties across Western Europe.

The Dutch Green Left, however, is still very small, especially compared to the strength of social movements in Holland. The Green Left's recent votes, in the European and local election, were over 7 per cent. They have 400 councillors, six MPs (out of a parliament of 150) and a membership of 13,000. Moreover, this new party is not proving to be the prime beneficiary of the demise of social democracy in Holland. The party that has grown fastest as a radical opposition party is the radical liberal party, Democracy 66 (known as D66), which is making the most electoral headway. For all its new structures, it is still the old faces of the leaderships of the original, failing parties which give the Green Left its image. This might be one explanation of their failure to gain from the clear desire for an alternative to the conservative of Dutch Labour. Another factor is that on economic issues D66 has been moving with the tide of neo-liberal economics. Perhaps as this economics is increasingly perceived as anti-democratic in its consequences, the Green Left, with a renewed leadership, will find its opportinity.

The island exception

In Northern Europe, Britain provides an exception. No new left or new left influenced party has secured any Britain-wide political representation.[20] Political representation of the left has been monopolized by the Labour Party, and the social movements on the left have had, with some short-lived success, to bang persistently on its door. Any breakthrough, usually at a local level, has, under the leadership of Neil Kinnock, led to metal reinforcements.[21]

However, as the British state begins, in its creaky manner, to break up, Labour finds itself unable to sustain its position, at least as far as Scotland and Wales are concerned. Both Plaid Cymru and the Scottish National Party have a significant radical left minorities,[22] and due to the geographic concentration of their support they have representation in the UK parliament as well as in local councils. Moreover, the Conservative Party's success, aided by the first-past-the-post electoral system, in driving Labour back to its North of England stronghold, has opened the Labour Party to the attractions of electoral reform. An increasing number of Labour politicians recognize that only with a pro-portional electoral system can Labour be re-established as a national party, albeit without its accustomed monopoly.

British exceptionalism is thus closely bound up with the particularly undemocratic character of its parliamentary system: the centralization of power in the hands of a Westminster executive, the first-past-the-post elec-toral system, a second chamber based in part on principles of inheritence and, protecting all of these, the unwritten character of its constitution at the heart of which are the powers that the Prime Minister wields through the royal prerogative.

British exceptionalism is also shaped by the founding institutions of working-class politics, which in turn developed a vested interest in the undemocratic character of the state it was seeking to govern. The British Labour Party never was in a full sense a social democratic party. As a creature of one of the strongest trade union movements in the world, it has had a dual and at times chimerical character.

On the one hand, as formally 'the party of the working class', it appears, especially at times of working-class militancy, to have the potential to bring about radical reform – far more radical than the reforms of a continental social democratic party lacking direct links with workers' organization. The hope that this potential might one day be realized has tended to make the left ultimately loyal to the party. On the other hand, the character of these linkages (in particular the fact that the locuses of power lie with the leadership of trade unions and parliamentary parties rather than, say, with the workplace organizations, local constituency parties and MPs) are shaped by the origins of the party as, literally, the Representation Committee of the trade unions. This has placed the party in a permanently defensive position, seeking to represent the interests of a class within the existing economic and political framework. Its rhetoric and, at times, many of its proclaimed policies are very much more radical in their scope. But without exception, Labour leaders have been preoccupied with proving their capacity and that of the party to govern; to govern, that is, with the instruments of the existing state. This has created a philistine political culture and centralized institutions, quick to repress activities that might offend existing parliamentary custom and practice.

Furthermore, it has protected itself from any electoral challenge from the left by stoutly defending the first-past-the-post electoral system.[23] This electoral system rebuffs the minority challenger from the left not only through the unscalable arithmetic that it requires to gain a representative, but also through the way that it pulls the political spectrum to the centre. The divisions within the Green Party in Britain are in part the product of this pressure. This party never aspired as clearly to be a voice for the movements of the left as Die Grünen or the Dutch Green Left. Its origins were much more politically heterogeneous. But the electoral system has undoubtedly further undermined its ability to establish a confident political identity.[24]

It was an electoral system that in Labour's view suited its immediate interest: to get into government, whatever the popular mandate. Labour made the assumption that office alone would enable it to carry out its commitments. At certain points, between 1945–7 in particular, it carried through important reforms, but within limits that later became fatally constraining (namely, the party tried to hold itself to reforms that would not interfere with the workings of the City). Any such challenge would require a genuinely popular mandate; without this, financial and industrial interests have always been able to call Labour's bluff.[25] Like an unfit runner with a licence to cheat,

Labour has always got to the winning post by a short cut. It has never had to win the support of the overall majority. Nor, once in office, has Labour ever developed a strategy of popular alliances – like those of the 1982 GLC – to use office to create a popular mandate, and popular initiative, for radical policies.

This diversion to a Western Island of the continent has implications for our map of the variations in the politics of the left shaped by the social movements. It means that in the nations and regions of Britain this left has a double task: to mobilize for a democratic constitution as a condition for then establishing their own independent voices. Charter 88 has provided a focus for a widely-based coalition for a democratic written constitution involving electoral reform, a bill of rights, and an end to a hereditary second chamber, the Royal Prerogative and centralized rule from Westminster. At the same time, the many activists on the green radical left are making a virtue out of necessity and working to create the infrastructure of a radical left with the resources of the extra-parliamentary movements but without the impetus of direct political representation. This non-party radical left is organized through a variety of overlapping networks and political associations: it tends to come together only at a local level in defence of public services, for instance, or around national and international issues, most notably in the last ten years: the anti-Cruise movement, the 1984 miners' strike, the opposition to the Gulf War, the 1992–3 resistance to pit closure, the movement for home rule in Scotland. A regular 'Socialist Conference' in Tony Benn's Chesterfield constituency, or elsewhere in the north of England, has provided a minimal focus for hundreds of these activists.

Communism's after-lives

These examples of new political forms come from the nations of North-Western Europe, where social democratic parties have been the predominant expression of the workers' movement: the Nordic states, the Low Countries, the German and English speaking lands.[26] Significant new left parties with a distinctive character are in the process of formation in Southern Europe, where labour's political allegiances have been more divided between social democracy and Communism. In Spain and Italy two organizations have emerged from splits in the Communist Parties and then teamed up with Red–Green and peace movement organizations named, at present, the United Left and Refundazione Communista (Communist Refoundation) respectively. The character of these organizations is still fluid; at present, they are significantly different from the parties just introduced and from each other. Both are the outcome of recent divisions and changes of strategy within national Communist Parties.[27]

The Spanish Communist Party experienced simultaneously two major splits following its electoral reversal in 1982, when its vote fell by well over a half and its number of parliamentary representatives went from 23 down to 4. In that year it split three ways. On the one hand its hardline pro-Moscow faction left to set up their own party. Santiago Carrillo, who led the Spanish party's move away from the Soviet party model and towards becoming a conventional parliamentary party, set up his own party and many of his supporters eventually joined the social democratic party, Partido Socialista Obrero Español (PSOE). What was left of the party (still a significant number, for it increased its vote marginally in the 1986 election and its number of seats went up to 7) put its energies into building what became a powerful coalition of left political parties – including a minority of the PSOE – and independent local peace movements, against Spanish membership of NATO. The popular vote was in favour (Gonzales had successfully tied membership of NATO to the question of joining the EC and the general modernization and democratization of Spanish society), though Catalonia and the Basque country had voted 'no'. The campaign itself, however, had been important in establishing a new degree of organization and contact amongst those to the left of social democracy.

Soon after the referendum, the Communist Party tried to build on this coalition to create the United Left, a primarily electoral alliance in which it joined with several much smaller left nationalist parties, the (also small) pro-Moscow Communist Party, and a small number of independent activists. Its membership is around 40,000, roughly 70 per cent of whom are members of the CP. At the most recent elections its share of the vote was over 8 per cent, a significant increase on the vote which the Communist Party had been winning on its own. A wide spectrum of leftists give it their vote at elections, but the majority of independent and 'movement' socialists active in local collectives and co-operatives of various kinds – of which there is in Spain a rich tradition – are wary of its Communist domination. This has meant that although the basic programme of the United Left has many similar themes to those of the new parties on the left in Northern Europe, its methods of organizing and policy making do not yet reflect the influence of the social movements. There are some signs that this is changing, particularly under the influence of radical nationalism (in Catalonia and the Basque country).

Catalonian members recently suggested that there should be primary elections amongst the United Left's supporters for the organizations' electoral list. Up until now the list has been chosen centrally, and almost everyone at the top of the list have been members of the Communist Party. The Communist Party talks of dissolving itself into the United Left. If this is genuinely done, it could hasten a process of thoroughgoing democratization, in which the networks of independent radical collectives might feel they could participate. But the prospects for this are uncertain.

In Italy, the Communist Party's slow suicide has taken the opposite form. The majority of the PCI have followed the party leadership's yearning for respectability and, in the hope of becoming a potential partner in government, deleted the offending word 'Communist' from its name. A minority, or rather a seemingly unholy alliance of disparate minorities, has launched a new party based on those amongst the PCI's active working-class base who were unwilling to let go of their Communist tradition; but appealing also, with some success, to non-Communist groups on the radical and green left. Refondazione Communista includes past supporters of the paper Il Manifesto, such as Luciana Castellina and Lucio Magri, who left the PCI in protest aginst the Soviet invasion of Czechoslovakia (but rejoined in 1984). It also includes a small pro-Moscow minority who supported, amongst other Soviet policies, the suppression of the Prague Spring. Whether such disparate political tendencies can build a common organization, and whether it will take a form which adopts principles drawn from the insights of feminism, shop-floor trade unionism and Italy's particularly sustained peace and ecology movements remains to be seen. Some signs are encouraging: the new party came out immediately against the Soviet Coup. The party is attracting activists from the non-Communist left. It won over 8 per cent of the vote in recent elections. And pro-Moscow politics nowadays can have little more than memories to keep it alive. Moreover, the unravelling of the corrupt, clientelist character of the Italian political system breaths life into anti-party politics. Refondazione works closely with the La Rete (Network) party, an anti-corruption party of left Catholic origins increasingly radicalized by social and economic issues and closely allied to civic movements concerned with human rights and democracy. The traditional methods of organization which have predominated in Refondazione, inherited from the PCI, are likely to be shaken by social movement activists bringing with them a more libertarian political culture.

The collapse of Communism, and its various forms of party suicide and reincarnation, will affect to a greater or lesser extent all the social movement parties of Western Europe. In the South, though, this experience, itself immensely varied, has been decisive in determining their initial character. The association of the Communist Parties with the anti-fascist resistance of

Southern Europe gave them a lasting moral credibility and popular support. So long as the Communist Parties in these countries were more or less united, there was little political space to the left of social democracy for a sustained alternative. In both Italy and Spain, small Green and radical left parties have existed but never gained more than 1 or 2 per cent of the vote.

The French Green Party, 'Les Verts', led by Antoine Waechter, at first had only slightly more success, winning only 3.8 per cent in the 1988 presidential elections. Moreover, it tended initially to define itself independently of the left. However, the collapse of the Socialist Party (largely because the failure of the Mitterrand government to live up to high expectations), and – one of the outcomes of the traditional left's collapse – the rise of Le Pen's National Front, has changed the political landscapes dramatically. It has both opened up new opportunities for the Greens as part of a realignment on the left and it has put pressure on them to define themselves more clearly against the right. In the past, the party's position, like that of the Greens in Britain, was 'neither right nor left, but ahead'.

The Socialist Party never was a party with a mass membership. Created by Mitterrand in 1970, it has always been a 'parti des notables'. Now, however it is a party 'des factions', or rather clubs (Delors has his Witness club) and 'movements' (for example, Rocard's initiative to create a new centre left movement). A new green party has already been spun off the collapsing edifice of the Socialists: Brice Lalonde, previously socialist environment minister, formed Génération Ecologie in 1990. Though standing separately from Les Verts, the 'green vote' totalled 14 per cent in the regional elections of 1992. In November 1992 these two green organizations formed a temporary electoral alliance for the Assembly elections in March 1993 – where their results were disappointing. Les Verts has moved more clearly to the left of the green spectrum. But unlike the new left and green left parties described earlier in Northern Europe, it is not the product of a long history of involvement in the extra-parliamentary movements of the left. Indeed, there has been no sustained legacy of this kind from France, the epicentre of the events of 1968. At first this appears surprising. The Socialist Party is so elitist and now shown to be corrupt, while the French Communist Party is so traditionalist, making no attempt to win the support of new social movements, that one might expect new left alternatives could be sustained. It is not for want of trying. However, there are features of the French political system – in particular its centralization and historical hostility to non-party civic associations – that make unfertile ground for such an alternative to put down the kind of lasting roots that have been vital to longevity in most of Northern Europe. Even when new social movements do gain a momentum, as briefly over nuclear power, the electoral system makes it difficult to gain a political foothold from which to consolidate.[28]

Neither reform nor revolution

My mapping of the political innovations of the social and radical trade union movements in Western Europe hopefully has become three-dimensional. I have tried to indicate the contrasting terrain in the different countries and the scale and position of the different new formations. In the process of delineating these features, however, I have indicated the distinctiveness of the new parties' ambitions and political character.

The map should show, through contrasts with the politically weaker positions of the social movement left in the South and in Britain, that the emergence of parties responsive to the aspirations and methods of the social movements in the North is influenced by the achievements of both liberal and social democracy. There are features of the existing state, therefore, which the movements defend implicitly and indeed press to extend, albeit under very different forms of management: these are the state's social provisions and its assemblies elected through the franchise.

These new parties could not therefore be said to be orthodox 'revolutionaries'. At the same time, in their policies and their practice they challenge an economic order driven by capitalist accumulation. They want the transformation of this economy not its amelioration. They cannot therefore be described as 'reformists'.

It is too early to judge whether the new left parties in Northern Europe – including others very similar to one or another of the three types that I described above, Norway[29] and Finland[30] – will establish themselves as a lasting distinct political force. If they do, and a label is needed, they might be called 'transformational' – though it is exactly the term for a popular logo.

Another feature emerges from this mapping process: the varying pattern of Green Parties. In two cases, Germany and Holland, the new left parties include 'Green' in their name. In Denmark, Spain and Italy, other left parties, influenced by the new left have made a left green perspective part of their politics and have become, with varying degrees of success, a focus for left green activists. In these countries there are Green parties but they are very small. This varied pattern stems from the character of the ecology movement or movements.

The contemporary ecology movement has been central to the development of the new left and vice versa. Collective action on ecological issues does not invariably take place within an egalitarian or radical democratic framework. Historically there is no shortage of right-wing ecologists,[31] and some of them have had a brief sojourn in contemporary Green parties dominated by an eclectic mix of the new left. In general, though, the contemporary ecology movements have tended towards the left. This is partly because in the West, from the late 1960s onwards, the tools for a critique of instrumental approaches to nature has come predominantly from the left, from its challenge to positivist science. The threat to the planet is seen by activists in the green movement as arising from those who exercise power and are so fixated on their commercial or political ends that they are blind to the consequences of the means that they adopt. On the other hand, the green movement, with its challenge to the politics and morality of every new technology, has sharpened the break of the new left with orthodox 'productionist' Marxism. Given shared egalitarian and democratic goals, the modern green movements' rejection of a Promethean (dominating and exploitative) relation between humanity and nature in favour of a harmonious one, tends to reinforce the impetus of the new left towards co-operative rather than command economic means of achieving these goals.

Each of the new movements (feminism, for instance; and the movements for sexual liberation) had an equivalent influence on the shaping of the new left. The ecology movement is distinct, however, in its totalizing vision; it is this that enables it to provide the basis for political parties. Although it is totalizing in the scope of the problems it addresses, and in that sense an appropriate framework for a political party, an ecological perspective does not in itself imply any one political approach. The result is that where an established political party proves responsive to ecological priorities, as the new left parties in Scandinavia have proved, there is little impetus on the left of the ecology movement to join or start a specifically Green Party.

Conditions for political influence

At their most successful these parties' methods illustrate radically distinct principles from those of traditional Communist or Social Democratic Parties of the Left. First, there is a recognition of diverse sources of power to change, stemming from the social movements' awareness of their role in reproducing and therefore potentially transforming social institutions. The second principle is an appreciation of sources of knowledge of social needs and possible solutions not encompassed by the kinds of scientific knowledge available to a state or party leadership. Knowledge and power are closely related instruments for any effective agency or process of social change. These parties have experimented with new methods of organizing which recognize that they have no monopoly of the knowledge and power necessary for changes they desire. But though there is much moral commitment to decentralization, grass-roots power and so on, there is not always a self-consciousness about the importance of some of these methods for the *effectiveness* of both party and movement.

The success, therefore, of the aspiring parties of the new left depends, firstly, on enhancing the capacity of the movements to achieve the social transformations for which they have unique power. It depends secondly on developing policies in a way which draws on the movements' (or the projects which have developed from them) unique expertise and networks. Their ability to do this depends on developing a methodology, even as part of their constitutions or rules, certaintly part of their culture, appropriate to the capacities and limits of the movements. And this involves a radical break from most of the methods enshrined, or rather encrusted, into the institutions of the traditional parties of the left.

The methodology of the traditional parties

The old methods of Social Democratic and Labour Parties on the one hand and Communist Parties on the other differ in important ways, and historically there are many varieties of each. But they share common roots which have produced features characteristic of both. Both kinds of parties, for instance, have traditionally tended either to take social movements under their wing: 'our women's/peace/tenants' movement', 'This Great Movement of Ours', or, if the movement is too stroppy to be embraced, to give them leper status and treat them as 'outside our movement', and presumably doomed. The role of old-fashioned father, into which the traditional parties of labour seem so naturally to fall, stems from their view of power. They are founded on the assumption that the power for change lies exclusively with the state, to which, for socialists, trade union and movement activists alike, they control the access. Thus they see themselves rather like the political embodiment of the sole (male) breadwinner. Those that are clamouring for bread/power are like their children or subordinate wives. The party knows what is good for them.

Robert Michels, in his investigation of what he described as 'the iron law of oligarchy', to be found even in a party with the most democratic of aspirations, described the essential features of these parties. His exemplary case was the early Social Democratic Party in Germany. He worked prior to the Russian revolution. However, since in Western Europe Communist Parties were mainly splits from Social Democratic Parties, many of whose basic organizational assumptions were taken for granted by both sides, much of what he says about the parties of the Second International are apposite to the Third. In a sense he is describing what he believes to be an unavoidable 'Taylorism' in political organization: a degree of specialized expertise owned by a professional elite which, whatever the formal democratic procedures, becomes autonomous from 'the masses', grass roots or base. The latter are understood as undifferentiated in their interests and passive in their knowledge. Michels assumes that they are capable only of knowing with which elite their interests lie, not of knowing, even partially, how those interests might be met.

Michels does not refer to Taylor, who was writing in the same period (on another continent) on industrial rather than political management. But he is discovering in politics similar principles at work, principles that in his view are an unavoidable outcome of efficient goal-oriented organization. Where Taylor was advocating these principles as the basis of efficient industrial management, Michels was discovering them at work in the political party which claims 'to struggle against elites in all their forms'.

He was making the same assumptions as Taylor about the character of organizationally relevant knowledge, namely that it had an exclusively scientific form — in the positivistic sense of codified laws and professional techniques — into which people had to be trained. He was making assumptions about the essentially uncreative character of the masses and about the unitary goal of the organization (to capture state power), which are similar to those made by Taylor in *Principles of Scientific Management* with regard to the mechanical, standardizable skills of the workers and the profit maximizing goal of the corporation. Efficiency in meeting these goals required that the specialized elite ruled as standardized an organization as possible. Creative autonomous activity undermined the party just as it did the corporation. Centralization made for economies of effort in party and in corporation alike.

Given the underlying political culture which he describes, the iron law of oligarchy does indeed, in all likelihood, hold. He was writing, however, from within this culture. He had the objectivity and perspicacity of a trained sceptic to identify its fundamental features, of which many a party cadre, believing its own democratic rhetoric, hardly would have been conscious. He treats these features as the unavoidable 'givens' of a mass party.

A collective will for a single centre of power

The first of the crucial 'givens' in Michels' description of the oligarchies of the traditional left is the assumption of the desirability of a collective will to take over a single centre of power, to take hold of the wheel of state to steer it towards socialism. Organization, it was assumed, is 'the only means for the creation of a collective will'. And organization according to Michels is based on 'the principle of least effort, that is to say, upon the greatest possible economy of energy'. The metaphors for the kind of party this produced were, not surprisingly, military and mechanical: the party is divided into the 'rank and file' and the 'officers' – an efficient party is also an effective 'electoral machine'. Michels' remarks from his observations that 'there is hardly one expression of military tactics and strategy, hardly a phrase of barrack slang which does not recur again and again in the leading articles of the socialist press'. The major social democratic and Communist Parties were not organizations which gave any positive place to autonomy of initiative, to developing by argument and common experience not so much a collective will but a convergence or negotiated agreement of different wills drawing on distinct sources of social power.

The supreme challenge to the former political method was a party made up, for historical reasons, of many disparate wills. The British Labour Party provides a good example. The history of its formation from different political and trade union organizations had left, from a traditional point of view, a messy legacy of outdated tools and regiments going their own way. But party strategists met the challenge with military ruthlessness. A constitution was drawn up which permitted the party's power – it's electoral monopoly on the left and its automatic receipt of trade union funds – to be exerted single-mindedly, as if by a single collective will. Those of different minds were marginalized, even if they did not realize the full extent of their fate. The constitution, drawn up by Sidney and Beatrice Webb, in Richard Crossman's words, 'apparently created a full party democracy while excluding party militants from effective power'.[32]

The specialized nature of knowledge and the incompetence of the masses

The second axiom tending to underlie parties of the left formed in the organizational culture of the early twentieth century is the assumption, as a matter of fact, of the exclusive importance of scientific or professional knowledge and the incompetence or ignorance of the masses. 'In all the affairs of management for whose decision there is requisite specialized knowledge . . . a measure of despotism must be allowed and thereby a deviation from the principles of pure democracy. From the democratic point of view this is perhaps an evil, but it is a necessary evil. Socialism does not signify everything by the people, but everything for the people.' Several important assumptions lead Michels to this conclusion. First is the idea that the only knowledge relevant to the efficacy of the party is a technical, positivistically construed scientific knowledge that is inaccessible to the ordinary member and, once learnt by an official of the party, sets him or her apart from the members. Possession of knowledge in Michels' terms 'emancipates [the officers] . . . from the masses and makes them independent of their control'.

Secondly, there is the assumption that facts and values are entirely separate: that the members are capable simply of establishing the party's values. The party then appoints or elects an official to collect the appropriate facts (which is imagined to be a purely technical matter) and depends on specialized knowledge. Parties based on these assumptions have structures for involving the members in taking decisions of principle, which are assumed to be entirely separate from questions of implementation. They also have an extensive staff which works with the executive to implement and elaborate these policies. A gulf develops between the members and the leadership because the former have little basis on which to judge the appropriateness of the executive's work from the standpoint of the principles in which they believe. Where they believe the executive to be wrong they have little basis on which to argue for an alternative. They are in effect politically deskilled.

How far does the methodology implicit in the new parties differ? These assumptions often are still implicit in the new parties. The practical consequences prevent these parties from realizing conditions for their effectiveness: namely, their need to draw on several sources of power, with a co-ordination rather than a fusion of different wills; and also their capacity to combine everyday, tacit knowledge with the knowledge of underlying structures based on theory. Old methods have a subtle, unconscious pulling power, drawing supposedly innovating organizations back into well established grooves, especially when the objectives of these organizations include public office. The old methods appear to present the easiest route, especially when, as with the parliamentary structures of West Germany, they are backed by enormous resources; or as in Britain, where beguiling shortcuts to office tempt social movement radicals to devote themselves to committee room manoeuvring.

The grooves of these methods run quite contrary to the creative potential of the new movements and the radical parts of the trade unions.

A common objective; different sources of power

The character of a party's own internal and external relations mirror its understanding of the relations between parliamentary and extra-parliamentary social power and the role of the party in activating and interconnecting the two. Two episodes in the German Greens' experience of coalition with the SPD in West Berlin between 1986 and 1990 illustrate that there are in the German Greens quite different understandings in this new kind of party, of power and therefore of the workings of their own organisation.

The majority of Greens share a belief that legislative bodies have limited but significant powers and that the social changes they desire depend on mobilizing sources of power in the wider society. But the way in which party activists interpret this varies significantly.

To illustrate my point I wish to recount two episodes in the recent history of the German Greens.

The first story suggests a strategy and way of organizing with a clear sense of the limits of the legislature and of a notion of differentiated sources of power for social change — even when, as in this case, what is wanted is legislative action. The second story illustrates the pressures on the Greens to succumb to conventional parliamentary pressures. It also illustrates that an interpretation of the party's 'grass roots democracy' which stresses only their control over the leadership, as distinct from their own capacity for initiative, can be self-defeating. It shows how easily these combined problems can lead to action which undermines the party's social movement base and therefore the electoral as well as social strength of the party.

The first story comes from the work of Heidi Bischoff Pflanz, Speaker of the Parliamentary Fraction of the Greens, on the rights of immigrants and 'guest workers'. The SPD was opposed to the Greens' policy of granting immigrants full rights, including the voting rights that go with German citizenship. After pressing the Greens position against the SPD's overwhelming hostility in the coalition, Pflanz decided that, for the time being, there was little more that could be done through government channels. So, using the public platform of parliament and her insider position in the government, she publicized the Greens' continued support for immigrants' rights, the SPD's opposition and the consequent impasse that the Greens had reached in the coalition. She went to the immigrants' organizations and they took the battle to the streets. The immigrants' organizations and the party worked together to wage a massive poster and propaganda campaign to morally isolate the SPD. The action was effective. It reverberated through the labour movement and left intelligentsia in West Berlin, causing divisions in the SPD. Pflanz and her parliamentary colleagues then took the issue back into parliament and won the first reading of legislation to give immigrants the vote. The role of the party outside the parliament was to support the mobilization organized primarily by immigrants organizations that had been involved in developing the Greens' policy on this issue. In the end the Supreme Court overruled the Berlin decision. But within Berlin, it was a victory for a strategy based on one policy but involving the mobilization of diverse sources of power under different but co-operating leaderships.

The second story concerns the Greens' Senator for Women, whose Department is also responsible for children's nurseries (kindergarten). In January 1990, the kindergarten workers went on strike to increase their low wages and to expand the number of teachers. Both were policies that the Green Party supported. Kindergarten workers were just the kind of public sector workers who normally supported the Greens. The SPD was against the strikers' demands. Anna Klein, the Green nominee for Senator for Women – she is not a member of the Green Party, but a leading feminist sympathetic to the Greens – was supportive but did not oppose the SPD approach, nor did she encourage the party to develop an independent strategy of the kind that Pflanz followed on immigrant rights. This would have involved mobilizing public support for the kindergarten workers (they were a popular group of workers) and widening divisions in the SPD. Neither did the Green Party executive take the initiative and attempt to organize this support; instead they became locked in a row with the Senator, as if she had the power to resolve the problem. At the executive meeting where Anna Klein was called to account for herself, and in the gossip round the Green's corridor of the town hall, all the energy concentrated on criticism of the Senator. Very little attention was given to the independent role of the party in building up a coalition of support for the kindergarten workers outside parliament, which would have exerted pressure on the Senator, probably emboldened her own approach and divided the SPD. The final outcome was unfavourable to the kindergarten workers and was one of many such concessions made to the SDP without a popular campaign. The episode problably contributed to the steady decline in support from the Greens' traditional base – without winning any votes from more moderate citizens of Berlin – that led in 1990 to the party being voted out of government.

Ironically, for a stronghold of the left of the Green party, the party, or at least the city executive, easily became fixated on what was going on in the Parliament and the Senate rather than on the role of the party in mobilizing other sources of power. The party's constitutional commitment to 'base democracy' tended in practice to mean exclusively the party executive and activists seeking to control the Senators. The alternative would have been a vital additional dimension, improvised by Heidi Bischoff Pflanz, in which the party worked with others to activate popular pressure in a way that could shift the balance of power at the top, in the Senate.

The possibility of a Red–Green coalition in Berlin took the Greens by surprise, as many of its electoral successes have done, including its first entry into the Bundestag. Some of their mistakes, both the premature compromises made on the Senate and the fixation of the party on its controlling rather than its campaigning role can be explained by a lack of strategic consideration of how its 'base democracy' should be applied according to differing balances of social and political power. Application in abstract forms leads either to giving up the methods of practical action and falling into old political patterns, or using them in a very formalistic way, rather than as principles by which the party through its independent action might influence the balance of power in office.[33]

Different kinds of expertise

Social movements have proved to be not only sources of power unreachable by parliamentary parties, but also sources of knowledge and expertise not discoverable from above. Again the experience of the last twenty-five years or so, has led to a questioning of another of the 'given' features of traditional parties of labour, identified by Michels: the technical superiority of the party leadership and the incompetence of the masses.

The work of the Dutch Green Left provides the clearest most self-conscious contrast. Take the issue of a basic income, an important part of the economic policy which they promote through their parliamentary spokespeople and through popular campaigns with other organizations. The way the new party developed its policy is revealing. It began with several principles concerning labour and the labour market: the extension of peoples' choices concerning their work at different times in their lives; the recognition of the unpaid labour normally done by women in the privacy of the home; the enhancement of people's dignity at work so that their labour is not reduced to the status of a commodity. They start from the assumption that the party does not itself have the knowledge to turn these principles into a credible policy and strategy for action. On this issue as with others their approach is to be 'continuously confronted with the knowledge, opinions and visions' from outside the party. The job of the party executive and staff is to create a 'working space' (e.g., on the question of a basic income) and approach all organizations with an interest in the issue and in working in some kind of collaboration with the Green Left.

In 1990 the Green Left provided facilities for regular meetings of the Dutch Women's Union which brings together employed and unemployed women workers (it is affiliated to the Dutch TUC; founded at the beginning of the century, it is at present going through a significant revival and becoming a powerful force); organizations of the unemployed and researchers working on labour market issues. This group produced a detailed strategy on the right to economic security, whether in or out of work – not a fully-fledged commitment to a basic income – which was supported at the Green Left conference.

Michels would have had difficulty in recognizing such a process. It is underpinned by three implicit assumptions which make it radically different from the left parties of old. Firstly, the 'masses', whether inside or outside the party, are understood as organized in a variety of ways independently of the party leadership, rather than as inert and undifferentiated. Party members and supporters are seen as sources of knowledge and experience or as means of access to wider networks of knowledge and experience. Secondly, the detail of policy making is seen as itself a political, interest and value-laden process rather than a technical matter to be left to neutral experts. From the issue of which groups are to be involved in the 'working space' to the question of where the policy should be campaigned for, mobilizing what sources of power: all were treated as intertwined questions of fact and value, and therefore as subjects of democratic debate. Finally, the party's leadership role rests not in its superior knowledge but in its determination and ability to use its presence within society's elected political institutions to create or strengthen favourable conditions for fundamental transformation through action independent of the party.

Moreover, the 'working spaces' idea starts from a recognition that the Green Left political party does not have a monopoly over the processes of transformation, nor of leadership. Whether its leadership is successful depends not on the unity of its will (its leadership's control over the membership), but on its relationship with those in society working for similar goals, and its ability to use its position within the party political system to add to the power of these people to bring about change. At certain times this might involve a unity of action; at other times it will require alliances at many levels of society involving different but complementary kinds of action.

This can sound smooth to write or read about but those who believe themselves to be working for democratic and egalitarian change often have conflicting interests and therefore contrary perceptions of what is involved. Drawing on the knowledge of independent movements can be a difficult, uncertain business: far easier to set up a research department and let bright young graduates produce impressive documents. Look at the experience of the Danish Socialist People's Party over the issue of wage levels for a shorter working week. The Party had long been committed to shorter working hours. But in 1985 feminist supporters of the party opened up a debate about how such a policy should be introduced and with what kind of wage levels. Drawing on research and ideas from the women's movement, including women's groups active in the trade unions, they proposed that the implementation of shorter working hours should not be left to the labour market and to free collective bargaining. Instead they insisted that it should be backed by legislation so that employers would have to introduce the change regardless of the bargaining power of the workers. They also argued that wage levels should be based on the principle of solidarity and a living wage, which would mean a reduction in differentials.

This went against the grain of many male trade unionists in the party, who prefered a strategy reliant on bargaining power and aiming for a wage system which did not disrupt differentials fought for in the past. After much debate the Party congress adopted the policy initiated by the feminists. The party's trade union conference, however, still passed a resolution backing the bargaining-based alternative. The party from its inception rejected democratic centralism so, the trade union conference had a right to continue to disagree and is under no discipline to implement the party decisions where it strongly disagrees. So the debate continues, with the party promoting its agreed position and supporting campaigns around it, and with the trade union conference reserving their right to disagree – though in fact the majority of trade unionists do in fact increasingly campaign for the party majority policy.'

A sign of weakness, a recipe for disaster, some might say. But since the party's notion of transformation is based on the pressure of popular movements and therefore depends on its policies being shared by these movements, there is not much to be gained by the party imposing a discipline on its members. The disagreements in the party reflect real debates in society: a party which takes a position but openly continues the debate is more likely to stimulate the consciousness of the movements than a party whose members regurgitate a line which they do not personally share. Again, the Danish SF like the Dutch Green Left has broken from the conventional assumption of the superiority of the leadership's knowledge: an assumption which turns a position produced by a debate in which everyone's knowledge is partial, into the imperatives of an all-knowing collective brain.

The recognition of the partial, fallible character of everybody's knowledge is the other side of recognizing the importance of knowledge arising from different kinds of experience. Through a conscious process of testing policies in the light of experience and new knowledge, the latter recognition can be used to overcome the limits presented by the former. These new left parties are about the sharing and the development of the knowledge required to change society. Parties are not research institutes, however. They are formed to take action. Their extension of knowledge thus has to involve a process of learning by doing.

An example of this comes from the German Greens in Baden Württemburg. There the Green faced a major problem over what to do with toxic waste. There is 200,000 tons of toxic waste in Baden Württemburg and no place to put it; no incinerator in which to burn it. In the past it had always been exported to the GDR. Since 1990 it had been taken to France. Then early in 1991 the Federal Government proposed that two incinerator plants be built in Baden Würtenburg, including one in Kehl, a city on the Rhine which already suffers from noxious emmissions. A campaign developed in which Greens participated in opposing the plant in Kehl. There were several opposing positions, however, held by members of the party and activists in local citizens' movements. On the one hand the party is in general against incineration plants because it provides an excuse for businesses to continue to produce toxics. What is needed, in the party's view, is regulations and help with conversion to prevent the toxins being produced in the first place. Others argued simply that there should be no incinerators in Baden Württemburg. Yet others argued that the region should accept responsibility for its own waste. At the same time as taking action to stop the building of any new incinerators, debate continued within the campaign and within the party. Eventually a solution was found which was put forward, so far successfully, in the negotiations with the Federal Government: that the regional government of Baden Württemburg would only discuss the building of an incinerator in Baden Württemburg if the Government and companies took measurable action to reduce the production of toxic waste. The outcome is still inconclusive, but the Greens have managed to unite the SPD, FDP and local campaigns around this position and to delay the building of an incinerator. The experience of the campaign itself, and the party's willingness to learn from this experience and the knowledge of others, was essential to the emergence of this strategy.

Conflicting pressures

The experience of the German Greens demonstrates most starkly the cultural and institutional weights that reinforce old models; the pressure pulling those in positions of privilege and responsibility away from political methods involving risk and uncertainty. To an observer the party offers an observation gallery from which both the conservative and the emancipatory forces influencing left politics can be seen at work and at war. There is no attempt to hide its internal debates and quarrels, difficulties and failings. The moderating influences on the parliamentary group in the Federal German Republic was particularly strong. Large salaries and allowances, media attention and a large staff, provide possibilities for modest personal aggrandizement that the rotation, sharing and accountability systems of the Greens have not been able entirely to resist. On the other hand, at the base of the party, local activities have their own strength. They benefit from Federal institutions of regional autonomy reinforced by a party constitution and culture in which independence of programme and initiative is a point of principle. It has proved to be a source of practical strength for the radical democratic traditions which the Greens aspire to practice. In fact it is a striking feature of all the new left parties that in the last two years or so they have become much stronger locally than nationally. Their distinctive relationship to efforts at social change outside the council or parliamentary chamber have a clearer meaning locally, where social movement organizations are known and understood, and where the outcome of co-operation with them is usually very practical and visible. The radical democratic traditions of Die Grünen also gain sustenance from the continuing legacy of a particular radical break of the first post-war generation from the Cold War politics of their parents and elder siblings.

The notably intense factional struggles of the German Greens, however, have often blocked the flows between local campaigning and Federal campaigning and policy making. The policy making of the party became, until very recently, increasingly sidelined by this factionalism. Every issue and every group has tended to become subordinated to the factional struggle. It became such an accepted part of party life, that at a recent conference a break was formally called to enable the different factions to retire and discuss their next moves – like a negotiation or football match. The explanation for this factionalism is complex, but one feature does stand out: the leadership of both sides came from the Maoist groups of the early 1970s and seemed to have pursued their new political cause with the same inflexibility and presumption of certain truth which they learnt in these groups.

It is the combination of these conflicting pressures which is so revealing. Each component is present separately elsewhere: the capacities of the British political system to tame rebellious spirits are rightly renowned. They are reinforced by a centralized and monarchical system of government which allows the executive to govern in hallowed secrecy and reduces the Opposition to deferential jelly. The result is a uniquely wide gap – compared to other parliamentary democracies – between the people, including their movements and organizations, and their political representatives. But unlike in Germany, resistance to them is not sustained by strong regional bases nor an electoral system that allows minorities electoral expression.

In comparison, in Holland, Denmark and Norway, where new left parties have become established, parliament does not pull its inmates quite so strongly away from the people.[34] A party that develops close working relations with extra-parliamentary movements is not rubbing quite so directly against the grain as they are in Germany, and even more so Britain. Even in the more ideal cases, however, there is a gravitational pull towards parliamentary activity and the parliamentarians. It is reinforced by a corporatist pull on social and trade union movements. These parties have divisions and continuing debates but they have not suffered from the permanent factionalism which has recently virtually paralysed the German Greens as a federal party.

As well as the external political power structures, two other factors influence the new parties' ability to break successfully from the traditional political methods that brought the orthodox left to an impasse: (1) the strength and development of the social movements which led to the creation of these parties, or at least greatly influenced their character; (2) the organization and constitution of the party and how effectively they reflect the diverse sources of power and varied forms of knowledge with which, to be successful, the party needs to work.

The ups and downs of social movements

There is no doubt that, whether the new left party is new or renewed, it has been social movements organizing in new ways amongst previously ignored sections of the population – usually for values that the left has at one time stood for – that have provided the impetus to start or to change. These movements are the main counterforce to the parliamentary state, and an important influence on Communist and Social Democratic institutions that have sustained the old political methods. This is not to say that all social movements have adopted new methods. Prior to 1968, and in a lingering way afterwards, some movements used methods adapted from the social democratic or Labour parties: a national committee and executive that holds all executive power; a central research department; branches to carry out the will of the national committee, under the supervision of as many professionals as the organization can afford. The British-based Campaign for Nuclear Disarmament would be a good example of this, especially at times of routine activity – until the independently arising movement against Cruise missiles, and especially the direct action of the Greenham Women, forced it to rethink its methods.

The new movements do not go on forever, or anyway not in the same form. Their strength and character is influenced by the responses they get from within the political system. In France, for instance, after 1981, the previously strong anti-nuclear and independent peace movements almost disappeared, and the women's and gay movements also went into serious decline: the former because their demands were completely rebuffed and they had no voice within the political system nor any realistic chance of creating one; the latter because many of their demands were conceded, though not in a way that enabled them to participate in the implementation and develop their ideas further. In Holland and Germany, by contrast, the eighties saw the biggest post-war mobilization of social movements, followed by considerable institutionalization and consolidation, in trade unions, in projects and services that gained public funding and in local and regional government. How have the new left parties adapted to these changes and still maintained an interactive relationship with the movements in their scattered, fragmented form?

Constitutions and cultures for grass-roots democracy

Like all social institutions, political parties are marked by the context of their birth. A significant trauma is usually involved in any major change of character – and even then the possibility of change depends on the responsiveness of the party's democracy. The Danish Socialist People's Party, for instance, had, from its birth as a split from the anti-parliamentary Third International, a primarily parliamentary emphasis. With the social movements and new trade union militancy of the late 1960s and early 1970s rebelling against the failures of parliamentary socialism, there was pressure for a political voice more sympathetic to independent and extra-parliamentary forces for change: though their scepticism about parliament was more pragmatic than the ideological antipathy of the Communist tradition. In Denmark, it took a breakaway and the defeat of most of the original leadership of the SF to shift the party in this direction. The result is a party with quite a sensitive and changing balance between parliamentary and extra-parliamentary strategies for change. The German Greens, by contrast, were born at a high point of the social movements. Admittedly, it was a sense that extra-parliamentary activity was insufficient that galvanized diverse movements into forming a party. But all that they wanted from a party was a voice. The problems of the German Greens reflect limits of transferring in a rather frozen form to a political party the organizational practices that social movements found appropriate in their first, most energetic phase.

Implicit in the notion of 'a voice' was the assumption that the important messages to convey and initiatives to spread originated outside the parliamentary system and would continue to do so. This assumption was built into the constitution of the German Greens with its idea of 'the democracy of the base'. It emphasises that the base organizations of the party must control the leaders; that the leaders and representatives must not lose touch with the base; that the base must be kept fully informed and must in principle have access to all the decision-making processes of the party. Policy making must be done with the base of the party and the social movements. The role of parliamentarians was to be to publicize the arguments of the social movements, to reveal information which the government is trying to hide, to press for political action in accord with the demands of the social movements. There was often an implicit assumption in the German Greens' theory of 'base democracy' that the base of the party in effect represented the social movements. At times this assumption led the activists of the party to substitute themselves for the movements. As the contrast between the party's action over the kindergarten strike compared with its action of the issue of votes for immigrants suggests, it is at the very least ambiguous about the relation between the party's own base and the wider social movements. There is an assumption sometimes that the party's own activists in some sense represent the social movements, and that therefore accountability to the party is equivalent to serving the social movements, or people in struggle. This implicit presumption was an influence in the debate over the kindergarten strike. It was an ambiguity which proved very damaging in the Green's conduct of the high-profile Red–Green coalition of Berlin.

These problems are worth reflecting on for a moment. There is pressure on the German Greens, as there will be on any new left party, to 'professionalise', meaning 'to become like other parliamentary parties'. To resist this pressure these parties need diagnoses of their problems that maintain the integrity of their original principles; and then they must seek to improve their organization in the light of *these* principles rather than the criteria of conventional politics. After all, if they accepted the latter, they would in effect be defining themselves out of existence and losing their constituency of support. It is their break with convention which has won the support of significant section of the public.

Many of the original procedures written into the Greens' constitution to ensure 'grass-roots' democracy no longer operate. Rotation mid-term has been generally abandoned, though it is a principle frequently followed after the end of each parliamentary term. The incumbents in one political office, however, often frequently move to another. So there does exist in the Greens a professional elite, even if its members do not hold the same job for as long as in a conventional party. Participation in the party is not as high as the idea of base democracy implies. It has declined steadily, even where votes for the party have risen.

One explanation for the failure of 'base democracy' to live up to its promise in the German Greens is that too much weight was put on the procedures within the party, especially between political office holders and the membership, to achieve what is in reality a political relationship between the party and independent social movements. The party was organized as if it contained both the movements and party activists; they were seen as virtually one and the same thing. Other new left parties in Northern Europe have proved more stable and in many respects successful by organizing in a way which includes both rules to make representatives accountable and avoid their domination, and also, just as importantly, rules formalizing the party's distinct but complementary role to that of the movements. These later rules include explicit and transparent mechanisms for working with the movements, like the Dutch Green Left's 'working space'.

These parties are constantly under pressure, both from the expectations of the movements and from their own rules, to look outwards, to work with people organizing outside the party as an essential source of political vitality. In such circumstances factionalism, as distinct from debate, does not thrive. Factionalism is the product of a party whose rules turn the party in on itself.

It follows from this analysis that the professionalism that is required is not that defined by the electoral consensus – the need for a charismatic leader, a bland message etc. – but the skills required by the distinct campaigning alliances of which the party is part, by the process of sustaining these alliances, and dovetailing the various sources of power.

A European response to scepticism from the East?

Can the experience of these parties answer the scepticism of Eastern democrats towards political parties, or prevent their reluctant acquiescence in conventional Western models? Can it avoid the choice many of them have felt they had to make between taking responsibility for political office and following their concern to establish strong civil movements?

The Western parties radically influenced by the social movements do not provide a cut and dried model of an alternative. On the basis of the movements' understanding of knowledge as social, diverse and impossible fully to centralize, they provide some of the founding principles of such an alternative, that could be applied according to specific circumstances. In a pragmatic way they see themselves as consciously trying to influence society according to ecological and social goals, but on the basis of partial knowledge, and therefore with the need consciously to experiment, to be open to external influence. They make no claims to be all-knowing or to desire to become all-knowing, but they are confident of acting in a purposeful way to bring about democratic and egalitarian change against the equally purposeful power of parties of the centre and right and the interests they promote. In the course of exploring the new parties that have emerged in some West European countries as radical challengers to traditional parties of the left, I have stressed the importance for the transformations they seek of close, respectful alliances with democratic citizens' movements or networks; that is, forms of political agency that are not organized primarily around electoral politics.

The shape that European integration is taking on and the strength of the international market forces that pull it, pose an acute problem of political agency for those, politicians and publically active citisens alike, who are pressing social needs and democratic principles against unaccountable centres of economic and political power. At this point in European history, the kind of left that could lay the basis for solving this problem is one whose main concern is not so much the seizure of state power but the creation of new forms of power. Such a left would not be reliant on any one, invariably flawed, level of political power. A distinctive political commitment that many of the social movement activists of the kind described in this book have in common, is a concern to build power through citizens' organizations and to attempt to win support from political structures at all levels. The differentiated view of democracy implicit in much of their practice, gives them some of the tools to respond to the problems facing democratic and egalitarian aspirations in the new post-Cold War Europe.

The importance – or more realistically, the potential – of social movement organizations in circumstances where democratic structures need to be created rather than presumed, stems from several characteristics highlighted by the argument of this book. They are not an alternative to political parties but they reach parts of society that parties and government cannot. They are, as I sought to show in this chapter, a necessary complement to party organization for any project of radical transformation.

A sub-theme of this book has been to explain how activists in social movement networks and projects see themselves as transforming society by virtue of their own activity rather than pressing others to take action on their behalf. Some might rest at a particular reform. Many are constantly making connections, practical and intellectual, following the threads that resistance in daily life unravels. In other words, they are personally and through their immediate networks, carrying out the functions that a party might focus in one single structure. They then take a pragmatic view of representation and political alliances.

There is a cluster of MEPs in the Green, Socialist and ex-Communist Groups who social movement groups treat as in some sense their representatives. Occasionally, a group of these MEPs will help to arrange conferences where activists and writers can reflect on and strengthen their campaigns and networks. These activists will have other alliances with supportive political representatives in their locality, region and nation. You might call it representation *à la carte*. But it does not imply a bounded particularism, a denial of the need constantly to arrive at a wider understanding, to make broader connection. It is rather that there is no one party that adequately encompasses the kind of changes that radical activists in these movements envisage; and anyway they are already engaged in changes which do not need any single political agent.

The pace of change in Europe, however, has stimulated two sustained attempts to co-ordinate green and radical left parties across the continent. In June 1993, 26 Green Parties from countries east and west of the Danube met in Helsinki to form the 'European Green Co-ordination'. This loose federation is based on a statement of agreed principles and statutes consolidating the results of two years of discussion. Later in the same month, a 'Forum of New Left Forces' met in Copenhagen. This was a gathering of most of the Western new left/green left parties discussed in this chapter, though it did not have significant representation from Central or Eastern Europe. It too agreed on guiding principles, almost identical with those of the European Green Co-ordination. A theme flowing through the principles of both groupings is a recognition of the limits of a purely governmental, legislative strategy for social change of the kind they desire, a general limit made stark by the character of West European 'integration'.

The processes of European integration have meant more areas of economic and social life are outside the realm of public legislative debate. In economics, this applies especially to questions concerning the generation of wealth, questions of production. The investment strategies of multinationals are largely beyond the reach of governments, and political parties in the European Parliament have little power to press such an intervention. Yet without some social control over production, there are few options for democratic control over the economy. The integration of exchange rates – a reality brought about by economic developments and only consolidated by political institutions – makes national monetary and to some extent fiscal measures blunt instruments of economic policy. Economic change will require the creation of new relationships in production itself (some created through internationally organized resistance, some through finding niches for democratic forms within the existing economy) before these constraints can be broken through.

Movements based inside production, have, as their activity in such diverse cases as the auto and textile industries demonstrates (see chapter 6), sources of power within economic institutions. Periodically they are driven by the immediate threats to their livelihoods to search out ways of mobilizing and exerting it. There will be a limit to what they can achieve without legislative or other political action to control the financial institutions and the markets on which the companies depend. This political action, however, cannot be most effective on an exclusively national level, which is one of the factors leading new left parties to seek greater co-ordination. This is combined with efforts to support democratic social movements as they strengthen their international networks (see the directory at the end of this book).

Social movements, whether they be innovative, grass-roots trade union organizations or movements based in the community, potentially have a distinctive mobility and flexibility of communication and contact. They have a problem of resources. But no entrenched national attachments slowed down the international networking of TIE, the Cruise missile watchers or European network of homeworkers. They faced the hostility of institutions from an earlier era, an era where Cold War divisions still policed the mind of the left. CND, for instance, was sometimes wary of contact with the independent peace movement in the East, and officials of British trade unions affiliated to the Cold War international trade union organizations would try to block contact between their members and members of Communist unions in Italy, Spain or France. But generally, their own drive and sense of direction had no national boundaries.

Central to the flexibility of social movements is their implicit but distinctive approach to knowledge – the main theme of this book. The innovative feature of their politics lies in the fact that they arose in disillusion with social democratic governments committed to use science in the interests of the people; a disillusionment that spread across virtually every area of life, from the factory to the fireside. From their own experience they had lost faith in the claims of science. Yet their approach was realist: they were reacting to material problems, or problems that had material consequences, so their instinct was to analyse to get to the roots of the problem; roots in which those with authority took no interest.

Part of the impetus behind the new internationalism is to 'socialize knowledge' (to put it somewhat pompously) around a set of issues and common problems that have, perforce, become international. Meetings of production and plantation workers across the chain of cocoa production; of women organizing amongst casual workers; of migrant workers; of designers and engineers in the arms industry: central to them all and many more is the exchange of information; often information uniquely available through these meetings.[35] By contrast, the traditional presumption of national parties that they know and, through the state, control the malleable variables of social and economic life, makes them ill-adapted to the diffuse inside information necessary for any social leverage over economic and social change.

A final argument for the immediate importance of democratic movements concerns the character of present sources of division and reaction in the new Europe, East and West. Political parties, however democratic their goals, cannot substitute for the social associations of daily life by which people gain both some power to shape their futures and a source of indentity that is not defined by its hatred of others. The visible strengthening of democratic civic movements, with roots amongst the most powerless or frustrated of society, will be essential if the racism and xenophobia poisoning European civic and political life is to be defeated.

Notes

1   For descriptions of these two movements see S. Wolchik, *Czechoslovakia in Transition* (London, 1990); G. Munnerup, 'The October Revolution in East Germany', *Labour Focus on Eastern Europe*, 3 (1989), and 'Kohl Hijacks East German Revolution', 1 (1990). *DDR Almanach*, ed. G. Fischbach, provides basic information (in German) on New Forum. B. Einhorn, *Cinderella Goes to Market* (London, 1993) provides an account of the activities and role of women in and independent of both movements.

2   M. Waller, B. Coppieters and K. Deschouwer (eds) *Social Democracy in a Post Communist Europe* (London, 1993), especially chapter by Waller. For writing on environmental politics in Eastern Europe, see P. Jehlička and Tomáš Kostelecky, 'Developments in the Czechoslovak Green Party Since the 1990 Elections', in *Environmental Politics*, 1, no. 1 (1992); M. Waller and F. Millard, 'Environmental Politics in Easter Europe', *Environmental Politics*, 1, no. 2 (1992).

3   Havel's speech to the Helsinki Citizens' Assembly is reprinted in *Europe from Below*, ed. Mary Kaldor (London, 1991).

4   Russell J. Dalton, *Citizen Politics in Western Democracies* (Chatham, New Jersey, 1988); Samuel Barnes, Max Kaase et al., *Political Action* (Beverly Hills, Calif., 1979).

5   See chapter 8 of *Political Parties*, ed. Alan Ware (Oxford, 1987); and chapter 5 of *The Future of Social Democracy*, eds W. Paterson and A. Thomas (Oxford, 1986). The voter/member ratio is an indicator not of the political passivity of voters for these new parties, but of the fact that a large number of them devote their political energies to campaigns and projects outside party politics.

6   Some traditional parties of the left, during the Cold War, did not even aspire to bring about change, most notably the German SPD. It simply monopolized working class political representation within the dominant consensus.

7   Perhaps one of the most damaging was in Portugal.

8   See C. Offe, *Contradictions of the Welfare State* (London, 1984) for a discussion of the problems of building power counter to that of the state.

9   There are a number of electronic bulletin boards especially established to serve social movement activists. Examples are 'Greenet' and 'Poptel' (the latter is used mostly by grass-root labour organizations).

10   See H. Kriesi, 'The Political Opportunity Structure of the Dutch Peace Movement', *West European Politics*, 11, no. 3, for an analysis of the relatively small influence of radical left parties on the peace movement in Holland.

11   Consequently, wherever they do win office, normally at a local or regional level, they tend to bring about changes to both the legislature and the executive by which extra-parliamentary movements and projects either gain representation alongside conventionally elected councillors or MPs, or become involved in a partnership in the implementation of policy.

12   For useful discussions of corporatism see P. Schmitter and G. Lehmbruch (eds) *Trends Towards Corporatist Intermediation* (London, 1979); and A. Cawson, *Corporatism and Political Theory* (Oxford, 1976).

13   Cited in chapter 3 of *Democracy from Below: New Social Movement and the Political System in West Germany* (forthcoming, Ruud Koopmans, 1994).

14   See E. Altvater, *The Future of the Market: An Essay on the Regulation of Money and Nature after the Collapse of 'Actually Existing Socialism'* (London, 1993) for a useful discussion of Marx and nature that contrasts Marx's own writings with later, especially Soviet, formulations.

15   For detailed histories of the German Greens see W. Hulsberg, *The German Greens*

(London, 1988); G. Langath, *The Green Factor in German Politics* (Boulder, USA, 1984); E. G. Frankland and D. Schoonmaker, *Between Protest and Power: The Green Party in Germany* (Boulder, USA, 1992).

16 T. Poguntke, *Alternative Politics: The German Green Party* (Edinburgh, 1993) provides sceptical analysis of the depth of this change, with extensive documentation.

17 John Logue, *Socialism and Abundance: Radical Socialism in the Danish Welfare State* (Minneapolis, 1982).

18 Green Left pamphlet. For a history of the Dutch Green Left and an especially useful examination of the merger, see H. Voerman, 'Changing Colours: The Dutch Small Left', in R. Richardson and C. Roots (eds) *The Green Challenge* (London, forthcoming 1994). The pamphlet entitled *Green Left* is available from Groen Links (Green Left) c/o Green in the European Parliament, Belliard Street 97–113, 1047 Brussels, Belgium.

19 Interview with the author.

20 There is a historical precedent worth further study, however: the Commonwealth Party, which briefly gave political expression to the radicalization that took place outside parliament towards the end of the Second World War, and whose economic and political programme contained a radical egalitarianism and commitment to grass-roots democracy that in some ways prefigured the contemporary social movement left.

21 For descriptions and analyses of these brief breakthroughs see K. Livingstone, *If Voting Changed Anything They Would Abolish It* (London, 1987), and H. Wainwright, *Labour, A Tale of Two Parties* (London, 1987). For a detailed documentation of the Kinnock leadership, see R. Heffernan and M. Marquesee, *Defeat from the Jaws of Victory* (London, 1992).

22 Indeed, socialists in Scotland talk openly about the SNP dividing into a Scottish social democratic party and a more radical red–green party, presumably with a minority also going off to a national party of the right.

23 Such a challenge would always have the paradoxical potential of strengthening from the outside the position of the left inside, as the success of Die Grünen strengthened the influence of the left in the SPD. In Berlin, for instance, the left of the SPD, discussing the period in the mid to late 1980s when their party was in coalition with the Alternative List (the West Berlin Greens), state very firmly that the pressure of the Greens meant that the SPD implemented its more radical manifesto promises, which would not normally have been the case.

24 See Richardson and Roots, *The Green Challenge*. For an early analysis, by a leading Green politician, of the Green Party in Britain and other Green Parties across the world, see S. Parkin, *Green Parties: An International Guide* (London, 1989).

25 For example, over the more radical industrial policies of the 1945 Government, the National Plan of Harold Wilson 1964/65 administrations and the modern-

ising industrial policies of 1975.

26   There are significantly different conditions facing social movements in Northern
Europe as distinct from the South. My generalizations are tentative and therefore
only for background consideration. Movements in Northern Europe grew in
extended periods of social democratic government. The working class in these
countries were also industrially the strongest in the continent, or had a close
alliance with a socially progessive rural population, as in Norway and Denmark.
(See Perry, Anderson's essay, 'The Singular and the Plural', *English Questions*
(London, 1992)). New left parties in the North have varied origins and characteristics, but the experience of social democratic governments – both of their
immediate post-war reforms and their later acceptance of the imperatives of an
increasingly international industrial and monetary order – has produced underlying features in common.

First, the prospect of parliamentary rule by a party supported by the majority
of the working class had lost its cure-all quality by the late 1960s for Northern
socialists and social movement activists. In France, for example, by contrast,
when a social democratic government was elected people danced in the street to
welcome what they thought would be a social revolution. Similarly in Italy,
many activists who in Northern Europe would have looked to a new party,
looked to the PCI in the hope that in government the PCI could bring about the
social and democratic reforms that had been promised as part of post-war
reconstruction but, in the course of virtually unbroken conservative rule, never
provided. The historical memory of the Communists in leading the resistence to
the fascists nourished this hope.

Secondly, the presence of strong social democratic parties made for a certain
moderation in employers' revenge for the challenges they faced from workers
flexing their bargaining power in the later days of the boom. Social movements
in Scandinavia, the Low Countries and Germany have gained a certain stability
and continuity through their influence amongst sections of a trade union movement that has remained relatively strong throughout the 1970s and 1980s. In
Italy, by contrast, the employers, notably Fiat, in one mighty attack, were able
virtually to destroy the shop floor organizations built up during the 1970s.
These organizations had been an important working-class base for the radical
politics developed in the late 1960s.

Thirdly, social democracy's material and political reforms had significant
consequences for the political demands and practice of the social movements.
The parties of the new left in the North have in their practice and their policies
a richness of ideas on the democratic management of public provision, state
intervention in industry and organization of local government which would be
exceptional in the South – or at any rate limited to regions of prolonged
Communist or other radical municipal government, such as Bolognia in Regio
Emilia, Italy; or of unique regional economic developments, such Mondragon in
Spain. These ideas depended on extensive social provision. They have been

concerned with the qualitative improvements, extension and democratization of this provision. Their campaigns for qualitatively better public provision have led both to continuing local initiatives and to continent-wide networks and lobbies to develop the pressure for new kinds of public intervention.

27 See M. Waller and M. Fennema (eds) *Communist Parties in Western Europe: Decline or Adaption* (Oxford, 1988) for recent histories of West European communist parties before the final shock of 1989; C. Boggs and D. Plotke (eds) *The Politics of Eurocommunism* (London, 1980) provides an earlier analysis of the emergence of Eurocommunism. For an analysis of the Italian left as the crisis of old order develops, see Tobias Abse, 'How Italians Have Been Cheated', *New Left Review* 199 (May–June 1993); and on Refondajione, an interview with Luciana Castellina, editor of its weekly newspaper, *Liberajione*, available from Dialogue for European Alternatives (see the directory at the end of this book).

28 For an examination of the Greens, see A. Cole and B. Doherty, 'Les Verts', in Richardson and Roots, *The Green Challenge*.

29 I refer to the Left Socialists, similar in many ways to the Danish Socialist People's Party in that they originated as a split from a traditional left party (in their case, a Labour rather than Communist Party).

30 The Finnish Leftwing Alliance is similar in many ways to the Dutch Green Left in that it is the result of a merger between several organizations to the left of social democracy and in support of social movement politics. Though (unlike in Holland) in Finland there is a separate, right of centre Green Party. The Finnish Left Alliance is made up of the Finnish Communist Party, the Finnish People's Democratic Alliance, the Finnish Democratic Women's Organization. Unlike the Dutch Green Left, the Communist Party is predominant in the Finnish left. It won 10.1 per cent of the vote at the last election.

31 See A. Dobson, *Green Political Thought* (London, 1990).

32 Richard Crossman, in his introduction to *The English Constitution* (London, 1963).

33 The Danish Socialist People's Party, through trial and error, argument and splits, arrived – at least during a period when social movements were strong at a national level – at an effective co-operation between parliamentarians and autonomous movements. The successful campaign against nuclear power in 1979–80 provides a further illustration of co-operation. Together, the extra-parliamentary anti-nuclear movement and the SF have kept Denmark free of any further development of nuclear power. The anti-nuclear campaign won popular support for their case through direct action and educational campaigns, and the SF drew up detailed parliamentary amendments to the government's pro-nuclear Bill and brought together an opposition coalition of MPs. They won an amendment, drawn up in close co-operation with the anti-nuclear movement, which effectively negated the Bill itself: stating that there would have to be another parliamentary debate before the Bill's commitment to nuclear power was implemented, and that no nuclear power station could be built without

approval by referendum in the locality concerned. Since then the government has withdrawn the nuclear programme. Throughout the period of this campaign SF MPs and representatives of the anti-nuclear movement met weekly, sometimes daily. The same kind of joint action took place with the independent peace movements against the deployment of cruise missiles in 1981. Denmark was not a country for deployment, but the Danish Government, as a member of the NATO Nuclear Planning Group, supported NATO's deployment strategy. The SF harvested in parliament the fruits of the peace movement's campaigning in the country. A divided Social Democratic Party reversed its support for cruise and joined with the SSP and the Radical Liberal Party to pass a series of anti-cruise resolutions through the Danish Folketung, against the wishes of the minority Conservative government and, of course, NATO.

34 My own experiences of conducting interviews in the Danish and Norwegian Parliaments compared to the equivalent contact with the British political system confirmed this relative lack of distance between parliament and the people (middle-class people, at least). In the Danish Folketung the Prime Minister conducted his regular press conference in a manner unthinkable in Britain. Anybody was allowed in, including uncredited riff-raff like myself. Everyone sat round a table, the PM almost indistinguishable from the rest, getting a journalist to light his cigarette, sharing jokes before giving his briefing, answering questions in a relaxed way. I would not guarantee that Paul Schuster, the PM, was any more truthful than Margaret Thatcher's Press Secretary, Bernard Ingham. It was the culture of the event that was remarkable. Similarly in Norway: after interviewing Helge Hernes, the feminist Foreign Minister, in 1989, I joined in the lift a rather glamourous looking woman who had also dropped in to meet Ms Hernes. Thinking she might be a senior assistant of some kind from which I could get another angle on the Foreign minister, I asked her whether she worked for Helga Hernes. 'No,' she said, 'I am the American Ambassador'. And after a few pleasantries about women in top jobs she took her limousine back to the embassy.

35 There is nothing new about international voluntary organizations. After the Second World War, the urge to prevent nationalism from ever again developing into a malign force led thousands of West Europeans to establish transnational networks: municipal twinning, cultural exchanges, transnational conferences and so on. The Society of Friends has consistently supported East–West dialogues of various kinds. Both the UN and the EC have special provisions for international 'non-governmental organizations' (NGOs) to play a consultative role in their affairs and have selected access to their budgets.

In the 1980s, however, there has been, in the words of a close observer of European voluntary organizations, 'a period of explosive growth in the international voluntary movement'. But it is not just the growth in their number which is important. It is also their importance for achieving social goals, that is, for policies that in any way press social needs in the face of the dominant commercial imperatives of an increasingly international market. See Brian Harvey, *European Networks* (London, 1992).

PART IV

WHY MOVEMENTS MATTER
IN THE NEW EUROPE

8

ENDING THE COLD WAR

Introduction

Do social movements really matter? Or are they just good for the souls, or egos, of those who participate? In this book, I have argued that a distinctive feature of the democratic movements that have developed since 1968 is socialization of practical and theoretical knowledge. What bearing does this have on their power? Do they in fact have any power?

The impact of citizens' movements tends to be invisible. Moments of riot or revolution are recognized when the political order, which is the day-to-day focus for conventional media coverage, breaks down. But the everyday, cumulative impact, if any, of all the meetings, leaflets – and in the East, the more arduous work of underground organizing – is rarely acknowledged. The only faint recognition of something stirring has been the occasional bland reference in the West to 'shifts in public opinion' or politicians 'constrained by public opinion' in the course of reporting that invariably is focused on the politicians and their parties.

Sustained citizens' movements that lack direct political representation are consequently rarely regarded as actors that actually influence political outcomes. Anyone expressing a belief in their importance is often treated as if they are believers in a mysterious political alchemy. Sometimes, it is true, activists and sympathetic theorists do tend to invoke 'social movements' or 'civic initiatives' as if they were the elixir of political life. But it is possible, by inquiring into the workings of those 'shifts in public opinion', to make an empirical assessment of a movement's impact. Moreover such an assessment provides clues to the possible importance of similar movements in the future.

This book is laying out an argument between political actors across Europe, who as well as confronting fundamental disagreements also share a commitment to democratic civic movements. I argue that much of the practice of these movements in the West, at least much of the practice with which I am familiar, illustrates an approach to knowledge which underpins their potential as a distinctive kind of political agent. This involves on the one hand conscious effort to share, exchange and gather practical as well as theoretical knowledge in order to be sufficiently knowing to achieve purposive and effective social change. On the other hand it entails, ideally, a self-conscious sense of the limits of their knowledge, a refusal to claim the all-knowing expertise frequently claimed by social reformers of the past. I have illustrated how this approach to knowledge is closely associated with a radical, participative approach to democracy. It also inclines much movement practice towards a distinct approach to power.

The movements' emphasis tends to be less on taking power in the sense of taking over existing centres of power – many established power structures would, whoever was in charge, be organically inhospitable towards participative notions of democracy – and more on breaking up established power structures and creating new forms of power; though as we have seen, this frequently involves footholds within the existing structures. In the process of breaking up established power structures recent movements have created and recreated their own shifting sources of power, within social, cultural and economic rather than within predominantly political institutions. The democratization of knowledge is not, clearly, their only source of power: they accumulate resources, sometimes from the public sector (for example women's centres; trade union resource centres; municipal authorities committed to nuclear-free zones; co-operative, and ecologically conscious enterprises in Germany funded by Die Grünen), sometimes through other socially committed foundations (radical trade union and peace organizations, for instance, have benefitted from the World Council of Churches), sometimes through servicing their own 'niche' market (alternative bookshops, newpapers, cafes, clubs, independent film producers, publishing firms) and sometimes through winning positions and space within established institutions. They win cultural and political influence, through direct political and/or media representation, or through alliances with other social and political groups, such as churches, social democratic leaders, or popular cultural figures who do not share their wider politics but converge on a specific goal.[1]

But their implicit approach to knowledge, that is, the high priority they give to collective development of individual skills for political change (flowing in part from their emphasis on direct action for change in daily life), the way they gather knowledge otherwise ignored, expose knowledge otherwise kept secret, share knowledge otherwise dispersed and under-utilized, are all vital to their capacity to exercise a distinct form of power. Can this dispersed power, however, affect the course of history? To answer this question and to gain a sense of the importance of recent social movements for the future of European politics, it would be useful to assess the importance of citizens' movements in the momentous events of Europe's recent past, the events that ended the Cold War – though they failed to destroy its Western institutions. My focus will be on the peace movements which grew up from diverse origins across Europe from the early 1980s.

I want briefly to assess this historical moment not because that history could repeat itself (whether seriously or as farce), but because certain actors, themes and kinds of activity frequently recur. The peace movement of the early 1980s grew so quickly and became so vast because of the widespread fear of extermination – a powerful unifying force. Such a unifying factor is not now visibly present. The problems we now face across Europe entail many interests which in the short-term conflict with each other. Efforts to build movements against racism, to resist unemployment, to overcome the marginality of women and homophobic responses to lesbians and gay men, come up against numerous cross cutting interests and sources of mistrust. If the peace movement organized in vain then there is even less hope for the new coalitions that are gathering. On the other hand, if its impact (however specific) was significant, then some of the conditions of its success might apply to the attempts of civic activists at further change from below.

The peace movement and the end of Cold War

Commentators on both the left [2] and right accept the importance of popular action in the final phases of the downfall of the old regimes, when economic sclerosis had blocked all room for manoeuvre in the old structures. The pre-1981 strikes of Solidarity, the mass exodous to the West after the opening of the Hungarian border, the push on the streets of Prague to topple the Communist Party in Czechoslovakia are examples. But many of the same analysts would maintain that organized movements, campaigning for several years with explicit objectives – like independent peace movements mainly in the West but also in the East – were not effective players in the dramas that ended the Cold War. They would point to the fact that the peace movement, after all, did not prevent any government from finally accepting cruise. And the peace and democracy movements in the East (New Forum and Charter 77, for example) which became famous during the revolutionary months of 1989 have, with the exception of FIDESZ, been marginalized or divided.

Such an analysis, however, invokes very superficial measures of change – rather like assuming that because there has not been an earthquake, nothing significant is happening beneath the earth's surface. The peace movements created pressures at the base of society and weakened the Cold War relationships which the European siting of US missiles were intended specifically to strengthen. The peace movement thereby helped to create a favourable international climate for *perestroika* – relative that is, to what it might have been if Reagan and the Pentagon had been unconstrained. This is a fact which, insiders report, had a significant influence on Gorbachev.[3] Moreover the Western peace movement's attempt to break out of bloc politics inspired and provided essential support for the unprecedented development of an independent peace movement in the East. This in turn became an influential catalyst to the unstoppable pressure for democracy. In the following summary of events from the deployment of Cruise in 1979 to the West's aceptance of Gorbachev's proposals for nuclear disarmament in 1986, I trace the effects of the peace movement as an influence in the negotiating chambers from which, physically, it was absent.

The decision to deploy cruise

The deployment in Europe of Cruise and Pershing missiles was decided upon at the end of the consensual regimes of Jimmy Carter and James Callaghan. The decision reflected the failure of détente. But it was announced in the terms of détente; the deployment of these new weapons was to be combined with negotiations over arms control: 'a twin track approach', the experts reassured us.[4]

With the electoral victory of the radical right on both sides of the Atlantic, détente gave way to a revival of the ideology and politics of the Cold War. As a result, the second track disappeared. Whether by design or unconstrained momentum, the strategy was escalation, intensifying the pressure on the already buckling Soviet economy.

Détente failed because the structures of the Cold War were intact on both sides: the military–industrial complexes, the secret state, the opposing alliances whose whole rationale was a permanent preparedness for war. The superpower war machines co-existed peacefully but the preparations for war continued uninhibited. Military technologies continued to be elaborated, making a new weapons system and an escalation of the arms race virtually inevitable.[5] The ideologies which justified the conflict had been moderated but not finally rubbished; social democratic governments had in effect kept them alive by deference to them. A confident rightwing political elite, actively seeking to give them new life, had been waiting in the wings.

Outside the political and media establishment, however, the period of détente had seen a weakening of the ideological hold of Cold War thinking. In the West, the revolts of 1968 and the movement against the war in Vietnam had produced a democratic tradition of radicalism defining itself against the military and industrial establishments that ruled either side of the Iron Curtain. As discussed earlier, this tradition gave birth to a plethora of social movements whose common stance involved both a profound alienation from the existing political system and the self-confident creation of new forms of political action. Moreover, influential groups within more conventional corners of civil society – churches, trade unions and the liberal professions – had taken the rhetoric of détente literally and come to reject all notions of 'the Soviet threat', believing that the only direction for the Cold War was disengagement and disarmament.

As news spread that Western Europe was to be the site of NATO's long-range weapons targetted on the Soviet Union, the critically minded public which had thrived in the West under the reassuring cover of détente, poured out in protest. In London, Hamburg, Bonn, Berlin, Paris, Amsterdam, Rome, and Madrid, demonstrators converged in numbers never before witnessed since the Second War ended and the Cold War began.

In the East, an unavoidably more restricted break from Cold War thinking had occurred. The Accords of the Helsinki Summit in 1977, marking the high point of détente, provided significant openings for critical citizens in the East. This was the founding moment of Charter 77 and of human rights groups of various kinds all over Central and Eastern Europe. Since the governments of these countries had signed the Helsinki Accords, it was difficult successfully to isolate and repress these free initiatives of independent citizens. After all, they were merely trying to hold their governments to their public commitments. Indirectly, these groups were precursors to independent peace organizations which sprang up in the early 1980s and attracted a far wider group of people who did not at first define themselves as oppositional. The importance of these discreet developments in the late 1970s did not become apparent until 1989, when many of their initiators became leaders of the movements for democracy.

Placating public opinion: the zero option

The unexpected emergence of the peace movement as a political actor in the otherwise highly predictable processes of arms negotiations caused considerable unease in NATO circles, especially amongst policy makers most in touch with public opinion. The German and Dutch governments felt particularly constrained by the pressures of a suddenly alert and active public. They in turn exerted pressure on the Americans to moderate their Cold War stance or at least disguise it under a position closer to the original twin track.[6] The result was what Reagan advisors no doubt considered to be a clever knight's move: to take over the 'zero option' of the peace movement as their negotiating stance. NATO would not deploy Cruise and Pershing if the Soviets would scrap their SS 20s. 'We got the idea from your slogans', one of Reagan's entourage told a European peace movement journalist.[7] Reagan's advisors were confident that no such response would be forthcoming from the Soviet gerontocracy, for whom land-based missiles were more important than for the West.

It was a gambit which enabled Chancellor Kohl and Dutch Prime Minister Lubbers to support the deployment of Cruise as if they had lent a sympathetic ear to the growing mutterings of public anxiety. And they gained some electoral advantage from doing so; both won elections in 1983 even though opinion polls showed that majority opinion was against the deployment of the missiles. Prime Minister Thatcher adopted a more belligerent approach. Her commitment to the new Cold War stemmed from conviction. Her party was newly united behind her in the aftermath of the Falklands War. She was not particularly impressed by Reagan's gesture towards the zero option – to her it was at best a harmless concession to continental sensibilities. She went on the offensive, smearing the peace movement as pro-Soviet with the classic Cold War logic that turns critics into allies of the enemy. With a divided opposition, the British electoral system gave her adequate protection against articulate and popular but nevertheless minority critics.

Amongst Cold Warriors and pragmatic practitioners of *realpolitik* alike, the intention of the zero option was to quieten down an unexpectedly agitated public opinion, rather than to make a serious negotiating move. As Reagan let slip, talking (off the autocue) about the zero option in 1983, 'It's not propaganda! It's public relations.'[8] The cognitive myopia induced by Cold War conditioning meant that although NATO governments realized and relished the increasingly decrepit economic state of the Soviet Union, under the weight of massive military spending and the restrictions of bureacratic planning, they could not conceive of serious moves for reform from the leadership of this system.

With the US announcement of the zero option, it appeared that on a continental and (with the American 'freeze' movement) an intercontinental basis, the arduous work of peace activists had made the peace movement a force to be reckoned with. They had not, however, succeeded in turning themselves into a constraint. They influenced NATO calculations about presentation, about the rituals and rhetoric which surround negotiations. But they did not at this stage alter the real negotiating agenda.

If the Greenham Women had folded up their 'bender' tents on the arrival of the missiles, rather than spreading their web of direct action;[9] if the 1984 Convention of the European Campaign for Nuclear Disarmament in Berlin had been a final reunion rather than the gathering which stimulated a new wave of East–West organizing; and if CND and other national peace movements had given up their regular demonstrations, press briefings and parliamentary lobbying; then this effect on the US presentation of its escalation of the Cold War, would have been the sum of the peace movements' impact on the end of the Cold War, and the end might not have been so speedy.

Reagan's dance of negotiating bravado in 1981 was taken over by Gorbachev in 1985 to relax East–West tensions and initiate a foxtrot of reform within the system over which he thought he ruled. It was then, when the zero option was for real, that Kohl, Thatcher and the inner core of the NATO mafia tried hard to block it. Such an option, as a serious negotiating move, broke with superpower negotiating conventions – according to which new weapons presented as bargaining chips are always in the end deployed and bargaining moves on, from a plateau of newly bristling weaponry, to a period of arms limitation. Here, in Gorbachev, was a Soviet leader without precedent, taking seriously a proposal for actually physically destroying the most sophisticated military technology available – in exchange for destroying an earlier generation of aggressive but inefficient missiles of their own. Even if Gorbachev personally were to be trusted, would he be in power long enough to see through his commitment? These and many other arguments were put up to protect the expensive objects lying demobilized in Greenham, Comiso, Muttlangen and Woensdrecht. Finally, Thatcher and Kohl reluctantly and 'under the pressure of public opinion' (elections were in the offing) followed Reagan's lead (he was nearing the end of his term of office; the moment to consider the judgements of history) and accepted Gorbachev's proposals.

Public opinion was such a powerful factor in Britain and Germany because a very widely supported peace movement, with all its unorthodox, widely shared political skills – the creation of telephone trees, the taking of symbolic direct action, the organizing of 'people-to-people' contact across the Iron Curtain, and the gathering and exposing defence intelligence – had kept the zero option in public debate. Across Western Europe, the peace movements had called Reagan's bluff. The movement's direct action, ambushing cruise convoys as they tried, in Heseltine's facile phrase, to 'melt into the country-side', gave headline publicity to the case for the West to deliver their zero immediately. Reagan had tried to twist the idea of double zero in his direction to expose the Soviets as war mongers. The common cause that an influential part of the peace movement made with independent peace and human rights groups across the Cold War divide enabled peace movements to weaken Reagan's impact. Without appearing to be tools of Moscow, they could deny the offensive intentions of the Soviet military, call convincingly for the initiators of the zero option to withdraw the missiles unilaterally, and show how this would strengthen the pressures in the Soviet bloc for democracy. Partly as a result of its contacts with Eastern oppositionists, the peace movement was far more in tune with the changing politics of the Soviet Union and the seismic shifts they were bringing about in international politics. NATO was in a state of considerable confusion, even though it was to be an immediate beneficiary of Gorbachev's reforms.[10]

Vital to this process was the fact that the peace movement entered the Gorbachev era already a political player in what turned out to be the endgame of the Cold War. It was even more important that most of the movement obstinately and actively kept the public eye on the zero option. The peace movement created a political climate – against the prevailing winds blowing from the strategists of NATO, the Pentagon, and the Ministries of Defence in Bonn and in London – that proved favourable to Gorbachev's dramatic moves towards disarmament. The freezing winds of the Reagan and Thatcher Cold War, if they had been able to let rip, could well have slowed down these initiatives, if not killed them, subjecting Gorbachev's stealthy strategy within his own party to impossible difficulties much earlier than it eventually was. The collapse of Communism would have come, but with violence, very likely on the Tienamen Square model planned by Honecker in East Germany, but avoided mainly through the intervention of Gorbachev.

The independent peace movement in the West also had an influence on the new thinking on foreign relations which flourished under Gorbachev. Tair Tairov had the job, as Soviet representative of the World Peace Council in Helsinki, of informing the Soviet leadership about trends in Western peace movements. Soon after Gorbachev became his boss, he found that he was required to report on the details of the movements' proposals rather than the ideological stance of its leaders. He believes that Gorbachev 'has been shaped, as far as foreign policy is concerned, by peace and new social movements in Europe.'[11]

The peace movements thus contributed to the end of the Cold War but not in quite the way that its activists intended. They eased the way for perestroika and the peaceful collapse of Communism. They damaged the Cold War consensus, or at least ensured that it could not be remade; but they did not fatally wound the Western institutions of the Cold War, as most of its activists wanted. These institutions remained essentially intact, as their role in the Gulf War demonstrated – even if their Atlantic foundations are shaky.

The erosion of the political culture of the Cold War?

What are the long-term implications of the partial character of the peace movement's success? How far can Cold War institutions, whose rationale no longer has a hold on people's consciousness, maintain their control over the processes of European transition, and determine to what kind of society they are leading? The answer to this depends in part on how far the peace movement challenged not only the weapons policy of the Cold War but also its deeper political and philosophical culture.

The distinctive character of the 1980s peace movement provides clues to how deeply it has really weakened the hold of Cold War institutions and culture on the people of the West. Peace movements through the Cold War years have had certain themes in common, but the movement of the 1980s had unique features.

Its size was extraordinary: it inspired more people to come out on to the streets and express their protest publically than any other movement in post-war years; in every country except France more people were demonstrating against Cruise than against the Vietnam war, or in support of the student revolt in the late sixties, or on trade union issues in the early seventies, or for the women's movement or anti-nuclear movement later in the seventies. It gained sustenance, however, from the roots which these movements had put down, the networks they had created. In particular, its quick footedness and self-confidence was enhanced by the large proportion of the politically aware members of a generation – the generation first politically active in the late 1960s and early 1970s – who never became devoted members of established political parties. An unusually large proportion of this generation, influenced by a significant smattering of individuals from earlier generations, had instead directed their energies to organizing independently, in their workplaces or localities, or to writing and educating from freelance lookout posts across the continent.

The new peace movement could draw on ready-made infrastructures, well-developed skills and accumulated knowledge of extra-parliamentary politics. Rebels from the Communist Party in 1956, student revolutionaries from 1968, feminists from the early days of Women's Liberation, radical trade unionists sharpened by the industrial militancy of the years before boom gave way to recession: all these disparate groups had kept alive organizing networks, a flow of ideas, debate, research and investigation, and the learning of new political skills. These were vital resources which the new peace movement was able immediately to mobilize. It was also able to draw on various religious and cultural institutions which had long established traditions of peace campaigning.

The motley range of people that came together to start a local group or initiate an action would usually consist – according to one survey – of 30 per cent who were new to any public political activity. Of the remaining 70 per cent there would invariably be a core who had learnt from the hard school of trial and error about starting a movement of protest and direct action. As a result, the 1980s peace movement was almost from birth an unusually skilled and articulate movement: skilled at digging out and disseminating information; at producing attractive literature; at the rapid organizing of meetings and direct action; and at reaching into the trade unions, social democratic parties and other parts of society with which a new, single issue movement would have difficulties making a connection.

As we have seen, the effort and energy of the movement was somehow sustained for six years, from 1981–7. There were moments of hesitation and a degree of demoralization, especially when, in all the five countries designated (except Holland and, for a period, Italy), the missiles were delivered as planned. There were divisions and squabbles and people went their own way – the peace movement was plural enough for that. Some people ran out of puff, but others joined at high points of popular influence. In 1984, at its height, CND had 100,000 members. And right until after the ceremonial signing of the INF, Cruisewatchers were still ambushing missiles on Salisbury Plain and monitoring Cruise launch exercises from the Peace House by the base in Florennes, not trusting those who had deployed them to actually destroy them.

People had come on the first demonstrations in 1981 in fear and anger. But such emotions cannot regenerate the energies of a movement for six years. From protesting against lethal weapons and the decisions that sited them on European soil, the movement developed a distinctive politics. When a private aeroplane circled endlessly over the demonstrators in Bonn on an October Saturday in 1981 saying 'Wie Demonstriert in Moscow?' (Who demonstrates in Moscow?), the crowd responded with a banner on helium balloons declaring in German: 'No to NATO and the Warsaw Pact'. The distinctive feature of the eighties peace movement was that it was for the end of the blocs, the end of the Cold War. This was undoubtedly a source of its wide appeal. Previous post-war peace movements had never clearly and publicly been able to break out of the Cold War mental bind: if you are for disarmament, you are supporting the enemy; the enemy represses freedom therefore you must be against freedom and all that 'the West' stands for. As Edward Thompson, one the movement's most persuasive advocates of this distinctive politics, put it: 'the great achievement of the Cold War is to separate peace and freedom, thereby paralysing activists on both sides. . . . The "West" claimed freedom and "the East" claimed the cause of peace. Crucial to the first is America's claim to be the custodian of that freedom and therefore in some sense for American society to epitomize that freedom. Crucial to the second is the Communist Party's monoploy of the meaning of peace and of the organization and orchestration of pro-peace activities.'[12]

The popular appeal of CND marches or their equivalent in West Germany, Holland and Belgium in the late 1950s and early 1960s was limited by this disabling logic and an inability convincingly to challenge it, as was the case to a lesser extent with the West European movement against the war in Vietnam ten years later. Governments attacked them all as pro-Moscow and the smear tended to stick, however loudly they protested their independence.

Reagan, Kohl, Thatcher and Lubbers tried again in the 1980s.[13] The private plane over Bonn is just a small example; similar planes with similar messages flew over demonstrations in London. Peace activists in Britain had their phones bugged and were the subjects of sustained campaigns of disinformation. We have the word of one of those who supervised this work, Cathy Massiter, to prove it.[14] Fortunately, the dirty tricks proved too dirty to handle, and the smears did not stick sufficiently to keep the movement in subcultural isolation.

Several factors are important. Firstly, the economic foundations of the Atlantic Alliance were beginning to crumble. American superpower leadership was central to the cohesion and credibility of the Western bloc and the apparent naturalness of the blocs as the basis of European politics; just as in a different form, Soviet economic power was central to the stability of the Eastern bloc. The economic strength of Western Europe and the economic decline of America meant that the basis for the Atlantic Alliance increasingly relied on America's military and in particular nuclear dominance rather than Western Europe's economic dependence. In the absence of any strong economic bond, acquiescence by West European populations in the need for such military dominance, when they had no democratic leverage over the US government, required widespread acceptance of virulently anti-Communist free-market ideology. Maestros of performance, Ronald Reagan and Margaret Thatcher did their best. But after ten years of détente during which an anti-Stalinist left established its own, if somewhat unstable, legitimacy (especially in countries with a proportional electoral system), and with every appearance of the Soviet bear in an old and decrepit state, rather than growling for a fight, their raw material was rather thin. The peace movement retaliated on many levels. There was no grand plan, but with an increasingly shared sense of direction as a movement for ending the Cold War different parts of the movement challenged the ideology and its props from every angle.

The props of cold war politics

Secrecy was the first prop to fall. A feature of parliamentary democracy, Cold War style, is that matters of 'national security' are never publicly debated – and guess who defines what is 'national security'? None of the last 40 years' decisions by NATO or member states concerning the acquisition of nuclear weapons has been taken, let alone debated, in public. The decision on 12 December 1979 to deploy intermediate nuclear missiles on European soil was no exception. What became exceptional was the public debate forced on governments and opposition parties across Western Europe.

On several occasions parliamentary debates in Holland, Britain and Germany were the result of peace organizations publishing information which the governments had kept secret. For instance, IKV, the Dutch Interchurch Peace Council, published for the first time information about its government's commitment to missions involving nuclear weapons. This led to an unplanned public debate and induced a government policy paper with a commitment to reduce the role of nuclear weapons in NATO. Similar secrets were dragged struggling before the public eye in Germany and the UK. Divisions within NATO, exacerbated by the Cruise decision, meant that the peace movement had friends in the most unlikely places.

The language of technological progress and scientific gobbledegook and its ability to obliterate the language of human values was a second prop which fell under the prose of writers like Edward Thompson, Vaclav Havel and Georg Konrad, and the songs of the Greenham Women. The parallel emergence of the green movement was important here: the whole notion of 'technological progress' was questioned and with it the positive connotations of words like 'modernization' and the promises of technical efficiency with which the military build-up of both sides had been glamorously cloaked.

The bipartisanship of the main parties had always been a condition of the Cold War. Parties that would not reliably collude, like the Italian and French Communist Parties, were constitutionally or through back room deals excluded from government. The most significant splintering of this powerful Cold War prop was the decision of the German SPD, against the wishes of ex-Chancellor Schmidt, to oppose the siting of missiles. The British Labour Party was divided. In fact, the first major divide in its Cold War history, with the formation of the SDP, was essentially over the risk that the party would break with its Atlanticist past. Although its life was brief, the SDP served its purpose by inducing the Labour leadership to look constantly to the right of the political spectrum, supressing all attempts to break the Labour Party from its historic loyalty to national security.

The significance of post-war bipartisanship over matters of national and European security was ideological: it tied political parties into the Cold War consensus. There was therefore no democratically legitimated voice providing a focus for critical debate. Consequently, a further challenge to the Cold War consensus emerged in Germany, Holland, Belgium and Denmark, in the form of political parties outside and to the left of this consensus. With Die Grünen, the Dutch Pacifist Socialist and Radical Parties, the two Belgium Green parties and the Danish Socialist People's parties – all with support ranging from 7 to 13 per cent of the popular vote – the peace movement had a political voice. Where it did not have this national electoral legitimacy, as in Britain, it sought with limited success to win it by other means: for instance, municipal councils declared themselves 'nuclear-free zones' to symbolize the aim of a nuclear-free Europe and eventually a nuclear free world; while the women's embrace of the Greenham base had extraordinarily widespread support.

The erosion of these various props of the Cold War consensus not only enabled the peace movement to enter deeper into the daily life of West European society than any other radical social movement in post war years, it also gave its activists an unusual self-confidence and courage. This reached its peak in the actions that regularly put Cruise out of service and kept the zero option dramatically in the headlines. 'The convoy was monitored lining up at 11pm. Red and white paint were sprayed onto the control vehicles at midnight,' an early issue of the *International Cruise Watch News* reports casually, as if describing a family outing. 'Ian climbed on top of the control vehicle whilst another man let down the tires, Ian leaned over and sprayed peace symbols on the windscreen and side windows . . . The Convoy struggled on towards

Bullingdon where it met a further demonstration.' And they were still at it when the poor old convoy returned to Greenham: 'At the yellow gate the women blockaded the convoy, Becky got on top of the launcher and rode into the base. She was arrested for trespass.' After a few preliminary skirmishes like this, the *Sunday Telegraph* on its front page quotes military authorities as being 'given great cause for concern' after another 'ambush' which these same authorities described as 'much better planned and executed than we had expected . . . [with the] use of radios, several vehicles and 200 people'.[15]

Through all these holes in Cold War defences, whether political, ideological or physical, the peace movement conveyed increasingly coherent challenges to the Iron Curtain's ideological foundation stones. They in effect dug up and broke the cement of these foundations: the cement that separates the cause of freedom and the cause of peace. In practical ways some part of the peace movement (not always the same part) challenged both the US claim to 'freedom' and the Soviet claim to 'peace'. On the one hand organizations concentrated their fire on the Reagan adminsitration and the US military establishment, exposing its activities worldwide. Victims and campaigners from the Pacific Islands where the US had tested nuclear weapons came to conferences in the West. West European peace organizations established close links with the Freeze movement in the States and with groups campaigning against American intervention in Nicaragua and El Salvador. The workings of NATO became the subject of public scrutiny. American military dominance in Europe and the institutions by which it is exerted became for the first time since the Marshall Plan the subject of popular debate and concern. Opinon polls in 1987 showed that more people considered the US to be a threat to world peace than considered the Soviet Union to be such.

On the other hand were organizations such as END and the German Greens, which sought to bring peace and freedom together by well publicized support for and dialogue with opposition groups and independent peace organizations in the East. The importance of this sensitive and persistent work was twofold. The more it became known in the West that peace movement leaders and activists were in the forefront of campaigning for democracy in Eastern Europe, the more ludicrous appeared the accusations that the peace movement peddled 'Soviet inspired anti-Americanism'. It also opened up the record of Western governments towards the East to scrutiny; and revealed a sickly syrup of hypocrisy. Behind the well-publicized pleas for mercy for particular dissidents was the firm priority of stability over anything so risky as democracy and freedom fought for from below.

Direct diplomacy: the basis of a political culture

The East–West 'people to people' diplomacy, engaging oppositionists to the blocs from both sides, provides perhaps the best illustration of the distinctiveness of the 1980s peace movement. It also demonstrates an application of the principles of direct action – autonomous of state and party, based on inside practical knowledge and theoretical insights – to international politics, at first sight an apparently distant sphere where such principles would seem particularly difficult to apply. The attendance of Western peace movement activists at clandestine meetings of oppositionists in the East, the debates published in samizdat and the occasional co-ordinated actions were all a form of direct action against the taboos of the Cold War and the language and institutions that sustained them. But they were more than protest; and in the West the peace movement was more than a single issue lobby. This corrosion of the Iron Curtain from below helped to create a political culture that lived independently and inevitably in conflict with the state – though in different forms East and West. The story of the emergence of this precarious culture of peace and democracy is interesting in itself, but for the argument of this book it provides an illustration of how the impact of the peace movements in the early 1980s, building in the West on the radical movements of the previous fifteen years, was not simply a matter of a brief mobilization of public opinion. It involved the creation over a period of five years or so of new relationships and institutions. At times these were very marginal and extremely shaky. At other times they proved to be alternative sources of power to those available within established politics. Moreover, it is the story of the origins of one of the lasting components of the pan-European networks of people organizing across the continents against the new curtains closing down on the lives of many of their fellow citizens or would-be citizens.

The independent peace movement in the West had an influence in the East whose precise importance in the democratic revolutions is difficult to measure. What is undeniable, however, is that organizations and individuals who founded independent peace movements in the East, or worked with (as far as possible) the independent peace movements in the West, played a leading role in the first moments of democratic transformation in Hungary, Czechoslovakia and East Germany. They were also influential amongst younger supporters of Solidarity.

In the late 1970s the opposition in Central and Eastern Europe began to take a more organized form than in the past with the groups that prised open the small space created by the Helsinki Accords. These organizations, Charter

77 among them, were at first suspicious of the Western peace movement. They had never known it to give support to their struggle for human rights against the militaristic regimes of the Soviet bloc. They had read about it in the past with bored, contemptuous eyes as its demonstrations against 'Western imperialism' were tediously paraded in the official press. In 1985 Havel wrote a whole essay, the 'Anatomy of Reticence', devoted to the problem. In it he said: 'When it comes to "dissidents" in east-central Europe, the prevailing mood [towards Western peace movements] seems to be one of reticence, of caution, if not outright distrust and uneasiness'.[16] When Edward Thompson went to Czechoslovakia to get support for the END appeal for a transcontinental movement against the Cold War, no one from Charter 77 wanted to meet him. For them peace without democracy was not worthy of the name.

The suspicion that the peace movement in the West did not understand this, and the desire to assuage this suspicion, stimulated an extraordinary correspondance between Thompson and Charter 77 founder, Jaroslav Sabota, who wrote from effective house arrest in Brno – extraordinary because both men had joined their respective countries' Communist Parties believing them to be a means of achieving a democratic peace. Thompson had left in 1956; Sabota had been a supporter of Dubceck on the Party's Central Committee in 1968, when he was the one member of the Central Committee to oppose the agreement with the Soviet Union that sealed the coffin of the reform movement. Both had seen the terms 'peace' and 'democracy' being drained of meaning in the East and trivialized in the West. Most important, both had seen them being wrenched apart; an outcome of the Cold War divide and the reason why two people of such similar values and, as Sabota eventually agrees, from 'movements which are essentially the same', should briefly be so estranged. In terms of language and political culture this exchange of letters and the pamphlet which spread their message were seminal – old fashioned as such exchanges might now, unfortunately, seem. They provided in appropriately immediate and personal terms the theoretical touchstone of the first peace movement East and West which broke, painstakingly and firmly, out of Cold War thinking.

After three years of such debate, Charter 77 (including Vaclav Havel and Jiri Deinspier) and END worked on a common appeal, the Prague Appeal, linking the struggle for democracy and human rights with the movements for peace. The importance of this linkage, both of the ideas (democracy and peace) and of the organizations (Charter 77 and END), is indicated by the exceedingly undiplomatic expressions of irritation by officials of both superpowers. US officials, including Reagan, used quotes from the minority of Charter 77 who disgreed with the Prague Appeal to discredit the peace movement. Soviet officials used every opportunity to abuse END spokespeople, such as Mary Kaldor and Edward Thompson.[17]

The impetus towards a new kind of peace movement in the East also came from young people, who did not see themselves as part of the opposition. The first positive Czechoslovak response to END's appeal came from the Prague Jazz Section of the Czechoslovak union of Musicians. Some of them formed the John Lennon Peace Group, some now work for *Respekt* and play in well-known rock groups.

In the late eighties young people founded the Independent Peace Association, and several of them briefly became MPs in the federal parliament supporting the Civic Movement, led by Jiri Dienstbier. In East Germany, the same generation organized in the early eighties what could truly be called a 'movement'. It grew under the protection of the Protestant churches, and was led by several different groups: among them 'Swords into Ploughshares' and 'The Initiative for Peace and Freedom'. In Hungary, too, young people inspired by the direct action of the peace movement in the West took their own initiatives in the early eighties. 'With Flowers Against Arms' was the name of one group; there was a group of artists called 'INDIGO' who drew up their own appeal; And an Anti-Nuclear Campaign began with the slogan, 'Let Us Melt Down the Arms'. They coalesced to create 'Dialogue'. Janos Laslo, 25 years old at the time and a cleaner in a small private enterprise, explained the meaning of this name: 'It indicates that we think of the Cold War as our prime enemy . . . we have got used to a divided Europe; it has become too much part of our consciousness, and it does not even occur to us that it can be changed. We want to start up plenty of lively human channels of relationships . . . so that we cannot be told "there are beasts over there" so that we cannot be sent to war because we cannot fight our friends'. Through END especially, the lively channels opened up. One of the first messages to come through was an embroidered banner of solidarity from Blaenau Festiniog in Wales which deeply impressed the young Hungarians. Later in 1988 Dialogue members joined with students and young lecturers to form FIDESZ. In Poland a group of young supporters of Solidarity formed a network of peace activists called Peace and Freedom.

In the first phase of these movements, from 1981 to the deployment of Cruise in 1983, they had active support from people well beyond dissident circles. They involved people who were trying to rescue some real meaning from the regime's rhetoric of peace and disarmament. Laslo Janos, a rebel in his daily life, a kind of Hungarian punk but not a dissident, again explained: 'We have a very difficult task. Both we and the State have to prove ourselves.

We have to convince it that we are not a cover organization for the overthrow of the social order; but the State will have to prove that its attempts for peace are not merely empty slogans. . . . There have to be guarantees so that the achievements of the anti-war movements in NATO countries will be followed by steps in Eastern Europe'. It is clear that a convergence with the peace movements in the West was part of this movement's character, and in the end was what made it so unacceptable to the authorities. In 1983 leading members of Dialogue were interrogated by the secret police and the organization was banned. At the same time leaders of the peace movement in the DDR were imprisoned.

A further feature of the peace groups that sprang up in 1981 that made almost inevitable their visits from the secret police, was their rebellion against the militarism that lay heavily on the institutions of the Eastern bloc. Campaigns against conscription were the main activity of these movements which so attracted young people. But they found that they experienced much of the same hierarchy, the same fear and humiliation, the same unchangeable power structure in civilian life. As a result these peace movements became the political engine rooms of an anti-authoritarian movement which is still very much part of the politics of its past members in the face of increasingly threatening authoritarian trends, post-1989.

Internationalist, anti-authoritarian, democratic: like the 1980s' peace movement in the West. But on both sides, their convergence was based on opposition to what these movements uniquely identified as a common enemy: the mutually reinforcing institutions of the two sides of the Cold War. Now they face problems of reconstruction and integration, problems which appear to be geographically and socially specific. Some of the common values shaped in dialogue against a common enemy are disintegrating in the face of new complexities and differences. What evidence is there of any lasting cohesion and influence of the movement networks created in the 1980s? What new 'people-to-people' organizations are being created to overcome the divisions provoked by the ideologically motivated meanness of the West and the political and economic opportunists gaining public and private power in the East? Can the distinctive view of knowledge and democracy identified in these pages contribute to developing a language and range of concepts with which to negotiate new forms of continental co-operation?

Notes

1 James Hinton provides a very thoughtful history of peace movements in Britain in *Protests and Visions* (London, 1989).
2 See Fred Halliday, 'The Ends of the Cold War', *New Left Review* 180 (March/

April, 1990); and the debate between Fred Halliday and E. P. Thompson in *New Left Review* 182 (July/August, 1990).

3   See Tair Tairov, 'From New Thinking to a Civic Peace', in *Europe from Below*, ed.Mary Kaldor (London, 1991).

4   D. Johnstone provides a well-informed analysis of the background to these developments in *The Politics of Euromissiles: Europe's Role in America's World* (London, 1984).

5   See Mary Kaldor, *The Imaginary War* (Oxford 1989) for a general analysis and her *Baroque Arsenal* (London, 1982) for a detailed analysis of the arms industry.

6   See chapter 9 of Thomas R. Rochan, *Mobilising for Peace* (London, 1988); and Gale Mattox, 'West German Perspectives on Nuclear Armament and Arms Control', *Annals of the American Academy of Political Science*, 469 (September, 1983).

7   See 'Alliance in Crisis Over INF Deal', *END Bulletin*, August 1987.

8   The monthly bulletin of END is a very useful source of information on the international dimensions of the campaigns against Cruise missiles. Back copies are available from END, 10 Goodwin Street, London W1.

9   For a fascinating history of women's role in different phases of the peace movement up to and including Greenham, see Jill Liddington, *The Long Road to Greenham: Feminism and Anti-Militarism Since 1920* (London, 1989).

10   See M. Kaldor, G. Holden and R. Falk (eds) *The New Détente: Rethinking East-West Relations* (London, 1989) for an excellent collection of articles on the 'new détente', the role of the peace movements and changes in the Soviet Union.

11   Tairov, 'From New Thinking to a Civic Peace'.

12   E. P. Thompson, *Beyond the Cold War* (Merlin, 1982).

13   For example, Michael Heseltine, Minister of Defence in the mid-1980s, set up a special department specifically to counter the impact of the peace movement. There also is evidence of contact between the Republican administration in the US and the British Conservative Party – for instance, during the 1987 election, Richard Pearle, a leading defence adviser to the Reagan administration, made what was seen by the British press as a direct attack on the Labour Party's defence policy.

14   Hugo Young Programme, 20 February 1985. This programme was banned, but the details came out in the press the following week.

15   The *Sunday Telegraph*, 9 November 1986.

16   V. Havel, 'Anatomy of Reticence', *Living the Truth*, ed. Jan Vladislav (London, 1986).

17   For example, they used a visit by Edna Healey and Glenys Kinnock to the headquarters of the Soviet peace movement to vent their hostility – such exasperation with the new peace movement probably had a familiar, more homely, ring to it for these two women. See D. Healey, *The Time of My Life* (London, 1990).

9

CONCLUSIONS: TRANSFORMING GOVERNMENTALITY

Introduction

Urgent pleas for a new partnership are coming from those in East Europe who feel that something has been lost as well as much gained, since 'those beautiful and crushing months in autumn 1989'. These are the words of Jan Urban, a leading Charter 77 activist, election campaign manager for the Civic Forum the movement that led the revolution in Prague, when it stood for the first post-1989 parliamentary elections in 1990. He is now a journalist. Urban went on to make this appeal on Western TV:

> Imagine us, East Europeans, like an ugly, worn-out male creature, waking up one morning and deciding that a lifetime spent on drinking was enough. There is an unclear memory of some better past a long time ago, maybe a slight feeling of shame and a will to wash, shave and go out to look for some work. In this particular situation, when moved by the combination of good will and a hangover, it is vital to have enough light, a mirror and someone who can help you convince yourself that you should open the window to get some fresh air. It is not just that someone shouts at you: "Stop drinking you beast. Just look at yourself. You will never make it among decent people!" We – ex-ideologyholics – need someone who knows us, who wants to know us better, we need a partner, not a teacher.[1]

Partners have been coming forward to work with civic activists like Jan Urban to overcome the hangover, counter xenophobia and resist war; to

overcome the 'golden curtain', as Gabriel Andreescu, a Romanian oppositionist, described the new economic divisions across Europe; and to develop
feasible alternatives to unemployment and ecological disaster. When there are
no democratic pan-European political institutions, the process of forging and
sustaining these partnerships is fraught with material difficulties (lack of
finance, of communication, of time), even before the deeper political complexities are addressed. To overcome these barriers people are drawing, ingen-
iously, on established resources, official and unofficial. Sympathetic factions in
the European Parliament and various funding programmes of the EC; the
networks established in the 1980s by peace, green and human rights movements and by feminist organizations; the limited spare capacities of the trade
union and co-operative movements, and voluntary organizations in the West;
the relatively well-resourced radical left and green parties of Northern Europe
– all are providing resources to create new means of international collaboration. This process is important to explain and study in itself.[2] What I have
been concerned to do in this book is to discuss the intellectual and political
challenges presented by this novel partnership to Westerners who consider
themselves part of a very broadly defined new left.

This might seem a description of a personal intellectual process, but it
has led me to conclusions which I think have a wider relevance. The
partnership began as something of a political shock. It has led, however,
to a clarification of a fuzzy cluster of radically democratic and (in my understanding of the concept) socialist aspirations. They amounted to a political
vision which aspired to a 'genuine socialism', as if this indicated clearly
a desirable and feasible alternative to the regimes that ruled in socialism's
name. These aspirations were a little imprecise about the character of
the break that was necessary with the presumptions that underlay the
state practice of socialism, East and West. And without the test of sustained
implementation – only of resistance and limited experimentation – these
aspirations could retain an innocent vagueness about the distinctive workings
of the alternative.

Encounters with young civic activists of 1989, whose rejection of Communism was so complete that it ruled out any consideration of a notion
of 'genuine socialism', was almost equivalent to the test of implementation.
It was the philosophical equivalent of my first few weeks in the echoing rooms
of County Hall, London, faced with implementing ambitious commitments to create jobs for tens of thousands of London's unemployed.[3] It required me to call on all the intellectual and political resources of the
unformed, inchoate political tradition in which I had an intuitive but
unscrutinized confidence.

It has been necessary to answer this challenge as a condition for pursuing this East–West partnership with any integrity, while at the same time persisting, on my home ground, with a renewal of socialist politics. I also believe that it is important for the future of a democratic, egalitarian and ecological European politics that leftists in the West and democratic civic activists in the East can not only collaborate practically, but can learn mutually from both the past failures of Communism and the present calamities brought about by the dogmatic pursuit of the free market.

My conclusion (which really only indicates the need for further study of an active and experimental kind) is that the Western movements of the left that have emerged independently of parliamentary politics over the last 30 years have in their practice, and sometimes in their theory, been pressing for and even illustrating a new kind of political method, new relations between state, economy and social life, and new forms of party and state organization.

The grounds for their transformation of politics and political economy lies in a rejection of the forms of rationality that have underpinned the dominant forms of both government and market throughout the Cold War years. In searching the theory and the practice of the would-be new left for an answer to the Eastern appeal of neo-liberalism, it became clear that it is in their presumptions concerning knowledge and its social organization that these movement activists break from the political methods that have dominated the governing parties of the left. In spite of many illusions and mistakes, the understanding of knowledge developing in the practice of the social movement left provides an impetus for a democratic transformation of existing political institutions, and for forms of socially owned, co-operatively organized and ecologically sustainable economies.

The left traditions that have shaped or been drawn on to justify the behaviour of the left in government, East and West, have rested, more or less explicitly, on understandings of knowledge of a positivist and instrumental character. The grounds for state action to meet the needs of the people were presumed to be given by social scientific laws based on constant correlations of social causes and effects. The character of government action was based on a calculation of the most effective technical means of mastering these social processes.

The movements that grew up in the West in the 1970s and 1980s outside the orthodox power structures, challenged not only the policies of 'the military and industrial complex', as C. Wright Mills famously described these structures,[4] but their very foundations and habitual methods.

A *common starting point*

I have sought to show that it is in the Western movements' fundamental rejection of existing power structures, Soviet as well as Western capitalist, that they have a common starting point with their would-be Eastern partners who have been so attracted to at least the philosophy, if not the policy prescriptions, of the free-market right. In very different ways, they have rebelled against political projects, however benignly intended, which implicitly as well as explicitly look to the agency of an all-knowing state or party to solve social problems on the people's behalf and without their close involvement. Both groups of movement activists were rebelling against, among other things, the appropriation of economic and social knowledge by the state and the party and, in the West, the private corporation. Each group, however, developed out of entirely different civil societies (or a lack of it, in the case of the East), and was drawn to a very different vision of society. In the Eastern vision, the private market has been central – as the basis of an escape from the state. In the Western vision, some kind of the market is presumed, but there is a stress on the common ownership of wealth and supportive action by the state as counter forces to unaccountable private wealth, and as necessary parts of an unspecified co-operative, self-managed economy. But in spite of such differences, both perspectives are based on an appreciation, in practice if not in theory, of the distinctive importance of 'everyday' or uncodified knowledge.

Under repressive regimes where private exile was the only means for the majority to retain any sense of personal identity and fulfilment, this everyday knowledge, the knowledge of the ordinary citizen, was easily understood as individual, inherently private. Hayek's challenge to the all-knowing state in the defence of the 'free market' consequently has an appeal to Eastern oppositionists as a political philosophy, even though these people would disagree with other social and political elements of the right-wing programme that generally accompanies such beliefs.

As I argued in chapters 3 and 4, there is an alternative basis on which to recognize and value uncodified knowledge. I contend that this alternative view values everyday knowledge more than Hayekian philosophy, in that it understands that such knowledge, when it is shared and combined with other forms of knowledge, can be the basis for purposeful social change. I have argued both against Hayek's atomistic understanding of experiential knowledge and against a positivistic, social-engineering understanding of theoretical knowledge. In doing so I have sought to retrieve retrospectively

from the practice of Western left movements the elements of radically different foundations to political action.

A *new politics of knowledge*

The starting point for many of the movements' explorations of alternative
conceptions of knowledge has been a belief that the character and organization of knowledge, including what kinds of knowledge are considered
publicly legitimate, are the outcome of social processes. Hence people can act
to transform the existing organization and hierarchy of knowledge if these
were seen as a foundation of present forms of exclusive power. This understanding generated the confidence that many of these movements shared, in
widening the range of ways of knowing recognized in economic and political
debate. In fact, in their early formation this was vital to the way the movements developed their sense of identity as a movement or political force.

Moreover, in their own practice they illustrated the importance of experiential and practical forms of knowledge, including the tacit knowledge
involved in exercising a skill, for the identification and resolution of social
problems. Such a widening of the field of relevant sources of understanding
broke down the fences that in conventional politics divided ends from means,
and facts from values, and which protected the clinical neutrality of instrumental reasoning.

The new movement politics, in its frustration with conventional politics, experimented with bringing about change directly, within whatever
relationships were oppressive. They came to discover limits to acting independently of the established power structures. But they had demonstrated the
possibilities of bringing about change through the actions of those who, as
victims, previously colluded, in apparent impotence, in reproducing the
social relationships through which they suffered. And movement activists
insisted that the perceptions and experiences of these previously marginalized
actors were therefore a vital source of the knowledge that should help to guide
strategies for change.[5]

Among the structures that many of these movements actively transformed
in this way has been the distribution and organization of knowledge itself. It
has often been the process of sharing of practical knowledge, combining and
connecting it with theoretical and statistical knowledge, that has imbued a
movement with power and social leverage. This has been combined, in the
most effective cases, with a self-reflexive awareness of their own fallibility, and
of the need constantly to reach out to sources of deeper and wider knowledge.[6]

In effect, many of the organizations produced through these movements presume that instead of acting on definitive, predictive social laws, they are themselves engaging in a form of experimental activity; with every significant action, they are revealing new clues to the character and contradictions of the institutions they are trying to transform.

The students' and workers' movement of the late sixties and again in Portugal in the mid-seventies, presented the virtues of a more or less undifferentiated, united and spontaneously self-organized alliance of the dispossessed, as an alternative to the military–industrial hierarchies of post-war Europe. From Paris 1968 to Portugal 1976, however, the actual trans-formation of state or industrial power through such popular movements proved elusive.

Yet the consequence of the defeats of the extra parliamentary left in the mid-1970s has not been – with several short-lived exceptions – a surge of energies into the established, Social Democratic, Labour and Communist, parties of the left.[7] From 1968 onwards, idealistically minded activists of a kind who in previous eras would have been the 'cadre' of traditional left-wing parties remained outside the mainstream party political system. Their extra-parliamentary efforts to transform society have been sufficiently real that many of them have continued to have more radical aspirations than anything these parties could satisfy. Throughout the 1970s and into the 1980s the rejection of authority spread with the radicalism of the women's movement and gay and lesbian minorities, all of which have to an uneven extent stimulated new ways of organizing, and new sources of collective self-confi-dence among working-class people and other subordinated groups.

As the Rousseauesque vision of direct participatory democracy emerging out of confident and self-conscious popular movements appeared increas-ingly unrealistic and problematic, left activists in the new movements faced two kinds of difficulties requiring further sophistication in their practical thinking.[8]

Firstly, as the unifying ideals of popular power faced defeat, whether in Portugal, Chile or in small ways nearer to home, they faced significant divisions, not simply of political tactics but of material experience and identity amongst those who they were seeking to involve, and amongst themselves. As they applied their radicalism to the intractable problems of everyday life and sought to build lasting organizations, they faced material forms of differentiation, between parts of the working class, among women, within a local community.

Sometimes the process of discovery and experimentation stopped short at the acknowledgement and celebration of differences. In part as a reaction to imposed unities, and heroic notions of a homogeneous working class as the agent of change, difference has became a source of identity and a sufficient basis for action.[9] There are others, however, involved in the practicalities of building lasting organizations in localities and work places, who are alert to the interconnectedness of these differences: the contradictory and the common interests, for instance, of low-paid casualized women workers and the higher paid, male employees of the same corporation; the common economic bonds alongside cultural differences between white working-class women in Europe and black women in Asia working in the textiles, electronics and other industries. Awareness of such inter-connectedness has led to ideas of political agency that rest on an under-standing of both the underlying structures involved and the significance of the different, sometimes conflicting, relationships that different groups of people have to these structures. Such an approach avoids false notions of unity and leadership by making the character (and hence political and organizational implications) of these connections in every context a matter of empirical inquiry, involving directly the people who experience them.

Secondly and most fundamentally, the failure of the directly participatory model (whose virtues were exemplified by the struggle itself, without requiring much further elaboration except as the stuggle developed) has faced movement activists with the problem of specifying an alternative. The question arises as to how the notion of popular self-government – essential to the democratic dimension of an egalitarian vision – could be retrieved and made into a feasible goal for the twenty-first century. Without a process of constantly envisaging and stretching towards such an alternative, there is a danger that the activities and organizations inspired by recent left social movements *would* collapse back, if not into the traditional party system, then into becoming part of an under-resourced, over-exploited voluntary and marginal sector.

An historic challenge to the mentality of government

The features of a new form of rationality implicit in the activity associated with recent left movements are not codified or universally shared. However, if they and the organizations for which they are the methodological foundation develop, they represent a historical transformation of the mentality of government, of government's relation to society in general and economics in particular.

The nature and significance of this transformation only becomes clear if one can see it in a historical context. In a course of unpublished but taped and partially reconstructed lectures, Michel Foucault analyses the history of what he called 'governmentality', the rationality of government.[10] He was concerned with questions raised by the historical existence and human creation of varied forms of reasoning and knowledge to be found over the centuries in the practice of government. He applies this theme to the doctrines of 'pastoral power' typical of government in antiquity and early Christianity; to the first secular doctrines of government in early modern Europe associated with the ideas of state and a science for every sphere of state policy; to the eighteenth-century beginnings of liberalism, considered as a conception of the art of limited government; and lastly, to post-war forms of neo-liberal thought in Germany, the USA and France, considered as ways of reasserting the limits of government.

A central implication of my argument is that the presumptions of post-war governments concerning knowledge and reason are historically specific and have over the past twenty years become increasingly unworkable and open to challenge. It would be stimulating, therefore, before summarizing the economic and political implications of the new political methodologies practised within the social movement left, to catch a glimpse of at least one writer's historical panorama of the variations in 'governmentality'. Conventional political theory, after all, pays too much attention to institutions and not sufficient to the underlying methodology of state control and organization.

I am not wholly convinced by Foucault's approach. A distinct research project would be necessary to develop his themes critically in relation to recent developments in governmentality. But by directly addressing questions of knowledge and power, he has opened the door to the cellars of government so that we can explore what can be done about the rotting foundations.

The starting point of modern governmentality, as autonomous from the cosmo-theological order of the world, came, according to Foucault, with the emergence of doctrines of 'reason of state' in sixteenth-century Europe. The sixteenth and seventeenth centuries also saw the rise of modern science, which helped to furnish an independent rationale for the principles of state. Etienne Thuau, an historian of the French 'politique' writers who theorized this new mentality, has summed it up: 'The notion of state ceases to be derived from the divine order of the universe. The point of departure for political speculation is no longer the Creation in its entirety, but the sovereign state. Reason of state seems to have perverted the old order of values . . .

Born of the calculation and ruse of men, a knowing machine, a work of reason, the state encompasses a whole heretical substrate.'[11]

This governmentality aspired to a knowledge of inexhaustible detail and continuous control. The task of political science and the state it guided was to supervise everything pertaining to man's happiness. This included social and economic activity. In conjunction with the allied knowledge of mercantilism and political arithmetic, this early modern understanding of the secular state was the first modern system of economic sovereignty, of government understood as an economy. The economy was seen as a machine to be continuously made, and not merely operated, by government. The aim (of mercantilist economic policy) was to maximize the quantity of bullion in the state's treasury, to ensure the happiness and prosperity of the subjects. At the same time mercantilist theory emphasizes that the real basis of the state's wealth and power lies in its population, in the strength and productivity of each and all. The central aim and paradox of early modern government was, according to Foucault, 'to develop those elements of individual lives in such a way that their development also fosters the state.'[12]

Foucault traces some elements of the welfare state back to this early modern conjunction of reason of state and the science of public policy. Other elements of the modern capitalist state stem from the advent of liberalism. What is distinctive about liberalism, for Foucault, is the transformation it brings about not only in political and economic thinking (the focus of most theorists) but also in the relationship between knowledge and government. For the early modern theorists and practitioners of reason of state, policy science and the state were inseparable. Liberal political economy, by contrast, as most comprehensively argued by Adam Smith in *The Wealth of Nations*, insists on the limits of the state as a knowing subject. Foucault sees liberalism as 'a doctrine of limitation and wise restraint, designed to educate state reason by displaying to it the intrinsic bounds of its power to know'.[13]

Foucault documents two stages in the politico-epistemological revolution brought about by liberalism. First, there were the French Physiocrates who based the limits of the state on the idea that the affairs of human society constitute a quasi-nature. Society and its economy, they argue, can and must only be governed in accordance with, and in respect for, the laws of that nature; that is, the autonomous capacity of civil society to generate its own order and prosperity. According to Physiocratic doctrine, however, the ruler can still know and monitor the totality of economic processes. It is on the basis of this knowledge that the sovereign grants economic subjects freedom of action. Adam Smith rejects this model of economic sovereignty and posits instead the idea of the invisible hand. He stresses that this benign economic randomness holds good not only for the individual but also for government. His liberalism breaks the immediate unity of knowledge and government. In his political economy the regularities of economic or commercial society display a rationality which is fundamentally different in kind from that of calculative state regulation. These are notions from which Hayek developed his critique of the social engineering state. Foucault updates his own study with a discussion of French, American and West German neo-liberals whose theories are very similar to, though not as comprehensive as, those of Hayek.

Now is not the place for an extended discussion of the different forms of neo-liberalism. There are two points to bear in mind from this sketch of Foucault's description of the major early modern transformations in the relation between knowledge and state, from which methodologies of modern government derive their basic principles.

The first point is simply that, whatever disagreements one might have with Foucault's detailed historical analyses, his historical comparisons do indicate convincingly the importance of theories of knowledge to the character of the state and its relation to society and the economy.

The second point to note is that in the transformations that he documents, the changes are in the *content* of economic and political science and the capacity of the state to be a scientific subject, rather than in presumptions made about the *character of science itself*.

From Francis Bacon in the seventeenth century and David Hume in the eighteenth until the middle years of this century, the generally accepted view of science, including social and political science, was fundamentally a positivistic one. Science was understood to consist in the description of recurring patterns of observable phenomena, in space and time. Scientific laws were constant conjunctions of phenomena. On most positivist accounts these laws constituted the only basis of valid knowledge. Positivist understandings usually have an instrumental twist, the understanding of these phenomena being a means of gaining mastery over them. Within this framework there have been many debates and disagreements, but not until the 1930s and 1940s, and more especially the 1960s and 1970s, was there any sustained challenge to the unitary notion of scientific understanding as laws that described regular combinations of observable phenomena, or to the related idea of scientific development as linear and monistic. In holding on to this latter notion, eighteenth, nineteenth and many twentieth-century liberal theorists, along with early modern theorists of state reason, and to a large extent the theorists of state socialism, all concurred. The liberals differed from various brands of statists not in their notion of scientific laws, but in seeing the laws describing economic phenomena as qualitatively different from those describing other spheres of society.

Several factors combined to make possible a significant challenge in the late sixties to the notions of science that underpinned both statist and liberal mentalities of government and economy.

There are no simple causal relationships between developments in science, in the philosophy of science and the radical social movements of recent years, with their transforming effects on governmentality and political economy. The scientific developments of the twenties and thirties – relativity theory and quantum mechanics – and their repercussions throughout the physical and natural sciences, stimulated an escalating and finally deadly challenge to positivist philosophy of science. The result by the late 1960s was a philosophical culture in flux and a radical broadening of the kinds of knowledge considered valid in what became seen as a many-angled process of scientific understanding.[14] Moreover, new generations desiring to take political action in the face of the dramatic economic and political developments of the late 1960s and early 1970s found the tools of positivistic social science wanting. The end of the post-war boom and the increasingly international integration of Western economies weakened the credibility of social-engineering methodologies which presumed the possibility of more or less closed economic systems. The social divisions made apparent by recession, the brutality of the war in Vietnam and of repression in Southern Africa, and the unfulfilled expectations of women and social minorities could not be comprehended through the political culture of the post-war consensus. In these circumstances, political action moved rapidly from specific issues into demands for a revolution in political reason, for which the radical developments in the philosophy of social science provided a source of intellectual confidence. Pulled apart by this unrest over its very instruments of government and public administration on the one hand and by material pressures on the other, the post-war social democratic consensus could not hold.

Implications of the critique of Hayek

Against the background of this breakdown of taken-for-granted governmentality, the importance of Hayek's philosophical underpinnings for radical conservativism – not quite the contradiction in terms that it sounds – is thrown into relief. He combined an orthodox view of science (a legitimate but limited compass for the state) with an advocacy of forms of experiential and practical knowledge ignored by orthodox economic theorists of all political colours. With this combination, he provided intellectual tools with which conservers of the capitalist economic order could adapt and modernize in the face of challenges from below, and at the same time reconsolidate the power of central government to maintain order; in fact, focus it to perform this function all the more single-mindedly. His theory of the knowledge of 'particular time and circumstance' provided the justification for deregulating and extending the private market. But his commitment to the idea of an exclusive form of scientific expertise able to classify the recurring patterns of social order justified an elite state to guard the order created by the unregulated market.

A critique of Hayek's view of knowledge and of science, of the relation between market and state, and the outline of an alternative has many implications for the character of government, of public administration, of political parties. It thus is not surprising that although Hayek formulated his theory of knowledge as a justification of the unregulated market as the most efficient way of utilizing the knowledge of the population, this book has moved some way beyond economics.

One reason for this is that my argument has followed the development of movements whose activity spans the divide between economics and politics. But this is in itself significant, for they in many ways were a rebellion against that divide. But they were not for a return to the old reasons of state, either in its pre-capitalist or its modern capitalist forms. The activities of many student, feminist, tenant and public sector worker organizations were a reaction to the forms of paternalism involved as state became increasingly involved with the market, despite claims to the contrary. Their demands fused social and economic because that was the reality of political economy. They both pressed for, and at times illustrated, non-paternalistic ways of providing infrastructure and services, as in the exemplary case of the Gothenburg women's school.

Part of my reason for dwelling on the experience of this school, and then the new parties of the left, has been to counter Hayek's influential notion that all forms of public provision and public intervention in economics have a necessarily negative, socially manipulative character to them, and to show another kind of rebellion, based on a different appreciation of practical knowledge.

After exploring these and other illustrations of an alternative view of knowledge drawn from the practice of the movements, I now wish to sum up in a theoretical manner the implications of my theses for an alternative view of the market, the state and the relation between the two, including, most importantly, the role of public associations independent of market and state.

A socialized market

Hayek's model assumes that a favourable economic equilibrium can be reached through the price mechanism alone. Other economists have long rejected this. The notion of 'externalities' – costs extraneous to the economic calculations of the firm – was introduced to deal with some of the flaws of the free-market model. 'Externalities' (including the costs of pollution, skilled labour, healthy labour etc.) are conventionally presumed to be the responsibility of government; to be outside strictly economic, that is, market, calculations. Within the framework of this conventional critique of Hayek, the new movements and the radicalization of the trade union movement could be said to have brought to light a further range of externalities, factors with an economic impact or economic causes not accounted for by the instrumental logics and individualist means–ends structures of either individual enterprises in Hayek's model of the market, or the somewhat limited agenda of social democracy. The influence of the new movements has drawn public attention to, for instance, the social consequences of wage and working time arrangements which contributed to the isolation of women with small children; the impact on local communities of factory closures; the impact on the quality of people's lives of long hours and mindless work routines; the consequences of the Cold War for post-war political economies East and West; the impact on the ozone layer and other necessary features of a safe environment of unregulated economic growth. Much of the action they have taken over these issues points to ways of coping with these externalities by using the powers of a sympathetic government in way that is guided by or shared with the workers and communities who suffer from the 'market'.

Perhaps more important, the new left especially through its influence at the base of the unions, has pointed often to ways of internalizing these 'non-economic' costs, of changing economic calculations so that other knowledges are part of an economic process that is wider than the market.

It is clear that the movements which have been the subject of this book have a dual character in relation to the economy: they have both pressed certain issues on to the public economic agenda and prefigured or illustrated new political, economic and social mechanisms through which these and other issues can be pursued.

They rarely hold out exact models. Political conditions have only exceptionally been sufficiently favourable for that (Sweden, for instance, in some respects, and briefly London). But there will always be a need for 'unofficial' movements, as a constant impetus for innovation and genuine democracy within the more permanent participatory public institutions which they might help to bring into being. Recent democratic social and trade union movements have illustrated the need and possibility of new political and economic mechanisms in two ways.

Firstly, they have inspired, originated and pressed for public backing for new kinds of institutions that, with political support, could address the failures of the market around which the movements initially organized: for example organizations that began as campaigns exposing poverty and low pay, have shown the need for non-state democratic groups trusted by the low paid, to monitor the implementation of legislation on a minimum wage; health and safety organizations and community environmental groups have shown the need for government to share power with organizations rooted in workplace and community to implement legislation on these issues; women's groups and community organizations campaigning to make health care more responsive to people's needs demonstrate the case for and the possibilities of patients and communities having a stronger voice in the running of the health service; international workers' organizations have shown their potential as a vital ally should governments genuinely committed to control, or even breakup, of the power of transnational corporations gain office.

Secondly, in much of their organizing they press in different ways against the disciplines of the market. Examples are: car workers co-operating internationally to level up wage rates and gain in bargaining strength over corporate investment; workers along the cocoa chain organizing against socially and environmentally harmful effects of pressures to cut the costs of labour and of raw commodities; home workers organizing for protection; co-operatives federating and sharing resources to be stronger on the international market; local and regional authorities establishing public investment boards and banks governed by social as well as commercial priorities. These people are not, on the whole, organizing against the market as such: that is, against the existence of means of exchanging goods for money. They are resisting what is aptly described as the 'anarchy of the market', the market as a determinant of life chances or the future of a community.[15] You could say such resistance is trying to take the sting out of the market. But where does that leave the market – or rather, the different markets, because the answer is different for labour, commodities and capital?

Can the market act as one means, amongst several, of conducting economic information without causing bankruptcy, unemployment and low wages? Drawing on the arguments of others, my conclusion is that they can on three conditions.[16] The first is that a significant part of the activity is independent of the market, or involves a co-operative response to the market; the second is that what is left of the market is socially regulated; and the third is that the information gathered through the market is but one source of knowledge in company decision making.

One solution argued for in relation to the labour market is, as I reported in chapter 7, the provision of a basic wage so that workers can, if they choose, live without participation in the labour market and yet when they do participate – and the incentives would be significant – they have a greater control over their future and the use they make of the information provided through the market. What is left of the labour market would be regulated according to minimum standards of training, health and safety, pay and hours, implemented through legislation guided in conception and implementation by labour organizations with inside knowledge of the kind that I described in chapter 6. The result would be a labour market that provided information to the would-be wage earner about where they might usefully use their labour and, within a limited range, with what incentive they could earn beyond their basic income.

In relation to the commodity market, there are some commodities whose distribution society decides to base directly on basic social needs and social rights rather than the market: for example housing, health care, certain forms of transport. This list could well be expanded according to the social surplus available: alternative and preventative health care, telephones for old-age pensioners, public uses of computers and faxes at non-market rates and so on. There would remain, however, a vast sphere of production and consumption for which information on needs, tastes and availability would be too diverse, variable and ephemeral to discover other than through the market. But we saw from the work of CITER (Centro Informazione Tessile dell' Emilia Romagna), of the Caja Laboral and the co-operative industrial groups in Mondragón, that there could be significant variations in how that information is gathered, how co-operatively and publically it is researched, and with what relations between enterprises and between enterprises and consumers. The information that the market, through the price mechanism, provides would be complemented and balanced by other forms of knowledge concerning other, employment, community and ecological objectives or obligations, and would not be the sole determinant of company decision making.

The consumer also would not take decisions only on the basis of privately determined prices. Chapter 6 showed how the work of consumer campaigns, drawn on by Diane Elson in proposals for opening up and regulating the process of price formation, demonstrates the pressure for a more public process.

My emphasis on the socialization of knowledge, practical and theoretical, and on the institutional mechanisms, networks and property relations that make this possible, leads me towards the idea of 'co-operative planning' between autonomous enterprises. Information on market exchanges would be one important, but not necessarily determinant, input into such a process. This would overcome the basis of the conventional opposition of Plan versus Market: that is, the opposition between *ex ante* co-ordination – achieved through the plan, an impossible task – and *ex post* co-ordination, achieved through the market, with all the consequent problems of recession and waste. Co-operative planning would be a process: it would be neither simply *ex ante* or *ex post*. It would be *ex ante* in the sense that the sharing of knowledge about market trends (illustrated by what CITER and various institutions in Mondragón are aiming to achieve) or the collaboration on research into market opportunities (illustrated by the work of Twin Trading for Third World producers) would be aiming to match supply with demand. This would be more likely to achieve an egalitarian and socially just equilibrium than ever atomized enterpise facing the market could do; but this would always be an approximation. Public and collaborative action *ex post* would be necessary to remedy any mal-allocation of resources. Local and Regional investment boards and/or banks could perform the function of the Caja Laboral in helping an ailing enterprise to restructure, while it and other co-operatives/self-managed enterprises found jobs for its workers elsewhere.

My argument puts much stress on the sharing and/or opening up of economic knowledge. The reason for this is not simply that this is the focus of my critique of neo-liberalism. It is also that it is an idea which provides a basis for co-operative economic co-ordination which does not make unrealistic assumptions about the possibility of total transparency nor of permanent popular participation beyond the institutions of everyday life.

Co-operative planning would not depend on the enterprises being state owned. It would be important, except for the very small ones, however, that in some form they were socially, communally or co-operatively owned. This in itself clearly would not ensure that their decisions were taken with regard to the wider community. Several further factors would be necessary: firstly the companies' dependence on collaboration with others for the knowledge, technology, training and know-how necessary for its ability to understand and meet market demand; and secondly, the companies' partial dependence, or possible future dependence on public – whether communal, as in Mondragón, or more likely, regional state – funds. The provision of such funds would depend on enterprise compliance with a framework of politically agreed economic, social and ecological objectives. Under these conditions the sharing of economic knowledge would become a powerful economic guiding mechanism indicating to enterprises where their productive energies could be efficiently and productively allocated.

The importance of co-operation across an economy made up of more or less autonomous co-operatively managed enterprises, for the sharing, among other functions, of practical and analytic knowledge, demonstrates that such wider co-operation has practical economic benefits. This is significant, because those who deny the possibility of non-market forms of economic co-ordination tend to view any form of co-operative non-market co-ordination as hopeless idealism. David Miller, for instance, equates such ideas with a primitive communalism, desired on purely moral grounds. He sees such commitments among today's socialists as an unscrutinized legacy of nineteenth-century utopianism, accusing advocates of such ideas of 'remaining romantically attached to a pre-industrial vision of community.'[17] The economic significance of the sharing of economic knowledge, strengthened by the extraordinary economic success of those local economies who have organized it, gives grounds for the practical, non-sentimental, economic function of non-market forms of democratic co-ordination.

At the same time, the socializing of economic knowledge on a collaborative basis indicates that, given social but not necessarily state property relations, there is an economic basis (I treat shared economic knowledge as a form of economic power) against those who insist on formal *ex ante* equilibrium, for collaboration between autonomous co-operatives for a wider common good.[18]

It is not a leap into the unknown. In fact an aspect of it (the co-operative identifying of market trends and opportunities) involves democratizing an extensive process common to every major corporation. Such corporations put massive resources into market research, a private version of what CITER shares with hundreds of entrepreneurs. Another aspect of it (the idea of a publically regulated process of price formation) involves democratizing an already highly institutional, conscious – as distinct from simply 'market taking' – corporate decision making process. (Which has already, through Prices and Incomes Policies in the 1960s, been subject to a half-hearted, but nonetheless revealing, process of public regulation.) Moreover, as we saw in chapter 6, there are many diverse and occasionally powerful, popular pressures for such a socialising of economic knowledge. Many of them are becoming increasingly sophisticated in the process, using electronic mail in a very democratic manner, constantly training new users, making it as straightforward as possible so that it does not become the basis of a new 'communications' elite.[19]

These popular pressures are blocked by major inequalities of wealth and economic power. A process of socializing economic knowledge could only be a basis for non-market driven forms of economic co-ordination under the conditions of economic equality that exist, for instance, between and within enterprises in Mondragón. Such equality is accompanied by mutual dependency on joint services, on local public sources of finance, training, and other forms of co-operation, all of which reinforce the role of shared economic knowledge as a form of non-coercive co-ordination. Like the economic networks described in chapter 6, they aspire to take such sharing of knowledge well beyond indicative planning which falls foul of the power and egoism of conventional private corporations.

The exact strategies by which present concentrations of economic power, and therefore economic secrecy, can be broken up are beyond the scope of this book. What I hope to have established is that an egalitarian distribution of wealth and common ownership of the means of production, distribution and exchange is possible on the basis of democratic economic and political institutions. Central to this possibility is the development of democratic public associations in the workplace and the community that recognize both the practical and theoretical dimensions of knowledge and organize to share it.

New forms of governmentality

In Mondragón, the processes of socializing knowledge of the market, of latest technological developments and other sources of economic understanding, have developed out of the needs of the early co-operatives with strong cultural and political commitment to a co-operative economy. Moreover, the co-operatives were, to a very significant extent, the means by which this part of Basque country developed. In the Carpi textile industry also – as with many other industries round Modena, Regio Emilia – the co-operation between the small entrepreneurs developed out of a strong co-operative tradition with its roots in agricultural co-operatives. Here, too, the process of industrialization was to a significant extent driven by this co-operativism, though there was far less effort to institutionalize this co-operative culture within the economy and society itself than in Mondragón.[20]

How can such a process develop in already industrialized regions, lacking well established indigenous co-operative traditions among entrepreneurs. If my argument (concerning the ways in which radical democratic movements of recent years have held out, sometimes prefigured, the possibility of a transformation in the forms of knowledge underlying politics and economics) has any validity, then there should be experiences which provide a glimpse of an answer to this question. The implication of my argument is that the co-operative elements of the Third Italy and the integrated character of the

Mondragón economy were developments ahead of their time, in terms of the official treatment of public knowledge. They are already becoming the subject of increasing attention. I reported in chapter 6 on several unfinished experiments that indicate how such principles might more self-consciously be spread. The most notable case was the incomplete efforts of the Greater London Council. As Henry Ford once remarked, 'the richest lessons come from failures'. The GLC's incomplete attempts to work with both entrepreneurs and trade unions to create non-market forms of co-operation across, for instance, the furniture industry, yields several lessons.

Lesson number one is that the strong support of a political authority with a commitment to a co-operative economy, and with power to invest and take a whole or part share in the ownership of industrial companies, is necessary to establish a counter to the dog-eat-dog dynamic of the competitive market. Lesson number two is that such political intervention is not sufficient: the elected political authority needs to make an alliance with those in the industry and, if appropriate, surrounding communities, who have a material interest in the industry developing a co-operative character. Furthermore, that alliance needs to be of a kind in which the government – at as decentralized a level as is appropriate to the present organization of the industry – helps the social groups concerned articulate and present that interest. So, for instance, as it became clear that the furniture employers in London were not seriously interested in breaking from their cutthroat competitive ways, driving jobs and skills further and further down, the GLC came to work closely with the trade unions. It was not simply a matter of patting them on the head and backing their existing strategies, but helping them develop industry-wide strategies. The GLC provided financial help via the trade union, for shop-floor leaders to have time off work for this purpose, providing research help and access to the information about the latest technology and design. The long-term aim was to carry out a pincer movement on an increasingly stubborn and yet beleaguered management, the trade union pressing from below for greater co-operation, the GLC using its limited financial clout 'from above'. The GLC had neither the time nor in fact the economic powers to carry it through. Had it been successful, the outcome would have involved the creation of commonly organized market research, design and technology services as well as the more conventional financial and export services. This in turn would probably have led to widespread changes in management and ownership as the traditional private companies found it difficult to adapt.

I have shared a glimpse in this book of four possible kinds of relationship whereby, to paraphrase Tom Paine, a considerable extent of popular capacity could be brought forward by quiet and regular operation – whether it is 'that extent which never fails to appear in revolution' is difficult to judge. There is the possibility exemplified by the Gothenburg School, where a public service is managed in a way which developed and utilized to the full the skills and understandings of everyone involved in any way in providing or using it. There is the possibility illustrated by the limited experience of health and safety legislation under the 1975 Labour Government, of government action to impose social considerations on management through empowering workers' representatives with inside knowledge and a vested interest in these social concerns, to guide and trigger the legal powers of the state. Then, rather similarly, there is the possibility, demonstrated in a small way by the Coin Street Development in Waterloo, of government socializing a material resource, in this instance, inner city land, and then supporting self-management by democratic organizations representing the people who live and work on that land. Finally, there is the possibility, just discussed, of government at every level supporting those social and economic organizations whose interests and values lead them to establish forms of co-operation across the divides otherwise created by antagonistic forms of competition.

All these possible relationships between elected political authorities, at different levels, presume a serious limitation in government's knowledge and skill to resolve problems which it has been elected to see resolved. On the other hand, against the arguments of the free-marketeers, these relationships presume that problems can consciously and legitimately be tackled by a combination of visible, democratic hands, constantly improving their efficacy by trial and error. These glimpses of possible new political and economic relationships have been arrived at *ad hoc*, out of experience of the failure of both state and market to satisfy social needs. Implicitly, these relations are based on an approach to science which combines many different sources and different kinds of knowledge to discover social solutions.[21] In the words of E. P. Thompson's lecture on the impulse to cultural as well as political *égalité*, politicians and state officials of various kinds face 'the abrasion of different worlds of experience.'[22]

It is worth inquiring further into the conditions for making that abrasion a sustained feature of the mentality of government. Firstly, in all the new political relationships whose possibility we have glimpsed, there was a sharing of power between one or several elected political authorities, and a popularly based civic organization or an alliance of such organizations. This, I would argue, is a necessary condition for combining different sources of knowledge or different worlds of experience in a common process of social transformation.

Gaining knowledge about a problem is more than gathering information. There are plenty of examples of government authorities having close relations with voluntary organizations simply to gather information. In these relationships the power of the political authority in unchanged, or if anything enhanced, however packaged the process is in terms of consultation and open government.[23] Information is storable knowledge, it is both one input and one outcome amongst many in a process of discovery. A process of gaining knowledge involves action, the exercise of power, and as a consequences the revealing of unpredicted problems or opportunities. If the process is a genuine alliance, the political authority is giving up some element of its power. If popular organizations are seen merely as a source of information, the old social engineering model is still at work; the experts are just being a little more outward-looking in their gathering of data. Cultural equality is still a long way off.

The other danger is a corporatism in which the political authority incorporates or undermines the independence of the organization respresenting the interests and combining the knowledge of a particular group. A condition of a popular organization's being able to contribute knowledge from a relevant experience, is the maintenance of their roots and daily involvement in that experience (their accountability to their base). A condition, then, for their efficacy as allies with a political authority is their autonomy from any particular part of that authority.

Autonomy is the basis of a relationship, not the synonym of separateness. It is clear from any cursory comparison of civic organizations and the state in different countries that political authorities, and political parties, in part shape the environment of these organizations, and hence have a significant influence on their strength and character. Many of these organizations are increasingly developing forms of funding that reduce their dependence on any one part of the state: through sympathetic trusts and foundations which are themselves developing forms of co-operation to enable them to support an emerging 'third sector' of non-profit, non-state organizations;[24] bankers orders from members; and though support from a variety of different levels of state authorities. A party committed to the kind of transformation I have illustrated, of the legacies of both free-market and social-engineering regimes, would need consciously to consider the ways (through grants, representation on committees, legal status, a public platform, public backing in negotiation with corporations blocking equality etc.) to enhance the strength of popular organizations without undermining their autonomy. The other side of this is that an elected political authority would have open criteria governing its relations with non-governmental bodies, and determining their own democracy, accountability and consistency with the basic principles of the elected authority.

No *popular will without popular knowledge*

These kinds of relationships could not simply be added on to representative government as it is exists today. Whether dominated by social democracy, the social market approach of Christian Democracy or the latest embodiment of the free-market right, the status quo rests on the assumption that the popular will can be executed without popular knowledge. Successive waves of reform of European states, from the eighteenth century onwards, democratized (that is, made more representative) the process by which government determined its will. But the mentality and culture of government itself, the institutions of execution and implementation, went through no such democratic transformation.

After the Second War, the scope of government grew as the people, largely through their labour movements, used their political rights to press their claims for greater social and, less successfully, economic rights. But the cultural presumptions regarding what kind of knowledge, held by whom, should guide the implementation of these new provisions, were as we have seen unchanged. The expertise was thought to lay with the government and its professional advisers who, it was presumed, had access to the relevant body of knowledge: social-scientific knowledge of a kind that was codified and straightforward to centralize.[25] In this process, the democratic element of government lay in making the Minister for whom these experts worked accountable for what they did. The Minister's concern (in theory) was that the chain of command from her or himself downwards, and accountability back upwards, was unbroken so that they could report reliably to Parliament. This, in the terms of representative government, was belived sufficient to ensure that Parliament's will was being implemented in a democratic manner.

The consequences are visible in the often well-intentioned legacy that post-war social democratic governments left to those who grew up during the post-war boom and since; a legacy for which these latter generations have appeared at times rudely ungrateful: university campuses on bleak parklands miles from city life, designed with little practical knowledge of students' needs and desires; medical training and hospital organizations developed with little knowledge of the particular concerns of women; transport systems worked out as if children did not exist; employment legislation passed as if the passing was enough, and the implementation could be left to the courts, without thought that the knowledge of the workers affected should be built in; investment grants made to keep jobs in a poor region, without consideration given to the inside knowledge needed to monitor their use. The list is infinite. The appeal of the radical republican Tom Paine has not been satisfied, as he hoped, by achieving a representative democracy. It is useful to pay attention to his words again:

> It appears to general observation, that revolutions create genius and talents; but those events do no more than bring them forward. There is existing in man, a mass of sense lying in a dormant state, and which unless something excites it to action, will descend with him, in that condition, to the grave. As it is to the advantage of society that the whole of its facilities should be employed, the construction of government ought to be such as to bring forward, by quiet and regular operation, all that extent of capacity which never fails to appear in revolution.[26]

Tom Paine was arguing for representative democracy against monarchy. But his appeal now stands as a critical appeal against existing forms of parliamentary government. Representative government cannot bring forward the full extent of human capacity. If the processes of 'doing' are democratized as well as those of deciding, so that popular knowledge is shared in order constantly to improve the implementation, and if political parties are opened up to determine the political will, then new questions of organization arise. In particular, the question arises of how practical knowledge of various sorts, including tacit knowledge – 'those things we know but cannot tell' – can feed into democratic processes.

In other words, genuinely democratic organization has to achieve conditions not only of popular representation, in Raymond William's terms, of 'making present'.[27] It also has to achieve conditions for the profoundest possible popular expression and for mutual attentiveness to what is expressed; conditions, that is, for 'making known' the experiences, problems and capacities lying dormant amongst the majority of the population.

Representative and participatory democracy

The resilient minority on the left, who have continued to aspire to achieving conditions for cultural equality as well as political and economic equality, have paid much attention to the implication of this aim for education and the media and, increasingly, many socialists and feminists have been thinking through its implications for the organization of work.[28] But very little attention has been paid to its implications for government. One result of this is that when parties of the new left, or new left groupings within established parties have gained office, usually at a local level, they have been disastrously unprepared to bring about changes in the administration itself.

The nearest thing to such concern has been a special alertness, some-times to the point of idealization, to those periodic moments of awakening to which Paine refers, through, if not revolutionary, at least extra-parliamen-tary activity: the outpouring of creativity during the years of student revolt in the late sixties; the newly revealed talents of public speaking and organ-izing amongst the most downtrodden groups of workers (such as night cleaners in the City of London, and then in 1984 and 1992 the same phenom-enon amongst the women in the pit communities); the expansive imagin-ation and ingenuity of the peace movement in the 1980s. These and other movements have provided for the new left a recurring source of inspiration and evidence of the extraordinary capacities of 'ordinary' people for self-government.

In the early years of the modern extra-parliamentary left, there was a tendency after 1968 to imagine that the direct forms of democracy that they created could be generalized to the government of society as a whole, without any differentiation for distinct kinds and purposes of decision. The Western new left often counterposed one single organizing principle of democracy to another. They called for 'participatory democracy' to replace 'representative democracy'. At times, in their concern to challenge the narrowed, positively anti-popular notions of democracy prevalent during the Cold War, and to widen democracy to include economic life and domestic relations, they lost sight of the questions of democratizing specifically governmental (legislative and ad-ministrative) institutions. There was an implicit assumption that these institutions could be bypassed; consequently, few people paid attention in the 1970s to the possible positive relations of government to democratic processes throughout society. There was little attempt, until recently, to consider feasible institutional forms for participatory democracy, and explore what structures for representative government create the best conditions for such participation.[29]

The problem with participatory democracy as a system of government, is that to retain the democratic character that it demonstrably has in situations of popular mobilization, the people have to retain in normal times the participatory spirit that they showed in crisis circumstances. In moments of crisis, working people have again and again organized their immediate mate-rial life, the distribution of food, the organization of work, transport and so on, through direct forms of democracy. Such activity, however, has never been sustained sufficiently to provide a complete democratic model for governing society.

We have the evidence from many 'micro' experiences, like the Women's School in Gothenburg, that direct participation can work in the everyday running of a moderately-sized institution. But it does not follow from such positive experiences that a legislative and executive process on a pyramid of such democratic units, sending delegates through different tiers up to the national and international levels, is the most direct and democratic means for people to influence the legal framework of their lives. The same level of participation cannot be sustained when the decision-making processes are so removed from everyday life.[30]

Some commentators have used this to dismiss the whole ideal of popular self-government. But perhaps the Council Communists, Guild Socialists and others who reject representative forms of democracy, have allowed themselves to be driven into a corner by making one particular institutional form a principle for the whole of society. What we need is not one integrated structure presupposing unrealistic levels of popular mobilization and activity. Rather, we need to consider a combination of structures in which the institutions of daily life are organized in a participatory manner, the means of economic and political co-ordination are as closely and transparently associated with these institutions as possible, and in which the legal framework is decided on by as representative a body as possible.

Reconstructing government

It is no longer academic or purely speculative to consider these issues in a practical way. In Europe at least, traditional levels, scope and forms of decision making are in flux. In these circumstances ideas of democracy that are not obsessed with national parliaments as the single focal point are very timely. So far, much of the running has been made by those who, whether for ideological or pragmatic reasons, favour an unregulated market and a minimum of political democracy.[31] The implication of my argument is that recent left movements have a record of tracking unaccountable centres of power that have been out of the effective control of elected government. In the process, networks and sporadic organizations have been built up which point to the role that different levels of representative government could play to exert democratic control over these centres of power. Unofficial organizations also illustrate the kind of civic allies that elected political bodies will need, and will need to foster, to achieve this control.

This contributes a criterion and a dimension to the debate about the appropriate levels of sovereignty for different purposes. My argument asserts the importance for democratic and effective government – including economic government – of utilizing the knowledge, including skills, of the whole of society. The full implications of this require much further work, but two flow directly from the arguments of previous chapters. The first is an implication of political principle: it would involve elected levels of government in a new kind of relationship with the people – a relationship which respects not only their political right but their competence to participate in government, or, in other words, to be self-governing. One must also add a new consideration in the process of constructing or transforming government: that government must be designed in such a way as to enable citizens to engage their capacities to the full in the governing of society, according to democratic principles. The second implication is that such an engagement cannot be achieved adequately either through the market or through the state. The practice of the social movement left illustrates the need to understand a level of interpersonal and institutional relations of economic significance which is neither part of the market nor of the state: a sphere of public activity which acts both to democratize the state and to socialize the market. As Western social movements organize to exert some social control over the market, they have created forms of organization with a social dynamic independent of the market and yet not aspiring to become a state.[32]

Across the world people are addressing these issues in practice: in addition to activists in Eastern and Western Europe struggling to fill the democratic vacuum in the government of their continent, there are all those in South Africa: ANC activists, organizers of the local civics, militants in the trade unions debating, organizing to construct new institutions of democratic government, while resisting the powerful forces of the racist right; the people building coalitions around basic needs in the inner cities of the US; the Sandinista supporters in Nicaragua struggling to defend the local institutions built up during the period of Sandinista government. It is not the time therefore to sign off with a conclusion. If my arguments have any relevance to these efforts to construct genuinely democratic and socially just forms of government, then they are part of a new beginning, a process of renewal.[33]

It remains simply to return to conversations which began this book, conversations in which the word 'socialism' acted as an interruption. As I implied in the preface, this book began as a response to Mísa Neubauer and other East Europeans to explore whether my idea of socialism could answer the appeal to them of the arguments of the free-market right. It was an attempt to get behind a word which so clearly had entirely different connotations for those who joined the conversation from East and West.

Many Western socialists who continue to hold to their beliefs, assume that the failure of past models of a socialist society puts the possibility of socialism off the political agenda for the foreseeable future. My approach is different. I do not deny the impact of these failures on when and how socialism becomes a widely acknowledged political option again, but I question whether the experience of past failures is the decisive factor. If, as I would argue, the motor of socialist transformation is the organization of people without private wealth to achieve equality, democracy, liberation and social justice, then future possibilities of socialism depend more fundamentally on the character and dynamic of people's struggles to be free of oppression and exploitation.

Such resistance is of course influenced by observation and direct experience of projects which began as struggles against injustice, but ended up producing new forms of subordination. But the struggle for socialism is a historical process of trial and error, and much depends on how quickly the errors are learnt and how urgent is the impetus to try again. The late nineteenth-century craftsman and socialist, William Morris, described this process in *The Dream of John Ball*. John Ball felt that his labour would not be in vain if the people continued to strive for social justice. But he is not sure that they will. 'Is it so that they shall?' he asked anxiously. To which the voice of Morris replies: 'Yes, and their remedy shall be the same as thine though the days be different. For if the folk be enthralled, what remedy save that they be set free? and if they have tried many roads towards freedom, and found that they led nowhither, then they shall try another.'

The confidence and sense of direction with which people try another road will depend amongst other things on how far they had anticipated dead ends and started to identify alternatives, before the final impasse was reached. It will also depend on how far the mapping and testing out of alternatives has been nourished by innovative struggles and a cumulative process of learning. This book has explored the ways in which there is a left influenced by different movements which *did*, in a variety of ways, anticipate that existing roads 'went nowhither', and *did* begin to map out alternatives.

This book also explores one sense at least in which this left had not questioned sufficiently deeply why those roads came to dead ends; and hence how this left did not have a full measure of the challenge it faced in mapping out an alternative. This is the importance, I believe, of my case for basing the maps of our next roads to freedom on a distinct politics of knowledge: rejecting both the view of knowledge which underpinned the state socialist experiments of the past, and that which provides a fatalistic justification of the hardships imposed by the capitalist market.

As to whether the mapping process has been stimulated by continuing resistance of an innovative character: certainly, the last twenty years in Western Europe have been years of recurring rebellion, social, economic and political. An underlying feature of these years has been the uncertainty of ruling institutions and their need to restructure themselves in the face of recession and the exhaustion of earlier technological advances. The insurgent movements of these years, however, were ill-served by traditional parties, organizations and state institutions of the left. Innovation has consequently been born of necessity.

This book has illustrated the kinds of innovation produced by movements organizing for social justice in an era when the instruments of the benevolent state have been tried and found wanting. The cumulative result has been in Western Europe the precarious growth of new kinds of institutions and associations of a co-operative, democratic and egalitarian kind. The process of their emergence has been chequered: workplace organizations of solidarity and strategic thinking have faced setbacks and defeats, and management has restructured with conservative governments on its side; attempts at democratic management of public services have been undermined by cuts in public spending. Nevertheless, memory and immediate experience of these alternatives is widespread, and as opportunities arise these memories will be signposts to new roads to be tried.

Whether the result will always and everywhere be called 'socialism' is an open question. But in addition to the word 'democracy', concepts, and in turn, words are needed to describe the co-operative, social dimension of the answer, and to capture the fact that such co-operation depends on a transparency of social life and the elimination of inequalities of wealth and power.[34]

Certainly, East, West and in the continents of the South, tentative and pragmatic interest in alternative co-operative ways of economic organization, especially at a regional level, is growing, out of necessity rather than confident optimism. Capitalism may have 'won' the Cold War, in the sense that Soviet socialism imploded; but its future is uncertain. It too was damaged by the Cold War. Its industrial structures are distorted by forty years of constant preparedness for war. Free-market economics has produced intolerable levels of unemployment and wastage of human capacity, yet a return to Keynesianism, even on a European scale, could merely begin again the cycle of stagflation that prepared the way for deregulation and economic *laisser-faire*. Moreover, international instabilities mount up as the consequences of

the brutality of international finance towards Third World debtors reverber-
ate throughout an already ustable world. In these circumstances, it is not
utopian to explore new roads to freedom, and to pick up maps which have yet
to be completed.

In most of Western Europe and in Asia, Africa and Latin America there
have been lively enough independent socialist traditions, albeit usually subordinate, for people who come from these traditions to use 'socialism' with
integrity, to describe possible new roads in spite of the governments that have
misruled in its name. Our underlying concern, however, should not be
directly with language but with finding means of co-operation between
movements North and South, as well as East and West, that share the same
egalitarian, democratic and ecological sense of direction. Only in this way will
the new roads get constructed – and in working to put common ideas into
effect we will develop the language necesary to communicate them.

Notes

1 Channel 4, September 1991.
2 A useful handbook of the initiatives is Brian Harvey, *Networking in Europe*
   (London, 1992). See also *Elf* (European Labour Forum), journal of the Socialist
   Group of the European Parliament; the Newsletter of the Helsinki Citizens'
   Assembly; *Green Leaves*, the bulletin of the Greens in the European Parliament;
   Civic Forum.
3 I worked in the Industry and Employment Branch of the GLC with the unduly
   grand title of Deputy Chief Economic Adviser. In fact my job was to create and
   then co-ordinate the Popular Planning Unit, a resource, research, education and
   information centre which ensured that the material and political resources of the
   GLC were shared with grass-roots, trade union and community organizations
   across London.
4 C. Wright Mills, *The Power Elite* (Oxford, 1956). The work of Mills was very
   influential in the thinking of the Anglo-American new left.
5 In many ways this insistence is a return to early socialist traditions. It is a return,
   however, after the experience of strategies for socialism which excluded the
   relevance of this knowledge, and with greater wisdom about how state power
   and knowledge could utilize everyday experience.
6 The work to establish, spread and train for the labour movement bulletin board,
   Poptel, is a very good example of this. See note 9, chapter 7.
7 There has been some attempt in Britain, which resulted in the radical politics of
   the GLC – something which would have been impossible without the participation of large numbers of activists from the movements that had their extra-
   parliamentary heyday in the 1970s. The Italian Communist Party also attracted
   a significant number of radical extra-parliamentary leftists. In both cases, these

parties were exceptions that confirm the rule: they were parties in a state of crisis and division. Their traditional leaderships were sufficiently unstable for activists looking for a political voice to think that the party could be pushed in a new direction. In both cases they were disappointed, though they left their mark on the character of the parties at local and regional if not national level.

8 See Anne Philips, *Engendering Democracy* (Cambridge, 1990) for a feminist analysis of participatory democracy and Sheila Rowbotham on 'Feminism and Democracy', in *New Forms of Democracy*, eds D. Held and C. Pollitt (London, 1986).

9 For perceptive criticism of identity politics see Mary Louise Adams, 'There's No Place Like Home: The Place of Identity Politics in Feminism', *Feminist Review*, 31 (Spring 1989).

10 The lectures are reconstructed in G. Burchell, C. Gordon and P. Miller, *The Foucault Effect: Studies in Governability* (Hemel Hempstead, 1991).

11 Etienne Thuau, *Raison d'état et pensée politique à l'époque de Richelieu* (Paris, 1966), quoted in Burchell et al., *The Foucault Effect*.

12 Quoted in Burchell et al. *The Foucault Effect*.

13 Burchell et al., *The Foucault Effect*, p. 15.

14 See Roy Bhaskar's entry on 'Knowledge, Theory of', in the *Encyclopaedia of Twentieth-Century Social Thought*, eds. W. Outhwaite and T. Bottomore (Oxford, 1992), which provides a useful summary of the field.

15 This approach is similar to a distinction made by Pat Devine, between *market exchange* (transactions between buyers and sellers, where what is being exchanged consists in goods and services produced by enterprises using their existing capacity), and *market forces* (the process whereby changes are brought about in the allocation and distribution of investment, through enterprise decisions based purely on their own objectives, reacting simply to the outcomes of market exchange). See Pat Devine, *Democracy and Economic Planning* (Cambridge, 1988).

16 Robin Murray, 'Rethinking Social Ownership', *New Left Review*, 164 (July/August 1987); David Purdy, *Social Power and the Labour Market* (London, 1988); Diane Elson, 'Socializing the Market: Breaking the Circuit of Capital', in *Socialism and the Market*, ed. J. Schwartz (London, 1993).

17 David Miller, 'Why Markets?', in *Market Socialism*, eds J. Le Grand and S. Estrin (London, 1989), p. 29.

18 See Ernest Mandel, 'In Defence of Socialist Planning', *New Left Review*, 159 (September/October 1986).

19 For details of these developments contact the Labour Telematics Centre, GMBU National College, College Road, Manchester M19.

20 The Italian Communist Party became its somewhat unreliable bearer. Organizations such as CITER were not part of a wider network as in Mondragón.

21 The practical knowledge of the students at the Women's School provided a test for the educational and feminist theories of the founding staff in the development of educational policy; more economic knowledge of the job market had to

be weighed up with considerations of personal development in the decisions over what courses to put on. The experiential knowledge gathered by workers' health and safety representatives combine with the theoretical knowledge of government inspectors or academic scientists in deciding what substances were dangerous; economic knowledge of gaps in the market combined with social and medical knowledge about aspects of the productin process in deciding alternative products. Again in the development of Coin Street the knowledge of residence built up, for some, from experience over decades, combined with the trained knowledge of GLC architects and economists. And in the analysing of market trends, the experience of retail managers and observers of fashion combines with that of economists studying the textile industry.

22   E. P. Thompson, *Education and Experience* (Leeds, 1968).

23   Cynthia Cockburn's *The Local State* documents this in a detailed case study of the relations of Lambeth Council with community groups in the 1970s when 'participation' was all the rage.

24   For discussion of this third sector see P. Ekins and M. Max-Neef, *Real-life Economics* (London, 1992); W. Streeck and P. C. Schmitter, *Private Interest Government* (London, 1985); H. E. Daly and J. Cobb, *For the Common Good: Redirecting the Economy Towards the Community, the Environment and a Sustainable Future* (London, 1990).

25   A. Dunsire provides a detailed description of the character of the processes of political implementation in Britain in *The Execution Process, Vol. 1: Implementation in a Bureaucracy* (London, 1978).

26   *The Rights of Man*, in *The Thomas Paine Reader* (London, 1987), p. 277.

27   See Raymond Williams, *Towards 2000*

28   See C. Marsh, *Hours of Work of Women and Men in Britain*, Equal Opportunities Commission (HMSO, 1991); C. Cockburn, *Machinery of Dominance* (London, 1985); U. Huws, J. Hursfield and R. Holtmaat, *What Price Flexibility?: The Casualisation of Women's Employment* (London, 1989); P. Hewitt, *About Time* (London, 1993).

29   See, for example, the debates reported in a special issue of *Politics and Society*, 20, no. 4 (December, 1992); John Mathews, *Age of Democracy: The Political Economy of Post-Fordism* (New York, 1989); Paul Hirst, *Representative Democracy and its Limits* (Cambridge, 1990); and the essays in D. Held (ed.) *Prospects for Democracy* (Cambridge, 1993).

30   Tim Wohlforth makes a similar critique of the idea of substituting direct democratic forms for representative ones in 'The Transition to the Transition', *New Left Review*, 130 (November/December 1981). Ann Philips makes perceptive points about the limits of participatory democracy as it was practised and advocated in the women's movement in *Engendering Democracy* (Cambridge, 1990).

31   And it has been the nationalist right rather than the internationalist left that has been a public focus to many of those who feel they are losing out from the present character of European integration.

32 Yet it is the issue where their development beyond orthodox Marxism can be most clearly seen. The break is over the implicit understanding of civil society, the economy and the state. Marx's analysis of these relationships understands the economy as the central feature of civil society and sees the state as reflecting the relations of power within the economy.

The movements' experience has led to lasting innovations: a process of small group discussion as a necessary part of democratic decision making; the importance, in mixed organizations like trade unions, of space and time for members facing particular forms of subordination and hardship to define their needs themselves and develop the self-confidence to articulate them in more formal democratic processes; the recognition of non-verbal, practical expression of ideas relevant to democratic decision making; the importance of a culture through which people gain the self-esteem to believe their knowledge is of public relevance.

33 For histories and political analyses of the Brazilian Workers' Party see M. Keck, *Workers' Party and Democracy in Brazil* (London, 1991). For regular information and analysis on the civics and the ANC see *Work in Progress*, Southern African Research Service, P.O. Box 32716, Braamfontein 2017, South Africa. On Nicaragua, see H. Smith, *Nicaragua: Self-Determination and Survival* (London, 1993). On grass-roots struggles in the US see J. Becher and T. Costello, *Building Bridges: The Emerging Grassroots Coalition of Labor and Community* (New York, 1990); M. Davis and M. Sprinker, *Reshaping the Left: Popular Struggles in the 1980s* (London, 1988); D. Reif, *Los Angeles: Third World City* (London, 1993).

34 See Raymond Williams' discussion of the ways in which the meanings of words change, in *Keywords* (London, 1988). Cf. also R. Bhaskar, *Dialectic* (London, 1993).

BIBLIOGRAPHY AND
FURTHER READING

As I followed through my main argument and as I discussed it with others, I found myself connecting with more and more debates which have generated vast literatures that I could not hope to address in a definitive manner. This select bibliography is consequently a list of writings which have been especially influential in the development and grounding of my argument; it also includes suggestions for further reading into controversies encountered in the course of work on this book.

Albert, M. and Hahnel, R. *Looking Forward: Participatory Economics for the Twenty-First Century*. Boston, 1991.

Albo, G., Langille, D., Panitch, L. *A Different Kind of State?: Popular Power and Democratic Administration*. Toronto, 1993.

Alcock, P., Gamble, A., Gough, I., Lee, P. and Walker, A. (eds) *The Social Economy and the Democratic State: A New Policy Agenda*. 1989.

Ali, T. *1968 and After*. London, 1978.

Allen, B. *Germany East: Dissent and Opposition*. Montreal, 1991.

Anderson P. *Considerations of Western Marxism*. London, 1976.

Anderson, P. *Arguments in English Marxism*. London, 1980.

Arato, A. 'Civil Society Against the State: Poland 1980–81', *Telos*, 47, pp. 23–47.

Arblaster, A. *Democracy*. Milton Keynes, 1987.

Arendt, H. *On Revolution*. London, 1973.

Aronowitz, S. *Science as Power: Discourse and Ideology in Modern Society*. Basingstoke, 1989.

Austin, J. *Philosophical Papers*. Oxford, 1962.

Bahro, R. *The Alternative In Eastern Europe*. London, 1978.

Barnett, A. *Soviet Freedom*. London, 1988.

Barratt Brown, M. *European Union: Fortress or Democracy?*. Nottingham, 1991.

Batt, J. *East Central Europe from Reform to Transition*. London, 1991.

Baudrillard, J. *In the Shadow of Silent Majorities . . . or the End of the Social*. New York, 1983.

Beetham, D. *The Legitimation of Power*. 1991.

Benton, T. 'Marx and Natural Limits', *New Left Review*, 178 (1989).

Berger, J. *Rendezvous* (especially Chapter 5). London, 1992.

Berger, S. *Organising Interests in Western Europe: Pluralism, Corporatism and the Transformation of Politics*. Cambridge, 1981.

Best, M. *The New Competition Institutions of Industrial Restructuring*. Cambridge, 1990.

Bhaskar, R. *A Realist Theory of Science*, 2nd edn. Brighton, 1978.

Bhaskar, R. *Reclaiming Reality*. London, 1989.

Bhaskar, R. (ed.) *A Meeting of Minds*. London, 1991.

Bhaskar, R. *Dialectic*. London, 1993.

Blackburn, R. *After the Fall: The Failure of Communism*. London, 1991.

Bobbio, N. *The Future of Democracy*. Cambridge, 1987.

Bobbio, N. *Which Socialism?*. 1987

Boddy, M. and Fudge, C. *Local Socialism? Labour Councils and the New Left Alternatives*. London, 1984.

Boggs, C. and Plotke, D. *The Politics of Euro-Communism*. London, 1980.

Bottomore, T. (ed.) *Dictionary of Marxist Thought*. Oxford, 1983.

Bottomore, T. and Outhwaite, W. (eds) *Dictionary of Twentieth-Century Social Thought*. Oxford, 1992.

Bowles, S. and Gintis, H. *Democracy and Capitalism*. 1986.

Brittain, S. *The Permissive Society*. London, 1973.

Brusco, S. 'The Emilian Model: Productive Decentralisation and Social Integration', *Cambridge Journal of Economics*, 6 (1982).

Burawoy M. et al. *Ethnography Unbound Power and Resistance in the Modern Metropolis*. 1991.

Burchell, G., Gordon, C. and Miller, P. *The Foucault Effect: Studies in Governability*. Hemel Hempstead, 1991.

Callinicos, A. *Against Post-Modernism*. Oxford, 1988.

Canovan, M. *The Political Thought of Hannah Arendt*. London, 1974.

Caute, D. *The Year of the Barricades: '68*. London, 1988.

Cawson, A. *Corporatism and Political Theory*. Oxford, 1986.

Claudin-Urondo, C. *Lenin and the Cultural Revolution*. Sussex, 1977.

Clode, D. *Towards the Sensitive Bureacracy: Consumers, Welfare and the New Pluralism*. 1987.

Cockburn A. and Blackburn, R. (eds) *Student Power*. London, 1969.

Cohn-Bendit, D. and G. *Obsolete Communism: the Left-Wing Alternative*. London, 1968.

Collier, A. *Critical Realism: An Introduction to Roy Bhaskar's Philosophy*. London, 1994.

Corrigan, P. and Sayer, D. *The Great Arch: English State Formation as Cultural Revolution*. 1985.

Cooley, M. *Architect or Bee: The Human Price of Technology*. 1987.

Costello, N., Michie, J. and Milne, S. *Beyond the Casino Economy*. London, 1989.

Dale, J. and Foster, P. *Feminists and State Welfare.* 1986.

Devine, P. *Democracy and Economic Planning.* 1988

Donnison, D. *A Radical Agenda After the New Right and the Old Left.* London, 1991.

Doyal, L. and Gough, I. *A Theory of Human Need.* London, 1991.

Doyal, L. *The Political Economy of Health.* 1979.

Eatwell, J. *The New Palgarve Dictionary of Economics,* vol. 13. London, 1987.

Einhorn, B. *Cinderella Goes to Market.* London, 1993.

Ekins, P. and Max-Neef, M. *Real-Life Economics, Understanding Wealth Creation.* 1992.

Elshtain, J. B. 'Feminist Discourse and its Discontents: Language, Power and Meaning', in N. Keohane, M. Z. Rosaldo, B. C. Gelp (eds) *Feminist Theory.* Chicago, 1981.

Elson, D. 'Market Socialism or Socialising the Market', *New Left Review,* 172, pp. 3–44.

Enloe, C. *Bananas, Beaches & Bases.* London, 1989.

Enzenberger, H. *Raids and Reconstructions.* 1976.

Epstein, B., Kauffman, L. A., Plotke, D. and Winant, D. 'Is That All There Is? Reappraising Social Movements', *Socialist Review,* January–March, 1990.

Esping-Anderson, G. *The Three Worlds of Welfare Capitalism.* 1990.

Eyerman, R. and Jamison, A. *Social Movements A Cognitive Approach.* 1991.

Feyeraband, P. *Against Method.* London, 1975.

Feher, F., Heller, A. *Eastern Left-Western Left.* Cambridge, 1986.

Flacks, R., Harrington, M. and Harber, B. 'Port Huron: Agenda for a Generation', *Socialist Review,* May–August, 1987.

Foucault, M. *The Archaeology of Knowledge.* London, 1966.

Foucault, M. *Power/Knowledge.* Brighton, 1980.

Fraser, N. *Unruly Practices: Power, Discourse and Gender in Conemporary Social Theory.* Cambridge, 1989.

Fraser, R. *1968.* London, 1988.

Freire, P. *Pedagogy of the Oppressed.* London, 1980.

Gamble, A. *The Free Economy and the Strong State.* London, 1988.

Geras, N. *The Legacy of Rosa Luxemburg.* London, 1976.

Giddens, A. *The Constitution of Society.* Cambridge, 1982.

Glenny, M. *The Rebirth of History: Eastern Europe in the Age of Democracy.* 1990.

Gorbachev, M. *Perestroika.* London, 1987.

Gorz, A. *Critique of Economic Reason.* London, 1989.

Gorz, A. *Farewell to the Working Class: An Essay on Post-Industrial Socialism.* London, 1982.

Gorz, A. *Strategy for Labour: A Radical Proposal.* Boston, 1964.

Gowan, P. 'Western Economic Diplomacy and the New Eastern Europe', *New Left Review,* 182 (1990).

Gramsci, A. *Selections from the Prison Notebooks.* London, 1971.

Gray, J. *Limited Government: A Positive Agenda.* London, 1989.

Gray, J. *Hayek on Liberty.* Oxford, 1986.

Habermas, J. *Knowledge and Human Interests*. London, 1971.

Habermas, J. *Toward a Rational Society: Student Protest, Science and Politics*. London, 1977.

Habermas, J. *Autonomy and Solidarity: Interviews with Jürgen Habermas*. London, 1986.

Habermas, J. 'What Does Socialism Mean Today? The Rectifying Revolution and the Need for New Thinking on the Left', *New Left Review*, 183.

Hall, S. and Jaques, M. *New Times: The Changing Face of Politics in the 1990s*. 1989.

Hanley, D. *Keeping Left: Ceres and the French Socialist Party*. Manchester, 1986.

Haraway, D. J. *Simians, Cyborgs, and Women* (especially chapter 9). London, 1991.

Harré, R. *The Principles of Scientific Thinking*. London, 1970.

Harvey, B. *Networking in Europe: A guide to European Voluntary Organisations*. London, 1992.

Harvey, D. *The Condition of Post-Modernity*. Oxford, 1989.

Havel, V. *Disturbing the Peace*. New York, 1991.

Hayek, F. A. *The Road to Serfdom*. Chicago, 1944.

Hayek, F. A. *Individualism and Economic Order*. London, 1949.

Hayek, F. A. *The Constitution of Liberty*. London, 1960.

Hayek, F. A. *The Fatal Conceit: The Errors of Socialism*. London, 1988.

Healey, D. *The Time of My Life*. London, 1989.

Held, D. and Pollit, C. *New Forms of Democracy*. London, 1986.

Held, D. *Models of Democracy*. Oxford, 1987.

Held, D. (ed.) *Prospects for Democracy: North, South, East, West*. Cambridge, 1993.

Hodgson, G. *Economics and Institutions*. Cambridge, 1988.

Holland, S. *The Market Economy: From Micro to Mesoeconomics*. London, 1987.

Hollis, M. and Lukes, S. (eds) *Rationality and Relativism*. 1982.

Horvat, B., Marković, M. and Supek, R. *Self-Governing Socialism: A Reader*. 1975.

Institute for Public Policy Research *A More Perfect Union*. 1992.

Kagarlitsky, B. *Farewell Perestroika: A Soviet Chronicle*. London, 1990.

Kaldor, M. *The Baroque Arsenal*. London, 1981.

Kaldor, M. (ed.) *The New Détente: Rethinking East–West Relations*. London, 1989.

Kaldor, M. *The Imaginary War: Understanding the East–West Conflict*. Oxford, 1990.

Kaldor, M. (ed.) *Europe from Below: An East–West Dialogue*. London, 1991.

Keane, J. *Civil Society and the State: New European Perspectives*. 1988.

Kelly, P. *Fighting for Hope*. London, 1984.

Kelly, J. *Trade Unions and Socialist Politics*. London, 1988.

Kemp, P., Antunes C., Juquin, P., Otto Wolf, F., Stengers, I. and Telkamper, W. *Europe's Green Alternative Manifesto For a New World*. London, 1992.

Konrad, G. *Antipolitics*. London, 1984.

Kornai, J. *The Road to a Free Economy*. London, 1990.

Korsch, K. *Marxism and Philosophy*. 1970.

Laclau, E. and Mouffe C. *Hegemony and Socialist Strategy: Towards a Radical Democratic Politics*. London, 1985.

Liebman, M. *Leninism Under Lenin*. London, 1975.

Lipietz, A. *Towards a New Economic Order: Postfordism, Ecology and Democracy*. Cambridge, 1992.

Loviduski, J. and Woodall, J. *Politics and Society in Eastern Europe*. London, 1987.

Lovibond, S. 'Feminism and Postmodernism' *New Left Review*, 178.

McLellan, D. and Sayers, S. (eds) *Socialism and Democracy*. London, 1991.

Macpherson, C. B. *The Real World of Democracy*. Oxford, 1973.

Macshane, D. *Solidarity: Poland's Independent Trade Union*. Nottingham, 1981.

Magas B. *The Destruction of Yugoslavia: Tracking the Break-up 1980–1992*. London, 1993.

Manicas, P. *A History and Philosophy of the Social Sciences*. Oxford, 1987.

Marcuse, H. *One Dimensional Man*. London, 1964.

Marcuse, H. *An Essay on Liberation*. London, 1969.

Marquesee, M. and Heffernan, R. *Defeat from the Jaws of Victory*. London, 1992.

Martinez-Alier, Juan *Ecological Economics*. Oxford, 1990.

Mellor, M. *Breaking the Boundaries: Towards a Feminist, Green Socialism*. London, 1991.

Melucci, A. *Nomads of the Present*. London, 1989.

Miliband, R. *Divided Societies*. Oxford, 1990.

Mole, V. and Elliott, E. *Enterprising Innovation: An Alternative Approach*. 1987.

Morrison, R. *We Build the Road as We Travel*. Philadelphia, 1991.

Norris, C. *What's Wrong With Post-Modernism: Critical Theory and the Ends of Philosophy*. Baltimore, 1990.

Nove, A. *The Economics of Feasible Socialism*. London, 1983.

Offe, C. *Contradictions of the Welfare State*. 1984.

Outhwaite, W. *New Philosophies of Social Science*. London, 1987.

Outhwaite, W. *Habermas*. Cambridge, 1994, forthcoming.

Oxford University Socialist Discussion Group *Out of Apathy: Voices of the New Left 30 Years On*. London, 1989.

Palmer, J. *Europe Without America*. Oxford, 1986.

Panitch, L. and Miliband, R. 'A New World Order?', *Socialist Register*, 1992.

Pateman C. and Gross E. (eds) *Feminist Challenges: Social and Political Theory*. Boston, 1987.

Pateman C. *The Disorder of Women: Democracy, Feminism and Political Theory*. Cambridge, 1989.

Phillips A. *Engendering Democracy*. Cambridge, 1991.

Piore, M. and Sabel, C. *The Second Industrial Divide*. New York, 1984.

Polan, A. *Lenin and the End of Politics*. London, 1984.

Polanyi, K. *The Great Transformation*. London, 1944.

Polanyi, K. 'Our Obsolete Market Mentality', in *Primitive and Archaic Economics: Essays of Karl Polanyi*. New York, 1968.

Quattrocchi, A. and Nairn, T. *The Beginning of the End: France, May 1968*. London, 1968.

Ray, L. J. *Rethinking Critical Theory*.

Rowbotham, S., Segal, L. and Wainwright, H. *Beyond the Fragments: Feminism and the*

Making of Socialism. London, 1981.

Rowbotham, S. *The Past is Before Us: Feminism in Action Since the 1960s*. London, 1989.

Rowbotham, S. *Women in Movement: Feminism and Social Action*. New York, 1992.

Rowbotham, S. *Homeworkers World Wide*. London, 1993.

Sassoon, D. *Contemporary Italy: Politics, Economy and Society since 1945*. London, 1986.

Sayer, A. *Method: A Realist Approach*. London, 1982.

Sayer, A. and Walker, R. *The New Social Economy: Reworking the Division of Labour*. Oxford, 1992.

Schorske, K. *Fin-de-Siècle Vienna: Politics and Culture*. London, 1961.

Scott, A. *New Industrial Spaces: Flexible Production Organisation and Regional Development in North America and Western Europe*. London, 1988.

Schumpeter, J. *Capitalism, Socialism and Democracy*. New York, 1950.

Segal, L. *Is The Future Female?* London, 1986?

Shavelson, J. *A Third Way: A Sourcebook, Innovations in Community-Owned Enterprises*. Washington, 1990.

Sinanni, C. 'Councils and Parliaments: The Problems of Dual Power and Democracy in Comparative Perspective', *Politics and Society*, 12, no. 1, 1983.

Sivandan, A. 'All That Melts into Air: the Hokum of New Times', *Race and Class*, January–March, 1990.

Smith, A. *The Theory of Moral Sentiments*. Oxford, 1976.

Sohn-Rethel, A. *Intellectual and Manual Labour: A Critique of Epistemology*. London, 1978.

Soper, K. *Troubled Pleasures*. London, 1992.

Soper, K. *The Idea of Nature*. Oxford, 1994.

Statera, G. *Death of a Utopia: The Development and Decline of Student Movements in Europe*. New York, 1975.

Strawson, P. *Individuals*. London, 1966.

Szelenyi, I. and Szelenyi, S. 'The Vacuum in Hungarian Politics', *New Left Review*, 187.

Taylor, F. W. *Principles of Scientific Management*. New York, 1911.

Teague, P. and Grahl, J. *Industrial Relations and European Integration*. London, 1992.

Thompson, E. P. *Education and Experience*. Leeds, 1968.

Thompson, E. P. *The Poverty of Theory*. London, 1979.

Thompson, G., et al. (eds) *Markets, Hierarchies and Networks: The Co-ordination of Social Life*. London, 1989.

Thompson, M. *A Paper House: The Ending of Yugoslavia*. London, 1992.

Touraine, A. *Le Mouvement de mai ou le Communisme utopique*. Paris, 1968.

Wainwright, H. *Labour, A Tale of Two Parties*. London, 1987.

Wainwright, H., Burke, P. and Thompson, M. *Democracy and Movement Politics in the New Europe*. London, 1991.

Wall, D. *Getting There: Steps to a Green Society*. London, 1990.

Ward, A., Gregory, J. and Yuval-Davis, N. *Women and Citizenship in Europe: Border, Rights and Duties*. Stoke, 1993.

Wheaton, B. and Kavan, Z. *The Velvet Revolution: Czechoslovakia 1988–1991.* Oxford, 1992.

Watson S. (ed.) *Playing the State: Australian Feminist Interventions.* London, 1990.

Widgery, D. *The left in Britain, 1956–68.* Harmondsworth, 1976.

Widgery, D. *Beating Time.* London, 1986.

Widgery, D. *Preserving Disorder.* 1989.

Williams, G. *Proletarian Order: Antonio Gramsci, Factory Councils and the Origins of Communism in Italy 1911–1921.*

Williams, R. *Keywords.* London, 1988.

Williams, R. *Resources of Hope.* London, 1989.

Williams, R. *What I Came to Say.* London, 1989.

Wittgenstein, L. *Philosophical Investigations.* Oxford, 1953.

Women Working Worldwide *Common Interests: Women Organising in Global Electronics.* London, 1991.

Wootton, B. *Freedom Under Planning.* London, 1945.

Wright, N. *Assessing Radical Education.* Milton Keynes, 1989.

DIRECTORY OF INTERNATIONAL CAMPAIGNS, NETWORKS AND NEWSLETTERS

GENERAL

Agenor
Rue de Toulouse 22
1040 Brussels
Belgium
32 2 230477 (T)
32 2 2305957 (F)

A Europe-wide left communication group, looking critically at issues of European politics and society. It publishes pamphlets and organizes annual conferences.

Dialogue for European Alternatives
c/o Agenor
rue de Toulouse 22
1040 Brussels
Belgium
32 2 230477 (T)
32 2 2305957 (F)

Publish "Opposition Papers"

European Dialogue
11 Goodwin Street
London
N4 3HQ
UK
44 71 272 9092 (T)
44 71 272 3044 (F)

Independent organization whose purpose is 'to help bring into being a new Europe united not simply by a common market but by common rights for all its residents'. Priorities are human rights, cultural diversity, social justice and environmental responsibility. Individuals and group membership.

European New Left Forum
c/o Joost Lagendijk
Postbus 700
1000 AS Amsterdam
Netherlands

See chapter 7.

Helsinki Citizens' Assembly
Panská 7
Praha 1
CZ 11669
Czech Republic
42 2 220181 (T)
42 2 220948 (F)

See the introduction and chapter 1. Produces a regular bulletin.

Left European Forum
c/o Guy Haworth
5a Alma Square
London NW1
UK

Links Europa
Dhr Albert Marks
Joubertweg 15
Oosterbeek
Netherlands

Network of Left Wing Journals
c/o Tamas Krausz
Frankel Leo utca 68B
1023 Budapest
Hungary

Red–Green Network
Cabin W
25 Horsell Road
London
N5 1XL
UK
44 71 700 3853 (T)

A broad based network of all those committed to eco-socialism and who want to be involved both in the development of eco-socialist ideas and in practical campaigning work.

ANTI-RACIST

Campaign Against Fascism in Europe
PO Box 3104
London
SE13 6EU
UK
44 71 252 5122 (T)

Its purpose is to publicize and inform about
the danger of Eurofascism and organize mass
action to stop the activities of Euro-fascists.
Individual and group membership.

Charta 91
Wellingstraat 89
B-9000 Gent
Belgium
32 191 225 2142 (T&F)

Citizens' movement which has come about as
a reaction against the gains of the racist extreme right in the Belgian elections of 1991.
The aim of the initiative is to raise the level of
citizens' involvement in European matters. It

is an 'independent movement of individual
citizens who want to act together pluralistic-
ally for freedom, equality and solidarity'.

Churches Committee for Migrants in
Europe (CCME)
European Ecumenical Centre
Rue Joseph 11, 174
1040 Brussels
Belgium
32 2 230 2011 (T)
32 2 231 1413 (F)

Citizen's Movement Against Racism
6 Fitiou Street
10678 Athens
Greece

European Action for Racial Equality and
Social Justice
76A Stroud Green Road
London
N4 3EN
UK

European Communities Migrants' Forum
A-1/6-30 Rue de la Loi 200
B-1049 Brussels
Belgium

Initially funded by the EC - sees itself 'as a
consultative body and a fighting unit.'

European Consultation on Refugees and
Exiles (ECRE)
The Refugee Council
Bondway House
3-9 Bondway
London SW8
UK
44 71 582 9928 (T)
44 71 582 9929 (F)

Migrants   Associations   Information
Network in Europe
(MAINE)
Hoogbrugstraat 43
6221 CP Maastricht
Netherlands
31 43 216724 (T)
31 43 255712 (F)

Mouvement Contre le Racisme, l'Anti-
semitisme et la Xenophobie
(MRAX)
Rue de la Poste 37
1210 Brussels
Belgium
32 2 2182371 (T)
32 2 2196959 (F)

SCORE
Standing Conference on Racial Equality in
Europe
Unit 303
Brixton Enterprise Centre
Bon Marche Building
444 Brixton Road
London
UK
44 71 274 4000 x303 (T)

Network of organizations in UK, Italy, Spain,
Denmark and Germany to work for equality
regardless of colour, race, nationality or reli-
gion; to promote legislation to ensure equal
treatment of black people; to outlaw racial
harassment; and to liaise with other organizations across the EC.

SOS Racisme
14 Cité Griset
Paris 75011
France
33 1 4806 4000 (T)
33 1 4355 9463 (F)

United for Intercultural Action
Postbus 413
NL-1000 AK Amsterdam
Netherlands

It produced a directory of internationalist,
anti-racist movements across Europe —
mainly youth movements. It organizes conferences on networking against racism.

Youth Against Racism in Europe (YRE)
PO Box 858
London
E2 79R
UK
44 81 533 4533 (T)

BLACK AND MIGRANT WOMEN

Babaylan – Philippine Women's Network
in Europe
c/o Women's Programme CFMW
Haarlemmerdikj 173
1013 KH Amsterdam
Netherlands
31 20 625 4829 (T)

Black Women in Europe Network
Nilgun Canver
c/o Women's Equality Unit
Islington Town Hall
Upper Street
London N1
UK
44 71 477 3133 (T)

European Women's Network for Inter-
cultural Action and Exchange
124-128 City Road
London
EC1V 2NJ
UK

Latin American Women's European
Network
c/o Latin American Women's Rights
Service,
Wesley House,
4 Wild Court
London
WC2B 5AV
UK

Migrants Forum Women's Committee
33 rue de Treves
B-1040 Brussels
Belgium
32 2 230 1414 (T)
32 2 230 1461 (F)

Turkish Women's European Network
c/o Enise Yaylali
7 Risborough Court
Muswell Hill
London N10
UK

An informal network of Turkish-speaking women.

DEMOCRACY, HUMAN AND SOCIAL RIGHTS

Amnesty International
9 rue Berkmanns
B-1060 Brussels
Belgium
32 2 537 1302 (T)
32 2 537 4750 (F)

Basic Income European Network
Bosduifstraat 21
B-2018 Antwerp
Belgium
32 3 220 4181 (T)

Link between individuals and groups 'committed to or interested in basic income unconditionally granted to all on an individual basis'.

European Alliance with Indigenous Peoples
c/o Rue Marché aux Poulets 30
1000 Brussels
Belgium
32 2 217 8225 (T)
32 2 218 4569 (F)

European Citizens Action Service (ECAS)
Rue Defacqz 1
B-1050 Brussels
Belgium
32 2 534 5166 (T)
32 2 534 5275 (F)

An information and advocacy service – a 'citizen's watchdog' on corporate lobbying in the EC which provides an open lobbying advice service for members of the public.

European Network of Older People in Poverty
(Euro Link Age)
Rue du Trône 98
B-1050 Brussels
Belgium
32 2 512 9360 (T)
32 2 512 6673 (F)

'A European network concerned with older people and issues of aging'. It campaigns, for example, for concessionary travel passes and legislation against age discrimination.

European Network of One Parent Families
325 Bunratty Road
Coolock
Dublin 17
Ireland
353 1 481872 (T)
353 1 481116 (F)

Network of self-help groups, researchers and academics working on the issue of the changing family.

European Social Action Network
rue du Trône 98
1050 Brussels
Belgium
32 2 512 7411 (T)
32 2 512 6673 (F)

To ensure that the social concerns of the national voluntary sectors are argued in Brussels.

European Youth Forum
Europees Jeugdforum
Dhr Egbert de Vries
Jozef straat 120
1040 Brussels
Belgium

Initiative Citoyens en Europe
18 rue de Chatillon
75014 Paris
France

Interrights
International Centre for the Legal Protection of Human Rights
5-15 Cromer Street
London
WC1H 8LS

UK
44 71 278 3230

UK based international lawyers network providing free advice on all aspects of international human rights law and assistance and representation to the European Court of Justice.

Helsinki Citizens' Assembly
Panská 7
Praha 1
CZ 11669
Czech Republic
42 2 220181 (T)
42 2 220948 (F)

See the introduction and chapter 1.

Mobility International
228 Borough High Street
London
SE1 1JX
UK
44 71 403 5688 (T)
44 71 378 1292 (F)

Represents disabled activists at a European level.

Statewatch
Tony Bunyan
PO Box 1516
London
N16 0EW

EMPLOYMENT, TRADE UNIONS AND ECONOMIC DEVELOPMENT

ATD Quart Monde
Av V. Hugo 12
B-1040 Brussels
Belgium
322 647 9900 (T)
322 640 7384 (F)

A network concerned with community development.

CAITS/FAST/SOMO
404 Camden Road
London
N7 0SJ
UK
44 71 607 7079 (T)
44 71 700 0362 (F)

Centre for Alternative Industrial and Technological Systems have an informal partnership with two other research institutes in the Netherlands and Germany. They work on socially useful and worker controlled production and company and sectoral research for trade unions and shop stewards.

European Anti Poverty Network
Rue Belliard 205
Boite 13
B-1040 Brussels
Belgium
32 2 230 4455 (T)
32 2 230 9733 (F)

Aims to establish a democratic network of anti-poverty groups across Europe which will bring together people experiencing poverty to influence and effect change in social, economic and political structures.

European Committee of Workers' Co-operatives
(CECOP)
Avenue de Cortenberg 62
B-1040 Brussels
Belgium
32 2 736 2030 (T)
32 2 732 1897 (F)

European Homeworkers' Network
c/o Jane Tate
Yorkshire and Humberside Low Pay Unit
102 Commercial St
Batley
Yorks
WF17 5DP
UK
44 924 443850 (T)

European Labour Forum
c/o Spokesman

Bertrand Russell House
Gamble Street
Nottingham
NG7 4ET
UK

A forum for socialists in the European Parliament which produces a monthly magazine.

European Network for a Better Working Environment
c/o European Work Hazards Conference
Mudford's Building
37 Exchange Street
Sheffield
S2 5TR
UK
44 742 765693

An alliance of workers and health and safety advisors which organizes annual conferences and co-ordinates their activities.

European Network of Unemployed
NUCC
24 Hardman Street
Liverpool
L1 9AX
UK
44 51 709 3995 (T)
44 51 708 8862 (F)

This network brings together national and local organizations of unemployed and has produced a Charter for Rights of the Unemployed. It aims to represent the interests of the unemployed and exchange information and experience.

European Trade Union Confederation
rue Montagne aux Herbes Potagères 37
B-1000 Brussels
Belgium
32 2 218 3100 (T)
32 2 218 3566 (F)

European Trade Union Confederation
Women's Committee
rue Montagne aux Herbes 37
B-1000 Brussels
Belgium

32 2 218 3100 (T)
32 2 218 3566 (F)

International Labour Organisation
CH-1211 Geneva 22,
Switzerland.
41 22 799 6111 (T)
41 22 798 8685 (F)

International Restructuring and Educational Network Europe (IRENE)
Stationstraat 39
5038 EC Tilburg
Netherlands
31 13 35 1523 (T)
31 13 35 0253 (F)

Examines effects of international restructuring in industries and services on jobs, the environment, technology and housing conditions. It includes a research group on large multinational companies (mainly Dutch).

KAS–KOR
Po Box 16
Moscow 129642
Russia

A trade union information network which produces a newsletter.

Labour Industrial Fund
c/o Milka Tyszkiewicz
Rekodzielnicza 16
50-501 Wroclaw
Poland

Socialist network in Eastern Europe.

Reseau Européen d'Economie Alternative et Solidaire
Mme. Pascale Turlotte
61 rue V. Hugo
F93500 Pantin
France

Trade Union Rural Network (TURN)
Joe Mitchell Associates
136 Middleton Road
Heywood
Lancashire
OL10 2LU

UK
44 706 68691
44 706 626059

Trans-European rural network.
(TERN)
Rue de Trone 98
B-1050 Brussels
Belgium
32 2 512 9360 (T)
32 2 512 6673 (F)

Transnational Information Exchange
Paulus Potter Straat 20
1071 DA Amsterdam
Netherlands
31 2066 42191 (T)
31 20673 0179 (F)
E-Mail: Geo Net GEO2:TIE

Produces educational materials, occasional newsletters, booklets and conference reports, and puts workers into contact with each other internationally. Their focus is on labour in international corporations. They are based in Brazil, Kuala Lumpur, Moscow, Detroit and Frankfurt.

Workers' Health International Newsletter (WHIN)
PO Box 199
Sheffield
S1 1SQ
UK

Reports workers' struggles and actions all over world. It is produced quarterly and there is a Spanish edition.

GREEN AND ENVIRONMENTAL

Alliance of Northern People for Environment and Development
c/o WEED
Berlinerplatz 1
5300 Bonn 3
Germany

49 228 696479 (T)
49 228 696470 (F)

Arose out of 1992 UN Conference on Environment and Development. People active in NGOs and social movements in Europe and the US. Working groups on, for example, EC single market, Women and Commission on Sustainable Development.

ASEED Europe
(Action for Solidarity, Equality, Environment and Development)
PO Box 40066
1009 BB Amsterdam
Netherlands
31 20 6650166 (T)
E-mail: ASEEDEUR@antenna.nl

A coalition of youth groups around the world working at local, national and international level for social change, the emancipation of the oppressed and ecologically sustainable relations between humans and nature and northern and southern parts of the planet.

CEAT
Friends of the Earth, European Coordination
29 Rue Blanche
1050 Brussels
Belgium
32 2 537 7228 (T)
32 2 537 5596 (F)

European coordination office of FoE 24 national members groups from Western and Eastern Europe.

CEEWEB
c/o Ivan Gyulai
Kossuth 13
Miskolc
Hungary 3525
36 46 352010 (T&F)

Citizens' groups networking to preserve Central and Eastern European biodiversity in the face of traumatic political and social change.

European Ecological Consumer Co-operation (EECC)
3rd Floor

5-11 Worship Street
London
EC2A 2BH
UK

An affiliation of nearly 100 European organizations concerned with the development of sustainable forms of consumption.

European Federation of Green Parties
Information Office of European Greens
Rue Bellirard 97
1047 Brussels
Belgium
32 2 284 5135 (T)
32 2 284 9135 (F)

See chapter 7.

European Network of Coalitions for Sustainable Agriculture
c/o SAFE
21 Tower Street
London
WC2H 9NS
UK
44 71 240 1811 (T)

Network of farmers, ecologists, consumers and people concerned with development in the Third World for promoting more equal ways of production and to lobby at a European level. Includes EC and Scandinavian countries.

Greenpeace International
Keizergracht 176
1016 Amsterdam
Netherlands
31 20 523 6555 (T)
31 20 523 6500 (F)

Pesticides Action Network Pan Europe
c/o The Pesticides Trust
23 Beehive Place
London
SW9 7QR
UK
44 71 274 9086 (T)
44 71 274 9084 (F)

International coalition of citizens' groups and individuals who oppose the misuse of pesticides and support reliance on safe, sustainable pest management methods.

Taiga Rescue Network
TRN Coordination Centre
AJTTE
Box-116
S-962 23
Jikkmokk
Sweden

Network of individuals, NGOs and indigenous peoples. Aims to strengthen and support those concerned with the protection, restoration and sustainable use of forests.

Women's Environmental Network
Aberdeen Studios
22 Highbury Grove
London
N5 2EA
UK
44 71 354 8823 (T)
44 71 354 0464 (F)

Networks of individuals and groups mainly in UK but also across the world. Dedicated to educating, informing and empowering women who care about the environment.

LESBIAN AND GAY

International Gay and Lesbian Association (ILGA)
Information Secretariat
Rue Marché au Charbon 81
8100 Brussels 1
Belgium
322 502 2471 (T&F)

Worldwide federation of national and local groups dedicated to achieving lesbian and gay rights throughout the world. Publishes newsletter and organizes conferences.

International-Gay and Lesbian Organization (IGLYO)
P.O. Box 1662
22101 Lund
Sweden

PEACE AND DISARMAMENT

Campaign to Free Mordechai Vanunu and for a Nuclear-Free Middle East
6 Endsleigh Street
London
WC1H 0DX
UK
44 71 387 5096 (T)

European Bureau for Conscientious Objection (EBCO)
35 Rue Van Elewyck
1050 Brussels
Belgium
32 2 640 5220 (T)
32 2 640 0774 (F)

European Convention on Nuclear Disarmament
30 Rue de Vlessingue
1210 Brussels
Belgium
32 2 428 2217 (T&F)

Established in the early 1980s to campaign against arms race and for peace. Individual and group membership. Not to be confused with END (below).

European Nuclear Disarmament (END)
11 Goodwin Street
London
N4 3HQ
UK
44 71 272 9092 (T)
44 71 272 3044 (F)

European Network Against the Arms Trade
c/o Campaign Against the Arms Trade
11 Goodwin Street
London
N4 3HQ
UK
44 71 281 0297 (T&F)

A network of groups that campaign against arms production and export and a monitor of European military co-operation.

Foundation Balkan Peace Campaign Hudaibaya
SPIOR
Heemraadssingel 241
3023 CD Rotterdam
Netherlands
31 10 476 2022 (T)
31 10 478 1213 (F)

An initiative taken by the Islamic community to send international peace convoys to Zagreb, appeal to UN to take effective and just measures in the Balkans, show solidarity to the Muslims and show how people with different cultural backgrounds can work together.

International Committee for European Security and Cooperation (ICESC)
Rue Major Pétillon 18
1040 Brussels
Belgium
32 2 732 1550 (T)

International Peace Bureau
Rue de Zurich 41
CH 1201 Geneva
Switzerland
41 22 731 64 29 (T)
41 22 738 94 19 (F)

International Peace Communication and Co-ordination Centre
Anna Pavlownaplein 3
PB 18747
2502 Den Haag
Netherlands
31 70 469756 (T)

International Trade Union Committee for Peace and Disarmament
PO Box 514
11121 Praha 1
Czech Republic
42 2 235 4422 (T)

North Atlantic Network (NAN)
c/o Nei Til Atomvapen
Youngstorget 7
0181 Oslo 1
Norway
Nuclear Disarmament.

Peacework
c/o Ian Graham
International Federation of Chemical, Energy and General Workers' Unions
Ave Emile de Beco 109
B-1050 Brussels
Belgium

Work on arms conversion.

Stockholm International Peace Institute
Pipers Vag 28
17173 Solna
Sweden

Transnational Working Group for a Global Peace Policy in Europe
c/o BSV
Friedensplatz 1a
W4950 Minden
Germany
49 571 24339 (T)
49 571 23019 (F)

Verona Forum for Peace and Reconciliation on the Territory of the Former Yugoslavia
c/o European Parliament
Bel 3007
Rue Bellirard 97–113
B-1040 Brussels
Belgium
32 2 284 5456 (T)
32 2 284 9456 (F)

An organization of all groups dedicated to facilitate dialogue and co-operation among democratic and peace oriented forces in all states and regions of the former Yugoslavia.

War Resisters International
55 Dawes Street
London
SE17 1EL
UK
44 71 703 7189 (T)
44 71 708 2545 (F)

Network of organizations of conscientious objectors, non-violent activists and pacifists, across Europe and the world.

WOMEN

Centre for International Women's Issues (CEWI)
Fr Nansenspl.6,
0160 Oslo
Norway
47 2 42 62 45 (T)
47 2 42 32 05 (F)

Co-ordinates campaigns on international issues.

Centre for Research on European Women
CREW
Enter SA
21 rue de la Tourelle
B-1040 Brussels
Belgium
32 2 230 5158 (T)
32 2 230 6230 (F)
E-mail: MCRI=CREW

Specializes in consultancy and research into equal opportunities in the fields of employment, enterprise creation and training. Publishes CREW reports and co-ordinates IRIS, the European network of training schemes for women in the European Community.

East–West European Women's Network
OWEN
Prenzlauer Allee 36
0-1055 Berlin
Germany
372 4200215 (T)
372 2812315 (F)

Women's forum producing newsletters and organizing conferences. Prioritizes questions of democracy and anti-racism from a women's perspective.

European Forum of Left Feminists
c/o Enise Yaylali
10 Risborough Court
London N10
UK

Network of individuals from most countries of Europe, loosely linked through a mailing list, an occasional newsletter and a series of conferences. They are not associated with any one political party and they are 'committed to the involvement of black, ethnic minority and migrant women'.

European Network of Women
2 Wesley Street
Castleford
West Yorkshire
WS10 1AE
UK
44 977 603165 (T)

Pan-European organization campaigning for women's rights in the EC, but will soon decide to extend membership to the rest of Europe. Membership is made up of individuals and groups.

European Women's Lobby
Rue du Méridien 22
B-1030 Brussels
Belgium
32 2 217 9020 (T)

Funded principally by the European Commission, they aim to exert influence and put pressure on European and national institutions to ensure women's interests are adequately defended and represented. It involves women from across the political spectrum.

Feminist Network
c/o Maria Adamik
Szerb Utca 8
1056 Budapest
Hungary

Women in Development Europe
c/o Irish Commission for Justice and Peace
169 Booterstown Avenue
Blackrock
Co Dublin
Ireland

Network of women development workers and researchers working in Europe which promotes contact with women from developing countries to lobby European and interna-

tional institutions on gender and development issues.

Women's Global Network for Reproductive Rights
Nieuwe Zijds Voorburgwal 32
1012 RZ Amsterdam
Netherlands
31 20 620 9672 (T)
31 20 622 2450 (F)

Women Working Worldwide
c/o Sociology Department
Manchester University
Oxford Road
Manchester
M13 9PL

DIRECTORIES AND PUBLICATIONS NOT INCLUDED ABOVE

Repertoire des Associations Immigrées dans la Communauté Européenne, 1991. Available from:

Centre d'Information et d'Etudes sur les Migratures Internationales (CIEMI)
46 rue de Montreuil
75011 Paris
France
33 14 372 4934 (T)
33 14 372 0140 (T)
33 14 372 0642 (F)

'Everywoman Directory' of women's organizations including women's organizations and networks in Europe. Produced annually.

Everywoman
34a Islington Green
London
N1 8DU
UK
44 71 359 5496 (T)
44 71 226 9448 (F)

'Global Labour', an independent magazine committed to the promotion of independent and democratic trade unionism. An open forum inviting debate and discussion.

Global Labour
BCM Box 2001
London
WC1N 3XX
UK
44 71 972 9060 (T)
44 71 972 9061 (F)
E.Mail: MCR1/Global-labour

'Housman's diary': Produced annually with a very comprehensive international directory of pacifist, green and third-world organizations.

Housman's Bookshop
5 Caledonian Road
Kings Cross
London
N1 9DX
UK
44 71 837 4473 (T)

'Ethnic minority and migrant organisations - European directory.'

Joint Council for the Welfare of Immigrants (JCWI)
115 Old Street
Islington
London
EC1V 9JR
UK
44 71 251 8706 (T)
44 71 251 8708 (T)
44 71 253 3832 (F)

Labour Focus on Eastern Europe: An independent socialist magazine providing coverage of events in Eastern Europe and giving special attention to labour movements and political currents which are usually marginalized.

Labour Focus on Eastern Europe
30 Bridge St
Oxford
OX2 OBA
UK
44 865 723207 (T)

Protecting the Community: a worker's guide to health and safety in Europe, by Mike Allan, Cleia Matte and the London Hazards Centre

(1992). Contains full list of contacts in Europe.

London Hazards Centre
Headland House
308 Gray's Inn Road
London
WC1X 8DS
UK
44 71 837 5605 (T)

Provide access to the POPTEL database of non profit-making citizens' and workers' organizations. Organizations and individuals can subscribe for a mail-box:

Manchester Host
Soft Solution Ltd
30 Naples Street
Manchester
M4 4DB
UK
44 61 839 4212 (T)
44 61 839 4214 (F)
EMail: GeoNet MCR1:ADMIN

Consumer Advice Services in the European Community: a Directory, by National Consumer Council for the EEC (1992).

National Consumer Council
20 Grosvenor Gardens
London
SW1W OBD.
UK

Networking in Europe: a Guide to European Voluntary Organisations, by Brian Harvey (1992). Available from:

NCVO Publications
NCVO
26 Bedford Square
London
WC1B 3HU
UK

A regular information bulletin on peace movement events, organizations and publications across Europe is available from:

Network Information Project
30 Westwood Road

Southampton
SO2 1DN
UK
44 703 554434

'The Network' – a newsletter for the equal exchange of information on trade and technology:

Third World Information Network TWIN

5–11 Worship Street
London
EC2A 2BH
UK

Meeting the Corporate Challenge: A Handbook on Corporate Campaigns (Amsterdam, 1993).

Transnational Information Exchange
(For address see 'Labour' section above.)

INDEX

Note: page references in italics indicate footnotes